FEMINIST INTERPRETATIONS OF JANE ADDAMS

RE-READING THE CANON

NANCY TUANA, GENERAL EDITOR

This series consists of edited collections of essays, some original and some previously published, offering feminist re-interpretations of the writings of major figures in the Western philosophical tradition. Devoted to the work of a single philosopher, each volume contains essays covering the full range of the philosopher's thought and representing the diversity of approaches now being used by feminist critics.

Already published:

Nancy Tuana, ed., *Feminist Interpretations of Plato* (1994)
Margaret Simons, ed., *Feminist Interpretations of Simone de Beauvoir* (1995)
Bonnie Honig, ed., *Feminist Interpretations of Hannah Arendt* (1995)
Patricia Jagentowicz Mills, ed., *Feminist Interpretations of G. W. F. Hegel* (1996)
Maria J. Falco, ed., *Feminist Interpretations of Mary Wollstonecraft* (1996)
Susan Hekman, ed., *Feminist Interpretations of Michel Foucault* (1996)
Nancy Holland, ed., *Feminist Interpretations of Jacques Derrida* (1997)
Robin May Schott, ed., *Feminist Interpretations of Immanuel Kant* (1997)
Céline Léon and Sylvia Walsh, eds., *Feminist Interpretations of Søren Kierkegaard* (1997)
Cynthia Freeland, ed., *Feminist Interpretations of Aristotle* (1998)
Kelly Oliver and Marilyn Pearsall, eds., *Feminist Interpretations of Friedrich Nietzsche* (1998)
Mimi Reisel Gladstein and Chris Matthew Sciabarra, eds., *Feminist Interpretations of Ayn Rand* (1999)
Susan Bordo, ed., *Feminist Interpretations of René Descartes* (1999)
Julien S. Murphy, ed., *Feminist Interpretations of Jean-Paul Sartre* (1999)
Anne Jaap Jacobson, ed., *Feminist Interpretations of David Hume* (2000)
Sarah Lucia Hoagland and Marilyn Frye, eds., *Feminist Interpretations of Mary Daly* (2000)
Tina Chanter, ed., *Feminist Interpretations of Emmanuel Levinas* (2001)
Nancy J. Holland and Patricia Huntington, eds., *Feminist Interpretations of Martin Heidegger* (2001)
Charlene Haddock Seigfried, ed., *Feminist Interpretations of John Dewey* (2001)
Naomi Scheman and Peg O'Connor, eds., *Feminist Interpretations of Ludwig Wittgenstein* (2002)
Lynda Lange, ed., *Feminist Interpretations of Jean-Jacques Rousseau* (2002)
Lorraine Code, ed., *Feminist Interpretations of Hans-Georg Gadamer* (2002)
Lynn Hankinson Nelson and Jack Nelson, eds., *Feminist Interpretations of W. V. Quine* (2003)
Maria J. Falco, ed., *Feminist Interpretations of Niccolò Machiavelli* (2004)
Renée J. Heberle, ed., *Feminist Interpretations of Theodor Adorno* (2006)
Dorothea Olkowski and Gail Weiss, eds., *Feminist Interpretations of Maurice Merleau-Ponty* (2006)
Nancy J. Hirschmann and Kirstie M. McClure, eds., *Feminist Interpretations of John Locke* (2007)
Penny A. Weiss and Loretta Kensinger, eds., *Feminist Interpretations of Emma Goldman* (2007)
Judith Chelius Stark, ed., *Feminist Interpretations of Augustine* (2007)
Jill Locke and Eileen Hunt Botting, eds., *Feminist Interpretations of Alexis de Tocqueville* (2008)
Moira Gatens, ed., *Feminist Interpretations of Benedict Spinoza* (2009)
Marianne Janack, ed., *Feminist Interpretations of Richard Rorty* (2010)

FEMINIST INTERPRETATIONS OF JANE ADDAMS

EDITED BY
MAURICE HAMINGTON

THE PENNSYLVANIA STATE UNIVERSITY PRESS
UNIVERSITY PARK, PENNSYLVANIA

Library of Congress Cataloging-in-Publication Data

Feminist interpretations of Jane Addams / edited by Maurice Hamington.
    p.   cm.—(Re-reading the Canon)
Includes bibliographical references and index.
Summary: "A collection of articles that address Jane Addams (1860–1935) in terms of her contribution to feminist philosophy and theory through her work on culture, art, sex, society, religion, and politics"—Provided by publisher.
ISBN 978-0-271-03693-9 (cloth : alk. paper)
ISBN 978-0-271-03694-6 (pbk. : alk. paper)
1. Addams, Jane, 1860–1935.
2. Feminist theory.
3. Feminist theology.
I. Hamington, Maurice.

HQ1190.F46   2010
202.082—dc22
2010006208

Copyright © 2010 The Pennsylvania State University
All rights reserved
Printed in the United States of America
Published by The Pennsylvania State University Press,
University Park, PA 16802-1003

The Pennsylvania State University Press is a member of the Association of American University Presses.

It is the policy of The Pennsylvania State University Press to use acid-free paper. Publications on uncoated stock satisfy the minimum requirements of American National Standard for Information Sciences—Permanence of Paper for Printed Library Material, ANSI Z39.48-1992.

Dedicated to
all feminist pragmatists,
and particularly the "Jane Collective"
of the Society for the Advancement of American Philosophy

Contents

Preface ix

Acknowledgments xiii

Introduction 1

Part 1: Culture and Art

1 Reading Jane Addams in the Twenty-first Century 31
    Katherine Joslin

2 Cultural Contradictions: Jane Addams's Struggles with the
    Life of Art and the Art of Life 55
    Charlene Haddock Seigfried

3 Trojan Women and Devil Baby Tales: Addams on
    Domestic Violence 81
    Marilyn Fischer

4 Addams's Philosophy of Art: Feminist Aesthetics and Moral
    Imagination at Hull House 107
    L. Ryan Musgrave Bonomo

Part 2: Sex and Society

5 Sex and the City: Jane Addams Confronts Prostitution 125
    Victoria Bissell Brown

6   Toward a Queer Social Welfare Studies: Unsettling
    Jane Addams   159
        Shannon Jackson

7   Love on Halsted Street: A Contemplation on Jane Addams   181
        Louise W. Knight

Part 3: Religion and Politics

8   The Theology of Jane Addams: Religion "Seeking Its
    Own Adjustment"   201
        Eleanor J. Stebner

9   Social Democracy, Cosmopolitan Hospitality, and
    Intercivilizational Peace: Lessons from Jane Addams   223
        Judith M. Green

10 Community Organizing: Addams and Alinsky   255
        Maurice Hamington

11 Examining Addams's Democratic Theory Through a
    Postcolonial Feminist Lens   275
        Judy D. Whipps

12 Engendering Democracy by Socializing It: Jane Addams's
    Contribution to Feminist Political Theorizing   293
        Wendy Sarvasy

    Selected Bibliography   311

    List of Contributors   323

    Index   327

Preface

Nancy Tuana

Take into your hands any history of philosophy text. You will find compiled therein the "classics" of modern philosophy. Since these texts are often designed for use in undergraduate classes, the editor is likely to offer an introduction in which the reader is informed that these selections represent the perennial questions of philosophy. The student is to assume that she or he is about to explore the timeless wisdom of the greatest minds of Western philosophy. No one calls attention to the fact that the philosophers are all men.

Although women are omitted from the canons of philosophy, these texts inscribe the nature of woman. Sometimes the philosopher speaks directly about woman, delineating her proper role, her abilities and inabilities, her desires. Other times the message is indirect—a passing remark hinting at women's emotionality, irrationality, unreliability.

This process of definition occurs in far more subtle ways when the central concepts of philosophy—reason and justice, those characteristics that are taken to define us as human—are associated with traits historically identified with masculinity. If the "man" of reason must learn to control or overcome traits identified as feminine—the body, the emotions, the passions—then the realm of rationality will be one reserved primarily for men,[1] with grudging entrance to those few women who are capable of transcending their femininity.

Feminist philosophers have begun to look critically at the canonized texts of philosophy and have concluded that the discourses of philosophy are not gender-neutral. Philosophical narratives do not offer a universal perspective, but rather privilege some experiences and beliefs over others. These experiences and beliefs permeate all philosophical theories whether they be aesthetic or epistemological, moral or metaphysical. Yet this fact has often been neglected by those studying the traditions of philosophy. Given the history of canon formation in Western philosophy, the perspective most likely to be privileged is that of upper-class white males. Thus, to be fully aware of the impact of gender biases, it is imperative that we re-read the canon with attention to the ways in which philosophers' assumptions concerning gender are embedded within their theories.

This series, Re-Reading the Canon, is designed to foster this process of reevaluation. Each volume will offer feminist analyses of the theories of a selected philosopher. Since feminist philosophy is not monolithic in method or content, the essays are also selected to illustrate the variety of perspectives within feminist criticism and highlight some of the controversies within feminist scholarship.

In this series, feminist lenses focus on the canonical texts of Western philosophy, both those authors who have been part of the traditional canon, and those philosophers whose writings have more recently gained attention within the philosophical community. A glance at the list of volumes in the series reveals an immediate gender bias of the canon: Arendt, Aristotle, Beauvoir, Derrida, Descartes, Foucault, Hegel, Hume, Kant, Locke, Marx, Mill, Nietzsche, Plato, Rousseau, Wittgenstein, Wollstonecraft. There are all too few women included, and those few who do appear have been added only recently. In creating this series, it is not my intention to rectify the current canon of philosophical thought. What is and is not included within the canon during a particular historical period is a result of many factors. Although no canonization of texts will include all philosophers, no canonization of texts that excludes all but a few women can offer an accurate representation of the history of the discipline, as women have been philosophers since the ancient period.[2]

I share with many feminist philosophers and other philosophers writing from the margins of philosophy the concern that the current canonization of philosophy be transformed. Although I do not accept the position that the current canon has been formed exclusively by power relations, I do believe that this canon represents only a selective history of the tradition. I share the view of Michael Bérubé that "canons are at once the location, the index, and the record of the struggle for cultural representation; like any other hegemonic formation, they must be continually reproduced anew and are continually contested."[3]

The process of canon transformation will require the recovery of "lost" texts and a careful examination of the reasons such voices have been silenced. Along with the process of uncovering women's philosophical history, we must also begin to analyze the impact of gender ideologies upon the process of canonization. This process of recovery and examination must occur in conjunction with careful attention to the concept of a canon of authorized texts. Are we to dispense with the notion of a tradition of excellence embodied in a canon of authorized texts? Or, rather than abandon the whole idea of a canon, do we instead encourage a reconstruction of a canon of those texts that inform a common culture?

This series is designed to contribute to this process of canon transformation by offering a re-reading of the current philosophical canon. Such a re-reading shifts our attention to the ways in which woman and the role of the feminine are constructed within the texts of philosophy. A question we must keep in front of us during this process of re-reading is whether a philosopher's socially inherited prejudices concerning woman's nature and role are independent of her or his larger philosophical framework. In asking this question attention must be paid to the ways in which the definitions of central philosophical concepts implicitly include or exclude gendered traits.

This type of reading strategy is not limited to the canon, but can be applied to all texts. It is my desire that this series reveal the importance of this type of critical reading. Paying attention to the workings of gender within the texts of philosophy will make visible the complexities of the inscription of gender ideologies.

Notes

1. More properly, it is a realm reserved for a group of privileged males, since the texts also inscribe race and class biases that thereby omit certain males from participation.

2. Mary Ellen Waithe's multivolume series, *A History of Women Philosophers* (Boston: M. Nijhoff, 1987), attests to this presence of women.

3. Michael Bérubé, *Marginal Forces/Cultural Centers: Tolson, Pynchon, and the Politics of the Canon* (Ithaca: Cornell University Press, 1992), 4–5.

Acknowledgments

The excellence of this collection is the result of the generosity of the authors who contributed to it. I had many lengthy phone conversations and electronic correspondence with the authors, and I want to thank them for sharing their time and effort on this project. Nancy Tuana also deserves a copious amount of praise. She is not only the series editor, but also my mentor and friend. The many insights Nancy shared with me paved the way for a smoother editorial process. The professionals at Penn State Press, including Sandy Thatcher, Patty Mitchell, Laura Reed-Morrisson, Kathryn Yahner, and Cherene Holland, contributed tremendously to the quality of this anthology. One of the most overlooked aspects of successful publishing is copyediting. In this respect, Romaine Perin made this book much more intelligible than my original manuscript. I would also like to express my appreciation to Dean David Glassman of the College of Liberal Arts and all the folks at the University of Southern Indiana who granted me reassignment time to work on this book. Finally, special thanks go to my family, Stephanie and Rosemary, for supporting me through my research addiction.

Introduction

The Re-Reading the Canon series performs the important function of taking a fresh feminist look at classic texts in the Western tradition. In regard to the works of Jane Addams, "re-reading" takes on the added dimension of exploring a corpus of texts that until recently was relegated to the dustbin of American history. Although her *Twenty Years at Hull-House* is considered an American classic (and has never gone out of print), Addams's dozen books and hundreds of published articles have sometimes been thought of as quaint examples of an overly optimistic era. Beginning in the 1990s, feminist scholars rediscovered the vitality of Addams's social philosophy and challenged the traditional marginalization of her ideas.¹ Today, following a war-laden twentieth century, and the failure of militarism and "get tough" approaches to solve domestic and global problems, Addams's social theorizing, which emphasizes cosmopolitan experiences and sympathetic connections, provides a provocative alternative to Western notions of individualism, transactional relations, and spectator epistemology.

This volume brings together many of the leading Addams scholars in North America to consider Addams's ongoing relevance to feminist thought. For decades, Addams has been a troublesome figure for feminists to identify as one of their own. Clearly, she advocated for women's suffrage, supported the advancement of women's social and political standing, and was the most visible female public figure of her era. However, her pragmatist proclivities, avoidance of ideology, and inclusive approach has masked her original contributions to theorizing about society and gender. For example, the feminist credentials of Addams's contemporary Charlotte Perkins Gilman are unquestioned. Although Gilman, like Addams, eschewed the title of "feminist," she made gender a central organizing principle for many of her works and was not afraid to make pointed criticisms of the behavior and institutions of men. Addams's feminism is more complex and subtle. Always careful to avoid antagonism that might alienate participants, Addams interwove her critique of masculinity into her concern for social advancement. Where Gilman lambastes men's religious organizations, for example, Addams cajoles them to act differently without categorically rejecting them. The contributors to *Feminist Interpretations of Jane Addams* have the benefit of decades worth of development in feminist analytical tools to see past many of the biases and fully consider Addams's intellectual legacy. In this Introduction, I provide a brief overview of Addams's life and work, as well as describe the subjects and themes developed by the contributors to this volume.

The Snare of Preparation

Addams took up the task of writing the autobiography that became *Twenty Years at Hull-House* when she was nearly fifty years old.² She viewed her personal development as a prelude, "the snare of preparation," to her mission in the social settlement movement. Having achieved national recognition, she interpreted her life as culminating in the founding and running of the social settlement Hull House. This interpretative lens is consistent with the romantic notion of social heroism that she adapted from reading Thomas Carlyle and John Ruskin. Yet Addams was both humble enough and sufficiently secure in her convictions to write about her foibles and move beyond individual heroism. The last part of *Twenty Years at Hull-House* is less personal and focuses entirely on the achievements of the social settlement, which is indicative of Addams's inseparable identification with it. At a time when Horatio Alger stories, triumphant of personal effort, capitalism, and material success, were all the rage, Addams told an alternative tale of social morality rooted in a life dedicated to social progress.

Laura Jane Addams was born in Cedarville, Illinois, on September 6, 1860. She grew up in the shadow of the Civil War (which ended in 1865) and during a time when Darwin's *Origin of Species* (1859) was achieving widespread influence. As a child, she benefited from the material advantage of being the daughter of a politician and successful mill owner, John Addams. When Jane was two years old, her mother, Mary, died giving birth to her ninth child. Subsequently, the precocious Addams became devoted to her father and benefited psychologically and intellectually from his attention. John Addams sent his daughter to college at what was then Rockford Seminary. Addams became part of a generation of women who were among the first in their family to attend college. At Rockford, she experienced the empowerment of living in a women-centered environment, and she blossomed as an intellectual and a social leader. Addams's college experience foreshadowed the sense of purposeful community she created at Hull House.

As was true for those of many women of her time, Addams's prospects after completing college were limited. Following a failed attempt at medical school, Addams slipped into a near-decade-long malaise regarding the course her life should take. Because she was a woman living in the late nineteenth century, her college experience did not translate into any clear career path, particularly given that she had rejected marriage and religious life. Her lack of personal direction was punctuated by chronic physical illness. She made two trips to Europe during this period. On the second, she visited Toynbee Hall, a community of young men committed to helping the poor of London by living among them. Inspired, Addams formulated a plan to emulate aspects of Toynbee Hall to benefit those in the United States. She had found her way out of her malaise.[3]

Reinvigorated, Addams enlisted a college friend, Ellen Gates Starr, in a plan to found a social settlement in Chicago, a city facing unparalleled immigrant influx. On September 18, 1889, Hull House opened its doors amid the squalor of Chicago's West Side. Settlements are unfamiliar organizations today; few social institutions currently engage in the range of endeavors or are driven by the level of passion of these Progressive Era communities. One way to describe them is as a mix of research and service. Hull House became an incubator for numerous social programs. Settlements responded to the needs of their neighborhood by initiating community projects. The reputation of Hull House quickly grew, and women, as well as a few men, from all over the country came to live and work there. Ostensibly coeducational, Hull House was clearly a woman-identified space. A few of the residents were married but many were single, and many women, including Addams, were in committed relationships with other women.

From the outset of the settlement's operation, Addams theorized about the identity and function of Hull House. The language she used in her descriptions reflected her philosophical training and insight. For example, she described the application and reorganization of knowledge as the fundamental problem of modern life and then claimed that settlements were like applied universities: "The ideal and developed settlement would attempt to test the value of human knowledge by action, and realization, quite as the complete and ideal university would concern itself with the discovery of knowledge in all branches."[4] Inspired by her experiences at Hull House, Addams became a prolific author and a sought-after public speaker. Eventually, she extended her cosmopolitan-based analysis to issues of race, education, and world peace.

Addams became one of the most respected and well-recognized figures in the nation, playing a key role in numerous progressive endeavors. She was a founding figure in the National Association for the Advancement of Colored People, the American Civil Liberties Union, and the Women's International League for Peace and Freedom. Her popularity was such that Theodore Roosevelt asked her to second his nomination for the presidency in 1912, the first time a woman had participated in such an act. There was, however, a gendered dimension to her popularity. Her work at Hull House has sometimes been referred to as "social housekeeping" in that she took on a number of projects deemed socially acceptable to women: cleaning up the neighborhoods and providing for the well-being of children. As such, she had only mildly challenged the division between the gender-identified public and private spheres. After World

War I broke out in Europe, her outspoken pacifism and refusal to endorse the war or the U.S. entry into it was more gender role transgression than the public was willing to tolerate. Her popularity fell and she became the victim of vicious public criticism. Ever reflective, she took this opportunity to write about the social function of citizenship and the nature of patriotism.[5] Late in her life, her worldwide efforts on behalf of peace were somewhat vindicated through her reception of the Nobel Peace Prize (1931). Addams died of cancer on May 21, 1935, leaving behind a tremendous intellectual legacy that has only recently begun to be fully appreciated.

In what follows I will address Addams's public social philosophy and specifically her epistemology, pragmatism, and ethics.

A Public Philosopher

George Cotkin described William James as a public philosopher, or one who "attempted to capture the nature of the cultural crisis of his era and to present solutions to it in accessible philosophical manner."[6] Addams took this definition one step further. Not only did she couch solutions in ethical, metaphysical, epistemological, and aesthetic terms, she also attempted material solutions and provided further reflections upon her efforts. Addams was a public philosopher who engaged and actively invested in a cycle of experience, reflection, and action through her books, articles, and speeches.

Although Addams was recognized for her social settlement efforts, her work was usually mapped onto conventional gender understandings: male philosophers such as John Dewey, William James, and George Herbert Mead were believed to provide original progressive thought, while Addams administered their theories. Nevertheless, the almost half century in which she lived and worked as the leader of Hull House gave her an opportunity to bring her commitment toward social improvement, feminism, diversity, and peace to direct action while she continually reflected and refined her ideas. The diversity and oppression in the neighborhood surrounding Hull House was staggering, and it is a wonder that reflective work could be done in the face of such dire need. However, Addams viewed her settlement work as a grand epistemological endeavor, although she never forgot the humanity of her neighbors. She was indeed a public philosopher—one who was not afraid to get her hands dirty in drawing her social theories from social experience.

Addams's philosophy combined feminist sensibilities with an unwavering commitment to social improvement through cooperative efforts. Although she sympathized with feminists, socialists, and pacifists, she refused to be labeled. This refusal was pragmatic rather than ideological. Addams's commitment to social cohesion and cooperation prompted her to eschew what she perceived as divisive distinctions. Active democratic social progress was so essential to Addams that she did not want to alienate any group of people from the conversation or potential participation. Accordingly, her writing is not readily recognizable as "philosophical." Her audience varied as she directed her writing toward influencing different constituencies of the public. She did not intend to engage in philosophical narratives directed at specialists who were removed from civic engagement. Her writing is replete with examples from her Hull House experience addressing topics that are not the centerpiece of traditional philosophical debate, such as garbage collection, immigrant folk stories, and prostitution. Recovering Jane Addams as a philosopher requires appreciating the dynamic operating between theory and action that is reflected in her writing. However, within Addams's work, a wellspring of nascent feminist philosophical insight can be found.

Epistemology and Context

Traditionally, Western philosophy has not problematized the authoritative voice from which it speaks. Extrapolating the Cartesian mind/body split, philosophers used theory to develop moral systems that speak to all people for all times. Kant's duties apply to everyone, Mill's consequential calculus works for everyone, and Locke's rights protect everyone . . . at least if that everyone is a member of the dominant group in society. Consequently, differences of time, power, and place matter little, because abstract theory is not mired in circumstantial issues.

Feminist philosophers, among others, have argued vigorously that context does matter. Although there are lively debates within feminist philosophical circles regarding the nature of objectivity, many, including Dorothy Smith, Nancy Hartsock, Hilary Rose, Alison Jaggar, and Sandra Harding, have developed the notion that knowledge is indeed situated.

In particular, *feminist* standpoint theorists valorize the perspectives and theories derived from oppressed positions in society such as from women's experience. Harding describes a feminist standpoint as something to be achieved rather than a passive perspective. All women have lived experience in a woman's body and therefore have a woman's perspective, but a feminist standpoint requires an effort at stepping back to gain a holistic picture of power struggles. Through the understanding of the perspectival aspect of truth claims, standpoint epistemology can create libratory knowledge that can be leveraged to subvert oppressive systems. One of the challenges of standpoint theory is how to give voice to multiple positions without falling back on hierarchies that favor certain standpoints over others.

Addams demonstrates an appreciation for the spirit of standpoint theory through her work and writing at Hull House. Despite the privileged social position she was born into, her settlement avocation immersed her in disempowered communities. Addams poetically describes her moral mandate to experience others: "We know, at last, that we can only discover truth by a rational and democratic interest in life, and to give truth complete social expression is the endeavor upon which we are entering. Thus the identification with the common lot which is the essential idea of Democracy becomes the source and expression of social ethics. It is though we thirsted to drink at the great wells of human experience, because we knew that a daintier draught would not carry us to the end of the journey, going forward as we must in the heat and jostle of the crowd."[7]

One might object that although these are admirable sentiments, they are still spoken by an outsider. What constitutes an outsider? Addams lived the better part of a half century in the diverse immigrant neighborhood of Hull House in Chicago. She did not go home to the suburbs or return with her data to a university office. She lived and worked among the crime, civic corruption, prostitution, sweatshops, and other ills of the community. When they first started Hull House, Addams and Starr were involved outsiders—an oddity that neighbors looked upon suspiciously. However, time, proximity, and an earnest desire to learn and help won the trust and respect of the neighborhood. The outsiders became insiders. Addams's work and theorizing resonates with what Patricia Hill Collins refers to as the "outsider-within." Usually applied to members of oppressed communities who must understand and negotiate within privileged communities to survive, this term describes Addams, who transgressed her privileged position to become an "outsider-within" in the immigrant communities around Hull House while simultaneously helping to empower those populations. When Addams wrote or spoke about single women laborers, child laborers, prostitutes, or first- and second-generation immigrants, she employed firsthand knowledge gained from her own social interactions. She leveraged her experiences to give voice to standpoints that were marginalized in society to foster what Collins describes as "distinctive oppositional knowledges that embrace multiplicity yet remain cognizant of power."[8] Simultaneously, Addams worked to give the oppressed access to privileged language through college extension courses, English language courses, and social clubs that fostered political and social debate. Addams was self-conscious about speaking for others: "I never addressed a Chicago audience on the subject of the Settlement and its vicinity without inviting a neighbor to go with me, that I might curb my hasty generalization by the consciousness that I had an auditor who knew the conditions more intimately than I could hope to do."[9] She did not try to develop universal moral truths but recognized that the standpoint of Hull House neighbors mattered.

In an 1896 article in the *American Journal of Sociology*, "A Belated Industry," Addams addressed the plight of women in domestic labor. People engaged in this work were the most powerless of laborers; they were predominantly women, many of whom were immigrants with limited English-language skills and in jobs that afforded little legal protection or organizing possibilities. Addams begins the article with a footnote claiming that her knowledge of domestic laborers came from her experience with the Woman's Labor Bureau, one of the many Hull House projects. She goes on to address the powerlessness of domestic work, particularly as it entails isolation and overwhelming power relationship: "The household employé [sic] has no regular opportunity for meeting other workers of her trade, and of attaining with them the dignity of corporate body."[10] She identifies the gendered dimension of this oppressive work: "Men would . . . resent the situation and consider it quite impossible if it implied the giving up of their family and social ties, and living under the roof of the household requiring their services."[11] Extrapolating her experience of these workers to help her readers imaginatively inhabit a standpoint, she writes, "An attempt is made to present this industry [domestic labor] from the point of view of those women who are working in households for wages."[12] She repeatedly gave recognition to the experiences of oppressed people whom she came to know, in an effort to have them participate in the social democracy she was trying to foster.

Addams's approach to standpoint theory is characteristically functional. She believes that recognizing alternative standpoints is important in promoting lateral progress through sympathetic understanding. Accordingly, if a voice is given to individuals inhabiting marginalized positions in society, it fosters the possibility of a better understanding between people as well as actions that can lead to improving their lot. Addams engages in the tricky balance of honoring standpoints while simultaneously seeking connections and continuities from which to build upon, as is exemplified in her book on young people, *The Spirit of Youth and the City Streets*, and that on elderly women, *The Long Road of Woman's Memory*. The latter work is a surprising look at the memories of first-generation immigrant women and is markedly atypical of philosophical writing. Rather than writing about famous women or theorists or women writers—and Addams knew most of the prominent women of her day—she addressed the women who were her neighbors at Hull House. By "addressed," I do not mean that Addams began by positing a theory about these women. Instead, she retold a number of stories she had heard from them and then drew out conclusions about the function of memory. For Addams, theory follows experience. She was in the minority among her peers in philosophy or feminism to believe that working-class immigrant women not only should be given a voice but also had something important to contribute to the community of ideas.

Feminist Pragmatism

Addams was the least elitist and the most radical of the American philosophers of her era. She consistently took inclusive positions that sought the benefit of society, and eloquently supported them. Although pragmatists typically advocated for social progress, she radicalizes the extent of that social progress. Rather than defining progress by the achievements of the best and the brightest, Addams advocates the betterment of all, in what she calls "lateral progress." This seemingly oxymoronic term highlights the tension in Addams's thinking over promoting social progress but in a widespread rather than elitist manner. Addams explains:

> The man who insists upon consent, who moves with the people, is bound to consult the "feasible right" as well as the absolute right. He is often obliged to attain only Mr. Lincoln's "best possible," and then has the sickening sense of compromising with his best convictions. He has to move along with those whom he leads toward a goal that neither he nor they see very clearly till they come to it. He has to discover what people really want, and then "provide the channels in which the growing moral force of their lives shall flow." What he does attain, however, is not the result of his individual striving, as a solitary mountain climber beyond that of the valley multitude but it is sustained and upheld by the sentiments and aspirations of many others. Progress has been slower perpendicularly, but incomparably greater because lateral.
>
> He has not taught his contemporaries to climb mountains, but he has persuaded the villagers to move up a few feet higher.[13]

Whether one refers to capitalists negatively as "robber barons" or positively as "captains of industry," the rise of commerce at the turn of the nineteenth century in the United States was defined by the winners of the game: those who amassed wealth. The wealthy enjoyed tremendous progress in health care, education, and material well-being. Addams was not satisfied with narrow social development and redefined progress according to the common person's experience. Ironically, she is often chastised for expounding middle-class values, which was her point of reference as she started Hull House, but her experiences pushed her to more fully understand and appreciate the immigrant poor in the neighborhood.

Addams applied lateral progress, or what might better be understood as inclusive social advancement, to numerous issues. When she discusses the role of labor unions, she argues that they are fulfilling a function that society has declined in their attempt to improve working conditions for all. Addams, who had a track record of supporting labor, makes it clear that she does not view collective bargaining as an end in itself. She sees unions as trailblazers that obtain working conditions that eventually benefit everyone in society: "Trade unions are trying to do for themselves what the government should secure for all its citizens; has, in fact, secured in many cases."[14] Addams is not interested in improving the lot of one group of workers over another: "Any sense of division and suspicion is fatal in a democratic form of government, for although each side may seem to secure most for itself, when consulting only its own interests, the final test must be the good of the community as a whole."[15] For Addams, unions are important inasmuch as they improve working conditions, raise wages, reduce hours, and eliminate child labor for all Americans.

An inclusive or lateral progress was also a gender issue, in Addams's view. Real progress could not be understood as the achievements of a select group of society—men. Just as Addams couched women's progress as participation in the overall progress of society, she viewed progress as incomplete if it were not extended to women. This dual sense of the benefits of progress can be seen in her claim about suffrage that "as the governing classes have been enlarged by the enfranchisement of one body of men after another, government itself has not only become enriched through new human interests, but at the same time it has become further democratized."[16] For Addams, feminism, egalitarianism, and lateral progress are all cut from the same cloth.

Although the first chapter of her *Democracy and Social Ethics* is ostensibly a critique of charity workers and their preconceived notions of the needs of the destitute, it also reveals her disposition toward the poor and oppressed. She decries the historical position of blaming the victim: "Formerly, when it was believed that poverty was synonymous with vice and laziness, and that the prosperous man was the righteous man, charity was administered harshly with a good conscience; for the charitable agent really blamed the individual for his poverty, and the very fact of his own superior prosperity gave him a certain consciousness of superior morality."[17] Such a judgment serves to separate the wealthy from the poor. Accordingly, the rich can make progress intellectually, materially, and technologically, while the poor are left behind largely because it is their own fault. Addams argues that the poor are victims of circumstance and that it is the responsibility of society to first understand those who are marginalized and then develop means for their participation in lateral progress.

For Addams, charity, although a good, is not lateral social progress. A temporary transfer in wealth, while noble, does not constitute real progress in alleviating economic disparity. She never viewed herself as a charity worker, nor did she characterize the work of Hull House as charity: "I am always sorry to have Hull House regarded as philanthropy."[18] What Addams sought was an inclusive progress that could be brought about by the collective will and manifested through social institutions. She believed that there would be no need for settlements if "society had been reconstructed to the point of affording equal opportunity for all."[19] Addams is not advocating a laissez-faire capitalism version of equal opportunity that is abstract and rights based. Addams's approach to equal opportunity is set in a context of active democracy in which citizens and social organizations look out for one another because they all have a stake in lateral progress.

Addams's notion of lateral progress can be summarized in four points. First, lateral or inclusive social progress is preferred over individual progress. Addams views the solidarity necessary for lateral progress as a prerequisite for social philosophy: "It is always easy to make all philosophy point one particular moral and all history adorn one particular tale; but I may be forgiven the reminder that the best speculative philosophy sets forth the solidarity of the human race; that the highest moralists have taught that without the advance and improvement of the whole, no man can hope for any lasting improvement in his own moral or material individual condition."[20] In this respect, Addams is against social Darwinism, which runs counter to her own ideas about social evolution. Social Darwinism celebrates the success of individuals as a manifestation of a type of natural selection. Accordingly, the best and brightest should receive fame and fortune because they are the most efficient users of social resources. Lateral progress means that all should advance together but not necessarily in lockstep. Addams is not against social leadership or philanthropy, but they must be tempered by widespread social cohesion and participation. Second, Addams's notion of inclusive progress assumes *circumstances* to be the major difference between the haves and have-nots. Here she employs a positive human ontology, in that people are not good or bad but circumstances can lead to good or bad situations. This approach leaves open the possibility for greater understanding because the essence of humanity is shared. Addams will assiduously avoid making individuals into "others" through labels of good and evil. Third, because human beings do have much in common, the experiences of others can lead to greater understanding, which in turn can lead to a mechanism, such as social advancement, that creates lateral progress. This valorization of proximity describes Addams's purpose for the Hull House settlement. Finally, Addams's lateral progress assumes that social reform for the betterment of all is possible. She believes that public and private institutions can institute programs that are the means for social advancement. Hull House incubated numerous public programs, among them the juvenile court system, labor union housing cooperatives, and the Labor Museum, that represented a means for citizens to be caring and accountable to one another while seeking benefits for all. Ultimately, the notion of lateral progress is not discontinuous with Addams's pragmatist philosophy, but it highlights an inclusive element and a radical edge.

Addams's radical pragmatism ultimately had a feminist dimension: she continually gave voice to women's experience, addressed women's issues, and saw a vibrant social democracy as possible only if there were full participation by both men and women. When it came to issues such as women's suffrage, she exhibited a feminist pragmatism: "If women had no votes with which to select the men upon whom her social reform had become dependent some cherished project might be so modified by uninformed legislatures during the process of legal enactment, that the law, as finally passed, injured the very people it was meant to protect. Women had discovered that the unrepresented are always liable to be given what they do not want by legislators who merely wish to placate them."[21] Note that Addams did not argue for the application of abstract human rights but instead made a functional claim about the role of voting in proper democratic representation. It is not that Addams opposed rights; rather, she continually opted for pragmatist arguments on feminist issues. Her male pragmatist colleagues were sympathetic to these positions but did not make the claims as forcefully or consistently as Addams.

Feminist Care Ethics

Addams's ethical philosophy was guided by the notion of sympathetic knowledge, which she described as "the only way of approach to any human problem."[22] Sympathetic knowledge is a mingling of epistemology and ethics: knowing one another better reinforces the common connection of people such that the potential for caring and empathetic moral actions increases. Addams not only theorized on this idea, she also lived it. Sympathetic knowledge underwrites her approach to the diversity she confronted in the immigrant neighborhood surrounding Hull House and allowed her to develop a precursor to standpoint epistemology. Her leadership among the American pragmatists in understanding the poor and oppressed resulted in a more critical form of pragmatism, imbued with a class and gender consciousness. Ultimately, Addams operates and theorizes about what today is described as a relational approach to morality derived from feminist theory known as "care ethics."[23] Although it is difficult to capture in a short statement, Virginia Held describes caring as "a relation in which carer and cared-for share an interest in their mutual well-being."[24] In her version of care ethics, Addams does not privatize caring relationships in metaphors of parent-child relationships, as did early care theorists, but assertively extends the notion to community and society.[25]

An analysis of Addams's moral philosophy suggests at least three claims about her relationship to feminist care ethics. First, her approach to the important social issues of her day reflects the relationality and contextualization consistent with what is called care ethics today. Second, while Addams employs caring in response to the needs of others, she contributes an active, even assertive, dimension to care ethics not commonly found among care ethicists. Third, she advocates what might be called "socializing care": systemically instantiating the habits and practices of care in social institutions.

Although *care* is a simple and widely invoked word, many feminist theorists have invested it with a particular meaning as it applies to ethics. The original motivation for developing care ethics was an acknowledgment that traditional forms of morality, in particular principle-based and consequence-based ethics, did not adequately capture the richness of the human condition. These approaches typically bracket out emotions, relationships, temporal considerations, reciprocity, and creativity to focus on immediate adjudication of moral conflicts. Accordingly, the use of rules or consequences can become a reductionist and formulaic response resulting in short-sighted responses to complex and systemic issues. Nevertheless, care ethicists do not generally advocate anarchy. Principles and consequences have an important place in moral deliberation, but care theorists seek a more robust sense of morality. For example, the claim that people who spray-paint graffiti on a building ought to be punished because they have damaged someone else's property (rule/principle violation) will likely receive widespread assent. Care ethicists will not necessarily deny such an assertion, but they want to know more. The person doing the spray-painting is a human being, and his or her motivations and circumstances may reveal other variables not sufficiently addressed by the mere recognition of rule violations. There may be systemic issues involving social opportunities or discrimination or lack of voice that have contributed to this behavior. Care ethicists shift the moral focus from abstract individuals and their actions to concrete, situated people with feelings, friends, and dreams—persons who can be cared about. Care ethics demands effort, experience, knowledge, imagination, and empathy for the totality of the moral context to be effectively understood. The result is not exoneration of personal responsibility but a richer understanding of the human condition whereby we are all actors and acted upon.

Addams consistently moves beyond formulaic moral accounts of principles or consequences to apply care ethics to her experiences in the Hull House neighborhood. Proximity is once again crucial, as she has direct experience of individuals, which better provides the resources for a caring response. However, as a philosopher, she extrapolates her experiences to theorize about others of similar circumstances. For example, in *The Spirit of Youth and the City Streets*, she addresses juvenile delinquency. She recounts charges against young men who were brought before Chicago's juvenile courts (which Hull House had helped establish). The charges were categorized by type, such as that of stealing, which included the pilfering of pigeons, blankets, and a bicycle. Another category was disorderly conduct, examples of which were picking up coal from railroad tracks, throwing stones at railroad employees, and breaking down fences. Yet another type was vagrancy, which covered among other things loafing, sleeping on the streets all night, and wandering.[26] Addams does not deny the seriousness of some of these infractions, but she does not rush to judgment, instead choosing to investigate the context further. She talks to the young men and asks them about their motivations. She identifies listlessness and a desire for adventure not quieted by what the city has to offer: "Their very demand for excitement is a protest against the dullness of life, to which we ourselves instinctively respond."[27] Addams views the city as built around factory production but ignoring the needs of future workers. She finds in "juvenile delinquents" young people who simply seek adventure and excitement because their lives have little of them. Had Addams merely abstracted youth as a category of individuals who seem to be prone to breaking the law, she could easily have found principles to place a negative judgment on them. However, she viewed them as human beings, many of whom she witnessed growing up in the neighborhood, and she cared for them beyond the alienating label of "troubled youth."

More than merely applying care ethics, Addams infuses a high level of social responsibility into this moral approach. She creates a virtual duty to care. Generally, care ethicists are wary of traditional formulations of abstract notions of duty.[28] Moral duties have historically entailed an agreement regarding what actions a person is required to offer on behalf of another. Because the "other" is an abstract other and the requirements are universalized (i.e., I must act in such a way in all cases), duties toward others have tended toward moral minimums of obligation. For example, if someone's life is in peril and minimal effort is required to prevent it, such as in an infant's being in danger of drowning in three inches of bathwater, a moral obligation to act is present. Although in such cases there is widespread agreement, it becomes more difficult to ascertain what obligation one has to distant others with unclear correlations of success. For example, many Americans have disposable income that could save the life of someone in a poverty-stricken country on a distant continent. Do they have a moral obligation to give that person money, and to what extent? Addams constructs the "duty" to care differently. Hers is an epistemological demand. She demands that good citizens actively pursue knowledge of others—not just facts but a deeper understanding of others—for the possibility of caring and acting on their behalf: "If we grow contemptuous of our fellows, and consciously limit our intercourse to certain kinds of people whom we have previously decided to respect, we not only tremendously circumscribe our range of life, but limit our scope of ethics."[29] For Addams, care ethics must be actively pursued, not passively fostered. Her language is more assertive than that of much current care ethics discourse.

Finally, Addams extends care ethics to the public realm. She is not content to compartmentalize personal and social morality. Caring is what she desires for democracy and its various institutions. She views the residents of social settlements, for example, as having "an opportunity of seeing institutions from the recipient's standpoint" because they are not distant "others" but neighbors. She regards this perspective as significant and one that should ultimately "find expression in institutional management."[30] Furthermore, she differentiates the epistemological project of the settlement from that of the university in language that acknowledges a caring element: "The settlement stands for application as opposed to research; for emotion as opposed to abstraction; for universal interest as opposed to specialization."[31] Although social settlements epitomize a democratic endeavor for her, she applies the same caring values to other institutions. The creation of the juvenile courts in Chicago represents an example of socialized caring for young people. The development of adult education in which tangible and contemporary issues were employed demonstrates a caring regard for the needs of Hull House neighbors. Perhaps most of all, care ethics are manifested in the comportment of the Hull House residents, in their willingness to listen, learn, and respond. Addams views socializing care as participating in a rich ideal of democracy.

The chapters in *Feminist Interpretations of Jane Addams* address many of the themes mentioned above. Because Addams was a fluid thinker who found connections across issues, the authors in this collection often address multiple themes, making clear categorization challenging. Nevertheless, the chapters of this volume are divided into three broad categories. Part 1, "Culture and Art," contains chapters that draw attention to the interplay between aesthetics and social theorizing in Addams's writing. Part 2, "Sex and Society," is an eclectic mix of chapters that address prostitution, the queering of social categories, and Addams's place in sociology. Part 3, "Religion and Politics," includes chapters that confront Addams's unique positions on Christianity and democracy as developed within a cosmopolitan framework.

Part 1: Culture and Art

For Addams, culture had robust implications, including as a motivational force or energy and as a wellspring of meaning, encompassing ethical insight. In the pragmatist cycle of experience, reflection, and action, she negotiates the implications of culture with her desire for social moral progress. As a feminist, she had to loosen culturally sedimented ideas about women. Her goal was to facilitate progress for women and society without alienating cultural constituencies. The first four chapters in this collection explore the intersection of gender, culture, and art in Addams's work.

Katherine Joslin, author of *Jane Addams, a Writer's Life,* brings the perspective of a writer to construct a narrative of Addams's career. In "Reading Jane Addams in the Twenty-first Century," Joslin investigates Addams's books, articles, diary, letters, and even telegraph messages to document the development of Addams's feminist sensibilities. From Addams's senior college essay "Cassandra" (1881) to *The Excellent Becomes the Permanent* (1932), Joslin notes how Addams's writing evolves over time as she ultimately finds her voice as a woman: "Her earlier books had relied heavily on the sound of male voices as authorities who gave volume and credence to what she had to say. In *The Second Twenty Years*, Addams seems content to talk like a woman." Joslin engages in literary contextualization by addressing how Addams responds to ideas she read, from the Declaration of Sentiments to the work of Virginia Woolf. Although philosophers have only recently acclimated to Addams's work as philosophically provocative, Joslin contends that Addams "wrote hybrid texts that seem modern, even postmodern to our eye and ear. . . . We who are living a century later would feel at home in such prose." Joslin views Addams's eclectic cosmopolitan mind as attractive and provocative for contemporary feminists.

No one has done more for advancing Addams as a pragmatist feminist philosopher than Charlene Haddock Seigfried. Her 1996 book *Pragmatism and Feminism: Reweaving the Social Fabric* inspired both feminist and nonfeminist scholars to rethink Addams's position in American intellectual history. In "Cultural Contradictions: Jane Addams's Struggles with the Life of Art and the Art of Life," Seigfried addresses how, through cultural reflection, Addams works out the relationship between theory and practice. Seigfried describes how Addams saw culture stifling women's progressive activism: "Addams complained that literature in the curriculum for young, well-to-do women of her time acted as a substitute for the direct engagement with the world denied them because of their gender." Of course, Addams was not against the development of culture, but as in so much of her connective analysis, she viewed artifacts of culture as misplaced when not seen in light of the social and political circumstances that they are drawn from. Seigfried provocatively parallels this analysis of culture with a commentary on philosophy and its proclivity toward disconnection with social context. Situating Addams within pragmatist thought, Seigfried notes that "the expansive sense of culture that Addams develops, the need to share it and to use it to build bridges between different classes, adds new dimensions to the pragmatist understanding of philosophy as a criticism of culture." Seigfried is equally interested in the role of gender in Addams's cultural analysis. She traces threads of Addams's evolving feminist reflections and discusses the important role of women's associations in this period. Despite Addams's acknowledged power and influence, Seigfried wonders "how much Addams's belief that the best approach to social transformation was through unobtrusive, small steps was caused by the felt restrictions of being a woman in a patriarchal society." This is a fascinating piece of conjecture, given contemporary theories of the epistemic privilege of the oppressed. Seigfried draws from writings throughout Addams's life to develop her theories of culture.

While Joslin provides sweeping analysis of Addams's literary career, and Seigfried offers far-reaching examination of Addams's relation to culture, Marilyn Fischer presents a close reading of a specific captivating event in Addams's life and finds provocative themes embedded within. In "Trojan Women and Devil Baby Tales: Addams on Domestic Violence," Fischer describes the power and subtlety of Addams's feminist pragmatism through Addams's analysis of the "Devil Baby" stories. For six weeks in 1913, the Hull House community was inundated with requests from their immigrant neighbors to view an alleged devil baby hidden there. The local papers denounced the incident as primitive superstition, while Addams found a deeper meaning in the phenomenon. Fischer, the author of *On Addams* as well as the coeditor of three anthologies of Addams's works, characterizes Addams as respectfully listening to and reflecting upon the women perpetuating the devil baby tale. Addams discovers "a form of moral instruction that had evolved and been refined through a long historical development" and then was used by these women to combat domestic violence. Attending to the intricacies of the historical moment, Fischer explains how Addams weaves together the devil baby story with a popular play she helped to underwrite, *The Trojan Women*, as well as theories about "race memory" to find and communicate deep meaning from the immigrant narrative in a manner intelligible to her white, educated audience. This chapter reveals the connective nature of Addams's philosophy that is both feminist and pragmatist. Fischer explains, "The theory of race memory enabled Addams to connect the ancient Egyptians, the women of Troy, and her immigrant neighbors to herself." It is this connectivity that is the touchstone of Addams's cultural analysis. For Addams, cultural expressions in art and literature are not entertainment for the privileged, but touchstones of insight into the humanity of the past, present, and future that can inspire and provoke.

In "Addams's Philosophy of Art: Feminist Aesthetics and Moral Imagination at Hull House," L. Ryan Musgrave Bonomo explores the epistemologically integral role of the arts in Addams's effort to build "cosmopolitan awareness" and global citizenship at Hull House. Musgrave Bonomo suggests that Addams and Ellen Gates Starr developed a unique epistemological approach to moral imagination using practices of arts engagement in a collective manner to facilitate cosmopolitanism and a sense of global ethics. As they drew on relational arts praxis as an essential tool to help residents facilitate new knowledge, American citizenship, *and* what Addams often calls an "international mind," they developed a feminist epistemology concerning the arts. Given this, Musgrave Bonomo suggests that both pioneers warrant immediate inclusion within pragmatist aesthetics—a field in which feminist perspectives remain marginalized. According to Musgrave Bonomo, "What Addams and Starr uniquely contributed to pragmatist aesthetics is their distinctively collective and communitarian emphasis on imaginative thinking." Further, as in the work of Locke and Du Bois, theirs is a pragmatist approach connecting the arts with democracy, but with a feminist dimension. Finally, Musgrave Bonomo offers their practice of integrating learning-through-arts-engagement at Hull House as a nuanced and robust alternative to a commonly held model of fostering individualized moral imagination. Musgrave Bonomo compares Addams's approach to Martha Nussbaum's cosmopolitan ethic.

Part 2: Sex and Society

This section's chapters are connected by themes of sex, gender, and society. It is only relatively recently that Addams has been recognized as an important social theorist, and for that exclusion, sexism is in part to blame. However, exclusion is not the only way that gender plays out in Addams's theorizing. In Lorraine Code's *What Can She Know?* a powerful case is made for the significance of gender in the formation of knowledge. By extension, does Addams's women-identified character further affect her social theorizing? How does this play out when she addresses particular social issues that involve sex? The chapters in this section confront these issues.

In "Sex and The City: Jane Addams Confronts Prostitution," Victoria Brown, author of *The Education of Jane Addams*, addresses Addams's "most vexing book," *A New Consciousness and an Ancient Evil*. Published in 1912 when Addams was well established as a national reformer, *A New Consciousness* raises questions about her grasp of the prostitution issue and, perhaps more important, what her feminism advocates. As Brown points out, *A New Consciousness*, fueled by the muckraking movement against white slave trafficking, contains numerous contradictions and inconsistencies. Brown explores these contradictions with a sympathetic, ironic, and critical eye. For example, Brown claims that "Addams's proposed solutions to prostitution derived more from her ideological commitment to sexual purity than from the realities of prostitution and urban sexual practices," which in part explains why *A New Consciousness* does not stand up to modern feminist scrutiny. Nevertheless, Addams's conclusion that social and economic reforms are needed to abate the proliferation of prostitution remains relevant. Furthermore, even though Addams argues for what Brown characterizes as a "female standard of sexuality" that is empowering and self-directed, the former values the primacy of marital sexuality in such a manner that her "personal path of unmarried service was not a path she could—or would—recommend to the mass of young women in Chicago." Brown demonstrates how feminism is a historical process and pioneering women such as Addams are pushing some boundaries while leaving others intact.

One of the least studied aspects of Addams's feminism is the relationship between the woman-identified community she created and her social theories. Addams's sexuality remains something of a mystery, but what is clear is that she lived a woman-centered life.[32] Shannon Jackson is less concerned with whether Addams was a lesbian than with how Addams's work can be understood through the lens of queer theory. In "Toward a Queer Social Welfare Studies: Unsettling Jane Addams," Jackson finds the notion of "settlement" illuminating. Addams was the leader of a social settlement, but in the process of settling in her neighborhood, she unsettled traditional publicly gendered boundaries as well as familial categories. Jackson suggests that "settling at Hull House was a daily lesson in undoing gendered and classed conventions of privacy and publicity." By applying queer theory, Jackson contends that Addams's work can be viewed as destabilizing social understanding of the feminine in ways that she claims are overlooked in Addams biographer Jean Bethke Elshtain's approach of revaluing the private sphere. For Jackson, the claim of "social housekeeping" was a strategy of Addams and her cohort to transgress social boundaries. Accordingly, Jackson finds that queer theory can "unsettle Jane Addams" while simultaneously "an unsettled Jane Addams speaks back to these fields." For Jackson, Addams's work stands counterposed to queer theorists' concern that supporting the welfare state necessarily results in a force for normalization. Addams was able to negotiate institutional structures of social support during socially repressive times while still queering ideas of community and family. Ultimately, Jackson suggests that Addams may be a founding mother of another discipline: queer welfare studies.

What of Addams's sexuality? Is it an important topic of serious intellectual reflection and potential influence on Addams's thinking or is it a prurient concern of a society that clings to heterosexual normativity? In "Love on Halsted Street: A Contemplation on Jane Addams," Louise W. Knight directly takes up the vexing topic of Addams's sexuality. For so many years this subject was avoided by biographers and commentators despite the evidence of Addams's two long-term relationships with women at Hull House. The highly connective philosophy of Addams makes it likely that her personal relational experiences cannot be separated from her social and political thought. Knight, the author of *Citizen: Jane Addams and the Struggle for Democracy*, claims, "Addams thought about, and explored, three functions of love: intimate love; affectionate, cooperative love; and love of humanity, sometimes called love of the stranger." Knight carefully negotiates the challenges of addressing contemporary understanding of same-sex relationships with that of late nineteenth- and early twentieth-century American society. She discusses the nature of Addams's relationships with Ellen Gates Starr and Mary Rozet Smith, but more important, she discusses the implications of Addams's relationships to her thinking. Knight views the experience of affinity that grows through interaction as contributing to her social theories: "[Addams] came to see that possessing a wide range of affectionate personal relations was what loving humanity meant and was the only way to strengthen democracy. Our first task as citizens, Addams believed, was to get to know one another." Furthermore, Knight observes how what is said or not said about Addams's sexuality indicates as much about the time and circumstances of the people making the commentary as it does about Addams.

Part 3: Religion and Politics

Two spheres of immense masculine derivation are religion and politics. In the final section of *Feminist Interpretations of Jane Addams*, the chapters address Addams's feminist religious and political theorizing. Given the notion of separate spheres, the climate of the late nineteenth and early twentieth century makes Addams's work in these areas particularly extraordinary. What is perhaps even more surprising is that the authors in this section find in Addams alternative perspectives on religion and politics that remain intriguing a century after they were evidenced in her writing.

As with her sexuality, Addams's religiosity has been the subject of much speculation. Addams was well versed in Christianity and valued religion, but she was clearly not an orthodox Christian. In "The Theology of Jane Addams: Religion 'Seeking Its Own Adjustment,'" religion scholar Eleanor Stebner, author of *The Women of Hull-House*, addresses Addams's ambiguous relationship to Christianity. By tracing Addams's youth and early adulthood, Stebner reminds the reader of how close Addams's connections to Christianity were, as shown in her baptism at age twenty-five. Stebner explains that Addams was "biblically literate, but she was not a biblical literalist." She proceeds to recount how commentators and biographers have wrestled over the depth of Addams's religious commitment. Stebner offers three important contextualizations for understanding Addams's religiosity. First, she describes Addams's work in light of the social gospel movement, which was contemporaneous and shared much of the social goals of the Progressive movement, with which Addams is associated. Second, Stebner analyzes Addams's unique relationship to religion when Addams is compared with other feminist pioneers: Matilda Joslyn Gage, Elizabeth Cady Stanton, and Charlotte Perkins Gilman. Finally, Stebner discusses the striking connections between Addams's beliefs and those of modern feminist theologians. For example, Stebner observes that Addams's "desire for religions to adjust and recognize their culpability in supporting systems of injustice is similar to the emphases of later twentieth-century feminist theologians and the connections they identified between traditional religious teachings and systems of sexism, racism, classism, and heterosexism." Addams's comfort in summoning Christian values to encourage social progress while simultaneously criticizing religious institutions for their failures is a refreshing alternative to the modern tendency toward absolute polarization over religion.

Addams connected grassroots efforts with institutional change to actualize social progress. In "Social Democracy, Cosmopolitan Hospitality, and Intercivilizational Peace: Lessons from Jane Addams," Judith Green develops the notion of Addams's approach to peace as a robust intertwining of the local and the national, of the experiential and the theoretical.

Green views "hospitality and peace" as the fundamental aims of Addams's work, but in the organic nature of Addams's methodology, these are two aspects of the same endeavor. Addams viewed her hospitality work with her immigrant neighborhood in Chicago as directly connected to her efforts to bring about world peace. Green favorably compares Addams's writing on peace to that of contemporary political scientists Seyla Benhabib and Samuel Huntington. Both Benhabib and Huntington have conjectured the potential of a cosmopolitan world capable of mitigating violent international conflict. What Green contends is that both Benhabib and Huntington lack an explicit theoretical connection to local peace, which undermines their international project. As Green puts it, "Without such a social expansion of the meaning and practices of democracy to include daily obligations of hospitality as well as those that arise in times of emergency, a 'bounded community' of angry and frightened individuals has no motives and no intellectual resources for opening its doors to outsiders at all, much less for treating them as new neighbors." In a statement resonant with Cornel West's notion of prophetic pragmatism, Green suggests that an undertheorized aspect of Addams's work, her "renascent Christianity," supports her ability to link the experiential and the theoretical. According to Green, Addams's "minimally propositional, antidogmatic take on Christianity" draws on the best of religious traditions that seek to change hearts as well as minds.

It is easy to forget that before Addams was an international peace activist and agitator for racial justice, she was a community organizer. Hull House was an early settlement house, and Addams quickly ascended to leadership in the settlement movement. For Addams, all her subsequent social theory is grounded in the settlement experience. However, male "founding" figures often overshadow pioneering women, and that was the case in the settlement movement, as it is in many other fields. When it comes to community organizing, the most recognizable name is Saul Alinsky, who came to inner-city Chicago a generation after Addams. In "Community Organizing: Addams and Alinsky," I suggest that despite efforts, many led by Alinsky, to differentiate these two, both community organizers shared a number of ideals. Furthermore, because Addams was influential in the early years of the "Chicago School," at the University of Chicago, where Alinsky ultimately studied, the intellectual connection is stronger than one might think. What does differentiate the two community leaders is methodology and metaphors. While Addams viewed her role as that of a good, long-standing member of a neighborhood, Alinsky viewed local justice as a battle to be won, followed by moving on to the next fight. Ultimately, I claim that Addams offers an approach to community organizing that resonates with contemporary local feminist organizing because it values "fluidity and cosmopolitanism" while attempting "to create lasting social relationships."

Judy Whipps observes that modern U.S. military incursions often maintain the claim of "bringing democracy" to the world, which begs the question of what democracy means in this context. In "Examining Addams's Democratic Theory Through a Postcolonial Feminist Lens," Whipps claims that Addams's definition of democracy is useful in reconsidering the contemporary political climate, given the number of military actions and the critique of postcolonial feminists. Accordingly, Whipps traces the development of Addams's democratic ideal. Inheriting a traditional notion of liberal democracy from her upbringing and education, Addams reframes it as an organic community and an ethical system in her first book, *Democracy and Social Ethics*. Her expansive notion of democracy became the scaffolding for all her subsequent work. As Whipps describes it, "Democracy had become a concept large enough to serve as a beacon to Addams in the many re-creations of her career." Whipps, the coeditor of two anthologies of Addams's work, engages in a comparison between Addams's philosophy and that of contemporary feminist postcolonial theorists Chandra Mohanty and Mary E. Hawkesworth. Although Addams did not begin with a postcolonial perspective, her cosmopolitan experience of the city gave her sensitivity to power and privilege. According to Whipps, "By the first decade of the twentieth century Addams had begun to see that democracy can only exist as a living principle, in particular localities and times." Simultaneously, Addams "warned of equating democracy with nationalism," including in a critique of capitalism consistent with some feminist postcolonial analysis. Addams is not always consistent, but she develops a democratic theory that is much more inclusive than those of her pragmatist contemporaries.

One of the challenges in placing Addams in the philosophical tradition is that her work does not fit neatly into established intellectual categories. Hence, the hybrid term *feminist pragmatist* has the greatest resonance with Addams's philosophy. In "Engendering Democracy by Socializing It: Jane Addams's Contribution to Feminist Political Theorizing," Wendy Sarvasy offers the term *theory/activist dynamic* to describe Addams's method of generating new feminist theories through action. Applying this approach to the notion of citizenship, Sarvasy views Addams as employing a "gendered path" to renegotiate public/private boundaries: "Daughters would grasp the nature of social justice only by joining social reform movements." For Addams, private, familial ethics are inadequate in fostering democratic citizenship, because they lack the diverse social interactions that can only come from confronting others in the public arena. According to Sarvasy, the gendered path for women of privilege seeking social progress entails establishing "what feminists today call an intersectional location" by forming solidarity with working-class women. Sarvasy finds in Addams a sense of class responsibility: "I cannot find any evidence that Addams expected the working-class daughter to practice sympathetic understanding toward her well-off sisters." It was through the activism of working with and on behalf of others that Addams developed a theory of engaged citizenship.

The chapters in this volume suggest that there is something valuable in rereading Addams as a feminist and an intellectual whose work has ongoing relevance. The efforts of the authors in this collection are a testament to the notion that if contemporary postmodern sensibilities allow us to entertain the idea of an intellectual canon, Jane Addams deserves to be a part of it.

Notes

1. Recent works on Addams acknowledging feminist issues include Victoria Bissell Brown, *The Education of Jane Addams* (Philadelphia: University of Pennsylvania Press, 2004); Mary Jo Deegan, *Jane Addams and the Men of the Chicago School, 1892–1918* (New Brunswick, N.J.: Transaction Books, 1988); Jean Bethke Elshtain, ed., *Jane Addams and the Dream of American Democracy: A Life* (New York: Basic Books, 2002); Marilyn Fischer, *On Addams* (Toronto: Wadsworth, 2004); Maurice Hamington, *Embodied Care: Jane Addams, Maurice Merleau-Ponty, and Feminist Ethics* (Urbana: University of Illinois Press, 2004); Katherine Joslin, *Jane Addams, a Writer's Life* (Urbana: University of Illinois Press, 2004); Louise W. Knight, *Citizen: Jane Addams and the Struggle for Democracy* (Chicago: University of Chicago Press, 2005); and Charlene Haddock Seigfried, *Pragmatism and Feminism: Reweaving the Social Fabric* (Chicago: University of Chicago Press, 1996).

2. An earlier version of portions of the following text appears in Maurice Hamington, "Jane Addams," *The Stanford Encyclopedia of Philosophy* (Summer 2007 edition), ed. Edward N. Zalta, http://plato.stanford.edu/archives/sum2007/entries/addams-jane/.

3. Jane Addams, *Twenty Years at Hull-House* (1910; Urbana: University of Illinois Press, 1990), 53.

4. Jane Addams, "A Function of the Social Settlement" (1899), reprinted in *The Social Thought of Jane Addams*, ed. Christopher Lasch (Indianapolis: Bobbs-Merrill, 1965), 187.

5. Jane Addams, *Peace and Bread in Time of War* (1922; Urbana: University of Illinois Press, 2002), 79; Jane Addams, Emily G. Balch, and Alice Hamilton, *Women at The Hague: The International Congress of Women and Its Results* (1915; Urbana: University of Illinois Press, 2003), 41.

Introduction   27

6. George Cotkin, *William James: Public Philosopher* (Baltimore: Johns Hopkins University Press, 1990), 88.
7. Jane Addams, *Democracy and Social Ethics* (1902; Urbana: University of Illinois Press, 2002), 9.
8. Patricia Hill Collins, *Fighting Words: Black Women and the Search for Justice* (Minneapolis: University of Minnesota Press, 1998), 8.
9. Addams, *Twenty Years at Hull-House*, 80.
10. Jane Addams, "A Belated Industry," *American Journal of Sociology* 1, no. 5 (1896): 538.
11. Ibid., 540.
12. Ibid., 536.
13. Jane Addams, "A Modern Lear" (1912), reprinted in *Jane Addams and the Dream of American Democracy*, ed. Elshtain.
14. Addams, "A Function of the Social Settlement," 456.
15. Ibid., 461.
16. Jane Addams, "The Larger Aspects of the Woman's Movement," in *Women in Public Life* (Philadelphia: American Academy of Political and Social Science, 1914), 1.
17. Addams, *Democracy and Social Ethics*, 11–12.
18. Jane Addams, "The Objective Value of the Social Settlement" (1893), reprinted in *Jane Addams and the Dream of American Democracy*, ed. Elshtain, 45.
19. Addams, "A Function of the Social Settlement," 185.
20. Jane Addams, "The Subjective Necessity for Social Settlements" (1893), reprinted in *Jane Addams and the Dream of American Democracy*, ed. Elshtain, 127.
21. Jane Addams, *Second Twenty Years at Hull-House* (New York: Macmillan, 1930), 89–90.
22. Jane Addams, *A New Conscience and an Ancient Evil* (1912; Urbana: University of Illinois Press, 2002), 7.
23. Care theory has evolved a great deal since Carol Gilligan first coined the term in 1982. A quarter century later, the definition of care ethics continues to be negotiated. For a discussion of Jane Addams as a care theorist, see Maurice Hamington, *Embodied Care: Jane Addams, Maurice Merleau-Ponty, and Feminist Ethics* (Urbana: University of Illinois Press, 2004), chap. 5.
24. Virginia Held, *The Ethics of Care: Personal, Political, and Global* (New York: Oxford University Press, 2006).
25. Mother-child dyads permeated much of the early care theorizing, including in Nel Noddings, *Caring: A Feminine Approach to Ethics and Moral Education* (Berkeley and Los Angeles: University of California Press, 1984), and Sara Ruddick, *Maternal Thinking: Toward A Politics of Peace* (Boston: Beacon Press, 1989). Recent work by care ethicists has moved away from emphasizing the mother-child model. See, for example, Nel Noddings, *Starting at Home: Caring and Social Policy* (Berkeley and Los Angeles: University of California Press, 2002), and Maurice Hamington and Dorothy Miller, eds., *Socializing Care: Feminist Ethics and Public Issues* (Lanham, Md.: Rowman and Littlefield, 2006).
26. Jane Addams, *The Spirit of Youth and the City Streets* (1909; Urbana: University of Illinois Press, 1972), 56–57.
27. Ibid., 71.
28. Care ethicists have eschewed abstract notions of universalizable moral duties as offered by Kant. Nel Noddings, for example, suggests that obligation (an inner sense of "I must") arises from an encounter with another person in need. Noddings, *Starting at Home*, 49–52.
29. Addams, *Democracy and Social Ethics*, 8.
30. Addams, "The Objective Value of the Social Settlement," 39.
31. Addams, "A Function of the Social Settlement," 189.
32. Lillian Faderman states, "Jane Addams—whether or not she knew to use the term about herself—was what our day would consider lesbian. She devoted her entire emotional life to women, she considered herself married to a woman, and she believed that she was 'delivered' by their shared

28   Introduction

love." Faderman, *Odd Girls and Twilight Lovers: A History of Lesbian Life in Twentieth-Century America* (New York: Penguin Books, 1991), 28. Addams's recent biographers are much more guarded about her sexuality. Victoria Brown identifies the mystery: "Whether Jane and Mary [Rozet Smith] expressed their love for each other sexually is a secret that was buried with them." Nevertheless, according to Brown, the evidence suggests that they had "the sort of mutual admiration and devotion that typifies any strong marriage." Brown, *The Education of Jane Addams*, 257. From what personal letters Addams did not destroy, Louise Knight concludes that "the two friends experienced moments of emotional and physical intimacy together, but nothing is said that could be interpreted as explicitly sexual." Knight, *Citizen*, 218. Whether Addams was a lesbian is less important (although it perhaps influenced her thinking) than the evidence that suggests that she queered the notion of family in her own life, which is the basis for Jackson's project.

Part One

Culture and Art

1
Reading Jane Addams in the Twenty-first Century

Katherine Joslin

We read Jane Addams because, for all the years that separate us from her, she still seems one of us. The truth is that her issues, the vexing social and political questions of her day, remain unresolved, for the most part, a hundred years later. Her books are not merely polemical and are decidedly not academic, and yet they are not wholly imaginative either, never quite fiction. Her writing blends the voices of ordinary people together with those of sociological, political, philosophical, and literary writers and, by amplifying common voices and setting them into dialogue with established authorities, she creates in print the very world she sought in fact.

The goal of this collection of essays is to look with fresh eyes on Jane Addams as a philosopher, a woman worthy of inclusion in the American canon. Such a project comes from the call to action among feminist scholars in the late twentieth century to retrieve female thinkers and artists from their forgotten places in our collective past and reconsider their contribution and appeal across time. This chapter participates in that feminist endeavor by looking closely at Jane Addams as a literary woman. "Literary women have worked in every available form and style, have exhibited every mood and character, have been radical and conservative, narrow and wide-ranging, tragic and comic in their writings," Ellen Moers had proclaimed in 1963. "There is no point saying what women cannot do in literature, for history shows they have done it all."[1] The feminist retrieval work I am doing crosses disciplines by moving Addams, a peripheral writer in literary studies, to the center of a discussion of American literature. Her writing, I am arguing, is her most enduring legacy.[2]

In becoming a literary woman, Jane Addams experimented with language and genre, bringing together what she thought of as male and female modes of expression. Early in her professional life at Hull House, she worked with colleagues to craft the language of sociology, a quasi-scientific prose, associated at that time and indeed over the twentieth century with the male voice. Desire for a wider audience moved her toward more literary modes of expression that were tuned, she believed, to a female voice. She experimented with dramatic techniques of presentation, using vivid street scenes and distinctive immigrant voices to create narratives that advanced her argument and embodied her ethics. During the years of the Great War, she responded in her most poetic voice—a minor key—transmuting story into song. At the end of the 1920s as her progressive causes unraveled, she relaxed into modern, even modernist, expression that she called "honest reminiscence," feeling comfortable at last with the sound of her own voice. In this chapter I will consider the relationship between her ethics and prose as well as changes in her writing over time in *Democracy and Social Ethics* (1902), *The Long Road of Woman's Memory* (1916), and *The Second Twenty Years at Hull-House* (1930).

Philosophers and poets alike have admired her as a storyteller. In 1902, the year in which he published his book of storytelling, *Varieties of Religious Experience*, William James settled into his armchair to read *Democracy and Social Ethics*. He later wrote to its author, Jane Addams:

"[*Democracy and Social Ethics*] seems to me one of the great books of our time. The religion of democracy needs nothing so much as sympathetic interpretations to one another of the different classes of which society consists; and you have made your contribution in a masterly manner. I have learned a lot from your pages."[3] Likewise, Harriet Monroe, who would later found and edit *Poetry* magazine, rose from the comfort of her chair with *Democracy and Social Ethics* in hand to enthuse in a review that the book was "as interesting as a novel" in large part because "the style is so easy and familiar, so much like gracious talk, that one follows it over the heights and depths of a great subject scarcely conscious of the author's mountaineer venturesomeness."[4]

What made her book sound like a novel to Harriet Monroe's ear was the interweaving of voices. The Russian literary theorist Mikhail Bakhtin (born in 1895) differentiated between what he called "authoritative discourse"—the inflexible monologic rhetoric of, say, scientists and businesspeople—and fiction, the dialogic intermingling of voices contending for credence, leaving the reader to interpret meaning. In the essay "Discourse in the Novel" Bakhtin views the genre of the novel as containing "a diversity of social speech types (sometimes even diversity of languages) and a diversity of individual voices, artistically organized."[5] His definition of the novel comes very close to describing the literary form Addams was doing much to create as a mode of didactic storytelling. Over the course of her writing career, she would move away from the monologic prose of science and toward the dialogic or polyvocal possibilities of fiction.

Jane Addams wrote ten books on her own and collaborated on another three. At the beginning of the twentieth century, she wrote three radical and wide-ranging studies of ethical possibilities for culture in the United States: *Democracy and Social Ethics*, *Newer Ideals of Peace* (1907), and *The Spirit of Youth and the City Streets* (1909). She became over those years an iconic figure, almost something of a saint, giving her a stage for her autobiography, *Twenty Years at Hull-House* (1910), a characteristically American tale of individual success amid the broader triumph of the institution she led. Before her fall from grace in 1915, she wrote a last book about the nature of our culture, *A New Conscience and an Ancient Evil* (1912), an ominous study of female sexual vulnerability in the capitalist marketplace. During the Great War, as publishers rejected her pacifist essays, she fell out of favor with her readers and wrote her most literary book in response, *The Long Road of Woman's Memory*, this one, too, about female vulnerability and the sway of the female voice. At the beginning of the 1920s, she looked back on her pacifist efforts in *Peace and Bread in Time of War* (1922). Later, she adopted the mood and mode of literary modernism in *The Second Twenty Years at Hull-House*, and before her death in 1935 she collected funeral orations in *The Excellent Becomes the Permanent* (1932) and experimented with biography in *My Friend, Julia Lathrop* (1935). At times in her career when she was least sure of her own voice, she collaborated with other writers, as she did in *Philanthropy and Social Progress: Seven Essays by Miss Jane Addams, Robert A. Woods, Father J. O. S. Huntington, Professor Franklin H. Giddings, and Bernard Bosanquet* (1893), a collection of essays that established her as an ethicist, and in *Hull-House Maps and Papers: A Presentation of Nationalities and Wages in A Congested District of Chicago, Together with Comments and Essays on Growing Out of the Social Conditions* (1895), an early sociological study she edited with Florence Kelley. As the Great War escalated in 1915, she worked with Emily Greene Balch and Alice Hamilton to write *Women at The Hague* (1915), a justification of their pacifist activism in the Women's International League.[6]

Recent attention to her suggests that she is a writer for our time. The truth is that her way of looking at the world is very like our own. She wrote hybrid texts that seem modern, even postmodern, to our eye and ear, folding personal narrative together with fragments of stories she collected from the streets of Chicago; reporting them from her memory rather than from notes; embroidering them with her considerable imagination; and augmenting them, at times, with sentimental narratives. Her writing is not journalism, not entirely memoir, not scholarly sociology, not often political diatribe, not exclusively philosophy, and yet not quite fiction, not wholeheartedly art. We who are living a century later would feel at home in such prose, I am arguing. We would agree with the way she had of telling the story of her own life as though it signified the larger tale of her neighborhood, the nation, even the enduring human saga. And we would trust in her acknowledgment, later in life, that she could speak only for herself and only from her perspective, the bead she could draw with her own eye.

Reading her early diaries gives us a sense of the writer and philosopher she would become. We find the seed of her ethics, for example, in a diary draft of a letter she was writing, dated December 5, 1880, to E. G. Smith, a Bible salesman who knew her father. In the entry, she struggles with language to articulate what will become the very heart of her ethics. "I was embarrassed and unnatural most of the time I talked with you the other day," she began in apology. "Perhaps it was because I had never before tried to define my purposes and ideals and . . . saw how shallow . . . they were. Feeling . . . that I was neither accurate or just in my representation of myself in trying to become . . . clearer my expressions and ideas were bungling."[7] The page is full of scratched-out words and phrases as she worked to find clear language for a wooly idea. "I am much obliged to you for what you said," she offered as she looked for ways to distance her idea from his. "I see that my idea of that so much as I embody . . . Truth in myself that much I could attract from other people and bring out what was best in their lives a[s] well as my own, can never be carried out unless I have the sacred flame to start with."

Smith was pressing her to commit herself more deeply and openly to the sacred flame of Christian Truth (capital T) but she sought a subtler, synthetic truth. Jane had been writing that year to her former classmate and future professional partner Ellen Gates Starr that she felt "preverted" because she loathed going to prayer meetings. "I do not know that I have grown very much in spiritual things," she acknowledged.[8] What the letter to Smith tells us is that very early in her life Jane had a core idea nearly within the grasp of her mind if not quite within the grasp of her tongue: "So much as I embody . . . Truth in myself that much I could attract from other people and bring out what was best in their lives a[s] well as my own." She would continue to hone that idea as she worked with Ellen to establish the Hull House settlement and create social work and, too, as she constructed a literary voice by blending the voices of others into her own.

Her first professional essays, delivered as speeches at the School of Applied Ethics in Plymouth, Massachusetts, in the summer of 1892 and then published in the collection *Philanthropy and Social Progress*, reveal her thinking about ethics and writing. The school used a comparative model to analyze the world's "great" religions and ethical systems that have "given color to different epochs of history."[9] The third branch of the school studied the practical "rights and wrongs" of industrial economics. The theme that summer was the idea of social progress, and over the six weeks, participants looked specifically at economics, sociology, law, philanthropy, industry, and labor. In *Twenty Years at Hull-House*, she claimed, "I doubt if anywhere on the continent that summer could have been found a group of people more genuinely interested in social development or more sincerely convinced that they had found a clew by which the conditions in crowded cities might be understood."[10] Looking back at the end of her life, she joked that her lectures were "a fine Victorian example of rose water for the plague."[11] Henry C. Adams, a professor of political economy and finance at the University of Michigan, edited a volume of essays from the week on philanthropy and selected Jane Addams as the lead writer.

She was the only contributor to divide her fifty pages into two essays: "Subjective Necessity for Social Settlements" comes first and tells the story of her experience; this is followed by "Objective Value of a Social Settlement," a report on Hull House itself. The very fact that she articulated the settlement movement in twin essays, one from a subjective and the other an objective point of view, suggests a tension that will run throughout her writing career. Over time, Jane Addams will move away from objective, rational, linear expression toward subjective, imaginative, associative prose.

"The Subjective Necessity for Social Settlements" is a persuasive essay that works emotionally on a "bewildered" armchair reformer who shies away from urban poverty because city neighborhoods look dangerous and chaotic. Her reader must have been unsettled and chagrined as she asserted, "I believe the men who lose most are those who thus stay away" (5). The essay takes up the cause of people on the economic and social margin: immigrants, children, and former slaves. Much of her career as a social thinker and a writer will focus on such peripheral groups and notions of social justice. Even her skittish reader, she claims, desires "to share in the race life." Here, too, she turns the configuration on its head by asserting, "To shut one's self away from that half of the race life is to shut one's self away from the most vital part of it; it is to live out but half the humanity which we have been born heir to and to use but half our faculties" (11). She describes a vivid street scene and admonishes her reader, "The stream of laboring people goes past you as you gaze through the plate-glass window of your hotel." It is here that she first uses what will become a dominant metaphor in her writing: "A more poetic prayer would be that the great mother breasts of our common humanity, with its labor and suffering and its homely comforts, may never be withheld from you" (11–12). Again, she deftly turns the tables, leaving her reader to ponder the difference between what certainly feels breastlike in the comfort of a leisure-class hotel and the homely comforts of the throng that he or she is nervously eyeing on the other side of the plate-glass window.

Addams enters the narrative as a young woman eager to share the homely comforts of the "race life," as her family and society offer only "pleasure and freedom from care." Later in her autobiography, Addams will call this the "snare of preparation," the curious tendency of adults to curb the creative energy of the young (65–89). The college-educated woman "is besotted with innocent little ambitions, and does not understand this apparent waste of herself, this elaborate preparation, if no work is provided for her" (13). What she fears is that the vitality of youth itself will wither as an unused muscle may in an otherwise healthy leg. When the young girl returns from college and travel, she finds the "family claim," a ritual of duties that require her to stay at home, tethered—we might say hobbled—a safe distance from the homely throng.

The singing of the Hallelujah Chorus in Handel's *Messiah* becomes a trope for her ethics as well as her writing style. All voices in the chorus, lifted by concerted effort, create a unity of purpose that blends together the voices of professional and novice singers. Likewise, the settlement house attempts to bring voices together. "It aims, in a measure, to lead whatever of social life its neighborhood may afford, to focus and give form to that life, to bring to bear upon it the results of cultivation and training," she reports, "but it receives in exchange for the music of isolated voices the volume and strength of the chorus" (21).

The question for her as she took up the pen was how to amplify "the music of isolated voices." We come back to her letter to the Bible salesman: "[S]o much as I embody . . . Truth in myself that much I could attract from other people and bring out what was best in their lives a[s] well as my own." Throughout "Subjective Necessity for Social Settlements" she synthesizes the voices of an odd assortment of thinkers, beginning with John Locke, Johann Heinrich Pestalozzi, Walter Besant, Samuel Barnett, Jesus, Leo Tolstoy, and Mrs. Humphrey Ward. None of these experts, with the exception of Jesus and he only in paraphrase, gets to talk. She absorbs the voices into her own, amplifying what she has to say. At times in the essay, she uses seemingly disembodied quotes from the Hull House charter, declaring, for example, at the outset that "'the social relation is essentially a reciprocal relation, it gives a form of expression that has peculiar value'" (1–2).[12] Later in the essay, she allows Giuseppe Mazzini to speak: "Education is not merely a necessity of true life by which the individual renews his vital force in the vital force of humanity; it is a Holy Communion with generations dead and living, by which he formulates all his faculties. When he is withheld from this Communion for generations, as the Italian peasant has been, we point our finger at him and say, 'He is like a beast of the field; he must be controlled by force" (9–10). In support of Mazzini's claim for the humanity of the peasant, Addams finally lets us hear the voice of a neighbor, the sort of voice that will become stronger in her later writing. "I remember one man who used to shake his head and say it [settlement work] was 'the strangest thing he had met in this experience,' but who was finally convinced that it was not strange but natural" (25). The subjective essay brings these "isolated voices" together, and here we can see the beginning of her literary style.

She sorted out the sociological data into "Objective Value of a Social Settlement," an essay that works hard to measure, map, and calculate the realities of Hull House in ways that male sociologists were learning to do. It is the approach she and Florence Kelley will later use in crafting *Hull-House Maps and Papers*.[13] She reports that South Halsted Street is thirty-two miles long, for example, and that the Hull mansion was built in 1856. The neighborhood is made up of Neapolitans, Sicilians, Calabrians, Germans, Polish and Russian Jews, French Canadians, and the Irish, all of them living in the fourteenth precinct of the nineteenth ward, containing 50,000 people, 7,072 of whom vote. The ward, an assemblage of small wooden houses and newer tenement buildings, is home to 255 saloons, averaging one for every twenty-eight voters. No one but Addams talks in the essay, although she claims to have heard or remembered or seen many of her neighbors. "The residents of a Social Settlement," she assures her readers, "have an opportunity of seeing institutions from the recipient's standpoint, of catching the spirit of the original impulse which founded them" (46). She lists the many activities housed in the settlement, college extension courses, a kindergarten and nursery, a reading room, an art gallery, a kitchen and coffeehouse, and clubs of all sorts; among this last were labor unions and the Working People's Social Science Club. And she ends with a warning: "The only possible danger from this commingling of many theories is incurred when there is an attempt at suppression; bottled up, there is danger of explosion; constantly uncorked, open to the deodorizing and freeing process of the air, all danger is averted" (53). The chorus works, as democracy works, when all voices have authority and freedom to speak.

As a young woman, Addams was especially sensitive to the silencing of her generation of women, the first to be educated in the United States. As she graduated from Rockford Female Seminary, she considered the timbre of the female voice in the public arena she hoped to enter. She graduated at the head of her class and wrote her senior essay, "Cassandra," as a sober warning to her classmates, who looked and sounded to her like the Greek heroine: "The frail girl stood conscious of Truth but she had no logic to convince the impatient defeated warriors, and no facts to gain their confidence, she could only assert and proclaim until at last in sooth she becomes mad."[14] The young women of her generation—females who had heard tales of the Seneca Falls Convention in 1848, perhaps read the Declaration of Sentiments, and had taken schooling seriously—would live and many die with little civic or political power and few chances to enter professional life. Half the women who went to college in her generation would never marry and many would suffer from depression, a malady in women that went by the name of "hysteria." The malady clouded eight years of her life, making her a literal and figurative Cassandra herself.

Addams distinguished between female and male patterns of thinking and talking in the essay. She believed that a woman, by her very nature, has the power of intuitive knowledge, but a man, by dint of training, holds the power of scientific expression. As she put it, "I would call this a feminine trait of mind, an accurate perception of Truth and Justice which rests contented in itself, and will make no effort to conform itself, or to organize through existing knowledge." Intuitive Truth—the idea that she struggled to define for the Bible salesman—without language of expression is bound, as Cassandra discovered, to fail. How might a woman come to talk like a man? Addams concluded that women could learn to conform to male modes of expression by studying science, even if they were to take only a single class in the sciences. A woman, that is to say, can be taught to talk like a man. After her female schooling at Rockford, she took her own advice by moving to Philadelphia to study medicine.

In the first book that Addams wrote by herself, *Democracy and Social Ethics*, she struggles to give Cassandra a legitimate public voice by synthesizing what she saw as male and female modes of expression. Culling characters from her experience and imagination, Addams dresses, redresses, and even cross-dresses the Cassandra figure.[15] She dresses first as a "daintily clad" young volunteer who, for all her feminine attire, sounds like a businessman when she insists that the poor "must work and be self-supporting, that the most dangerous of all situations is idleness, that seeking one's own pleasure, while ignoring claims and responsibilities is the most ignoble of actions."[16] A second character, this one a more mature charity worker, has grown to understand the subtler levels of difference among her neighbors. In passages that echo Tolstoy's *What to Do?*

the social worker "discovers how incorrigibly bourgeois her standards have been, and it takes but a little time to reach the conclusion that she cannot insist so strenuously upon the conventions of her own class" (38).[17]

Beyond the volunteer and the worker stands a third figure, the writer who observes the larger situation, listens to everyone, and stages the drama for the reader. She hears the voice of "pseudo-science" in the ideas of the dainty volunteer who stumbles and falls as she tries to "push forward the mass" of men and women in the Hull House neighborhood (69). She chronicles the tales of various patriarchs, including Shakespeare's King Lear; the capitalist George Pullman; and finally, closer to home, the alderman of the Nineteenth Ward, Johnny Powers, a figure that she surprisingly sees as more democratic because he does not try to foist middle-class manners and morals on the workers he represents. The experienced writer emerges in the final scene "with the muscle to thrust forward with the crude men of the street" (67). Oddly, those crude men of Halsted Street move forward "irrationally and emotionally, and often at the expense of the well-settled standards of morality" (67). Such men sound like Cassandra in cross-dress.

Readers got the metaphoric switch of costume. Praising the book, Edwin Seligman wrote to tell Addams that "no other book by a woman shows such vitality—such masculinity of mental grasp & surefootedness."[18] Oliver Wendell Holmes wrote to the series editor, Richard Ely, that Addams is "a big woman who knows at least the facts and gives me more insights into the point of view of the workingmen and poor than I had before."[19]

Addams's literary style of advancing argument through narrative, full of the voices of various people, embodies her ethics. Listening to those most different from ourselves, we come to know our social identity, and writing in many voices, we entice readers. The heart of her radicalism—unsettling to self-satisfied readers of her day as well as ours—is that "the idealism fitted to our industrial democracy will be evolved in crowded sewer ditches and in noisy factories."[20] Ethics grow naturally from the melding of cultures, the rich with the poor, the native-born with the immigrant, the old with the young, and especially the male with the female. "To attain individual morality in an age demanding social morality, to pride oneself on the results of personal effort when the time demands social adjustment, is utterly to fail to appreciate the situation," she cautions her reader. "Morally healthy society grows from associated, not individual, effort and through cooperation, not competition" (63).

As she was thinking about how to write a book, she was reading a surprising variety of prose, including Stanton Coit's *Ethical Democracy*, W. E. B. Du Bois's *The Souls of Black Folk*, and the speeches of Teddy Roosevelt and Senator Robert M. La Follette (she would join them in the Progressive Party), but she was also reading the letters of ordinary women from places like Paw Paw, Michigan; Syracuse, New York; and Ontario, Canada. All the voices, those from acknowledged authorities, creative artists, and earnest politicians, blended in her mind with the voices of utterly common folks; and she added to those literate voices the stories of people in the streets, many of them immigrants with traces of various languages mixed into their Chicago dialect. The conversation that she amplified illustrates her ethical argument that "the cure for the ills of Democracy is more Democracy" (11–12), the very idea that caught the eye of William James.

Democracy and Social Ethics began a string of books that illustrate her argument for democracy. *Newer Ideals of Peace* took many years to write, perhaps because she was not sure she was in truth a writer or that she had much else to say. Letters between her and Richard Ely reveal the considerably widening difference between the academic writing he wanted and the more literary style she had in mind. Her favorite book, *The Spirit of Youth and the City Streets*, is openly dialogic and is an especially good book for our time. The underlying argument that capitalism feeds on the vitality of youth, paying them little for their labor and then taking the money back from them in the marketplace, is perhaps truer today than it was a hundred years ago. The one of her books that has achieved the status of a literary classic is *Twenty Years at Hull-House*, an autobiography that, as Carolyn Heilbrun has pointed out so well, is uncomfortable with telling the story of a woman's life, moving quickly away from Jane Addams and toward the institutional story of Hull House.[21] *A New Conscience and an Ancient Evil* marks the end of her early dramatic critique of American capitalism. Here the stories are sensational, stylized plots found in "white slave" narratives, and the voices are sentimental, coming secondhand from court proceedings, because Addams broke her own rule by not listening to sexual or "white" slaves and seasoned prostitutes.[22] We might expect that her career as a writer would have ended here.

Scholars rarely go beyond her first fifty years as a thinker, reformer, and certainly writer. The truth is that two of her best books, *The Long Road of Woman's Memory*, written as the United States moved toward active involvement in the Great War, and *The Second Twenty Years*, written in the wake of the stock market crash, mark significant changes in her writing over time.

In the spring of 1915, Jane Addams fell from favor as she worked together with an international group of women to bring an end to the fighting in Europe. Jeered at as peacettes, the women traveled to the Women's International Congress at The Hague, and their leaders, including Addams, fanned out to talk with world leaders in an effort to bring both warring and neutral nations into mediation. As she returned from Europe and waited to talk with President Woodrow Wilson, she spoke at Carnegie Hall. Failing to read the crowd, she ended the speech with stories about the bloody business of bayoneting. The speech itself set the stage for her gaffe when she cautioned, "The situation is so confused, so many wild and weird things are said about it that you are afraid to add one word that is not founded upon absolute first-hand impressions."[23] And then she herself said a "wild and weird thing" by claiming that a young soldier had told her he refused to do the bayoneting; "'That is what we cannot think of.'" She moved comfortably into the character of the young soldier, a pose that had always worked well in her writing. "We heard in all countries similar statements in regard to the necessity for the use of stimulant before men could engage in bayonet charges," she claimed, adding what quickly became the sound bite: "They have to give them the 'dope'"—rum in England and absinthe in France. The headlines blazed, "Troops Drink-Crazed, Says Miss Addams." She never quite recovered as a national icon and social leader after the press moved sharply against her, although the Nobel Committee finally turned to her in 1931 with a peace prize.

During the difficult years of the Great War when censors warily eyed her pacifism, Addams revived herself by writing a collective memoir of female experience, *The Long Road of Woman's Memory*. Addams was never happy with the book, cobbled together as it was from bits and pieces of things she had been working on as her voice and persona became very much out of favor with a public fascinated by the fighting in Europe. "Of course," she once confided to her editor, "one composes a book out of all the old stuff one has on hand."[24] Her writing process typically began with speeches that she reworked into essays and finally compiled and revised as books. An essay on the devil baby at Hull House and another account of a trip to Egypt anchor a book that reveals her pacifism in subtle ways.[25]

Silenced, or nearly so, this time as an aging Cassandra, Jane Addams worked to "transmute into song traditional tales of sorrow and wrongdoing."[26] The idea of writing as song goes back to the analogy of the Hallelujah Chorus, this time sung in a mournful tone. The tone had much to do with her being out of favor with readers and, too, in her being ill; she wrote "The Devil Baby at Hull-House" in the summer of 1916 as she traveled away from Chicago to Colorado and California to recover from tuberculosis of the kidney. Ellery Sedgwick, editor of the *Atlantic Monthly*, found "The Devil Baby at Hull-House" on his desk as he returned to New York from his own vacation in the West and was delighted to publish what he read as apolitical prose: "This is the Miss Addams in whom we all believe—militarists, pacifists, progressives, and the rest of us—and I shall take very greatest pleasure in publishing this paper."[27]

The essay ponders the many meanings of a six-week rumor that the ladies of Hull House were somehow sheltering the devil's own baby. The book brings together the poetry of Euripides, the psychology of William James, and the folklore of William Butler Yeats to consider the possibilities of collective memory as part of what she thought of as "the race life." Does a subconscious or semiconscious reservoir of memory exist? And, as a pragmatist might put it, does the urban myth of the devil baby reveal the imaginative possibilities of collective memory? She offers sociological and psychological analysis together with variations on the tale itself.

Addams speculates that the older women in her neighborhood carry the tale because the female mind may be especially receptive to memory, and thus she moves from male authorities to Diotema, "the wisest woman of antiquity," who explained to Socrates that the life worth living "must be discovered by faithful and strenuous search for ever-widening kinds of beauty" (82). The tale reinforces the notion that muses, after all, are female, "thrusting their ghostly fingers into the delicate fabric of human experience to the extreme end of life" (173). The older the woman, the more powerful the voice.

What she tells us about aging women as storytellers suggests a thinly veiled self-portrait. "During the weeks of excitement it was the old women who really seemed to have come into their own, and perhaps the most significant result of the incident was the reaction of the story upon them. It stirred their minds and memories as with a magic touch, it loosened their tongues and revealed the inner life and thoughts of those who are so often inarticulate" (8). The art of storytelling, the loosening of the tongue, gave the old women "a moment of triumph." Because they were the only ones in their community who knew the stories, the old women moved to the front of the stage, everyone eager to hear versions of the devil baby tale.

Addams gives many versions of the narrative, smoothing them into her own cool voice. Italian women tell a variety of stories about an atheist man who tears a holy picture from his wall and curses his pregnant wife, who, as a consequence, gives birth to the devil baby, an uncontrollable demon, much like his earthly impetuous daddy. The father repents by taking his baby to Hull House and then to church, where the urchin runs "lightly over the backs of the pews" (3). Jewish women likewise blame the father, who in their version so resents having six daughters that he swears he would be better off with a devil baby than another girl. His curse delivers the devil's son. "Save for a red automobile which occasionally figured in the story and a stray cigar," Addams quips, "the tale might have been fashioned a thousand years ago" (173). The urban myth is useful for "domestic instruction" in warning young men and women about the results of bad behavior. The random stories woven together, Addams avers, become art. "In the midst of the most tragic reminiscences, there remained that something in the memories of these mothers which has been called the great revelation of tragedy, or sometimes the great illusion of tragedy; that which has power in its own right to make life palatable and at rare moments even beautiful" (52).

On a deeper level, Addams sounds like a modernist when she sees "interpretative art" arising from what William James calls "the stream of consciousness." Her female voices, at times, break free of linear narrative and reveal sorrow in random, associative patterns, much like those of other experimental writers. Addams explains, "At moments, however, baffled desires, sharp cries of pain, echoes of justices unfulfilled, the original material from which such tales are fashioned, would defy Memory's appeasing power and break through the rigid restraints imposed by all Art, even that unconscious of itself" (35). The song, Addams understood, was at times inexpressibly sad.

The tale she wanted to tell was itself nearly inexpressible, one about the unfolding tragedy of the Great War in Europe, the poignant story everywhere around her. The penultimate chapter finally arrives at the war itself. What is especially revealing in this chapter is that she admits her fictionalizing technique. She tells readers in a footnote that the voice she uses is, in truth, a "composite made from several talks held with each of two women" (115). The character she creates is a mother of a soldier who paraphrases his letters to her. Oddly, the language sounds like a political speech, the very polemical writing that her editors did not want to publish. What battlefield letter would sound like this one? "He wrote that whenever he heard the firing of the huge field-piece he knew that the explosion consumed years of the taxes which had been slowly accumulated by some hard-working farmer or shopkeeper, and that he unconsciously calculated how fast industrial research would have gone forward, had his department been given once a decade the costs of a single day of warfare, with the government's command to turn back into alleviation of industrial conditions the taxes which the people had paid" (119). The voice is shrill and fairly openly Addams's own.

The last chapter, one she had crafted before the war (and would publish again as a eulogy, of sorts, for herself in *The Excellent Becomes the Permanent*), reports a vacation Addams had taken with her partner Mary Rozet Smith to Egypt, a trip that got her out of Chicago after the failure of the Bull Moose Party to bring Teddy Roosevelt back to the White House in 1912. As she journeyed through modern Egypt viewing relics of the ancient world, Addams returned in memory to her early life in Cedarville, giving readers the most personal account she ever gave of her own life. At the very end of the travelogue, she leaves readers with a shudder: "These records also afford us glimpses into a past so vast that the present generation seems to float upon its surface as thin as a sheet of light which momentarily covers the ocean and moves in response to the black waters underneath it" (168). Nothing so reminds us of the current world, perhaps, than this grim reminder of the Great War, a conflict not unlike ours in the twenty-first century.

Addams spent the 1920s out of public favor and clearly struggled to articulate what getting old was like for her. As she celebrated twin birthdays in 1930, one for her at seventy and another for Hull House at about forty, the United Press telegraphed eleven questions for her to answer about what seemed to everyone an august age. "NO SPECIAL WISDOM COMES AT SEVENTY," she retorted in a telegram. "CAN BE SECURED ONLY THROUGH ADAPTATION TO CHANGING WORLD STOP IMPOSSIBLE TO REPLY TO ELEVEN QUESTIONS IN SO SHORT A SPACE."[28]

Her cryptic message, adaptation to change, is pretty good advice. The truth is that Jane Addams watched most of her causes wane during the 1920s. "I cannot tell just when we began to have a sense of futility," she concedes in *The Second Twenty Years at Hull-House*, the companion to her autobiography and a book that tells the story of twenty years she spent largely away from Hull House.[29] Addams, over that time, established herself as a suffragist, a progressive politician, a pacifist, the leader of the Women's International League for Peace and Freedom, and eventually a Nobel laureate.

What changed around her was the national mood toward the textured community she had sought in *Democracy and Social Ethics*. Social work as a profession for women, to take the most telling example, lost ground. The Russell Sage Foundation released a study of salaries, tracing pay from 1914, when yearly income for social workers averaged eight hundred dollars, the same amount earned by elementary teachers, and noted that by 1925, during a supposed financial boom, a social worker earned fifteen hundred dollars, which was three hundred dollars less than the salary of an elementary school teacher.[30] Addams supported the 1924 presidential campaign of fellow Progressive Robert La Follette, although the third-party effort was doomed from the start. As women won suffrage in 1920, their long effort left them, as a group, enervated and at odds with one another. Jane traveled with Mary to Asia in the 1920s and later watched from home as anarchy and revolution washed over China. The movement toward a lasting peace floated on the surface of a deeper political chasm, one that was leading inevitability toward another World War. The Red Scare, following the war in Europe and the Bolshevik Revolution in Russia, had at its core the fear of aliens, and immigration law contracted as a measure of public suspicion.

Personal attacks on Addams as a "Red" continued long after the war. Lieutenant Joseph Hurley, in explaining his refusal to act as marshal for the 1925 Armistice Day Parade in Boston, characterized the pacifist women of the Women's International League for Peace and Freedom (WILPF) as "pregnant with evil portent" and Jane Addams as "a dangerous radical."[31] Helen Palmer Dawes, chair of the International Relations Committee of the National Federation of Women's Clubs, traveled to Grand Rapids, Michigan, to celebrate Armistice Day, 1926, by likewise attacking WILPF and charging Jane Addams with un-American activity: "I speak so freely of this because Miss Addams herself does not conceal the fact that she does not believe in our ideas of American loyalty."[32] Captain Ferre Watkins, commander of the Illinois department of the American Legion, accused Addams, who was recuperating from a heart attack at the time, of advocating that military uniforms be stripped from cadets at West Point. Friends and colleagues rallied around her and urged that she charge the American Legion and the Daughters of the American Revolution with libel. Sounding perhaps like the only adult in the conversation, Addams responded, "It seems to me however so desirable to drop the whole matter that I should deprecate prolonging the publicity which has been much exaggerated on both sides."[33]

In *The Second Twenty Years*, Addams acknowledged that she could finally speak only for herself. The book presents social and cultural history as what she calls "honest reminiscence." We might think of this book, written in her deep sixties, as the companion to *Spirit of Youth and the City Streets* in that this time she makes the argument that age itself has vitality and imagination. "Even if we, the elderly, have nothing to report but sordid compromises," she reports of her generation, "nothing to offer but a disconcerting acknowledgement that life has marked us with its slow stain, it is still better to define our position" (6). We hear the voice of a woman content with her age: "With all our errors thick upon us, we may at least be entitled to the comfort of Plato's intimation that truth itself may be discovered by honest reminiscence" (6). The muse, here as in *The Long Road of Woman's Memory*, is memory, what one may call to mind after time has passed. The very word *truth*, we note, is subjective, given the small t and not the capital T of surety we find in her early writing.

Her earlier books had relied heavily on the sound of male voices as authorities who gave volume and credence to what she had to say. In *The Second Twenty Years*, Addams seems content to talk like a woman. During the 1920s, she and Mary Smith had been reading the novels of Virginia Woolf, including *Mrs. Dalloway* and, perhaps, *Orlando*. In October 1929, they were reading *A Room of One's Own*, originally a series of lectures that, as Mary Gordon puts it, came "at a time when feminist writing was so little in vogue as to be effectively moribund, when the Feminist Movement, connected as it had come to be almost exclusively with female suffrage, considered its work finished."[34]

Much in the spirit of the essay, Addams loosely quotes Woolf in *The Second Twenty Years* on the nature of reality as "something very erratic and very undependable, sometimes it seems to dwell in shapes too far away from us to discern what their nature is, nevertheless whatever it touches, it fixes and makes permanent" (81). Addams quotes from memory and thus leaves out whole sentences. Woolf's graceful passage in *A Room of One's Own* actually reads:

> What is meant by "reality"? It would seem to be something very erratic, very undependable—now to be found in a dusty road, now in a scrap of newspaper in the street, now in a daffodil in the sun. It lights up a group in a room and stamps some casual saying. It overwhelms one walking home beneath the stars and makes the silent world more real than the world of speech—and then there it is again in an omnibus in the uproar of Piccadilly. Sometimes, too, it seems to dwell in shapes too far away for us to discern what their nature is. But whatever it touches, it fixes and makes permanent. That is what remains over when the skin of the day has been cast into the hedge, that is what is left of past time and of our loves and hates. Now the writer, as I think, has the chance to live more than other people in the presence of this reality.[35] (110)

Addams elides the middle section of the quote, apparently feeling utterly free to use Woolf's voice in her own way.

Toward the end of her life, Addams's style of writing has the texture and tone of literary modernism, following Woolf's call to writers to live in the reality of a deeper life beneath the skin. The modernist manifesto gave Addams freedom to write the way she always tended and, thereby, to live in the presence of subjective reality. *The Second Twenty Years* is conversational in tone and relaxed in style, an erratic patchwork of memories and articles and talks with friends. She had spent eight long years thinking about what she might have to say in another book as she looked back over essays and letters and the reading she had been doing. The book comes as an assemblage of voices, mostly her own. She is much more content, as a woman of seventy, to let the voices of others intrude as full paragraphs and less inclined to speak for them.

Had she also read Virginia Woolf's essay "Women's Fiction" in the *Forum* of March 1929, and she may well have, she would have been pleased by Woolf's insistence that women no longer "squint askance" for the right to see the world through female eyes. Addams knew what Woolf meant by the desire of women writers to "alter established values—to make serious what appears insignificant to a man, and trivial what is to him important."[36] Addams had been doing that throughout her career as a settlement founder and as a writer. She knew, too, that women often come under fire for being weak or trivial or sentimental, men being "genuinely puzzled and surprised by an attempt to alter the current scale of values."

Most of all, Addams would have noted with satisfaction that Woolf called women into intellectual and political debates, "the sophisticated arts" that male writers have always felt confident in pursuing. She predicted that women would move to "the writing of essays and criticism, of history and biography," just the direction that Addams had moved in over the course of her long career as a writer. The book Addams was writing in 1929 was, for the most part, a history, and her last book, one she was working to finish as she died, was a biography. As Ellen Moers would reiterate, women writers come in all voices and genres. Addams's backward glance, at seventy, left her with a strong sense of the writer she had become. She signed an American Civil Liberties Union petition to Herbert Hoover in 1928 as "Jane Addams, writer, social worker, Chicago, Ill." with literary work foremost in her mind.[37] The twenty-first-century feminist retrieval work of this study and of this collection as a whole situates Jane Addams comfortably in the canon of American writers, just as it places her quite rightly in the canon of American philosophers.

Readers in the twenty-first century may indeed want to find her books and curl up with them at home. The very questions she pursues remain at issue today. We find her writing about such morally vexed human problems as labor and sexual trafficking, environmental toxicity, international war, and immigration policy, all issues currently in the news, as well as the perennial desires of a democracy to provide a living wage, affordable housing, public education, safety in the workplace, health care, unemployment compensation, and protection for children. It remains as true in our time as in hers that "the cure for the ills of Democracy is more Democracy." Jane Addams, especially the older, wiser woman, sounds like one of us, too, when she cautions, "We have learned that life is never reasonable, at least a surface reasonableness is often misleading as to the profounder trends underneath."[38] Nearly a hundred years later, her voice resonates.

Notes

1. Moers, *Literary Women*, xiii. Moers and other feminist scholars, notably Elaine Showalter, in the 1960s and 1970s set the retrieval task of a generation of new women in the academy who sought ways to deconstruct and reconstruct the canon of writers, nearly all of whom were men, taught in

American literature classes. They looked specifically at poets and fiction writers, beginning with identifiable feminists and, over time, moving outward to include women who did not seem, at first blush, to have women's civil and social rights foremost in mind.

2. See Joslin, *Jane Addams, a Writer's Life*. Over the years, Addams biographers and editors have all noted her abilities as a writer. Her nephew James Weber Linn in *Jane Addams: A Biography* (1935) notes her graceful style; in *A Centennial Reader* (1960), William O. Douglas calls her prose a real tonic, Helen Hall sees her as an artist, and Ashley Montagu places her, rightfully I think, alongside Emerson and Thoreau; Christopher Lasch in *The Social Thought of Jane Addams* (1965) admires the radicalism of her storytelling; and Allen F. Davis in the landmark biography, *American Heroine: The Life and Legend of Jane Addams* (1973), considers her a heroine and a mythmaker. Women scholars and biographers who have followed the call to retrieve and reassess Jane Addams's life and work talk about her considerable ability as a writer, although their work focuses more specifically on her activism. Jill Conway in "Jane Addams: An American Heroine" (1964) and Anne Firor Scott in her introduction to *Democracy and Social Ethics* (1964) began the feminist retrieval work on Addams in the 1960s. Over the past decade several biographies have emerged: see Barbara Garland Polikoff, *With One Bold Act: The Story of Jane Addams*; Gioia Diliberto, *A Useful Woman: The Early Life of Jane Addams*; Jean Bethke Elshtain, *Jane Addams and the Dream of American Democracy: A Life*; Victoria Bissell Brown, *The Education of Jane Addams*; and most recently, Louise W. Knight, *Citizen: Jane Addams and the Struggle for Democracy*. Knight says that Addams's sentences "sparkle with condensed wisdom" (400). Considerable new work is being done by philosophers who focus on her writing about ethics: see Marilyn Fischer and Judy D. Whipps, eds., *Jane Addams's Writings on Peace*; Charlene Haddock Seigfried's introductions to the University of Illinois editions of *Democracy and Social Ethics* (2002) and *The Long Road of Woman's Memory* (2002); and Maurice Hamington, *Embodied Care: Jane Addams, Maurice Merleau-Ponty, and Feminist Ethics*. Scholars in composition and rhetoric are currently discussing Addams's contribution to education at meetings of the Four C's in panels such as "Jane Addams: Intellect and Influence" (2006). Ellen Condliffe Lagemann has edited *Jane Addams on Education*. Wendy Sharer in *Vote and Voice: Women's Organizations and Political Literacy* analyzes the rhetorical strategies of women who wrote for the Women's International League for Peace and Freedom and the Woman's Peace Party, among other organizations, at the turn of the last century. David Schaafsma is editing a collection of essays, *Jane Addams, Hull-House, and the Call to Education*, that promises fresh approaches to Addams and the teaching of writing.

3. William James, letter to Jane Addams, September 17, 1902, Jane Addams Papers Project (JAPP) 4–444.

4. Harriet Monroe, review of *Democracy and Social Ethics*, JAPP 11–22.

5. Bakhtin, *The Dialogic Imagination*, 262.

6. Mary Lynn McCree Bryan, Nancy Slote, and Maree de Angury have collected her papers in the Jane Addams Papers Project (JAPP), which contains eighty-two reels of microfilm on Addams and Hull House. The University of Illinois Press is bringing her books back into print with new introductions and is publishing editions of her papers. See Bryan, Bair, and de Angury, eds., *The Selected Papers of Jane Addams*, vol. 1, *Preparing to Lead, 1860–81*, and vol. 2, *Venturing into Usefulness, 1881–88*.

7. What we have is a diary draft of a letter she was writing, dated December 5, 1880, to E. G. Smith. The diary is located in JAPP 28–1482 through 28–1735. I am grateful to Mary Lynn McCree Bryan for first showing me this letter years ago as I began to read Addams's papers at the University of Illinois at Chicago.

8. Jane Addams, letter to Ellen Gates Starr, January 29, 1880, JAPP I-473–76.

9. Henry C. Adams, ed., *Philanthropy and Social Progress*, vi. Subsequent references will be cited in the text.

10. Jane Addams, *Twenty Years at Hull-House* (1910), 114. Subsequent references will be cited in the text.

11. Jane Addams, *My Friend, Julia Lathrop* (1935), 60–61.

12. The other quotations that come without citation or even a clear sense of the speaker are "The social spirit discharges itself in many forms, and no one form is adequate to its total expression" (6) and "There is nothing after disease, indigence, and a sense of guilt so fatal to health and to life itself as the want of a proper outlet for active faculties" (12). These voices seem strangely attached to her essay and suggest how she is experimenting with the use of other voices, a technique that she will refine in her later writing.

13. See Deegan, *Jane Addams and the Men of the Chicago School*. Deegan argues that male colleagues at the University of Chicago excluded women from their programs and, until the late 1920s, considered collecting quantitative data "women's work," the very sort of work that Addams and the women of Hull House began doing in the 1890s.

14. Jane Addams, "Cassandra," JAPP 46–267; also in Bryan, Bair, and de Angury, eds., *The Selected Papers of Jane Addams*, 428.

15. For a longer analysis of rhetorical dressing and cross-dressing in the book, see Joslin, *Jane Addams*, 58–68.

16. Jane Addams, *Democracy and Social Ethics*, 17. Subsequent references will be cited in the text.

17. Jane Addams read Leo Tolstoy's *My Confession* and *What to Do?* as she worked to design Hull House. She and Mary Smith (as they became life partners) traveled to Russia in 1896 to visit Tolstoy and talk with him about pacifism. Addams marked passages in her copies of his books that detail experiments with philanthropy. At times, as in this passage, her prose echoes his.

18. Edwin Seligman, letter to Jane Addams, April 26, 1902, JAPP 4–0348.

19. Oliver Wendell Holmes, letter to Richard Ely, July 10, 1906, JAPP 4–1408.

20. Jane Addams, *Newer Ideals of Peace*, 95.

21. Heilbrun, *Writing a Woman's Life*. In retrieving and reading women's autobiography, Heilbrun finds that women tell a markedly different story from that which men tell about themselves. The usual pattern for male autobiographies, such as Benjamin Franklin's, is to focus on the male himself and his struggle upward. American women before the 1960s shied away from telling a personal story and instead told narratives about other people or, as is the case with Addams, an institution. Addams tells a success story, one that has always pleased American readers but deflects attention away from her triumphs to those of the wider group.

22. For background and analysis of this book, see Katherine Joslin, introduction to *A New Conscience and an Ancient Evil*.

23. Jane Addams, "Carnegie Hall Address," JAPP 47–1180.

24. Jane Addams, letter to Paul Kellogg, November [16,] 1921, JAPP 14–464.

25. Jane Addams, "The Devil Baby at Hull-House," *Atlantic Monthly* 118 (October 1916): 441–51; "The Unexpected Reactions of a Traveler in Egypt," *Atlantic Monthly* 113 (February 1914): 178–86.

26. Jane Addams, *The Long Road of Woman's Memory*, ix–x. Subsequent references will be cited in the text.

27. Ellery Sedgwick, letter to Jane Addams, February 23, 1916, JAPP 9–1070.

28. Jane Addams, telegram to United Press, September 4, 1930, JAPP 21–0852.

29. Jane Addams, *The Second Twenty Years at Hull-House*, 20. Subsequent references will be cited in the text.

30. Russell Sage Foundation, New York, Department of Statistics, study of social worker and elementary school teacher salaries, JAPP 17–768A.

31. See reports in the *Boston Herald*: "Peace Societies Deny 'Red' Ties," "Hurley Replies to Critics of Speech," and "Parade Bodies in League with Soviet, Says Hurley," JAPP 17–1311, 17–1312, and 17–1313.

32. See newspaper account, "Mrs. Dawes Scorns Peace Society in Armistice Day Talk," JAPP 18–0740.

33. See attacks and counterattacks in newspaper account, "Hull House Residents Protest," JAPP 18–0747; see also "More or Less Personal," *Progressive*, December 1, 1926, JAPP 18–0755.

34. Mary Gordon, introduction to Virginia Woolf, *A Room of One's Own*, vii. Subsequent references will be cited in the text.
35. Woolf, *A Room of One's Own*, 110.
36. Woolf, "Women and Fiction," 49–52.
37. ACLU, petition to Herbert Hoover, November 21, 1928, JAPP 20–0535.
38. Addams, *The Second Twenty Years at Hull-House*, 271.

References

Adams, Henry C., ed. *Philanthropy and Social Progress: Seven Essays by Miss Jane Addams, Robert A. Woods, Father J. O. S. Huntington, Professor Franklin H. Giddings, and Bernard Bosanquet*. New York: Thomas Y. Crowell, 1893.
Addams, Jane. *Democracy and Social Ethics*. Citizen's Library Series. New York: Macmillan, 1902.
———. *The Excellent Becomes the Permanent*. New York: Macmillan, 1932.
———. *My Friend, Julia Lathrop*. New York: Macmillan, 1935.
———. *The Long Road of Woman's Memory*. New York: Macmillan, 1916.
———. *A New Conscience and an Ancient Evil*. New York: Macmillan, 1912.
———. *Newer Ideals of Peace*. Citizen's Library Series. New York: Macmillan, 1907.
———. *Peace and Bread in Time of War*. New York: Macmillan, 1922.
———. *The Second Twenty Years at Hull-House*. New York: Macmillan, 1930.
———. *The Spirit of Youth and the City Streets*. New York: Macmillan, 1909.
———. *Twenty Years at Hull-House*. New York: Macmillan, 1910.
Addams, Jane, Emily Greene Balch, and Alice Hamilton. *Women at The Hague*. New York: Macmillan, 1915.
Addams, Jane, and Florence Kelley, eds. *Hull-House Maps and Papers: A Presentation of Nationalities and Wages in a Congested District of Chicago, Together with Comments and Essays on Problems Growing out of the Social Conditions*. New York: Thomas Y. Crowell, 1895.
Bakhtin, Mikhail. *The Dialogic Imagination: Four Essays by M. M. Bakhtin*. Ed. Michael Holquist. Trans. Caryl Emerson and Michael Holquist. Austin: University of Texas Press, 1981.
Brown, Victoria Bissell. *The Education of Jane Addams*. Philadelphia: University of Pennsylvania Press, 2004.
Bryan, Mary Lynn McCree, Barbara Bair, and Maree de Angury, eds. *The Selected Papers of Jane Addams*. Vol. 1, *Preparing to Lead, 1860–81*. Urbana: University of Illinois Press, 2003.
———, eds. *The Selected Papers of Jane Addams*. Vol. 2, *Venturing into Usefulness, 1881–88*. Urbana: University of Illinois Press, 2009.
Bryan, Mary Lynn McCree, Nancy Slote, and Maree de Angury, eds. The Jane Addams Papers Project (JAPP). 82 reels. Ann Arbor, Mich.: Microfilming Corporation of America and University Microfilms International, 1984–85.
Conway, Jill. "Jane Addams: An American Heroine." *Daedalus* 93, no. 2 (1964): 761–80.
Davis, Allen F. *American Heroine: The Life and Legend of Jane Addams*. New York: Oxford University Press, 1973.

Deegan, Mary Jo. *Jane Addams and the Men of the Chicago School, 1892–1918*. New Brunswick, N.J.: Transaction Books, 1988.
Diliberto, Gioia. *A Useful Woman: The Early Life of Jane Addams*. New York: Scribner, 1999.
Douglas, William O. Introduction to *A Centennial Reader*, by Jane Addams. Ed. Emily Cooper Johnson. Consulting ed. William L. Neumann. New York: Macmillan, 1960.
Elshtain, Jean Bethke. *Jane Addams and the Dream of American Democracy: A Life*. New York: Basic Books, 2002.
Farrell, John C. *Beloved Lady: A History of Jane Addams's Ideas on Reform and Peace*. Baltimore: Johns Hopkins University Press, 1967.
Fischer, Marilyn, and Judy D. Whipps, eds. *Jane Addams's Essays and Speeches*. New ed. Bristol, U.K.: Thoemmes Continuum, 2006.
———. *Jane Addams's Writings on Peace*. 4 vols. History of American Thought. Facsimile ed. Bristol, U.K.: Thoemmes Continuum, 2003.
Hamington, Maurice. *Embodied Care: Jane Addams, Maurice Merleau-Ponty, and Feminist Ethics*. Urbana: University of Illinois Press, 2004.
Heilbrun, Carolyn. *Writing a Woman's Life*. New York: Norton, 1988.
Joslin, Katherine. Introduction to *A New Conscience and an Ancient Evil*, by Jane Addams. Urbana: University of Illinois Press, 2002.
———. Introduction to *Peace and Bread in Time of War*, by Jane Addams. Urbana: University of Illinois Press, 2002.
———. *Jane Addams, a Writer's Life*. Urbana: University of Illinois Press, 2004.
Knight, Louise W. *Citizen: Jane Addams and the Struggle for Democracy*. Chicago: University of Chicago Press, 2005.
Lagemann, Ellen Condliffe, ed. *Jane Addams on Education*. New York: Teachers College Press, 1985.
Lasch, Christopher, ed. *The Social Thought of Jane Addams*. Ed. Leonard W. Levy and Alfred Young. American Heritage Series. Indianapolis: Bobbs-Merrill, 1965.
Linn, James Weber. *Jane Addams: A Biography*. New York: D. Appleton-Century, 1935.
Moers, Ellen. *Literary Women: The Great Writers*. New York: Doubleday, 1963.
Monroe, Harriet. Review of *Democracy and Social Ethics*, by Jane Addams. *Chicago American*, April 19, 1902, n.p.
Polikoff, Barbara Garland. *With One Bold Act: The Story of Jane Addams*. Chicago: Boswell Books, 1999.
Schaafsma, David, ed. *Jane Addams, Hull-House, and the Call to Education*. New York: Teachers College Press, forthcoming.
Scott, Anne Firor. Introduction to *Democracy and Social Ethics*, by Jane Addams. Cambridge: Harvard University Press, 1964.
Seigfried, Charlene Haddock. Introduction to *Democracy and Social Ethics*, by Jane Addams. Urbana: University of Illinois Press, 2002.
———. Introduction to *The Long Road of Woman's Memory*, by Jane Addams. Urbana: University of Illinois Press, 2002.
Sharer, Wendy B. *Vote and Voice: Women's Organizations and Political Literacy, 1915–1930*. Carbondale: Southern Illinois University Press, 2004.
Woolf, Virginia. *A Room of One's Own*. 1929. Introduction by Mary Gordon. New York: Harcourt Brace Jovanovich, 1981.
———. "Women and Fiction." In *Women and Writing*, ed. and with an introduction by Michèle Barrett. San Diego: Harcourt Brace Jovanovich, 1979.

2

Cultural Contradictions

Jane Addams's Struggles with the Life of Art and the Art of Life

Charlene Haddock Seigfried

Jane Addams called her culture to account and found it wanting. In her first book, *Democracy and Social Ethics* (1902), she begins with an observation of how unhappy women and men are "in regard to their attitude toward the social order itself; toward the dreary round of uninteresting work, the pleasures narrowed down to those of appetite, the declining consciousness of brain power, and the lack of mental food which characterizes the lot of a large proportion of their fellow-

An earlier version of this chapter, called "Is Culture Responsible? Jane Addams Calls It to Account," was given as the John Dewey Lecture, the John Dewey Society, American Educational and Research Association, Chicago, April 8–11, 2007.

citizens."[1] Like others of her era, she detects a pervasive unease and claims that "these men and women have caught a moral challenge raised by the exigencies of contemporaneous life; some are bewildered, others who are denied the relief which sturdy action brings are even seeking an escape, but all are increasingly anxious concerning their actual relations to the basic organization of society."[2] And toward the end of *My Friend, Julia Lathrop* (1935), Addams's last work, she extends her observations worldwide.

Whereas in the first analysis, Addams emphasizes the subjective sense of cultural malaise, in the later selection, she addresses the concrete conditions and attitudes that narrow expectations and restrict accomplishments. In a variation on the belief that travel broadens the mind, she recalls how she and Lathrop agreed instead that it "toughens and objectifies life experience." Far from being uplifting, their journeys too often "gave a view of life's limitations caused by geographic and economic conditions that so often circumscribe action and suppress aspiration. We came back with a poignant knowledge of the bitter poverty in which so large a proportion of the world population lives; of the massive weight of heredity; of the despotism of those old women in complete control of eastern households who are so insistent that outworn ideas and usages must be meticulously observed; of the widespread bigotry which would bring the 'divine multiplicity of human life, under one yoke.'"[3]

While Addams's remarks address culture in the most expansive sense of human life or civilization, she also often reflects on the relation of culture, in the restricted sense of the fine and popular arts, especially literature, to society or culture in the larger sense. In both senses, she sees culture as badly needing reform and also as providing welcome avenues to, or instruments for, that reform. These ambivalent views can be explained both biographically, as she worked her way out of a restricted, gender-inflected liberal arts education and the constraints of middle-class Victorian respectability, and theoretically, as the development of her ever expanding interpretation of the meaning and scope of cultural accomplishment. In this chapter, I explore these various facets of Addams's approaches to culture as art and as structures of life because they illuminate not only her struggles to reconcile competing perspectives and values, but also because these issues are recurring features in the development of feminist analyses of culture.

Art and Social Reform: Help or Hindrance?

Addams complained that literature in the curriculum for young, well-to-do women of her time acted as a substitute for the direct engagement with the world denied them because of their gender. She devotes the chapter "The Snare of Preparation" in her masterpiece, *Twenty Years at Hull-House*, to decrying this immersion in culture as a distraction or a paralyzing force and as distorting reality by "lumbering our minds with literature that only served to cloud the really vital situation spread before our eyes."[4]

It is somewhat ironic, however, that Addams used literary accounts to criticize literature and demonstrate how it can undermine resolve and throw a veil over harsher aspects of reality. She explains that in her first encounter as a tourist with the desperate plight of the poor in London in 1883, she was appalled that there was nothing she could think of doing at the moment to relieve their misery. Addams says she was immediately reminded of De Quincey's work "The Vision of Sudden Death," the moral of which she takes to be that, while traveling through rural England on a mail coach, De Quincey could not act to save a pair of lovers in the direct path of a runaway vehicle until he could remember the exact lines from the *Iliad* that expressed an appropriate warning cry.[5] She uses this anecdote to express her own frustration about the fact that the many years she had spent studying literature obscured rather than illuminated the actual situation she was so painfully observing. It disturbed Addams that she was like De Quincey in that her first thoughts on seeing the horrific lives of those crushed by the industrial revolution were literary rather than practical.

But even as Addams laments how, after graduation, she spent years on the Continent in a "feverish search after culture" and was becoming increasingly disillusioned about the effects of an intense intellectual life upon moral development, she makes an exception for art that develops moral insight. She was turning away from aesthetic standards to moral ones. She railed against "the paralyzing sense of the futility of all artistic and intellectual effort when disconnected from the ultimate test of the conduct it inspired."[6] Addams admired Albrecht Dürer, for instance, because he did not record the smooth surface of life, but intimated the coming of the Reformation and the Peasants' War. She sees in his pictures pity for the downtrodden and attributes to him one of her constant themes, namely, that violence is sure to follow when we "forget how complicated life is and insist upon reducing it to logical dogmas."⁷

This reductively moralistic approach suits her purpose of explaining her growing distaste for the cultured life of the well-to-do lady that she was ostensibly pursuing in her two long travels abroad and her eventual assumption of the unconventional role of female reformer, but it does not do justice to the broader view toward the arts she developed over the years. Addams believed that literature had a moral function because it had a deeply social one, in that it has the power to move us to imaginatively enter into the lives of other persons in ways that foster understanding and sympathy and thus motivate us to act on their behalf. Victoria Bissell Brown recounts an incident in which this link of literature with social action operated in Addams's own life. It seems that in the same week in which she visited Toynbee Hall, Addams had read Walter Besant's popular 1882 novel, *All Sorts and Conditions of Men: An Impossible Story*. The novel's wealthy heroine went to live and learn among the working classes "and built there a People's Palace as a haven for recreation and culture. . . . Jane visited the real 'People's Palace,' a new East London youth center. . . . The Palace's classrooms, meeting rooms, billiard rooms, music and dance rooms, and library were an important model for Hull House."⁸

The same amalgam of understanding, sympathy, and transformative social action that literature at its best encompasses cannot be claimed with such confidence for philosophical theories. In the first place, few theories in philosophy directly aim at analyzing and responding to the social evils of poverty, torture, racism, militancy, and so on, rather than at developing better arguments in a number of areas, such as moral reasoning, logic, epistemology, the history of philosophy, metaphysics, or philosophy of mind. The exceptions are ethics, applied ethics, and social and political philosophy, but even in these cases the aim is commonly less to arouse the motivating emotions of sympathy or anger and to propose directed action than to develop good arguments.

However, the same seems true of literature, which can aim at pure entertainment or distraction or even have the effect of arousing dangerous or biased sentiments, instead of enlarging our understanding of others. But even so, there is a difference, if we restrict the phrase *literary culture* to great or enduring exemplars of literature, which are so called just because they continue to illuminate and challenge the human spirit. Philosophical theories, by contrast, can be great because they raise or solve some rational conundrum or argue some point of view especially well, without necessarily enlarging the human spirit in any sense except in developing or sharpening mental acuity.

But what about philosophical theories that do aim to reflect on and provide guidance for the betterment of human society and the environing world? There is no reason why they could not also foster such socially beneficial aims as encouraging benevolent association among diverse people, but even in such cases, not often with the emotional and imaginative power of great literature.[9] If, as Barbara Sicherman explains, culture for Addams is "not a luxury, but rather something to be cultivated in every human being of whatever origin or class," can the same honestly be said for philosophy once we get beyond vague platitudes of learning to think clearly?[10] Many of us hope so, but has this belief been tested in the public sphere or has it become a comforting background belief? Becoming better acquainted with the way Addams wrestled with the relationship of culture and social reform is one way of recognizing a necessarily uneasy tension and keeping it a live issue for us.

As we have seen, the young Addams seems to value literature only when it is didactic and morally uplifting. George Eliot's writings are praised, for example, because they strongly motivate her to work for the greater good of society, and Michelangelo's sculptures lose their attractiveness to the extent that they do not seem to be of any use or accomplish any good. Even the mature Addams approvingly recommends the antiwar writings of Tolstoy and the antiwar paintings of Vasily Verestchagin, commenting that they "hold their art of no account save as it serves moral ends."[11] But for most contemporary artists and cultural critics, this moralizing attitude strikes at the heart of what makes art art. It ignores the power of art to enlarge our perceptions and attitudes and to expand human possibility and, above all, to remind us of the creativity at the center of all human experience. Art, as the paradigmatic expression of culture, should be taken in this expansive sense if its relation to practical affairs is to be explored in any depth.

But Addams was well aware of the more diffuse transformative power of art as well, and she often appeals to it in her writings. After her chapter "The Snare of Preparation," for example, it comes as somewhat of a surprise that in the last couple of pages of *Hull-House*, she defends her experiential approach to social work by invoking the advantages gained from the aesthetic culture she had criticized so strongly in that chapter. When later residents of Hull House came with formal training in social work administration, there may have been some friction between those who were considered professional and the first residents, with their more amateur approach. Addams and her fellow residents had had no choice but to learn as they went along. In place of formal training, Addams asserted that they use "not only their linguistic ability, but all the resource they can command of travel and reading to qualify themselves for intelligent living in the immigrant quarter of the city."[12] But learning foreign languages, reading good literature, and taking the grand tour abroad define the traditional culture that well-to-do young women were expected to embrace. Only by breaking out of the social constraints that that culture also assumed was Addams able to reaffirm its values. Intelligent living, therefore, seems to require an aesthetic component. And yet the sense of alienation set up between an immersion in art and an engagement in practical affairs that Addams perceived so deeply as a young woman, searching for a meaningful role in life unrestricted by gender stereotypes, is also indicative of the way that culture and everyday life is often actually experienced. It informs John Dewey's criticism of the mistaken belief that art is paradigmatically "museum" art rather than continuous with the concernful doings, makings, and enjoyments of everyday life.[13]

Valuing the Fine Arts

Addams's most striking use of literature as an agent of social change is found in her essay "A Modern Lear," written in 1895 and first given many times as a speech.[14] Both her analysis of the violence of the 1894 Pullman strike, which brought home the brutal realities of industrial relations to a wider public in and around Chicago, and her suggestions for a just and lasting resolution of the underlying problems are developed through an extended analogy with Shakespeare's tragedy. Especially noteworthy is that as a result she subverts the public/private distinction by which women were restricted to the private sphere by using what is basically the dynamics of the domestic sphere in the relations of fathers and daughters as a model for explaining the equally coercive public sphere of George Pullman, the owner of the Pullman railroad and its company town, and his disgruntled employees, a significant number of whom were black men.[15] In both cases, it is the patriarchal social system with its paternalistic values that needs to be overturned and replaced by a more egalitarian, cooperative system if justice is to prevail and relationships developed peacefully instead of violently. Addams's article was refused publication as too incendiary, primarily because it sided with the striking workers and not with Pullman as an exemplar of capitalistic philanthropy, and it was only published seventeen years later (1912), when it was still thought to be too controversial. That it was believed to be beyond the capacities of a woman to understand the complexities of the industrial system and totally inappropriate for her to publicly criticize a prominent industrial leader is a measure of the longevity and pervasiveness of the social system being exposed.[16]

According to Addams, art has many functions. These range from traditional, middle-class ones, as when she says that "the play instinct comes to fruition in beauty and decorum" and encourages unselfishness, to its Marxist sense of the creativity that constitutes being human.[17] The transfigurative possibility of art could be expressed even in the seeming superstitions of uneducated, laboring people. Addams, for example, drew insightful lessons from the strange case of the "devil baby," a story recounted as actual fact by many immigrant women of diverse ethnic backgrounds.[18] Although the details vary, the story is told as a warning to men who have engaged in domestic violence. In one Italian version, an atheist husband tears down a holy picture from the bedroom wall, saying that he'd as soon have a devil in the house as that image, whereupon his wife gives birth to a devil baby, who immediately chases her husband around the room; in a Jewish version, a father of six daughters declares he'd rather have a devil in the family than another girl, and a devil obligingly appears. For some weeks, Hull House was thrown into a frenzy when it was inundated by people who believed wild rumors that the devil baby itself had taken refuge there. Eschewing the typical dismissal of the incident as a reflection of the primitive superstitions of immigrants, Addams made the radical claim that abused and long-suffering women kept the myth alive as a means of asserting power through the tale's threat of a preternatural retribution visited on abusive husbands and sons. In trying to understand this phenomenon, Addams points out that the story, "like all interpretive art, was one of those free, unconscious attempts to satisfy, outside of life, those cravings which life itself leaves unsatisfied."[19]

But the fine arts, as such, were also attractive to the working classes, and Addams was convinced that making them widely available was an important aim of Hull House. Helen Horowitz argues that Addams's conviction that art was rightfully the possession of all levels of society distinguished her approach from that of the elite cultural institutions of Chicago and that through the involvement with Hull House of Charles Hutchinson, a leading cultural philanthropist and president of the Art Institute of Chicago, she directly influenced the outreach of those institutions beyond the middle classes to the working classes.[20] Many arts projects flourished at Hull House, and over the years there support was given to a whole range of art, including painting, sculpture, pottery, drama, batik making, and musical performance and composition. The residents envisioned the settlement's programs as experiments that could have wide applications, especially across "the entire system of public education."[21] Even the interior decoration at Hull House was carefully undertaken, since Addams and her Hull House cofounder, Ellen Gates Starr, believed that beautiful surroundings were uplifting for rich and poor alike. According to the "new aestheticism" and following the lead of John Ruskin, they idealized craft done by hand and believed that "all luxury is right that can be and is shared."[22]

In a chapter titled "Play Instinct and the Arts," in *Second Twenty Years at Hull-House*, Addams explains in detail how the various immigrant groups produced distinctive art. In this way, she joined other dissident voices, such as those of Ida B. Wells, Frederick Douglass, and Eugene V. Debs, who directly challenged the common belief that culture was the special prerogative of the upper classes. In commenting on the World's Columbian Exposition of 1893, Alan Trachtenberg remarks that by its exclusion or subordination of laborers, blacks, women, and non-Anglo-Saxon ethnic groups, the exposition "seemed the victory of elites in business, politics, and culture over dissident but divided voices of labor, farmers, immigrants, blacks and women. . . . The power to say what was real, what was America, seemed now safely in the hands of property, wealth, and 'the word Culture.'"[23] Hull House residents were inspired by the Arts and Crafts movement, and Ellen Gates Starr, cofounder of Hull House, opened a branch of the Society of Arts and Crafts there. Those teaching art hoped that developing artistic skills and freeing the imagination would eventually compel industry itself to move away from deadening mechanization and lead to more variation in the products made. To motivate the leaders of industry to see the value of artistic expression and the play instinct, Addams argued that the monotony of factory work was not just unpleasant, it could lead to serious accidents. Its deadening effects are illustrated by studies showing that whatever education working boys started with, they actually deteriorated after years of factory work.[24]

In one of the strongest contrasts with how art is viewed today, Addams never abandoned the distinction between high and low art. The contrast between high, or elitist, art, or art for art's sake, and folk art or hand crafts was not invidious, however, but emphasized both the continuity of creativity in making and appreciating in everyday objects and activities with specialized artistic productions and their differing contributions to enlarging human consciousness. Whether in regard to elitist or folk forms of expression, L. Ryan Musgrave Bonomo argues that Addams's and Starr's unique contribution to pragmatist aesthetics was their insight that "shared cross-cultural forms of arts engagement foster cosmopolitanism and communicate ethical ways of creative being and making that allowed residents not only to become American but to become broader global citizens in a meaningful way."[25] In "Education by the Current Event," for example, Addams explains that "the settlement makes a constant effort through books, through the drama and through exhibits, to connect passing experience with those expressions of permanent values which lie at the basis of world culture." Emphasizing the mutuality of interests across cultures and what we can learn from different ethnic groups at home as well as abroad, she continues: "If this is well done, it should heighten the sense of companionship in the neighbourhood itself."[26] Although, for Addams, self-expression in the arts was one of the benefits of education—or perhaps because it was—not just any self-expression was worth pursuing.

She and the other women involved in the arts at Hull House continually criticized as vulgar the 466 movie theaters in the city of Chicago, with their constant theme of revenge, as well as popular songs, with their lyrics of amusement parks and flirting. The problem was that these "debased forms" of art represented a starved imagination. Unlike for middle-class children, whose dreams and reveries were amply fed by reading, drama—especially the cinema—performed the office of art for the wage-earning child, who dropped out of school early. Movies were a veritable "house of dreams" that Addams believed influenced their interpretation of life.[27] To cling to the belief that life was noble and harmonious, in contrast to the sordid conditions of life they saw around them, laboring children had only the cinema to fire their imaginations. Not only did theatrical fare favor the sensational, it was so appealing that poor children sometimes stole to get money for tickets and landed in juvenile court, which was where their lives intersected with those of the settlement workers. The admirable thirst for adventure through which the cinema enticed young people gave them popularized heroic models for moral judgments that could not possibly prepare them for the intricacies of moral development that the best literature, like that of Ibsen, Shaw, and Hauptmann, could.

Nonetheless, these judgments can sound to us like antimodernist rants and excessive fear of the attractiveness of new media forces that were not part of the older generation's experiences growing up, especially in rural areas. These contrasting generational and class experiences cannot be discounted, but social reformers such as the Hull House residents also based their judgments on the actual conditions they encountered and the troubled behavior of the children they met in various social agencies. They were also reflections of the central role they accorded the arts in education and in enlarging and transforming the life of children and adults alike. They did not just complain about the debased values they saw as dominating popular media; they also tried to present other artistic outlets to feed the underdeveloped imagination of young people.

Many of these alternatives were participatory rather than passive and sought to involve an integrated sense of human well-being and behavior, rather than appealing to isolated or extravagant emotions and limited imaginative possibilities. They recognized that drama had more than educational value in the narrow sense. Above all, drama gave youth "a magic space" in which life could expand beyond the everyday; it had the power to reveal "that larger world which surrounds and completes our own."[28] It was the very centrality of the arts and play to a full human life that led Hull House to become involved in so many projects, such as creating the first public playgrounds and athletic fields and setting up dance clubs and theater, pottery, and drawing classes and literary reading groups for adult workers.

Addams summarizes her case against debased forms of art and the value of high art, while taking it away from the exclusive provenance of the upper classes and situating it firmly in the midst of the working classes, as follows: "After all, what is the function of art but to preserve in permanent and beautiful form those emotions and solaces which cheer life and make it kindlier, more heroic and easier to comprehend; which lift the mind of the worker from the harshness and loneliness of his task, and, by connecting him to what has gone before, free him from a sense of isolation and hardship?"[29] Addams often links the free play of the imagination, as the source of new perspectives and values, with the historical conditions that have led to present alienated situations in order to make the unfamiliar familiar. Along with the role of imaginative leaps in providing emotional connections to higher ideals and incentives to bring them about, she urges grounding such ideals in the actual situations experienced by workers. By helping them revision their present circumstances as being the result of concrete historical changes, they can connect their own cultural and historical associations with their new industrial situation and thus come to a better understanding of what needs to be done to bring about a better future. Addams thus develops the pragmatist reinterpretation of the ideal as extending what is good in the present situation and rejecting what is bad about it. Addams argues, for example, that the lack of a more cosmopolitan standard—by which she means a consciousness "founded upon creative imagination and historic knowledge"—"cruelly widens the gulf between immigrant fathers and their children who are 'Americans in process.'"[30]

Women as Cultural Emissaries

It has often struck me how Addams frequently submerges her beliefs in women's abilities in a more egalitarian, gender-neutral rhetoric. She insinuates women's lives, women's struggles, burdens, and accomplishments into a broader narrative of human suffering and achievement. Even when she does speak about women's particular needs and sufferings and the way women have successfully or clumsily dealt with them, with the possible exception of her later pacifist writings, you never get the feeling that men are being consciously or unconsciously excluded. By focusing on Addams's early struggles to find a place for herself in a male-dominated world, Sicherman gives us helpful insights into how Addams's perspective and rhetorical style were developed.

Sicherman emphasizes a passage in the young Addams's (1881) graduation address at Rockford Female Seminary as evidence of the growing problematic nature of using culturally inculcated male models of heroism for young women destined for lives of constrained domesticity.[31] In the context of her speech on Homer's Cassandra, Addams sought a way to validate female intuition that would gain respect, and not ridicule or rejection, from the perspective of more masculine approaches to knowledge. Urging women to learn a physical science so that their intuitions could to be expressed in a way that men would recognize as a valuable approach to truth, Addams continues: "The actual Justice must be established in the world by trained intelligence. . . . Only an intuitive mind has a grasp comprehensive enough to embrace the opposing forces."[32] The value of scientific training is to counter the widespread belief that women's sympathies could be engaged only by personal encounters with individual instances of suffering and not by more distant, and hence more abstract, situations of great human suffering.

But when in *Twenty Years at Hull-House* Addams recollects a similar passage from her college years, she attributes it to "an oratorical contest" and gives it as an example of her premature pragmatism, rather than as a defense of women's intuition. She quotes herself as saying, "The actual justice must come by trained intelligence, by broadened sympathies toward the individual man or woman who crosses our path; one item added to another is the only method by which to build up a conception lofty enough to be of use in the world."[33] Addams affirms that many experiences have reinforced this "schoolgirl recipe" and gives a long example of a perplexing struggle between a group of trade unionists and a nonunion employee. Her conclusion is that justice in industrial relations depends on a "wearisome effort to secure the inner consent of all concerned," particularly "those upon whom the present situation presses so heavily."[34] This is a mature pragmatist feminism, indeed, but does not seem particularly directed to valorizing women's intuition.

Only after referring to this "earlier speech" does Addams mention her graduation essay "Cassandra" and its musings on "the feminine trait of mind called intuition." But rather than seeking to justify intuition as a separate, female mode of knowledge that must be defended against male dismissal, she emphasizes that it must be critically questioned. Addams does define it the same way she had earlier, namely, as "an accurate perception of Truth and Justice," but she continues with the rest of the quote, saying that it "rests contented in itself and will make no effort to confirm itself or to organize through existing knowledge."[35] As Sicherman says of the earlier essay, Addams repeats her contention that intuition would grow accurate and intelligible through studying some branch of scientific knowledge, but Addams later continues her self-quotation to give as the reason for pursuing science the fact that only thus would a woman be able to "detect all self-deceit and fancy in herself and learn to express herself without dogmatism." Furthermore, only by "having thus gained accuracy, would woman bring this force to bear throughout morals and justice" and use her growing insights in actual work.

This last statement brings the mature Addams more in line with the intent of the earlier, student essay. But in the context of *Twenty Years at Hull-House*, she dilutes her earlier intention of developing "a strategy to give women a public mission," which Sicherman carries over into her interpretation of the student passages when they are repeated in *Twenty Years*. In the new context, Addams seems more critical than laudatory of women's attempts to enter the public sphere by the manner in which she stresses the shortcomings of woman's intuition and the self-deprecating way she then tells the story of her inability to follow her own advice because she was unable—despite heroic efforts—to understand the intricacies of Darwin's evolutionary theory. The coda to Addams's retelling of the "Boarding House Ideals" in the second chapter of *Twenty Years* is an avowal of her youthful self-conceit and the general lack of insight of college women at the time into the need for a tolerance and self-criticism that would open their minds so that they "might learn something of the mystery and complexity of life's purposes."[36]

It is not so odd to think, as Addams did, that women's authority would be enhanced if they studied science, if the role of science at the time is taken into account.[37] The natural history methodology of Darwin, which forcefully challenged received knowledge, was easily seen as confirming Emerson's appeals to carefully read the book of nature instead of getting knowledge secondhand from books.[38] In Katherine Joslin's account of Addams as a writer, she uses Addams's first book, *Democracy and Social Ethics*, as an example of her "turn toward the literary and away from the social-scientific," which is "perhaps the distinctive feature of her writing."[39] But Addams uses anecdote and dialogue to draw the reader/listener into engaging his or her experiences experimentally, which is an important contribution to pragmatic method. Joslin better captures what is distinctive of Addams's writing when she points out that *Democracy and Social Ethics* "synthesizes masculine and feminine modes of thought and speech, blending rational and intuitive knowledge, intellectual and visceral experience, objective and subjective points of view into patterns of rational and associative logic."[40]

For rebellious youth, science had an appealing aura conferred on it by Auguste Comte because of its power to undermine religious superstition and philosophical speculation by replacing them with careful observation and experimentation. It held the promise of finally ending the worldwide scourges of disease and social ills. For women, it provided a powerful tool for undermining gender stereotypes because they could appeal to the authority of science against the authority of tradition and predict that it would demonstrate that women's presumed inferiority caused by perceived differences was not based in reality. Women were even beginning to be attracted to the new sciences of pedagogy and psychology in order to carry out such gender experiments themselves.[41]

This recognition by some women that they could adapt the emerging power of science to their own emancipatory ends did not make them less critical of its misuse. In *Twenty Years at Hull-House* Addams recounts a poignant example of the dire consequences of her strict application of scientific methods recently adopted by the Bureau of Organized Charities. In her eagerness to conform to its new instructions, meant to bring charity work in line with scientific facts and precision, she failed to pay full attention to the particular needs of a shipping clerk seeking help for his family, and she unintentionally contributed to his death by pneumonia. In her criticism of blind adherence to scientific methods, Addams concludes that "life cannot be administered by definite rules and regulations; that wisdom to deal with men's difficulties comes only through some knowledge of his life and habits as a whole."[42] Dewey emphasizes the same approach in his 1908 *Ethics* when he says: "A moral principle, then, is not a command to act or forbear acting in a given way: *it is a tool for analyzing a special situation*, the right or wrong being determined by the situation in its entirety, and not by the rule as such."[43] The difference between the two explanations of Addams's attitude toward science is that she vividly conveys what happens when this principle of sensitivity to concrete situations is ignored by using her own failure to do so as an example. The benefits of her combined literary, autobiographical, and theoretical approach is especially evident in its power to motivate as well as enlighten and gives added weight to Dewey's arguments for the priority of art to science, despite his ubiquitous appeals to science as synonymous with method.

The different contexts and intentions of Addams's student essay and its partial incorporation into her narrative of Hull House, as well as what she had learned since her college days, may account for their different emphases. Addams still strongly contends that women—in contrast to widely held gender stereotypes—can extend their sympathy beyond their immediate circle to whoever needs help. And she still argues that women must not be content with vague aspirations for good, but must follow through by actually working on social problems. But she is also intent on undermining the smug complacency of the educated upper classes who believe that they already have the solutions to such problems as poverty, labor unrest, and ethnic and class animosity. Their middle-class morality, sense of intellectual superiority, and unquestioned right to power had to be punctured if they were to have any hope of recognizing the causes of social ills and proposing just and workable solutions and if they were to work with those less well off as equals and partners in empowerment instead of treating them as mere beneficiaries or as themselves the source of the problem.

Perceptive accounts of the context of Addams's earlier views are helpful in understanding her mature work. As philosophers, we are trained to analyze the actual texts before us, rather than to examine their place in the life of their authors or to compare them with private journals or letters. But if neglect of context is the besetting failure of philosophers, as Dewey claims, then biographical studies can be a great help in deciphering texts. This has special relevance to works like Addams's *Twenty Years at Hull-House*; Simone de Beauvoir's many books reflecting on the stages of women's lives; and Frederick Douglass's working and reworking of his slave narratives, in which philosophical analysis integrates conceptual issues and autobiographical reflection, theory and practice, justifying goals and actual consequences. Through accounts of Addams's early life demonstrating the discrepancies between events and feelings as recorded by Addams at the time in her journals and letters and the way they are recounted in her later published work, we can realize that in *Twenty Years at Hull-House*, she recasts her earlier self to bring it in line with her later understanding, a process of memory with both conscious and unconscious aspects. Neither the literary achievement nor the philosophical acuity of the book can be fully recognized if it is believed that she is merely giving a journal-like account of those years. This is not to say that Addams's story of her early years is simply a fable, as Katherine Joslin claims.[44] As an artist and thinker, she is recasting her life and the history of the Hull House settlement into a coherent expression of the insights and theories she has developed.

Christianity or Humanism?

Two of Addams's recent biographers disagree over the importance of religion in her life. Louise W. Knight argues that the primary motivation for

Addams's social activism is to be found in a version of an earlier or social Christianity, while Victoria Bissell Brown locates it in a more diffuse yearning for human solidarity.[45] Both influences can be seen throughout Addams's writings. Since nondenominational Christianity was the earliest influence, it informed her imagination, her sense of herself as a caregiver, and her sense of being a member of a worldwide community of equals. Humanism, social democracy, and liberal humanism gave her a continued incentive to be inclusive and nondogmatic and a vocabulary in which to express her aspirations and the goals of Hull House to a public riven by sectarian, political, ethnic, and class divisions. A possible clue to the different weight Addams herself gives to these influences can be gathered from a few passages in the concluding pages of the chapter "The Snare of Preparation," just before she recalls when the idea of founding a settlement house came to her.

At the age of fifty, when she wrote *Twenty Years at Hull-House*, Addams seemed almost at a loss to explain why, twenty-five years earlier, she decided to be baptized in the Presbyterian Church after resisting it for so long. She reports that it had not been from any outside pressure or compulsion to conform, but neither was it a result of any emotional "conversion." Addams insists on her sincerity, but oddly only in regard to taking up "the outward expressions of the religious life."[46] Significantly, the pastor did not require much assent to dogma or miracle, and Addams was content with a simple acceptance of the Christian Gospels, especially their concern for the poor and outcast members of society. But she gives as her strongest motive a longing "for an outward symbol of fellowship," a tangible sign of the unity of spirit that overcomes all differences. Indeed, in contrast to her muted approach to Christian baptism, she confesses to a growing sense of "an almost passionate devotion to the ideals of democracy." What she takes from the Gospel stories is the assertion that lowly fishermen and slaves are no less ennobled by faith than are the privileged few. Her dreams are plainly of universal fellowship, and its most obvious expression in the small village of her youth was the Christian Church, which was thus idealized as a bulwark against the resurgence of aristocratic distinctions.

Presenting a contrast to her rather reticent recital of her Christian baptism, Addams exclaims that she "was enormously interested in the Positivists during those European years" and in their "manifestation of 'loyalty to humanity.'"[47] At the time, she stayed up half the night writing in her notebook, enthusing over the cathedral in Ulm as a veritable cathedral of humanity, which, in its eclectic inclusion in its carved choir stalls of Greek philosophers and Hebrew prophets as well as of Christian saints and a builder of pagan temples, presented a vision of human solidarity. Once again, there is a discrepancy between her descriptions at the time, in which Addams is plainly excited that women—pagan sibyls as well as figures in the Old and New Testaments—were memorialized in the choir stall carvings, and her later recounting in *Twenty Years at Hull-House* of her emotionally moving experience. Addams had earlier remarked in a letter to a friend that "it was something for the early Germans to give so much place to 'die Frauen.'"[48] But no mention is made in *Twenty Years* of the inclusion of women among the other heterogeneous figures harmoniously brought together in the carvings on the choir stalls of Ulm Cathedral, a site she had deliberately sought out because she imagined from reading art books that they expressed "a medieval statement of the Positivist's final synthesis, prefiguring their conception of a 'Supreme Humanity.'"[49]

The explanation for the omission can be found in Addams's reason for recalling the formative experience. Although Addams disparages her earlier enthusiastic diary expressions as "smug," with their "feverish composition cast in ill-digested phrases from Comte," she is clearly searching for the roots of her "early hopes for the Settlement that it should unite in the fellowship of the deed those of widely differing religious beliefs."[50] Such an intention did not preclude women's participation, and the women/men juxtaposition was aesthetically as well as rationally a good fit with the other contrasts featured. However, her immediate aim was to show how her goal of founding a settlement house on the basis of human solidarity, a goal that required not discriminating on the basis of religious affiliation, was not alien to Christian beliefs and practices, however much it ran counter to the militant sectarianism of the time. And immediately after relating another episode of how her understanding of early Christianity was at odds with the religious bigotry she experienced in the early years of Hull House, Addams explicitly attributed its founding to her conviction that it would be a good thing for well-to-do young women to get their heads out of books and take on the pressing needs of those in the impoverished inner city. Women, no less than men, needed balanced lives of reflection and activism and ought to test the truth of their beliefs by the pragmatic criterion of "the ultimate test of the conduct it dictates or inspires."[51]

Sicherman explains that while in Rome on her second trip to Europe,

Addams had also reread George Eliot's *Romola*, "which has been interpreted as a Positivist allegory in which the heroine moves from egoism to altruism, through the three historical stages posited by Comte."[52] According to Sicherman, "Addams explicitly linked George Eliot to positivism in an important talk she gave to the Chicago Women's Club soon after founding Hull House: 'Positivism insists that the very religious fervor of man can be turned into love for his race, and his desire for a future life into content to live in the echo of his deeds. This is what George Eliot passionately voices.'"[53] In *Twenty Years at Hull-House*, Addams continues her comparison of religious and humanistic approaches by telling of an experience and its aftermath from this second trip to Europe, when she had an opportunity to study the Catacombs in Rome.

During her first winter in Chicago and for two more years, she offered a series of lectures on primitive Christianity based on this study at a Deaconess Training School. Its theme illustrates Addams's lifelong efforts to undermine class hierarchy and ethnic bias by explaining that we learn at least as much from those less well off with whom we work as they do from those of us who are more privileged and better able to help. The specific case was her explanation that the early Church was made up of the poor, and it was they who brought the good news to more prosperous Romans. But when she was invited to become one of the trustees of the school, she attended only one meeting because some of the older members objected to her membership on the grounds that she did not offer religious instruction at the Hull House settlement. This religious attitude is contrasted with the spontaneous goodwill shown by an Italian laborer who, as a sign of respect, paid her streetcar fare when she returned home from the meeting, despite the fact that he could ill afford it.[54] The lesson is unmistakable. The blessing of her work denied her by the members of organized religion was readily given by those without a proselytizing agenda, who appreciated her efforts to bridge the ethnic and class divisions that separate us.

The Strengths and Limits of Women's Association with Culture

Women's clubs provided outlets for women when most other areas of public participation were closed to them. Their earliest approaches to culture were mainly through the appreciation and criticism of literary works, which was often combined with participation in "good works" for the poor. In the suffrage era, however, they became organizational centers for more overtly political actions.[55] This trajectory, from at first emphasizing the high culture of poetry, history, science, art, drama, and music, to becoming engaged with issues of child labor, home economics and public health, housing and social hygiene, was one Addams herself had taken earlier.[56] Her early attitudes toward culture more closely resembled the uplift model of the women's clubs, although she was interested from the beginning in how women could gain authority in the public realm from their cultural activities. She also felt stifled by the restrictions upheld by the identification of women with culture and the home and worked tirelessly at Hull House to enlarge the realm of culture appropriate for women until it embraced all human concerns and activities.

Among the great strengths of the women's clubs were their large numbers and wide geographical reach. When organized into national federations of women's clubs, they became a powerful force in changing public opinion on the need to take political action on some of the worse social ills of the time. According to Theda Skocpol, in the early twentieth century, "not only were women's groups at the height of their own organizational prowess and ideological self-confidence, they could also credibly claim to be the broadest force of the day working for the public interest."[57] Because they were excluded from so many civic organizations, black women in the late nineteenth and early twentieth century often organized and worked through women's clubs, many of them connected with, but not subservient to, churches.[58] These clubs were also often the only acceptable social outlet for rural women and their urban counterparts, rich or poor, black or white.

The ones connected with the social settlements were not unique in encouraging the transition to a more expansive sense of cultural and social involvement, but they did benefit from their close connection to the reform-minded activist women facilitating their efforts.[59] At Hull House, the largest was simply called the Hull-House Woman's Club, composed of women of the neighborhood along with some well-to-do benefactors such as Louise de Koven Bowen; others were affinity groups, made up of such individuals as mothers whose children attended the kindergarten; and still others were organized on the basis of language or ethnicity, which included clubs for Mexican, Greek, Italian, and "colored women."[60] Addams noted that "their efforts were municipal, state, national and international in scope" and later recalled with obvious pleasure the excitement of the years when "cooperation among women was new and the companionship exhilarating."[61]

Because Addams's experiences were gendered female and middle or upper class and because of her acute reflections on the ways that these factors colored her perceptions and influenced her interactions with women and men who were both less and more important politically, economically, and socially, she was able to make important contributions to pragmatist theory. She demonstrated in her many writings that theory was the expression of intelligent practice. I wonder how much Addams's belief that the best approach to social transformation was through unobtrusive, small steps was caused by the felt restrictions of being a woman in a patriarchal society. She never lost this conviction, despite her growing confidence and power, and it melded well with pragmatist methodology, which can hardly be said to derive from the same source.

From Elitist Culture to Human Culture

We have seen that already in her college years, Addams was increasingly disturbed by what she called "the self-absorption" that a life deeply immersed in literature and the arts tended to produce. She chafed under the restrictions that hedged in the life thought proper for a cultured, upper-class woman of her time. Her theme that uplifting ideas that were not put into action sicken rather than enhance lives was already articulated in her private correspondence and school essays and prepared the ground for her enthusiastic embrace of the active life of the Hull House settlement and her recognition of the fitness of pragmatist philosophy to her own needs and vision. At the same time, she deeply absorbed literary and historical accounts of heroic actions and works of genius that epitomized the highest ambitions of the human race, and she sought ways to pass on this inspiration to take on great deeds or create artistic or environmental harmony and beauty for the sake of others to generations of young people who did not have her advantages. Her early struggles to combine an ideal of heroism, thought to be an exclusive male prerogative, with what was considered feminine were gradually worked out in the course of her efforts to take on the dire problems of the laboring poor. Her later experiences also led her to abandon the individualism and elitism that her class and education inculcated and to emphasize instead cooperation and egalitarianism in her life and writings.

Addams was not just being generous when she claimed that the poor and underprivileged were her teachers. For one thing, interacting on a daily basis with different classes and nationalities, expressing various religious beliefs, social attitudes, and political outlooks, totally transformed her understanding of culture. Rhetorically, she signals this transformation by recounting a similar experience of one of the members of the Hull House Woman's Club, which included affluent women who had the leisure to devote time to helping others. Since this was a Hull House enterprise, Addams saw to it that they worked together with members of ethnic minorities whom they would otherwise never have encountered, let alone associate with as equals. She remarks that there was scarcely a greater sense of social difference in the various ethnic groups in Chicago at the time than that between the prosperous Irish American club women, who had helped organize a social gathering for people in the neighborhood, and the southern Italian workers attending the event, who were among the most despised ethnic groups. The encounter was a revelation in more ways than one, as the club women had invited southern Italian wives and mothers, who, like women from the East in seclusion, sent their menfolk instead. Afterward, one of the upper-class organizers said to Addams: "Do you know I am ashamed of the way I have always talked about 'dagos,' they are quite like other people. . . . I have been nagging my husband to move off M Street because they are moving in, but I am going to try staying awhile and see if I can make a real acquaintance with some of them."[62]

Addams explains that this marked the moment when the woman had passed from being an uncultivated person to being a cultivated one. She then defines what she means by each term. The uncultivated person "is bounded by a narrow outlook on life, unable to overcome differences of dress and habit, and his interests are slowly contracting within a circumscribed area; while the [cultivated person] constantly tends to be more a citizen of the world because of his growing understanding of all kinds of people with their varying experiences."[63] Addams then pointedly compares the transformative possibilities of ordinary experience, of deliberately placing yourself in unfamiliar situations, of choosing one's experiences with full awareness of the challenges they might make to one's moral outlook and empirical perceptions, with the high-culture equivalents of traveling abroad to broaden one's experiences or attending college to gain a larger outlook.[64]

The conflict between the life of art and the art of life that so pressed upon Addams as she resisted the gendered restrictions of her times, turns out to have been an artifact of biased values that set up the conflicts between high and low art, between elitist and popular art, between museum art and folk art or artisanship, and between moralizing and moral art or an art of integrity. She came to understand that there was no conflict between the culture of fine arts and culture more broadly, but this understanding required a thorough reworking of the roles of art and culture in a democratic society. As Helen L. Horowitz puts it, for Addams, "art was an expression of the life of a society and was only healthy when the society creating it was healthy."[65]

The expansive sense of culture that Addams develops, the need to share it and to use it to build bridges between different classes, adds new dimensions to the pragmatist understanding of philosophy as a criticism of culture. It is one that bridges the often contentious divisions between local, national, and international outlooks. Following her usual approach of undercutting the elitist privileges of Anglo-Saxon ethnicity and nationality, Addams recognized the unique opportunities of Asian women attending the 1928 Pan Pacific Union Congress to take up the understanding of culture as a way of life that promotes equal respect for every person. Addams no longer hesitates in putting culture on a par with the modernizing forces of industrialization and the sciences as she tells the international gathering that "the cultural outlook on life must become as aggressive as the commercial if it hopes to be effective."[66] And to be successful, bolder arrangements in the distribution of education need to be "carried on with that same spirit of free thinking and outspoken publication that has won in the field of natural sciences."

Notes

1. Jane Addams, *Democracy and Social Ethics* (1902), intro. Charlene Haddock Seigfried (Urbana: University of Illinois Press, 2002), 6.

2. For more on this period of discontent, compare Francesca Bordogna on William James's worries "about the lack of self-mastery, general weakness and 'lack of inner harmony' of the modern self, which he diagnosed as effects of the hectic life prevalent in modern America." "Inner Division and Uncertain Contours: William James and the Politics of the Modern Self," *British Journal for the History of Science* 40, no. 3 (2007): 4.

3. Jane Addams, *My Friend, Julia Lathrop* (1935), intro. Anne Firor Scott (Urbana: University of Illinois Press, 1963), 140.

4. Jane Addams, *Twenty Years at Hull-House* (1910; New York: Signet Classic, 1981), 63.

5. Although the accuracy of this remembered passage has been challenged, Louise W. Knight defends its underlying veracity. See *Citizen: Jane Addams and the Struggle for Democracy* (Chicago: University of Chicago Press, 2005), 133–34.

6. Addams, *Twenty Years*, 66–68.

7. Ibid., 67.

8. Victoria Bissell Brown, *The Education of Jane Addams* (Philadelphia: University of Pennsylvania Press, 2004), 203.

9. See Martha C. Nussbaum, *Love's Knowledge: Essays on Philosophy and Literature* (New York: Oxford University Press, 1992), and Charlene Haddock Seigfried, "Has Passion a Place in Philosophy?" in "Philosophy in America at the Turn of the Century," ed. Hugh McCann and Robert Audi, APA centennial issue, *Journal of Philosophical Research* (2003): 35–54.

10. Barbara Sicherman, "Intellect vs. Experience: Jane Addams and Literature's Dual Legacy," Coss Lecture, Society for the Advancement of American Philosophy, Denver, Colorado, March 13, 2003, 2.

11. Jane Addams, *Newer Ideals of Peace* (1906), intro. Berenice A. Carroll and Clinton F. Fink (Urbana: University of Illinois Press, 2007), 6.

12. Addams, *Twenty Years*, 306.

13. John Dewey, *Art as Experience*, in *John Dewey: Later Works*, vol. 10, 1934, ed. Jo Ann Boydston (Carbondale: Southern Illinois University Press, 1989). Compare also Addams's method of intelligent living with Dewey's method of intelligence. See Charlene Haddock Seigfried, "Ghosts Walking Underground: Dewey's Vanishing Metaphysics," *Transactions of the Charles S. Peirce Society* 40, no. 1 (2004): 71.

14. "A Modern Lear," in *The Jane Addams Reader*, ed. Jean Bethke Elshtain (New York: Basic Books, 2002), 163–76.

15. See Larry Tye, *Rising from the Rails: Pullman Porters and the Making of the Black Middle Class* (New York: Henry Holt, 2004).

16. For the importance of "A Modern Lear" as marking the transition to Addams's mature pragmatist philosophy and a history of the varied responses to publishing it, see Knight, *Citizen*, 352–62. For an extended analysis of "A Modern Lear," see Louise W. Knight, "Biography's Window on Social Change: Benevolence and Justice in Jane Addams's 'A Modern Lear,'" *Journal of Women's History* 9, no. 1 (1997): 111–38.

17. Jane Addams, *Second Twenty Years at Hull-House* (New York: Macmillan, 1930), 350.

18. Jane Addams, *The Long Road of Woman's Memory* (Urbana: University of Illinois Press, 2002), 7–28; also in *Second Twenty Years*, 49–79.

19. Addams, *Second Twenty Years*, 67.

20. Helen L. Horowitz, "Varieties of Cultural Experience in Jane Addams' Chicago," *History of Education Quarterly* 14, no. 1 (1974): 70–72.

21. Addams, *Second Twenty Years*, 358.

22. Brown, *Education*, 220.

23. Alan Trachtenberg, *The Incorporation of America: Culture and Society in the Gilded Age* (New York: Hill and Wang, 1982), 208–34. Thanks to Purdue American studies graduate student Arslan Jumaniyazov for pointing this out in his paper "Decolonization of Imperial Knowledge and the Failure of Orientalism."

24. Addams, *Second Twenty Years*, 358–62.

25. L. Ryan Musgrave, "Cosmopolitan Ethics Through Art: Addams, Starr, and Hull-House Aesthetics," Society for the Advancement of American Philosophy, University of South Carolina, March 8–10, 2007, 7.

26. Addams, *Second Twenty Years*, 410.
27. Jane Addams, *The Spirit of Youth and the City Streets* (1909), intro. Allen F. Davis (Urbana: University of Illinois Press, 1972), 85, 75–103.
28. Ibid., 89–89.
29. Ibid., 101.
30. Addams, *Newer Ideals*, 44.
31. Sicherman, "Intellect vs. Experience," 16–17.
32. Addams, "Cassandra," graduation address (June 1881), in Mary Lynn McCree Bryan, Barbara Bair, and Maree de Angury, eds., *Selected Papers of Jane Addams*, vol. 1, *Preparing to Lead, 1860–81* (Urbana: University of Illinois Press, 2003), 429. As quoted in Sicherman, "Intellect vs. Experience," 17.
33. Addams, *Twenty Years*, 55. Actually, all the quotations from the "oratorical contest" or "earlier essay" are found in "Cassandra." With the exception of the substitution of one word ("our" path instead of "one" path), and the inclusion of the phrase "by broadened sympathies toward the individual man or woman who crosses our path" (the omission of which was indicated by ellipses), this is the same quotation as the one cited by Sicherman.
34. Addams, *Twenty Years*, 56–57.
35. Ibid., 57.
36. Ibid., 58.
37. Sicherman attributes this interest to purely biographical reasons, rather than a general cultural shift ("Intellect vs. Experience," 18–19). But for the increasing prestige of science as arbiter of knowledge and truth, see Francesca Bordogna, *William James at the Boundaries: Philosophy, Science, and the Geography of Knowledge* (Chicago: University of Chicago Press, 2009).
38. This also explains why pragmatists saw no necessary contradiction between trained intelligence and empathy. See Charlene Haddock Seigfried, *William James's Radical Reconstruction of Philosophy* (Albany: State University of New York Press, 1990), 139–70.
39. Katherine Joslin, *Jane Addams, a Writer's Life* (Urbana: University of Illinois Press, 2004), 15.
40. Ibid., 61.
41. See Charlene Haddock Seigfried, *Pragmatism and Feminism* (Chicago: University of Chicago Press, 1966), 70–72.
42. Addams, *Twenty Years*, 123.
43. John Dewey, *Ethics*, in *John Dewey: Middle Works*, vol. 5, *1908*, ed. Jo Ann Boydston (Carbondale: Southern Illinois University Press, 1978). This is repeated in his revised *Ethics*, in *John Dewey: Later Works*, vol. 7, *1932*, ed. Jo Ann Boydston (Carbondale: Southern Illinois University Press, 1989).
44. Joslin, *Jane Addams*, 109.
45. Victoria Bissell Brown, "The Sermon of the Deed: Jane Addams's Spiritual Evolution," in *Jane Addams and the Practice of Democracy*, ed. Marilyn Fischer, Carol Nackenoff, and Wendy Chmielewski (Urbana: University of Illinois Press, 2009), 21–39. Knight, *Citizen*, 137–38, 173–74, 253–54, 393.
46. Addams, *Twenty Years*, 68.
47. Ibid., 70.
48. Sicherman, "Intellect vs. Experience," 29–30.
49. Addams, *Twenty Years*, 71.
50. Ibid.
51. Ibid., 72. Addams herself puts this phrase in quotes, indicating that she is aligning herself with a particular position that would be recognized by her readers.
52. Sicherman, "Intellect vs. Experience," 26.
53. Ibid., 45n88. The quote is from Jane Addams, "Outgrowths of Toynbee Hall," Jane Addams Papers, 1890, reel 46.

54. Addams, *Twenty Years*, 71–72.

55. Kathryn Kish Sklar, "The Historical Foundations of Women's Power in the Creation of the American Welfare State, 1830–1930," in *Mothers of a New World: Maternalist Politics and the Origins of Welfare States*, ed. Seth Koven and Sonya Michel (New York: Routledge, 1993), 43–93.

56. Addams, *Second Twenty Years*, 94–99.

57. Theda Skocpol, *Protecting Soldiers and Mothers: The Political Origins of Social Policy in the United States* (Cambridge: Harvard University Press, 1992), 372.

58. Evelyn Brooks Higginbotham, *Righteous Discontent: The Women's Movement in the Black Baptist Church, 1880–1920* (Cambridge: Harvard University Press, 1993), 58.

59. On the woman's clubs' transition from appreciating culture in the narrow sense to active social reform, see Addams, *Second Twenty Years*, 94–99.

60. Louise de Koven Bowen, *Growing Up with a City* (1926; Urbana: University of Illinois Press, 2002), 82–88.

61. Addams, *Second Twenty Years*, 96, 99.

62. Addams, *Twenty Years*, 249.

63. Ibid.

64. For Addams's theory of experience, see Charlene Haddock Seigfried, "Has Experience Any Value?" introduction to Addams, *Democracy and Social Ethics*, xvi–xx, and Charlene Haddock Seigfried, "'The Courage of One's Conviction or the Conviction of One's Courage?' Jane Addams's Principled Compromises," in *Jane Addams and the Practice of Democracy*, ed. Fischer, Nackenoff, and Chmielewski, 40–62.

65. Horowitz, "Varieties of Cultural Experience," 76.

66. Addams, *Second Twenty Years*, 101.

3

Trojan Women and Devil Baby Tales

Addams on Domestic Violence

Marilyn Fischer

The knowledge of the existence of the Devil Baby burst upon the residents of Hull-House one day when three Italian women, with an excited rush through the door, demanded that he be shown to them. No amount of denial convinced them that he was not there, for they knew exactly what he was like, with his cloven hoofs, his pointed ears and diminutive tail; moreover, the Devil Baby had been able to speak as soon as he was born, and was most shockingly profane.

With this description Addams captivated her audiences with devil baby tales, folkloric stories believed by many Chicago immigrants. She published an account of these tales in the October 1916 issue of the *Atlantic Monthly*, with a revised version included as the first two chapters of *Long Road of Woman's Memory*.[1] In these accounts Addams set Greek tragedy and the violence of war alongside the violence her immigrant neighbor women experienced at home as a way of elevating the significance of

---

Materials marked as JAPM are in the microfilm collection of the Jane Addams Papers. The first number is the reel; the number following the colon is the frame number. In *The Jane Addams Papers, 1860–1960*, ed. Mary Lynn McCree Bryan (Ann Arbor: University Microfilms International, 1984).

domestic violence and the dignity of those who suffer. She used the scientific theory of race memory to present these women, not as passive victims, but as creative agents, and to help her audiences form a sense of connection with them. These claims may sound somewhat jarring to contemporary readers, as Addams does not explicitly name either Greek tragedy or race memory in her accounts.[2] However, Addams was acutely aware of the conceptual frames her audiences brought to their reading. Because many among her audiences were well acquainted with Greek literature and then-current scientific theories, Addams could make fleeting, implicit references to these bodies of knowledge and rely on her audiences to fill in the rest. In this discussion I will show how Addams used these bodies of knowledge in shaping a pragmatist-feminist analysis of the devil baby tales and of domestic violence. Pragmatists begin with people's concrete experience within specific, lived contexts and then return to experience to test their theories and concepts. Feminist pragmatists such as Addams give women's experiences central place.[3] In her analysis of the devil baby tales and domestic violence, Addams presents the most marginalized women, not merely as victims, but as agents and artists in their own right.

Writing About the Devil Baby

The devil baby incident took place in the fall of 1913. Addams reported that Hull House was overrun with inquiries for a period of six weeks, probably triggered by the birth of a baby with disabilities in the neighborhood. The *Chicago Tribune* labeled the phenomenon a case of "outcropping medievalism" and worried that if people's intelligence matched their curiosity, "Chicago and civilization would shake hands and say 'good night.'"[4]

Addams gave brief, public accounts of the devil baby incident in 1914. In the July 1914 issue of the *American Journal of Sociology*, she gave a basic description of the devil baby incident, which she repeated in all subsequent accounts. For a period of six weeks, thousands of people appeared at Hull House to see the rumored child, with descriptions already in hand. The Italian version involved an atheist husband who tells his pregnant wife that he would rather have the devil in the house than her religious pictures on the wall. His wish is granted when their baby turns out to be the devil himself. In the Jewish version, the devil appears as the seventh child of a husband who had threatened his wife not to add another daughter to the six they already had. Addams explained that the stories originated as fairy tales authored by women to soften their husbands' treatment of themselves and their children. Many of Chicago's immigrants, former European peasants, still believed and used these tales for family discipline.[5]

In June 1914 the General Federation of Women's Clubs held its biennial convention in Chicago. Attendance was estimated to be up to 150,000, representing the one million women's clubs' members in the United States.[6] At the convention, in a speech titled "Immigrant Woman as She Adjusts Herself to American Life," Addams used the story of the devil baby incident for the same purpose seen in so much of her speaking and writing: to "interpret," for prosperous, middle-class Americans, the immigrant as sensible and fully human and to seek from her audience some form of reciprocity toward immigrants.[7] In this speech Addams interpreted the devil baby tales, not as evidence of superstitions held by ignorant, backward folks, but as a form of moral instruction that had evolved and been refined through a long historical development. The tales, along with their art and music, were gifts the immigrants could offer to her audiences. She suggested that as immigrant women became more economically secure and did not need to work long hours, audience members could reciprocate by inviting immigrants to participate in women's clubs.[8]

Addams's 1914 presentations did not include the features that gave her accounts of 1916 so much power. Her earlier renditions say nothing about woman's memory, nor do they recount how domestic abuse was a staple feature of immigrant women's lives. What happened between the summer of 1914 and 1916 to lead Addams to change and deepen her interpretation so dramatically?

In August 1914 World War I broke out in Europe; in January 1915 Addams assumed the presidency of the Woman's Peace Party. That organization sponsored a national tour by the internationally acclaimed Chicago Little Theater Company of Euripides' *The Trojan Women*. Addams negotiated a five-thousand-dollar grant from the Carnegie Endowment for International Peace to help fund the tour and corresponded with British classicist and translator Gilbert Murray about his accepting reduced royalties; she had lunch with Murray while in Europe during the summer of 1915. The play was performed forty-two times in thirty-one cities on the fifteen-week tour; extended excerpts from Murray's book *Euripides and His Age* were included in the playbill.[9]

In publicity for the tour *The Trojan Women* was billed as "The World's Greatest Peace Play" and as "still the most vivid, the most poignant and the most beautiful illustration of war's utter futility and unmitigated evil, particularly as war affects women and children. The Woman's Peace Party sends it, not as an archaic curiosity, but as a direct message, inspiration and appeal, here and now to the men and women of America."[10] Audiences had the background to appreciate the play, as knowledge of the classics was pervasive among the elite and middle classes. Before the 1880s knowledge of both Greek and Latin were required for college admission in the United States. As those requirements were dropped, the humanities courses that replaced them contained heavy doses of classical literature, philosophy, and art. Classical subjects and texts figured prominently in Chautauqua movement lectures and on women's clubs reading lists, where ancient Egyptian, Greek, and Roman history was favored over more modern fare. Murray's translations of Euripides were widely known and enthusiastically received by audiences and readers on both sides of the Atlantic. His book *Euripides and His Age* was part of the Home University Library, a series of low-priced books written expressly for a popular audience that sold widely and well.[11]

In her 1916 analyses of the devil baby tales, Addams does not mention the Trojan War, Euripides' play, or the suffering of women then in the midst of ongoing slaughter in Europe. In 1915 Addams had met with these women and had spoken eloquently about war's devastation for women and children.[12] As she wrote the devil baby account of the brutality her neighbor women suffered at home, the suffering of war's victims lay heavy on her mind. Katherine Joslin, in *Jane Addams, a Writer's Life*, suggests that with the devil baby analysis, Addams may have been trying to "deflect public criticism of her pacifism."[13] Perhaps. But given the associations Addams makes between Greek tragedy and domestic violence, it is more likely she was asking her readers to appreciate her pacifism more fully and viscerally.

Greek Tragedy and Domestic Violence

"While I may receive valuable suggestions from classic literature," Addams notes in her introduction to *Long Road*, "when I really want to learn about life, I must depend upon my neighbors."[14] Addams's statement, though truthful, disguises the extent to which she draws from Murray's picture of Euripides depicted in *Euripides and His Age* and from Murray's translations of Euripides' plays to probe the significance of the devil baby tales. Citation practices in the early twentieth century were loose; many of Addams's unattributed quotations are from these sources, and many of her own sentences contain close paraphrases of Murray's material.

Addams was particularly drawn to the old women immigrants who came to see the devil baby. Living in silence, ignored by their Americanizing families, and unable to adjust to urban Chicago, the women felt their memories stirred by the possibility of such a creature, and they poured out the stories of their lives. In recounting these women's stories, Addams sometimes cast these women in the role of Euripides, for whom Murray invoked the authority of Goethe and Aristotle, calling Euripides "the most tragic of poets."[15] She also makes parallels between the old women and Euripides' tragic heroines, among them Medea and Hecuba. By borrowing in this way Addams places her neighbor women's suffering from domestic abuse alongside the sufferings that the women of ancient Greece experienced through war and betrayal. In the following section I will italicize passages from Addams and Murray to reveal where Addams quotes or closely paraphrases Murray's writings or translations.

In her introduction to *Long Road*, Addams names Gilbert Murray and thanks him for telling how Euripides

> could transmute into song traditional tales of sorrow and wrongdoing because, being long past, they had already *become part mystery and part music. "Memory, that Memory who is the Mother of the Muses, having done her work upon them."*

In this passage Addams borrows from Murray's description of how Euripides presents the cries of long-dead children, who

> are now at peace and whose ancient pain has *become part mystery and part music. Memory—that Memory who was mother of the Muses—has done her work upon it.*[16]

Throughout the analysis, Addams credits the figure of Memory with shifting elderly people's attention from the future to the past and then transmuting the past by softening bitterness and resentment and enhancing what is beautiful. Memory gathers the fruits of this process into "legendary wisdom."[17] She concludes her analysis with these lines:

> In the midst of the most tragic reminiscences, there remained that something in the memories of these mothers which has been called *the great revelation of tragedy, or sometimes the great illusion of tragedy; that which has power in its own right to make life palatable and at rare moments even beautiful.*

Note how heavily Addams draws from the penultimate paragraph of *Euripides and His Age*, where Murray gives a succinct statement of his conception of tragedy in Greek literature:

> The powers of evil and horror must be granted their full scope; it is only thus that we can triumph over them. Only when they have worked their uttermost will do we realize that there remains something in man's soul which is forever beyond their grasp and *has power in its own right to make life beautiful. That is the great revelation, or the great illusion, of tragedy.*[18]

In passages from *Euripides and His Age* excerpted in *The Trojan Women* playbill, Murray explains how the play is the story of the Greeks' great triumph over Troy, told from the perspective of its greatest victims, the women of Troy. The war is over; their city is destroyed; their loved ones are dead. The remaining women, including Hecuba, the Trojan queen; her daughter Cassandra; and her daughter-in-law Andromache, will become slaves and concubines to Greek chieftains. Murray describes Hecuba, holding her murdered grandson: "No friend among the dead, no help in God, no illusion anywhere, Hecuba faces That Which Is and finds somewhere, in the very intensity of Troy's affliction, a splendour which cannot die." Euripides' tragedy reveals "the crying of one of the great wrongs of the world wrought into music, as it were, and made beautiful."[19]

Addams adapts Euripides' pattern in her presentation of her old neighbor women. When we isolate her descriptions of their lives, the starkness shocks. These women "had been forced to face tragic experiences, the powers of brutality and horror had had full scope in their lives." Their faces were "worn and scarred by harsh living." Some lived "under the iron tyranny of that poverty which threatens starvation and under the dread of a brutality which may any dark night bring them or their children to extinction."[20] Yet Addams surrounds these brutal truths with an aura of sympathy and gives the women in full measure the humanity and dignity of Euripides' Trojan women.

In some passages Addams uses Murray's language to cast the old women in the role of Euripides himself. She likens the women's quiet endurance to

> *the age-worn minstrel who turned into song a Memory which was more that of history and tradition than his own.*

Here she is giving a close paraphrase to Murray's description of Euripides, when he officially became one of the "old men" upon completing his forty years of military service. Murray notes,

> Even yet *the age-worn minstrel can turn Memory into song . . . the saga of history and tradition, more than his own.*[21]

Addams further identifies the old women with Euripides through the way they told their stories. They spoke without anger or regret, yet they did not hide from the violence that had filled their years. Addams writes,

> Such old women do not *shirk life's misery by feeble idealism. . . .* They relate *without flinching the most hideous experiences.*

Murray had written,

> *The weak artist shirks the truth by a feeble idealism,*

while the great tragic poet

> *can touch without flinching any horror of tragic life*

and transform this material into poetry.[22]

Addams also draws from the choruses in Euripides' plays, both by quoting them and by paraphrasing Murray's account of the chorus's function to describe the women's stories. Murray calls the chorus "the very heart of Greek tragedy." In the chorus, "verisimilitude is simply thrown to the winds." By its "power of transfiguration" the chorus gives expression to "ultimate emotion," "the essence" of "something universal and eternal." Throughout her analysis, Addams uses similar language. She describes stories such as that of the devil baby as "careless of verisimilitude," as "expressing the very essence of human emotion," as dealing "with fundamental experiences."[23]

Addams quotes several passages from the chorus in Murray's translation of *Medea*, a play that Murray claimed was often cited in suffrage circles.[24] Medea, daughter of a king and mother of Jason's children, sacrificed much for Jason, including committing murder on his behalf. Jason then betrayed her to marry another woman. Addams borrows from *Medea* to describe the women and the conditions under which they raised children. Her succinctness makes the old women's pain palpable:

> Some of these old women had struggled for weary years with poverty and much childbearing, had known what it was to be bullied and beaten by their husbands, neglected and ignored by their prosperous children, and burdened by the support of the imbecile and the shiftless ones. They had literally gone "*Deep written all their days with care.*"

This phrase is taken from *Medea*, where the chorus sings,

> But they within whose garden fair
> That gentle plant hath blown, they go
> *Deep-written all their days with care—*
> To rear the children.[25]

Here the chorus sings Medea's lament about the enormous pain of bearing, rearing, and loving children and how the children then grow to be good or evil and to die. To Addams's ears, her neighbors' stories of children who died prematurely from lack of medical care or from unavoidable neglect while their mothers were at work echoed the following quotation, also from the chorus in *Medea*:

> *That God should send this one thing more*
> *Of hunger and of dread, a door*
> *Set wide to every wind of pain?*[26]

To capture the joy tangled with intense pain with which women in her own neighborhood brought forth and nurtured young lives, Addams uses the phrase

> *the precious vintage stored from their own agony.*

The poignancy of the phrase deepens when we note its source. As Medea prepares to kill her own children, the women of the chorus, desperately trying to beat down the barred door between them and Medea, cry out,

> Thou stone, thou thing of iron? Wilt verily
> Spill with thine hand that life, *the vintage stored
> Of thine own agony?*[27]

Addams was a very careful, intentional, and highly skilled writer. She reworked her material extensively; the four presentations of the devil baby story discussed above are one illustration of that.[28] I do not think that Addams relied on Murray to the extent that she did as a way to avoid crafting her own descriptions. My hypothesis is that the borrowing was intentional and done to help her communicate with an educated audience, who would, to varying degrees of precision, recognize the sources of Addams's borrowing. They would know the conceptions of Greek tragedy that Murray worked with; some would identify specific passages from Murray's translations of Euripides' plays. Addams's analysis is feminist in that she names women's oppression vividly, and she signals its significance to her readers by setting it alongside a form of literature they valued most highly.[29]

As I write this chapter, the layered parallels swirl in my mind. Euripides wrote *The Trojan Women* during the Peloponnesian War, immediately after the Greeks expressed their imperial hubris by slaughtering the Milesians and just as they set off toward their final debacle in Sicily. Murray translated Euripides during the height of the British Empire, just before two world wars led to the demise of European imperial hegemony. I sit here now, on the soil of the greatest military power on earth, a nation entangled in its own imperial debacles, in Iraq and Afghanistan. I read Murray quoting Thucydides, who said that "a democracy cannot govern an empire," and remember Addams's rhetorical query "Was not war in the interest of democracy for the salvation of civilization a contradiction of terms?"[30] I think of the explicit, tight connection between war and violence against women, with rape as a perennial weapon of war, and then turn to the implicit connection, that maintaining structures of patriarchy fuels both violence in war and violence against women in the home. I imagine that in 1916 some of these layered images swirled in Addams's mind, and in the minds of her readers, as well.

Evolutionary Theory, Race Memory, and "A Literature of Their Own"

In this section I will explain theories accepted as scientific in the early twentieth century regarding human social evolution, race memory, and folklore and demonstrate how Addams used these theories in her analysis of the devil baby. Addams placed these theories within a pragmatist-feminist perspective to form connections with and thus decrease distance between her "primitive" neighbors and her "civilized" audiences. As with Greek tragedy, Addams did not need to be explicit in using these theories. Just a few terms and phrases would give her audiences sufficient clues.

To late nineteenth-century anthropologists, *savagery*, *barbarism*, and *civilization* were technical terms. American anthropologist Lewis Henry Morgan used them to name three stages in human social and cultural evolution, roughly corresponding to, respectively, the period of hunter-gatherer bands, the stage of settlement and agriculture, and the stage in which writing developed and governance was based on territorial control rather than kinship.[31] Morgan and many of his colleagues believed that the various human "races" followed roughly the same developmental path, with different races being at different points along that path at any given time. *Race* was loosely defined and, in most accounts, contained a mix of physical and cultural characteristics. Traits that we today would call "cultural" were assumed to be heritable in a Lamarckian sort of way.[32] These scientists thought that many Native Americans, Africans, Pacific Islanders, and others living at that time were in the stages of savagery and barbarism, and that by studying them, "civilized" peoples could learn about their own deep past.[33]

British anthropologist Edward Burnett Tylor regarded folklore as a particularly fruitful resource for investigating human evolution, claiming that the popular narratives of European peasants gave evidence connecting "savage" and "civilized" peoples.[34] J. A. MacCulloch followed this approach in *The Childhood of Fiction: A Study of Folk Tales and Primitive Thought* (1905), calling folktales "the literature of early man and of primitive people." He studied these stories much as a geologist or archeologist would dig into the earth. A single story could carry elements from many generations and thus give evidence for the movements and mingling of many peoples and the development of custom over vast stretches of time. McCulloch noted that the practice of studying folklore as "the fossil survivals of the thoughts and customs of the past" was then well established among scientists.[35]

Many theorists at the time thought that more than oral transmission was at work as these tales passed from one generation to the next. In "The Gods as Embodiments of the Race-Memory," Edward Carpenter explains race memory as the evolutionary equivalent of Plato's theory of recollection. Over long stretches of time, people's experiences and emotions accumulate and are shifted and refined into images analogous to Platonic forms. These reside in the subconscious, in the "nerve-plexus or brain-centre of the human body" and are heritable. Jung called them archetypes of the collective unconscious; Carpenter and others associated them with basic instincts, such as pugnacity and sympathy. These images are not perceived in ordinary consciousness, but are manifest in myths, legends, and rituals, seen, for example, in the deep awe and devotion a people show toward even an unworthy monarch. Artists and poets can give these images form; in responding to art, a perceiver's race memory is touched by the artistic artifact. Unlike Plato's forms, the images of race memory are not fixed, but continue to evolve. Carpenter concludes that this evolutionary process "gives to each individual the power . . . to add a chisel-touch to their outlines."[36]

Although Addams does not use the term *race memory* in *Long Road of Woman's Memory*, her reviewers made the association. A review in the *Los Angeles Times* quoted text from the book's slipcover: "The underlying purpose of the book is to show wherein modern civilization goes back to old tribal customs, to explain, in other words, the scientific theory of race memory." Another commented that "modern psychology is virtually founded" on the theory of race memory. A third thought Addams was presenting her own version of Jung's collective unconscious.[37]

If we use the theory of race memory as an interpretive frame, many of the phrases in Addams's analysis lose the character of rhetorical hyperbole and become more straightforward. She identifies the devil baby tales "as subconscious memories" that "still cast vague shadows upon the vast spaces of life, shadows that are dim and distorted because of their distant origin." The theory of race memory offers a process for explaining how "the story seemed to condense that mystical wisdom which becomes deposited in the heart of man by unnoticed innumerable experiences" and how "the strivings and sufferings of men and women long since dead . . . are thus transmuted into legendary wisdom."[38]

Pairing Addams's devil baby analysis in *Long Road* with Murray's *Euripides and His Age* provides additional evidence that both Murray and Addams drew on the theory of race memory. This theory gives a different feel to Murray's claim and Addams's paraphrase, quoted in the previous section, where Murray writes, "Memory, according to Greek legend, was the mother of the Muses; and the 'memory' of which Euripides is thinking is that of the race, the saga of history and tradition, more than his own."[39] Tylor's anthropological investigations of primitive religion and marriage practices[40] gave scientific backing to Murray's claim about Euripides' morally austere tone in *Cretan Women*, where Murray comments,

> But *next to religion itself, the sphere of sexual conduct has always been the great field for irrational taboos and savage punishments.*

Addams gives a close paraphrase, in describing how the devil baby story still acted

> as a restraining influence in the sphere of marital conduct which, *next to primitive religion, has always afforded the most fertile field for irrational taboos and savage punishments.*[41]

In the devil baby chapters, Addams describes her neighbors as "primitive" and as "simple women, representing an earlier development." Murray uses similar vocabulary, referring to the Macedonians as "barbaric" and noting, "We seem in ancient Greece to be moving in a region that is next door to savagery."[42] Although this language was ubiquitous among intellectuals and in public discourse, scholars today often brush past it. For example, in her introduction to the reprint edition of *Long Road*, Charlene Haddock Seigfried writes, "It is true some aspects of her writings are dated," and "Addams was not completely immune to the new anthropological paradigm," but does not pursue the point. A few scholars, such as Sullivan and Jackson, interpret Addams's use of this language as reinforcing then prevalent hierarchical, racist stereotypes.[43]

We rightly criticize such language and its conceptual frames as inherently and morally repugnant. It was used to justify slavery, imperialism, exclusionary immigration policies, unjust labor practices, and forced sterilization. A focused, extended study of Addams's use of this language and its conceptual apparatus would be valuable, particularly to ascertain the extent to which it worked at cross-purposes to her commitments to reciprocity, inclusion, and social democracy. However, for this chapter, I would like to pose the question this way: given that this vocabulary functioned as the air that educated people breathed, how might someone within that air, communicating to others who shared the same air, bridge the distance it implies between "primitive" and "civilized" people? Biographer Louise W. Knight notes how Addams, in much of her writing, would "skillfully embed controversial ideas in a soft cushion of conventionality."[44] I think this aptly describes what Addams does in her devil baby analysis. Here, "conventionality" would be the conventional vocabulary of the day's anthropological theories, with their elaborate differentiations of "primitive" and "civilized" peoples, with theories of "race memory," and with the "science of folklore" as then understood. Addams draws on all these, to stunning effect. My intent is not to justify her use of these theories and vocabulary, but to clarify how she used them to do pragmatist-feminist work, creating a sense of connection rather than distance between her immigrant neighbors and her middle-class audiences.

Feminism, Pluralism, and Making Connections

Seeking connections through responsibility and care and ending oppressions that hinder human flourishing have been central projects for feminist ethics.[45] These projects also describe Addams's activism and theorizing. She founded Hull House to bring together the privileged classes and the immigrant poor. In *Democracy and Social Ethics*, written for members of privileged classes, Addams argues that sympathetic understanding and reciprocity are essential practices for enacting social democracy. The knowledge required to heal fractured relationships and bring needed industrial and social reform could only be obtained through sympathy and shared, concrete experience. Addams understands democratic equality in terms of reciprocity, that is, that all people can simultaneously learn from and teach one another. As sympathetic understanding and reciprocity are internalized in attitude and expressed in action, the attitudes and beliefs that maintain power structures of privilege will be undermined.[46]

A worry for feminists is that when members of a dominant group seek connections with groups of lesser power and social standing, their efforts may be paternalistic or smothering. Even with good intentions, members of the dominant group may not recognize or adequately respect the perspectives of the other.[47] The task is to seek connection while respecting pluralism. This is not easy to do. There is no neutral stance; invariably, one cannot "understand" another's perspective, without using constructs and terms that make sense within one's own perspective. One way to read Addams's devil baby analysis is as an attempt to work through this difficulty, to seek connection while simultaneously respecting the immigrant women's perspectives. Addams's task in her written accounts was to move her audience from believing that the devil baby story was merely a manifestation of "primitive" people mired in superstition, toward appreciating these people's perspectives and being able to learn from them. Addams does not romanticize her neighbors or endow them with a feminist consciousness. For example, her statement that her neighbors believed that a man "needs a woman to keep him straight" is discordant to modern ears.[48] Yet the overall pattern of Addams's analysis is feminist. First, she constructs the perspective of immigrant women by presenting them as knowledge makers and artists. That is, she searches for the patterns of meaning they constructed out of their experience with which to understand and respond to the circumstances of their lives. Second, she does not judge these responses per se. Instead, she attends to how these patterns of meaning are responses to universally shared circumstances—dealing with family life, suffering from injustice and violence, needing companionship, facing death—and sets her neighbor women's responses alongside those of her own and her readers. Finally, in reciprocity, she uses her neighbors' stories to widen, deepen, and reconstruct her own knowledge and that of her readers.

The Old Women as Artists and Knowledge Makers

Pragmatists and feminists describe how knowledge is constructed and how reflection on concrete experience is central to that process. In *Pragmatism and Feminism*, Seigfried describes commonalities that pragmatist and feminist orientations share. She stresses how concrete experience serves as the starting point for reflection and subsequently as the testing ground for beliefs and theories. Values and purposes are integral to and guide the process of inquiry. Knowledge is a fabric of beliefs and attitudes, with old threads pulled out, new threads inserted or reinforced, and the shape stretched in response to new experiences.[49] In her analysis of the devil baby tales, Addams presents the most marginalized of persons— old, unassimilated, uneducated women, whose sanity was often on the edge—as knowledge makers for whom folklore served as functional threads.

Throughout her analysis, Addams makes repeated references to how women used these tales "as a valuable instrument in the business of living." Women first designed the tales to soften male brutality against them; Addams saw the devil baby story's taming effect in the faces of men who came to inquire. Women had used such tales for centuries to instruct; to establish family discipline; to give them social standing; to feed their imaginations; and, for peasants not able to acclimate to the modern, industrial city, to keep them sane.[50]

For Addams to refer to folklore as "a literature of their own" was not, in itself, unusual. Yeats and other collectors of folklore made similar points. However, many such collections reveal the patriarchal biases of their collectors. The images in Carpenter's account of race memory are primarily of male heroes—kings, warriors, and athletes.[51] By contrast, Addams claims that women themselves authored folklore and used the tales to assert their own power. Addams writes that these women artists, who "had nothing to oppose against unthinkable brutality," used the one tool available to them: "the charm of words." To twenty-first-century ears, *charm* has a diminutive ring, but for Addams's reading public, it had a far stronger emotional valence. Murray, in *Euripides and His Age*, quotes Thucydides' account of Cleon's warning that an empire must stand firm over those it rules. "Do not be misled by the three most deadly enemies of empire, pity and charm of words and the generosity of strength." Here Murray presents the "charm of words" as a potent tool of the oppressed, against which oppressors must guard.[52]

Placing the "charm of words" within the theory of race memory, Addams claims that women, with access to subconscious memories, had the skill to craft their words into literary form, and that their art had potency. Subsequent generations of women, including her neighbors, contributed their artistry to these heritable images, or, in Carpenter's words, added their own "chisel-touches." Noting that "new knowledge derived from concrete experience is continually being made available for the guidance of human life," Addams interprets her neighbors' custom of insisting that their husbands give them their unopened paychecks as another example of the still-evolving practices of women creating domestic morality. These practices, Addams writes, "are put into aphorisms which, in time, when Memory has done her work upon them, may become legendary wisdom."[53] Understood in this light, the title of the book takes on new resonance. "The long road of woman's memory" was long indeed, and one on which women were active and creative travelers.

Patterns of Meaning

In addition to their practical use, these folkloric stories had a place in the larger patterns of meaning with which the women made sense of their lives. Philosophers, theologians, and poets have long sought ways to reconcile humans' desire for universal justice, where evil is punished and good rewarded, with the suffering that blind fate and calculated injustice bring to the innocent. The devil baby stories helped these old women make this reconciliation. Addams hypothesized that the stories appealed in part because their frank, demonic quality matched the women's experiences with abject poverty and brutal violence.[54] The devil babies appeared as just retribution for the fathers' brutality. The stories gave the women a way to understand ungrateful children who beat them, or children born with mental and physical disabilities. Today, we refer to chemical imbalances and neural deficits to help us understand and feel some sympathy toward perpetrators of untoward behavior. The devil baby performed an equivalent role; the women could see how the father's "ugliness was born in the boy" and how "the Devil himself gets them."[55]

But how could the women come to terms with the fact that the devil's ugliness was inside the children themselves, causing the innocent to suffer? Addams saw her neighbor women take comfort in their shared stories, realizing that those who walk with the "the piteous multitudes who bear the undeserved wrongs of the world . . . walk henceforth with a sense of companionship." In this passage, Addams's readers may have heard echoes of the chorus from *The Trojan Women*. In the playbill, Murray called the parting of Andromache and her son "the most absolutely heart-rending in all the tragic literature of the world." As the child is dragged away to be killed, members of the chorus tell how they also lost loved ones. As Hecuba prepares her grandson's body for burial, the chorus again provides companionship.[56]

By stressing companionship here, Addams takes seriously the claim from folklorists that such tales functioned as literature. Devil baby tales and Greek tragedy performed the same literary service by bringing companionship and comfort to those who suffered. She begins the last paragraph of the *Atlantic Monthly* version by paraphrasing Murray, who wrote that the chorus

> *will translate the particular act into something universal.* It will make a change in all that it touches, increasing the elements of beauty and significance and leaving out or *reducing the element of crude pain.*

Addams adds women as artists to her paraphrase:

> It has always been the mission of literature to *translate the particular act into something of the universal, to reduce the element of crude pain* in the isolated experience by bringing to the sufferer a realization that his is but the common lot, this mission may have been performed through such stories as this for simple hard-working women, who, after all, at any given moment compose the bulk of the women of the world.[57]

Addams identifies another literary text to set alongside her neighbors' experiences. She writes that in talking with some of the old women who were very close to death,

> one realized that old age has its own expression for the mystic renunciation of the world. The impatience with all non-essentials, the craving to be free from hampering bonds and soft conditions, was perhaps typified in our own generation by Tolstoi's last impetuous journey, the light of his genius for a moment making comprehensible to us that unintelligible impulse of the aged.[58]

Tolstoy was one of her favorites; she referred to him and to his writings frequently. Addams does not specify what she meant by Tolstoy's "last impetuous journey." She may have been referring to his literal last journey; he died in 1910 while traveling. However, given the context, I suspect that Addams had in mind Tolstoy's short story "Master and Man," a text she used to close *Democracy and Social Ethics*. Lost in the snow and close to freezing, the master covers his servant's body with his own. As he slips into his final sleep, his own lifetime strivings seem trivial; he feels at one with his servant and at peace with himself.[59] Addams's old neighbor women had revealed through their literature what Addams had learned from Tolstoy, that at the end of life, companionship brings healing and mystic unity, and that is the only thing that matters.

Demonstrating Reciprocity

Addams's devil baby analysis is in one sense a departure from previous writings. In *Democracy and Social Ethics* (1902), *Newer Ideals of Peace* (1907), *Twenty Years at Hull-House* (1910), and *A New Conscience and an Ancient Evil* (1912), Addams names patterns of social injustice and then responds by advocating social democracy to end that oppression. By contrast, in the devil baby analysis, Addams catalogs her neighbors' lifelong suffering from injustice, but then responds by dwelling on their "mystic renunciation" and 'emotional serenity." She found that many of her old women neighbors, in spite of their lives of hardship, were not bitter or resentful; Memory had softened their pain. Again, she borrows from Murray. "Apparently," she notes,

> the petty and transitory had fallen away from their austere old age.

Murray likewise describes Memory's power, and he quotes Bertrand Russell, who wrote,

> The Past does not change or strive. . . . What was eager and grasping, *what was petty and transitory, had faded away*.[60]

In describing these old women's sense of renunciation, Addams writes,

> I gradually lost the impression that the old people *were longing for a second chance at life, to live it all over gain and to live more fully and wisely.*

Trojan Women and Devil Baby Tales   99

Here Addams uses Murray's words to counter his interpretation. Murray paraphrases what some Theban elders said in the chorus of Euripides's *Heracles*,

> *A second life is what one longs for. To have it all again and live it fully.*[61]

Addams also finds materials in Murray with which to characterize the old women's attitude toward death and to reassess her own response. Commenting on Euripides' presentations of death in his plays, Murray suggests that at places, Euripides conveys that

> *death may be the state that we unconsciously long for, and that really fulfills our inmost desires.*

He goes on to quote from his translation of *Hippolytus*, where Hippolytus says,

> *We cling to this strange thing that shines in the sunlight, and are sick with love for it*, because we have not seen beyond the veil.

Addams comments that one of her old neighbors expressed

> *a longing for death, as if it were a natural fulfillment of an inmost desire*, with a sincerity and anticipation so genuine that I would feel abashed in her presence, ashamed to *"cling to this strange thing that shines in the sunlight and to be sick with love for it."*[62]

Why does Addams mull over mystic renunciation rather than call for social democracy in response to domestic violence? One possible explanation is that death was on Addams's mind when she wrote her 1916 versions of the devil baby tale. She worried about the injustices of war then raging in Europe and worried about the well-being of the many people she knew and cared about there. She was not well herself; newspapers reported she was undergoing a lengthy recuperation from tuberculosis of the kidney, complicated by diabetes.[63] While Addams does not explicitly call for social democracy in response to domestic violence, I do think that she was enacting the essential practices of social democracy—sympathetic understanding and reciprocity, or the willingness and openness to learn from others. Her neighbor women's stories set alongside Euripides' presentation of old age and Tolstoy's last impetuous journey gave her an occasion for furthering her own construction of knowledge. The old women's attainment of renunciation and serenity added density to truths about death and injustice that Addams had been constructing for some time.

Shortly before the devil baby reputedly put in an appearance at Hull House, Addams had used a trip to Egypt as an occasion to ruminate about death, an account published in the *Atlantic Monthly* in February 1914 and reproduced virtually unaltered as the last chapter of *Long Road*. In that essay, perhaps framed by the theory of race memory, she sets her own experiences of the deaths of loved ones, a constant in her life from an early age, next to those of ancient Egypt.[64] The characters and the narrative line in the devil baby analysis are different, but I see Addams making a parallel exploration. Euripides and the women in his tragedies replace the ancient Egyptians; her old neighbors stand in for herself. There are times to protest social injustice, but there also comes a time to respond to impending death under conditions of injustice and violence that one can do little to change. The theory of race memory enabled Addams to connect the ancient Egyptians, the women of Troy, and her immigrant neighbors to herself. In 1915 and 1916, her status as the most famous and admired woman in the United States was beginning to slide, as press reports mocked and ridiculed her stance against war. Perhaps she was gathering from her old immigrant neighbors the strength and serenity she would so soon need to face rejection by friends and colleagues and unmeasured hostility from the public.

While Addams does not *argue* for social democracy in her devil baby analysis, she *enacts* it through approaching her neighbors with sympathetic understanding and reciprocity. It is true that readers today can often identify Addams's feminism straight off the page. But it is also true that Addams was very much a woman of her time. Reading her works through the conceptual frameworks widely embraced in her time can reveal her feminism in surprising and powerful ways.

Notes

1. The quotation that opens this chapter is taken from "The Devil Baby at Hull-House," *Atlantic Monthly*, October 1916, 441. Nearly identical passages are in "A Modern Devil-Baby," 117; "Immi-

grant Woman as She Adjusts Herself to American Life"; and *Long Road of Woman's Memory*, 7–8. Addams included a version of the devil baby analysis in *The Second Twenty Years at Hull-House* (1930), abridged but otherwise unaltered, from *Long Road of Woman's Memory*.

2. Other scholars discussing Addams's devil baby analysis have not made these connections. See Charlene Haddock Seigfried's introduction to the University of Illinois reprint edition of *Long Road of Woman's Memory*, xx–xxii; Joslin, *Jane Addams, a Writer's Life*, 171–76; and Elshtain, *Jane Addams and the Dream of American Democracy*, 176–80.

3. For discussions of feminist pragmatism, see the Introduction in this volume; Sullivan, "Feminism"; and Seigfried, *Pragmatism and Feminism*.

4. *Chicago American*, June 16, 1914, JAPM 62:184; *Chicago Tribune*, November 1, 1913, JAPM 60:1072.

5. "A Modern Devil-Baby," 117–18.

6. *Advertiser* (Boston), June 9, 1914, JAPM 62:141.

7. For Addams's discussion on interpretation as a function of the settlement house, see *Twenty Years at Hull-House*, 134.

8. "Immigrant Woman as She Adjusts Herself to American Life," JAPM 47:906. See also the news account of the speech in *Chicago American*, June 16, 1914, JAPM 62:184.

9. Woman's Peace Party microfilm, reel 3, box 3, folder 7; on Addams and the Carnegie Endowment, see letter dated March 13, 1915, JAPM 8:460, and extensive correspondence in WPP microfilm, reel 3, box 3, folder 7. On Addams and Murray regarding discounted royalties, see letters of March 28, 1915, JAPM 8:548 and March 29, 1915, JAPM 8:556. In a letter dated August 27, 1915, Murray mentioned the lunch and congratulated and thanked Addams for the successful tour of *The Trojan Women*, JAPM 8:1446. For data on the theater tour, see Albert, "Gilbert Murray," 65.

10. JAPM 42:1633.

11. Winterer, *The Culture of Classicism*, 1, 119, 145–47. Albert writes that Murray's writings and translations "effectively revitalized Greek drama both on the stage and the printed page, bringing it to unprecedented popularity throughout the English-speaking world." "Gilbert Murray," 62. Murray was one of the editors of the Home University Library series. See West, *Gilbert Murray*, 139–41.

12. See Addams's Presidential Address at the first Woman's Peace Party convention, "What War Is Destroying" (January 10, 1915); her Presidential Address at the International Congress of Women at The Hague, "Women and War" (May 1, 1915); and her address at Carnegie Hall, "The Revolt Against War" (July 9, 1915). At the International Congress of Women at The Hague, Lida Heymann spoke explicitly and eloquently on the connection between rape and war. See Heymann, "Leiden der Frauen im Krieg."

13. Joslin, *Jane Addams*, 173.

14. Addams, *Long Road*, 4.

15. Ibid., 10; Murray, *Euripides*, 243.

16. Addams, *Long Road*, 3; Murray, *Euripides*, 240.

17. Addams, *Long Road*, 7, 11, 16, 19.

18. Ibid., 28; Murray, *Euripides*, 242.

19. Woman's Peace Party microfilm, reel 3, box 3, folder 7.

20. Addams, *Long Road*, 10, 16, 23.

21. Ibid., 11; Murray, *Euripides*, 103.

22. Addams, *Long Road*, 10–11; Murray, *Euripides*, 242, 240.

23. Murray, *Euripides*, 226, 226, 241, 228, 230–31; Addams, *Long Road*, 18.

24. Murray, *Euripides*, 32.

25. Addams, *Long Road*, 12; Euripedes, *Medea*, 484.

26. Euripides, *Medea*, 484–85; Addams, *Long Road*, 21.

27. Addams, *Long Road*, 19; Murray, *Euripides*, 240.

28. For a detailed presentation of Addams as a writer, see Joslin, *Jane Addams*.

29. W. E. B. Du Bois uses a similar technique in *The Souls of Black Folk*, where he begins each chapter by pairing European or Euro-American poetry with an African American spiritual.
30. Murray, *Euripides*, 107; Addams, *Peace and Bread*, 82.
31. See Morgan, *Ancient Society*, chap. 1, "Ethnical Periods."
32. See Stocking, *Victorian Anthropology*, 138, 141, 235. For the construction of "race," see Stocking, *Delimiting Anthropology*, chap. 1, "The Turn-of-the-Century Concept of Race."
33. Morgan, *Ancient Society*, 22–23.
34. Stocking, *Victorian Anthropology*, 163.
35. MacCulloch, *The Childhood of Fiction*, vii, 13–14.
36. Carpenter, "Gods as Embodiments," 269, 273, 270–72, 279. My favorite of Carpenter's examples is his attributing a chicken's instinct to hide, when a shadow moves overhead, to "the memory of a thousand and a hundred thousand occasions in the history of the chick's ancestors, when the dreaded claws and beak came from the sky and snatched or nearly snatched the cowering prey" (264).
37. *Los Angeles Times*, January 28, 1917, JAPM 82:1108; *Public Ledger* (Philadelphia), November 11, 1916, JAPM 82:1071; *Chicago Post*, February 2, 1917, JAPM 82:1115. Not everyone endowed the devil baby analysis with such serious academic credentials. In reviews of a collection of *Atlantic Monthly* essays that included Addams's 1916 account, one called it "amusing"; another said it was "absurd" and "belongs in a book of fiction." *Republican* (Springfield, Mass.), March 17, 1918, JAPM 82:1138; *America* (New York), March 28, 1918, JAPM 82:1140.
38. Addams, *Long Road*, 18, 10, 15.
39. Murray, *Euripides*, 103; Addams, *Long Road*, 11.
40. For Tylor's anthropological investigations, see Stocking, *Victorian Anthropology*, 188. Tylor and Murray overlapped at Oxford. On Tylor's influence on Murray, see West, *Gilbert Murray*, 132.
41. Murray, *Euripides*, 77; Addams, *Long Road*, 18.
42. Addams, *Long Road*, 8, 27; Murray, *Euripides*, 169, 198.
43. Seigfried, introduction to Addams, *Long Road*, x, xxxiiin27; Sullivan, *Revealing Whiteness*, 168–80; Jackson, *Lines of Activity*, 51, 224–28.
44. Knight, *Citizen*, 98.
45. The literature on feminist ethics is vast. See, for example, Held, *The Ethics of Care*, chaps. 1, 10; Walker, *Moral Understandings*, chaps. 3–4. Essays on ethics in Jaggar and Young, eds., *A Companion to Feminist Philosophy* contain extensive bibliographical references.
46. See Addams's introduction to *Democracy and Social Ethics*.
47. See Tronto, *Moral Boundaries*, 170; Held, *The Ethics of Care*, 165; and Jaggar, "Global Responsibility and Western Feminism," 185–86.
48. Addams, *Long Road*, 19.
49. See Seigfried, *Pragmatism and Feminism*, chaps. 1–2. See also Code, *What Can She Know?* and Alcoff and Potter, eds., *Feminist Epistemologies*. Entries on feminist epistemology in Jaggar and Young, eds., *A Companion to Feminist Philosophy* include many bibliographical references.
50. Addams, *Long Road*, 17, 10, 12, 14, 20.
51. Yeats, *Irish Fairy and Folk Tales*, xxvii. See Stewart's analysis of the ballads collected by Francis James Child, Bottigheimer's extensive analysis of gendered images in the Grimms' fairy tales, and Lundell's discussion of patriarchal biases in Aarne and Thompson's collections of folktale types and motifs. Carpenter, "Gods as Embodiments," 268.
52. Addams, *Long Road*, 18. Murray, *Euripides*, 107. See Frye's discussion of charm in literature in *Spiritus Mundi*, 123–47.
53. Addams, *Long Road*, 19.
54. Ibid., 25, 23.
55. Ibid., 11, 22
56. Ibid., 27; Woman's Peace Party microfilm, reel 3, box 3, folder 7; Euripides, *The Trojan Women*, 70–73.

57. Murray, *Euripides*, 230; Addams, "The Devil Baby at Hull-House," 451. Never one to waste good material, Addams placed this paragraph at the beginning of chap. 4 in *Long Road*.
58. Addams, "The Devil Baby at Hull-House," 445. The equivalent passage in *Long Road* is identical except for a few key words; see 16.
59. Tolstoy, "Master and Man," 577.
60. Addams, *Long Road*, 11; Murray, *Euripides*, 241.
61. Addams, *Long Road*, 15; Murray, *Euripides*, 102.
62. Murray, *Euripides*, 190, 191; Addams, *Long Road*, 16.
63. *Chicago Evening Post*, April 6, 1916 (JAPM 64:139).
64. Addams, "The Unexpected Reactions of a Traveler in Egypt."

References

Addams, Jane. *Democracy and Social Ethics*. 1902. Reprint, Urbana: University of Illinois Press, 2002.
———. "Devil Baby at Hull-House." *Atlantic Monthly* 118 (1916): 441–51.
———. "Immigrant Woman as She Adjusts Herself to American Life." In *Biennial Convention Official Report* (General Federation of Women's Clubs), 370–74. 1914. JAPM 47:902–7.
———. *The Long Road of Woman's Memory*. 1916. Reprint, Urbana: University of Illinois Press, 2002.
———. "A Modern Devil-Baby." *American Journal of Sociology* 20 (1914): 117–18.
———. *Peace and Bread in Time of War*. 1922. Urbana: University of Illinois Press, 2002.
———. "The Revolt Against War." 1915. In *Addams's Essays and Speeches on Peace (1899–1935)*, ed. Marilyn Fischer and Judy D. Whipps, 83–95. Bristol, U.K.: Thoemmes Press, 2003.
———. *Twenty Years at Hull-House*. 1910. Urbana: University of Illinois Press, 1990.
———. "Unexpected Reactions of a Traveler in Egypt." *Atlantic Monthly* 113 (1914): 178–86.
———. "What War Is Destroying." 1915. In *Addams's Essays and Speeches on Peace (1899–1935)*, ed. Marilyn Fischer and Judy D. Whipps, 61–64. Bristol, U.K.: Thoemmes Press, 2003.
———. "Women and War." 1915. In *Addams's Essays and Speeches on Peace (1899–1935)*, ed. Marilyn Fischer and Judy D. Whipps, 75–82. Bristol, U.K.: Thoemmes Press, 2003.
Albert, Sidney P. "Gilbert Murray." In *Modern British Dramatists, 1900–1945*, part 2: M–Z, ed. Stanley Weintraub, 61–71. Detroit: Gale, 1982.
Alcoff, Linda, and Elizabeth Potter, eds. *Feminist Epistemologies*. New York: Routledge, 1992.
Bottigheimer, Ruth. *Grimms' Bad Girls and Bold Boys*. New Haven: Yale University Press, 1987.
Bryan, Mary Lynn McCree, ed. *The Jane Addams Papers, 1860–1960*. Ann Arbor: University Microfilms International, 1984.
Carpenter, Edward. "Gods as Embodiments of the Race-Memory." *Hibbert Journal* 2 (1904): 259–79.

Code, Lorraine. *What Can She Know? Feminist Theory and the Construction of Knowledge.* Ithaca: Cornell University Press, 1991.

Du Bois, W. E. B. *The Souls of Black Folk.* 1903. Boston: Bedford/St. Martin's Press, 1997.

Elshtain, Jean Bethke. *Jane Addams and the Dream of American Democracy: A Life.* New York: Basic Books, 2002.

Euripides. *Medea.* Trans. Gilbert Murray. In *Fifteen Greek Plays,* trans. Gilbert Murray, Benjamin Bickley Rogers, et al., vol. 2. New York: Oxford University Press, 1943.

———. *The Trojan Women.* Trans. Gilbert Murray. New York: Oxford University Press, 1915.

Frye, Northrop. *Spiritus Mundi: Essays on Literature, Myth, and Society.* Bloomington: Indiana University Press, 1976.

Held, Virginia. *The Ethics of Care: Personal, Political, and Global.* New York: Oxford University Press, 2006.

Heymann, Lida. "Leiden der Frauen im Krieg." In *International Congress of Women Report,* 79–81. Amsterdam: International Women's Committee of Permanent Peace, 1915.

Jackson, Shannon. *Lines of Activity: Performance, Historiography, Hull-House Domesticity.* Ann Arbor: University of Michigan Press, 2000.

Jaggar, Alison M. "Global Responsibility and Western Feminism." In *Feminist Interventions in Ethics and Politics,* ed. Barbara S. Andrew, Jean Keller, and Lisa H. Schwartzman. New York: Rowman and Littlefield, 2005.

Jaggar, Alison M., and Iris Marion Young, eds. *A Companion to Feminist Philosophy.* Malden, Mass.: Blackwell, 1998.

Joslin, Katherine. *Jane Addams, a Writer's Life.* Urbana: University of Illinois Press, 2004.

Knight, Louise W. *Citizen: Jane Addams and the Struggle for Democracy.* Chicago: University of Chicago Press, 2005.

Lundell, Torborg. "Gender-Related Biases in the Type and Motif Indexes of Aarne and Thompson." In *Fairy Tales and Society,* ed. Ruth B. Bottigheimer. Philadelphia: University of Pennsylvania Press, 1986.

MacCulloch, J. A. *The Childhood of Fiction: A Study of Folk Tales and Primitive Thought.* London: John Murray, 1905.

Morgan, Lewis Henry. *Ancient Society.* 1877. Cambridge: Harvard University Press, 1964.

Murray, Gilbert. *Euripides and His Age.* New York: Henry Holt, 1913.

Seigfried, Charlene Haddock. *Pragmatism and Feminism: Reweaving the Social Fabric.* Chicago: University of Chicago Press, 1996.

Stewart, Polly. "Wishful Willful Wily Women: Lessons for Female Success in the Child Ballads." In *Feminist Messages: Coding in Women's Folk Culture,* ed. Joan Newlon Radner, 54–73. Urbana: University of Illinois Press, 1993.

Stocking, George W. *Delimiting Anthropology: Occasional Essays and Reflections.* Madison: University of Wisconsin Press, 2001.

———. *Victorian Anthropology.* New York: Free Press, 1987.

Sullivan, Shannon. "Feminism." In *A Companion to Pragmatism,* ed. John R. Shook and Joseph Margolis, 232–38. Malden, Mass.: Blackwell, 2006.

———. *Revealing Whiteness: The Unconscious Habits of Racial Privilege.* Bloomington: Indiana University Press, 2006.

Tolstoy, Leo. "Master and Man." In *The Short Novels of Tolstoy,* trans. Aylmer Maude, 527–80. New York: Dial Press, 1946.

Tronto, Joan C. *Moral Boundaries: A Political Argument for an Ethic of Care*. New York: Routledge, 1993.
Walker, Margaret Urban. *Moral Understandings: A Feminist Study in Ethics*. New York: Routledge, 1998.
West, Francis. *Gilbert Murray: A Life*. New York: St. Martin's Press, 1984.
Winterer, Caroline. *The Culture of Classicism: Ancient Greece and Rome in American Intellectual Life, 1780–1910*. Baltimore: Johns Hopkins University Press, 2002.
Woman's Peace Party. *The Collected Records of the Woman's Peace Party Microform, 1915–1920*. Wilmington, Del.: Scholarly Resources, 1988.
Yeats, William Butler, ed. *Irish Fairy and Folk Tales*. 1918. New York: Modern Library, 2003.

4

Addams's Philosophy of Art

Feminist Aesthetics and Moral
Imagination at Hull House

L. Ryan Musgrave Bonomo

A project examining the philosophical importance of the arts at Chicago's Hull House settlement and the philosophy of art that Jane Addams developed there is one that should, by all rights, be old news. Addams herself had a liberal arts education, as part of the first wave of American women to obtain one. She was a lover of the arts, and providing something of the arts and humanities to the workers who constituted the common life of Chicago was central to her mission at Hull House. She was a theorist whose intellectual work was grounded in the concrete, lived experiential practices around her, and as a keen observer of Chicago's turn-of-the-century labor practices, Addams wrote frequently about the toll industrialization takes on more creative and imaginative human practices of making. As Hull House expanded, the physical spaces reserved for the arts increased at the settlement, a sign of their centrality to the mission and to daily life there. Given these facts, it is surprising to find virtually no account of how Addams used arts practices at Hull House to develop an original feminist philosophy of art—one that is, I argue, integral to her ethics. For the purposes of this chapter, I mean *art* broadly, as Addams meant it: at Hull House, the term included the use of traditional art objects, art engagement practices that ranged from traditional Western distanced contemplation to practices well beyond this, and practices of artistic creative making—whether the making of art objects, crafts, meals, songs, or the like.

My aim here is threefold: first, to make a feminist contribution to the field of philosophy of art and aesthetics by revising the canon to include Addams's work as it should (on the model of Seigfried and others who have rewritten Addams back into her actual position as a legitimate philosopher and founder of classical American pragmatism). I hope to show up and correct this blind spot by indicating four scholarly areas where Addams's work has been absent but clearly warrants inclusion. Second, I will examine how her approach was original within both feminism and pragmatism and was actually more original in some ways than Emerson's pragmatist approach before hers. I will especially look at the feminist dimensions of Addams's concept of moral imagination and cosmopolitan sensibility. I conclude by arguing that with these contributions, her work in fact constitutes a coherent and original feminist aesthetics—one of the earliest, actually, in U.S. history. Long before contemporary talk of cosmopolitanism or feminist epistemology, Addams had developed a theory of learning, knowing, and ethical engagement through the arts within the Hull House context.

Addams's Absence in Relevant Fields

There are at least four places where one might expect to find consideration of Addams's aesthetics. The first is within feminist pragmatism and a body of work by Seigfried, Deegan, Minnich, Fischer, and Whipps, who have decisively established her central role as a feminist philosopher and contributor to the subfields of pragmatism, sociopolitical and ethical theory, and epistemology. Yet the arts receive little treatment here. This could easily be the result of a persistent but unfortunate tendency to relegate aesthetics to a back-burner field within philosophy, crowded out by attention to its bigger siblings of epistemology, ethics, and sociopolitical theory. Likewise, a rich body of scholarship now exists on pragmatist aesthetics—philosophical views on art from American transcendentalists, to Alain Locke and the Harlem Renaissance. Recent contributions in this area have blossomed as well: one might expect to find the Hull House laboratory of the arts considered in Thomas Alexander's *John Dewey's Theory of Art, Experience, and Nature*, or in Shusterman's *Pragmatist Aesthetics* or *Practicing Philosophy* or *Performing Live*, or in the 1993 collection *Philosophy and the Reconstruction of Culture* edited by Stuhr, or in Gunn's 1992 *Thinking Across the American Grain*. Yet this body of work has neglected the Hull House context as well, and from the works mentioned, one would have no clue that feminist approaches in aesthetics or pragmatism exist at all. And yet they do: third, the (now burgeoning) field of feminist aesthetics developed historically even earlier than that of feminism and pragmatism. Built mainly by scholars trained in traditional aesthetics, feminist approaches in aesthetics internally critique this tradition and add to it new approaches focused on how aesthetics, politics, and ethics intertwine. Little attention to Addams exists here. Last, general analyses of the arts at Hull House do exist. They tend, however, to merely describe the concrete practices, and do not question what (if any) relevance this might have to theories of philosophy of art.[1]

Addams's Aesthetics at Hull House

That Addams found the arts central to the Hull House enterprise and developed a coherent aesthetics should be signaled by the attention she pays to the arts in *Twenty Years at Hull-House*—namely, through the significance of Chapter 16, "Arts at Hull-House." Addams does many things in that book: autobiography, history, sociology, political theory, pragmatist philosophy, social ethics, gender studies. In fact, this chapter and her later essay "The Play Instinct and the Arts" both build on and extend the traditional aesthetics of her day. It is also an approach that shares much with pragmatist accounts of art in her time: she had read Emerson on art, and her work foreshadows Dewey's later work in *Art as Experience*.

All three of these thinkers espouse the general pragmatist method of deriving theory from lived experience, so the theories can in turn improve experience. Yet Addams's approach to Hull House fulfills this pragmatist dictum more fully: as we will see, the lab of Hull House informs her aesthetic theories far more intimately than lived experience did for other pragmatists. Ellen Gates Starr's chapters "Art and Labor" and "Art and Democracy" in the 1895 *Hull-House Maps and Papers* are relevant here, as are other writings of hers on the role of art in public education assembled by Mary Jo Deegan and Ana-Maria Wahl in the 2003 collection *On Art, Labor, and Religion*. No less art lovers than Emerson, Dewey, or Danto, Starr and Addams had in Hull House a laboratory that the first three thinkers did not. Instead, the closest parallel to their practices and theories arising from the Hull House arts laboratory might be Locke's and Du Bois's writings on the arts in the context of the Harlem Renaissance.[2] This vantage point offered them a unique opportunity to consider the social, ethical, and epistemological dimensions of art-in-action at their particular historical point of immigration and industrialization.

Feminist and Pragmatist Aesthetic Approaches: "Hungry for a Chance to See and Create Beautiful Things"

The first furnishings of Hull-House were therefore pictures.

—Addams, "Art Works"[3]

While Addams was familiar with pragmatist writings on aesthetics prior to Hull House, she broke new ground in feminist approaches to aesthetic practice and theory with her work there. Dewey had not yet developed his mature views on aesthetics when she and Starr opened the settlement in 1889; from Emerson's 1841 essay "Art" we have a clear sense of developing pragmatist aesthetics on which Addams drew (these themes can also be traced into Dewey's eventual writing on aesthetics). Once Hull House began, Addams and Starr immediately put on the walls the hallowed art they had bought on their European postcollege tour. Before her, Emerson had suggested a pragmatist view of artistic creation as a collective human enterprise from the outset—a process in which the artist must "employ the symbols in use in his day and nation, to convey his enlarged sense to his fellow men. Thus the new in art is always formed out of the old."[4] Addams drew on this notion that artistic creation was never purely personal, but instead had a collective dimension. She explored this in far more depth than Emerson before her or Dewey after her in the lab setting of Hull House. She likewise extended two other threads of Emersonian aesthetics: the macro lens on creativity as a process natural for the human organism, and a view of creative making as a transactional process between materials, inherited processes and forms, and the individual.

These pragmatist aesthetic commitments also arose as key tenets of feminist aesthetics in the later part of the twentieth century, and Addams honed both the theory and practice of them far earlier in Hull House. Her stated aim for the arts there was so simple and straightforward: "to secure for working people the opportunity to know the best art."[5] At the time, she understood this to mean the great canonical works of Western civilization, along with an understanding of the formal criteria constituting their greatness, so that Hull House dwellers could appreciate them properly (according to the norms of Western practice—distanced, contemplative appreciation). But as mentioned above, this appreciation of the art object is only one mode of the arts operating at Hull House. Art operated as both a *noun* and a *verb* at Hull House, in a sense: as objects, art involved canonical works to be appreciated. But it was also treated as an action, as active making in which the immigrants themselves engaged. On this view that Addams came to develop, art was not just an object to be duly appreciated with proper aesthetic distance and abstract, rational reflection (apart from political, cultural, personal, ethical investments or values); art was also an active process of laboring, making, creating. This process included materials, formal aspects, ideas, and personal creative insight. Especially in the Chicago industrial setting, Addams also thought intently about how industrial forms of making, creating, and laboring could affect processes of artistic making (and vice versa). This seemed to her an essential question for impoverished immigrants who spent sixteen-hour days laboring and creating via factory work, citizens who would never enjoy the liberal arts education to which she had been privy.

As it expanded on multiple city blocks, the physical buildings of Hull House reflected Addams's aim to employ art in multiple modes. The original Hull House art gallery grew to include an art studio, a bindery, a kiln, shop classes that we might today call vo-technical education, artisan training in crafts, a drawing room, and a gymnasium as performance space for concerts and plays. The Hull House music school was opened in 1893 and the Labor Museum in 1900. After realizing early on that her aim to bring "great art" to "the common people" was too naive and simple a strategy for arts engagement at Hull House, Addams began encouraging Hull House members to also practice and share various creative practices that had been part of their previous country and culture. This included cooking, making folk tunes, clothes, children's toys, furniture, fine lace or linens, or crafts; all were offered alongside more traditional Western arts of painting, sculpture, drawing, or classical music. The more Addams reconsidered the sort of great art she had originally envisioned for Hull House, the more laughable seemed her initial expectations that, for example, an Italian immigrant would need to draw on some Americanized mode of appreciation to meaningfully engage a landscape by an Italian artist.

So at first glance, the initial methods by which Addams and Starr literally built Hull House on the arts might look to us like a case study in cultural imperialism, an approach of well-intentioned but ultimately insensitive privileged do-gooders. Committed to social amelioration, these college-educated women began with a hypothesis: "Influenced by John Ruskin and William Morris, the Hull House group believed that one way to bring meaning and purpose into the drab lives of immigrant neighbors was to introduce them to things of beauty, especially great art."[6] Like Emerson, Addams found the imaginative power of art praxis to be socially reconstructive: she shared his sentiment that "when I have seen fine statues, and afterwards enter a public assembly, I understand well what he meant who said, 'When I have been reading Homer, all men look like giants.'"[7] By viewing what had been placed before them as great works of art, Hull House dwellers had the chance to draw on an imaginative power that Addams hoped might give them an enlarged sense of what humanity could accomplish. It invited Hull House immigrants into the common family of humanity that had produced such beauty and intimated that, with serious effort and the training available down the hall, they themselves might contribute to that story.

The invitation may seem laughable or ironic, given the daily experiences of immigrants: crippling poverty, high death rates, overcrowded slums, round-the-clock factory work, child labor, and serious xenophobia. Addams recognized this as well: "There is something pathetic about little immigrant girls hanging copies of Fra Angelico angels on the dreary walls of their tenement rooms, and about Miss Addams's conviction that the youngsters gained a heroic and historic impulse from viewing art reproductions. Yet the early settlement members, for all their esoteric art exhibits and art history classes, had captured a basic truth: the immigrants were hungry for a chance to see and create beautiful things."[8] As Addams eventually realized, this "noun" sense of art could not be the only mode in which the arts existed at Hull House—but it could be an important one. She knew already that impoverished immigrants would never gain the privilege of a formal arts and humanities education; yet given the reality of their energies spent making and creating via factory labor, she also understood that they were robbed of any chance to use creative powers in imaginative or contemplative ways. Addams aimed for Hull House opportunities to offset this.

Addams's recognition of this is quite significant in the field of aesthetics. Before Marxist aesthetics had truly developed as a field and before Theodor Adorno focused in the early twentieth century on this dynamic in the American context, Addams offered a critique of capitalism's impact on creativity and organic cultural growth. She saw that advanced industrialism begat workers run by the objects they are forced to make into commodities, rather than the other way around. Aesthetically speaking, she worried that producing solely in this way would eventually alienate humans from their creative, imaginative powers—both intellectually and physically. Further, it seems significant that she observed and theorized this while deeply enmeshed within Chicago factory life. She concluded that under such labor conditions, humans are locked into relating to objects (and practices of making generally) for mainly commodity value and profit. The difference was stark, Addams realized, between any artistic sort of making Hull House members might engage in and the sort of making and labor they did as work. Precisely at this moment in the United States, where immigrants were far away from whatever counted as home and faced massive pressure to assimilate quickly to the culture and the labor/making practices, the paintings on the walls posited and literally framed a community larger than the version of America they were under such pressure to embrace.

Just to mention one contemporary feminist parallel: in her book *Art on My Mind*, bell hooks critiques the view that the only proper African American aesthetic approach to art must focus heavily on politics, race, and oppression. She recognizes that this might be one valuable mode of thinking about art, and she raises the question of art for art's sake for black folks (or other minority groups long foreclosed from enjoying such a thing). She recognizes here that the Western "art for art's sake" distanced approach (inherited from Kant), though traditional, may still have some libratory aspects to it. She points out how this narrow understanding of the significance of black art has sadly been adopted by the persons it was presumed to benefit: "Taking our cues from mainstream white culture, black folks have tended to see art as completely unimportant in the struggle for survival. Art as propaganda was and is acceptable, but not art that was concerned with any old subject, content or form. And black folks who thought there could be some art for art's sake for black people, well, they were seen as being out of the loop, apolitical."[9] She relates her own story of falling in love with the arts as a child through just this sort of approach: how liberating it was for her to experience what Kant calls the "free play of the imagination," rather than the notion (above) that any art by people of color must focus on some particular lens such as race or politics. This theme is treated in significant depth by many authors in my edited collection *Feminist Aesthetics and Philosophy of Art: Critical Visions, Creative Engagements*, where I have written on this dynamic in feminist interpretations of Nancy Spero's artwork.[10] Yet more than a century earlier than hooks and this recent scholarship, Addams was exploring in both practice and theory how liberating the same art for art's sake could be for new, impoverished immigrants as an alternative to mind-numbing factory work.

Feminist Aesthetics and Ethics at Hull House: Democratic Citizenship and an "International Mind"

This "hunger to see and create" also had an ethical dimension, one that connected creative and libratory making with democracy and broader cosmopolitan awareness. In her writings, Addams frequently references an "international mind," which she considered a requirement for citizens of a democracy: she saw the arts as an essential avenue for developing this.[11] She was a good pragmatist in that, like Emerson and later Dewey, she valued an art of the everyday: she championed arts and crafts, encouraged immigrants to draw on their daily lives for material, and operated with a pluralist understanding of art and beauty not relegated just to high art or refined tastes. Again, these are markers of feminist aesthetic approaches that eventually developed half a century later in the United States (a good example is the 1995 *Feminism and Tradition in Aesthetics* by Peggy Zeglin Brand and Carolyn Korsmeyer). Addams followed Emerson in holding that the arts had a strong ethical dimension, one that involved liberty and responsibility in the face of creative freedom, that the artist "must not be in any manner pinched or hindered by his material, but through his necessity of imparting himself the adamant will be wax in his hands, and will allow an adequate communication of himself, in his full stature and proportion. He will not need cumber himself with a conventional nature and culture."[12] Again, such lofty dreaming seems ill suited to Chicago slum realities. But Addams was determined to democratize such creative dreaming and making, convinced that it was a necessary route to whole personhood and that the educative powers of beauty were not solely the birthright of the upper classes.

The field of feminist aesthetics has long considered the access historically denied to marginalized groups regarding training in formal artmaking and authoritative positions as art critics or curators. Philosophers as diverse as Christine Battersby, Peggy Zeglin Brand, Mary Devereaux, Hilde Hein, Carolyn Korsmeyer, Linda Nochlin, and others have offered nuanced analyses of such dynamics. Elsewhere, I have written specifically about this democratizing of the arts framed as a basic right in a liberal democracy.[13] Addams recognized early on the importance of this aesthetic agency, and posited that this agency and creative expression of it affects how one comes to be a citizen. To position immigrant factory workers as heir to the pastime of considering and creating beauty permitted them an agency—as person, citizen, lover of beauty, artist—that was typically nonexistent in their daily lives of factory work. Instead of mindless body factory labor for profit, it invited them into what Emerson called "the depth of the artist's insight of that object he contemplates."[14]

So for Addams, citizenship in a democracy entailed the right to access and agency in the common life of creative appreciation and creative making. But even more interesting is the ethical significance she thought the arts had beyond American citizenship. As she came to realize that immigrants could appreciate Western canonical works on the wall but that their overall concept of art included modes beyond mere distanced contemplation, she encouraged them to continue practices of making and aesthetic engagement learned in their home cultures. At first, many seemed to balk at this: given the rampant xenophobia of the time, engaging in traditional artistic or artisan practices seemed to fly in the face of their concrete need to pass as legitimately American. But Addams encouraged and wove these diverse arts engagement practices into the life of Hull House, and the community began sharing them internally.

In this way, she saw firsthand how such cross-cultural arts-engagement practices were central to the new immigrant Americans becoming global citizens more broadly. Even as Hull House members came to be and know themselves as American in some sense, the act of sharing their inherited diversity of creative arts practices grounded a cosmopolitan awareness at Hull House. And this multicultural, collaborative, and collective sharing of arts practices only radiated further out from Hull House as an epicenter: through the plays, productions, musical performances, books printed, pots fired, and rugs woven, the house modeled an international approach to the arts for the surrounding community and beyond. This cooperative laboratory of the arts that Addams facilitated can be seen as a precursor to feminist art collectives that arose in the United States in the middle of the twentieth century.

Even as Addams drew on these themes shared by feminist and pragmatist approaches to art, the feminist focus and originality of her approach becomes obvious if we look back again at Emerson's aesthetics. Emerson's artist is a lone he, an individual creating through genius in isolation. Such a vantage point would likely have made little sense to Addams and the immigrants inhabiting overcrowded slums, crushing factory work, and a noticeable lack of privilege involving education or leisure time to hone or indulge such genius. Another difference is that in Emerson's little piece, there is much talk of nature and of Emerson's ideal Art expressing nature. Addams watched the pragmatist approach in action as immigrants shifted conceptions of beauty and connected it instead to their own daily realities. Like the house itself, the arts at Hull House took on a collective and cooperative methodology, one that spread even beyond the doors of the house. The collective aspect stretched into facilitating cosmopolitanism for the community through cross-cultural experiences of arts engagement practices.

Learning and Knowing via Arts Engagement: Moral Imagination and Cosmopolitanism

It is not news that feminists and pragmatists both found creative self-expression and collective artistic expression central to a lively democracy. I am suggesting, however, that Addams's unique contribution to early feminist and pragmatist aesthetics is her distinctively collective, communitarian, and truly international emphasis on imaginative thinking.

Moral imagination enabled Hull House immigrants to dream and imagine collectively, not just individually; beyond connecting with one another, they connected with other cultures not just through the singular act of one reading the literature of some distant other country and thereby gaining sympathy for them, but through group acts (some within similar ethnic groups, some within mixed groups) of both making and engaging art that seemed foreign in some way.

Addams's feminist theory of moral imagination broke new ground in her day. A century later, it still shines as an original contribution in what has developed into extensive scholarship on moral imagination. We can compare hers to a contemporary popular view of moral imagination voiced by Martha Nussbaum, one that is not specifically feminist.[15] In an unpublished paper Marilyn Fischer presented at the 2006 annual meeting of the Society for the Advancement of American Philosophy (SAAP), Fischer compared Nussbaum's cosmopolitanism with that of Addams and noted the way the role of the arts (or what Nussbaum calls "narrative imagination") differed for each. She makes the case that while Nussbaum recommends the "sympathetic understanding of all outcast or oppressed people" that can come from reading poets and novelists (in a way that Nussbaum herself suggested is "lonely and abstract") Addams's arts practices were more—as Fischer puts it—"crowdedly social and concrete."[16] Nussbaum's lone reader here parallels, in some sense, Emerson's lone artist model mentioned earlier.

Since Addams encouraged sharing of native artisan craft methods, experiencing art and beauty at Hull House expanded to a multifaceted and robust practice, with many avenues into the progressive power of the arts. Art engagement also came through artisan craft: members of diverse nationalities watched and compared with their neighbors the techniques to combine foods, weave clothing, craft furniture, make pottery, and so on. In doing this, they not only reconnected with creative agency via pastimes they had thought were foreclosed from the American experience; many were reminded, sitting beneath the "little pictures" on the walls at Hull House, that they had in fact always had some relation to beauty in their home setting. "The exhibits afforded pathetic evidence that the old immigrants do not expect the solace of art in this country; an Italian expressed great surprise when he found that we, although Americans, still liked pictures, and said quite naively that he didn't know that Americans cared for anything but dollars—that looking at pictures was something people only did in Italy."[17]

Contra this, Addams facilitated at Hull House a space for American and cosmopolitan "solace of art." Some immigrants realized anew that passing into American culture did not require them to jettison practices of creative making, that one could be American and love the arts, that in being a good industrial American worker, one might also (though still in so-called leisure time, which in truth barely existed for Hull House immigrant workers) be an imaginative artisan of beauty. Sharing these inherited traditional forms of making fostered an international mind also, in this sense: not only did the techniques get taught, but so did the histories, values, ways of life, and arts-engagement practices of the immigrants' home cultures. The arts at Hull House had an ethical dimension insofar as members systematized this deeper form of human connection to materials, to their home communities, and to other humans in other cultures. This is exactly what Addams meant with her aim to foster a cosmopolitan international mind: by doing this, members rejected the pressures of sheer assimilation and found another way of relating both to objects and to each other. They stressed plurality in creative practices while simultaneously recognizing the commonalities across cultural ways of making.

Conclusions: Addams's Contribution to Feminist Pragmatist Aesthetics

Feminist aesthetics of the mid-twentieth century and beyond engages themes Addams had been considering at least fifty years earlier—ones of aesthetic agency, canon inclusion, democratic access, collective creating, gendered aspects of alternative forms of making, critiques of the individual model of the lone artist and critiques of a sex-specific notion of artistic genius. Addams also refigured Emerson's pragmatist views from a feminist angle and predated many points that Dewey would later explore in his aesthetics. Emerson in 1841 and Dewey nearly one hundred years later in *Art as Experience* were certainly correct to identify as a pragmatist problem the division between fine art and everyday existence and proposing to instead live life as art. But the dream of making industrialized life within the factory conform to their expectation that everyday experience would be an enhanced aesthetic experience is clearly far too much of a stretch when one begins in the context that was Hull House. We can trace Emerson's ideal of Art with a capital A infusing all experience into Dewey's eventual notion of "an experience." Of course both were right, in a sense, to call for all our experiences to be as thickly artistic as they ideally can. Yet Addams really addressed a question they did not concerning the practicality of implementing this approach: for immigrant factory workers, this effectively rendered 90 percent of their time somehow "not experiential" and therefore seemingly irrelevant to the pragmatist model. This dynamic flies in the face of general pragmatist aims.

Addams's aesthetics at Hull House, then, preview later feminist and pragmatist concepts of how the arts are libratory—while it simultaneously offers an internal critique of both feminist and pragmatist views of her day. It also makes a unique epistemological point: that shared, crosscultural forms of arts engagement foster cosmopolitanism and communicate ethical ways of creative being and making that allow immigrants not only to become American but also to become broader global citizens in a meaningful way. Addams took this decidedly un-ideal main lived experience of immigrants' factory and slum lives not as the end of feminist or pragmatist inquiry, but as the starting point. Given their context, they could not afford the pessimism with which Emerson had claimed, "The fountains of invention and beauty in modern society are all but dried up. . . . Art is poor and low."[18]

Another original feminist contribution exists in Addams aesthetics, one taken up by current philosophers (though not explicitly considered in the arts). Ultimately, the array of arts-engagement practices Addams wove into the Hull House setting constitutes an original approach to feminist epistemology concerning the arts. Women were at the helm of art praxis at Hull House, and despite the rigid gender constraints of turn-of-the-century America, women and men there shared something of an egalitarian access to artistic creation and appreciation. The deeper feminist consideration here, though, is one raised by Shannon Sullivan in her discussion of the dual impact of continental and pragmatist philosophy on feminism. She suggests that this dual impact "challenges the philosophical construction of sharp dichotomies and opposed binaries. Such a challenge is feminist because even when dualisms do not explicitly refer to women, gender, or sexuality, they tend to be implicated in and to produce male privilege."[19] Even within a patriarchal Chicago and United States ruled by the iron law of wages and profit drive, there are seeds, here, of a feminist-pragmatist epistemological lens. Addams suggests that knowledge-seeking practices can be most fruitful when they start in a context involving a plurality of creative practices, when these practices speak back to oppressive social conditions, and when they are shared collectively.

To date, feminist epistemology has largely focused on the sciences and reframing the objectivity-versus-subjectivity debate. Physicist Evelyn Fox Keller and others critique the model of lab science that bills scientific process to be objective (male) rationality "taming" fluctuating (female) nature into submission.[20] The feminist-pragmatist alternative model Keller and others favor assumes kinship rather than competition as the starting point of inquiry, where the knower begins with "a feeling for the organism" under study. Addams developed a similar feminist epistemology, where relational arts-engagement practices helped members facilitate new knowledge and citizenship. They saw that scientific knowledge-gaining is deeply enmeshed in, and not divorced from, creative art-making practices. Starr and Addams realized that immigrants collectively teaching one another foreign arts-engagement practices led simultaneously to their retaining a home nationality, becoming American, *and* becoming cosmopolitan. I would argue that this awareness let Addams, more effectively than other feminists or pragmatists of her day, develop concrete strategies to help the most disenfranchised populations fulfill the pragmatist quest of "living life like art"—but globally, not merely as an American.

Notes

1. See, for example, Ganz and Strobel, eds., *Pots of Promise*.
2. Leonard Harris has written on this other pragmatist arts context in "The Great Debate."
3. Addams, "The Art-Work Done by Hull-House," quoted in Davis and McCree, *Eighty Years at Hull-House*, 50.
4. Emerson, "Art," in *Essays: First Series*, 318.
5. Addams, *Twenty Years*, 213.
6. Addams, "Art Works," quoted in Davis and McCree, *Eighty Years at Hull-House*, 50.
7. Emerson, "Art," 292.
8. Davis, *American Heroine*, 142.
9. hooks, *Art on My Mind*, xii.
10. See my forthcoming edited collection, *Feminist Aesthetics and Philosophy of Art: Critical Visions, Creative Engagements* (New York: Springer Press), one of the six volumes in Springer Press's new feminist philosophy series and the only volume to collect current scholarship on feminism and aesthetics. For more on this debate about art for art's sake in minority and feminist aesthetics, see particularly the introduction and my essay "Feminist Art Objecting: Spero's Alternative Modernism" in the volume.

11. For example, Addams speaks of this in terms of a community of scientists building a global fellowship of knowledge in *The Long Road of Woman's Memory*, 60.
12. Emerson, "Art," 294.
13. Musgrave, "Liberal Feminism, from Law to Art."
14. Emerson, *Works of Ralph Waldo Emerson*, 78.
15. Nussbaum, *Cultivating Humanity*, 1998.
16. Fischer, "A Pragmatist Cosmopolitan Moment," 10.
17. Addams, *Twenty Years*, 226.
18. Emerson, "Art," 299.
19. Sullivan, "Intersections Between Pragmatist and Continental Feminism."
20. Fox Keller, *A Feeling for the Organism*.

References

Addams, Jane. "The Art-Work Done by Hull-House, Chicago." *Forum* 19 (July 1895): 614–17.
———. *The Long Road of Woman's Memory*. 1916. Intro. Charlene Haddock Seigfried. Chicago: University of Illinois Press, 2002.
———. *Newer Ideals of Peace*. 1907. Ed. Marilyn Fischer and Judy Whipps. Bristol, U.K.: Thoemmes Press, 2003.
———. *Twenty Years at Hull-House, with Autobiographical Notes*. Urbana: University of Illinois Press, 1990.
Alexander, Thomas. *John Dewey's Theory of Art, Experience, and Nature: The Horizons of Feeling*. Albany: State University of New York Press, 1987.
Battersby, Christine. *Gender and Genius: Towards a Feminist Aesthetics*. Bloomington: Indiana University Press, 1990.
Brand, Peggy Zeglin, and Carolyn Korsmeyer, eds. *Beauty Matters*. Bloomington: Indiana University Press, 2000.
———. *Feminism and Tradition in Aesthetics*. University Park: Pennsylvania State University Press, 1995.
Davis, Allen F. *American Heroine: The Life and Legend of Jane Addams*. New York: Oxford University Press, 1973.
Davis, Allen F., and Mary Lynn McCree. *Eighty Years at Hull-House*. Chicago: Quadrangle Books, 1969.
Devereaux, Mary. "Beauty and Evil: The Case of Leni Riefenstahl's *Triumph of the Will*." In *Aesthetics and Ethics: Essays at the Intersection*, ed. Jerrold Levinson. Cambridge: Cambridge University Press, 1998.
Dewey, John. *Art as Experience*. New York: Perigee Books, 1934.
Deegan, Mary Jo, and Ana-Marie Wahl. *Ellen Gates Starr: On Art, Labor, and Religion*. New Brunswick, N.J.: Transaction Books, 2003.
Emerson, Ralph Waldo. *Essays: First Series*. Boston: James Munroe, 1850.
———. *Essays: First Series*. London: Macmillan, 1883.
———. *Works of Ralph Waldo Emerson*. New York: Routledge and Sons, 1883.
Fischer, Marilyn. "A Pragmatist Cosmopolitan Moment: Reconfiguring Nussbaum's Cosmopolitan Concentric Circles." Paper presented at the ninth annual meeting of

the Society for the Advancement of American Philosophy, San Antonio, Tex., March 2006.

Fox Keller, Evelyn. *A Feeling for the Organism: The Life and Work of Barbara McClintock.* New York: Henry Holt, 1983.

———. *Reflections on Gender and Science: Tenth Anniversary Paperback Edition.* Binghamton, N.Y.: Yale University Press, 1995.

Ganz, Cheryl, and Margaret Strobel, eds. *Pots of Promise: Mexicans and Pottery at Hull House, 1920–1940.* Chicago: University of Illinois Press, 2004.

Gunn, Giles. *Thinking Across the American Grain: Ideology, Intellect, and the New Pragmatism.* Chicago: University of Chicago Press, 1992.

Harris, Leonard. "The Great Debate: W. E. B. Du Bois vs. Alain Locke on the Aesthetic." *Philosophia Africana* 7, no. 1 (2004): 13–37.

Hein, Hilde, and Carolyn Korsmeyer. *Aesthetics in Feminist Perspective.* Bloomington: Indiana University Press, 1993.

hooks, bell. *Art on My Mind: Visual Politics.* New York: New Press, 1995.

Musgrave, L. Ryan. "Liberal Feminism, from Law to Art: The Impact of Feminist Jurisprudence on Feminist Aesthetics." Special issue on feminist aesthetics, *Hypatia: A Journal of Feminist Philosophy* 18, no. 4 (2003): 42–44.

Nochlin, Linda. *Women, Art, and Power and Other Essays.* New York: Westview Press, 1989.

Nussbaum, Martha. *Cultivating Humanity: A Classical Defense of Reform in Liberal Education.* Cambridge: Harvard University Press, 1998.

Seigfried, Charlene Haddock. *Pragmatism and Feminism: Reweaving the Social Fabric.* Chicago: University of Chicago Press, 1996.

Shusterman, Richard. *Performing Live: Aesthetic Alternatives for the End of Art.* Ithaca: Cornell University Press, 2000.

———. *Practicing Philosophy: Pragmatism and the Philosophical Life.* New York: Routledge, 1997.

———. *Pragmatist Aesthetics: Living Beauty, Rethinking Art.* 2nd ed. New York: Rowman and Littlefield, 2000.

Stuhr, John, ed. *Philosophy and the Reconstruction of Culture: Pragmatist Essays After Dewey.* Albany: State University of New York Press, 1993.

Sullivan, Shannon. "Intersections Between Pragmatist and Continental Feminism," *Stanford Encyclopedia of Philosophy* (2002), http://plato.stanford.edu/entries/femapproach-prag-cont/.

West, Cornel. *The American Evasion of Philosophy: A Genealogy of Pragmatism.* Madison: University of Wisconsin Press, 1989.

Whipps, Judy. "Jane Addams's Social Thought as a Model for a Pragmatist-Feminist Communitarianism." *Hypatia* 19, no. 2 (2004): 118–33.

Part Two

Sex and Society

5

Sex and the City

Jane Addams Confronts Prostitution

Victoria Bissell Brown

I have been writing in the most energetic manner upon "A New Conscience and an Ancient Evil" but seem to have reached the point just now where I very much doubt the value of the whole thing.
—Jane Addams to Sophonisba Breckinridge, July 27, 1911

For anyone seeking to measure the reach of Jane Addams's gender vision or locate her on any map of feminism, A *New Conscience and an Ancient Evil* is an illuminating—and vexing—piece of work. Walter Lippmann's 1913 pronouncement that Addams's 1912 book on prostitution was "hysterical" sounds suspiciously sexist, of course, and Allen Davis's endorsement of that view in his prefeminist, 1972 biography of Addams only heightens the impulse to discover and defend the womanly wisdom these

---

The quotation that opens this chapter is from Jane Addams to Sophonisba Breckinridge, July 27, 1911, Sophonisba Breckenridge Papers, Library of Congress. Included in Jane Addams Papers, 1860–1960, microfilm edition, reel 6, frame 377.

men overlooked.[1] But modern social historians' evidence on the fluid range of working-class women's sexual conduct—from dating to treating to selling—force us to question her construction of the sexual situation on the ground in 1912, and modern feminist debates over the ethics and legality of prostitution force us to look critically at Addams's call for the total abolition of prostitution and the institution of an ostensibly female standard of sexual purity. Examination of *A New Conscience and an Ancient Evil* through the dual lenses of social history and feminist theory reveals a text that is far less wise, and far less honest, than we have come to expect from Addams's writing.

Most of Addams's books hold up well under modern scrutiny. Today's readers still appreciate her artful arguments for an active, peaceful state dedicated to ensuring that citizens have a standard of living that will foster political democracy and harmonious civil society. In the series of new editions of Addams's works, published by the University of Illinois Press, noted scholars have written substantive, positive introductions to *Democracy and Social Ethics*, *Newer Ideals of Peace*, *The Long Road of Woman's Memory*, and *Peace and Bread in Time of War*.[2] In every case, they praise Addams's twin abilities to write stories that could evoke the dignity of the most impoverished immigrant and to craft analyses that could blend communal sacrifice and individual freedom into a compelling national vision. Only Katherine Joslin's introduction to *A New Conscience and an Ancient Evil* strikes a fundamentally negative chord, arguing that Addams's stories and analyses in this book "could not be convincing" because they perpetuated the "urban myth" of widespread female abduction, recoiled from the "unfettered, working-class female," and answered patriarchal exploitation with matriarchal protection.[3]

Although Joslin's comments, by definition, offer only an introduction to the problems in *A New Conscience*, they certainly reinforce the sense that this is Jane Addams's least persuasive book—sloppy, contradictory, sentimental, hyperbolic—and is, for that reason, a rich and complicated vehicle for discussing the connections Addams drew between sexual conduct, morality, social justice, and American women. This chapter intends to place those connections within two contexts: modern feminist theory on prostitution and modern social history on heterosexual activity in the urban working class of the early twentieth century. Attention to both the theoretical and historical context is useful for exploring the three key elements of the text: the ideological assumptions guiding Addams's approach to nonmarital sex in general and commercial sex in particular, the evidence Addams offered to support her arguments, and the solutions she advocated to combat prostitution.

The conclusion of this exploration is that *A New Conscience and an Ancient Evil* directly opposes the modern "liberal feminist" position on prostitution and presages select elements of the modern "radical feminist" position but, in the end, does not actually engage in a feminist analysis of gender power or propose profeminist reforms. Presuming chastity as women's natural state, Addams envisioned progress as female power to create a sexually pure society in which women would protect and patrol the borders of patriarchal marriage. And while the book purports to use sociological data to make its arguments, it is not a work of social science insofar as its claims are either not testable or not consistent with independent data on prostitution at the time. Because Addams's proposed solutions to prostitution derived more from her ideological commitment to sexual purity than from the realities of prostitution and urban sexual practices, the book's public policy proposals were largely irrelevant to the lives of the women Addams sincerely sought to help. Ultimately, *A New Conscience and an Ancient Evil* is not a very good book on the topic of early twentieth-century urban prostitution, but it is an excellent book for understanding the ideological importance Addams placed on female-dictated sexual purity as a means to achieving the communal goals she defined for the Progressive Era. It is also an invitation to further empirical study of the ways in which Addams's sexual attitudes may have interfered with her ability to connect with the young urban women she sought to assist and even empower.

A New Conscience and an Ancient Evil (hereafter referred to as *A New Conscience*) was published at the height of the national frenzy over the "white slave traffic," which vice crusaders defined as an international crime network whose profiteers, pimps, and petty thieves kidnapped young girls off the streets, stripped them of their virtue as well as their clothing, and held them in virtual slavery through a mix of seduction, isolation, violence, addiction, and moral degradation. American moral reformers since the early nineteenth century had decried the evils of prostitution, but in the years between 1910 and 1915, the cause took on a wholly new energy. As Mark Connelly put it, "Prostitution became a master symbol, a code word, for a wide range of anxieties engendered by the great social and cultural changes that give the progressive era its coherence as a distinct historical period."[4] A New York grand jury issued a report on the white slave traffic in 1910, the U.S. Immigration Commission followed with a report on the subject in 1911, and a book-length study by the Chicago Vice Commission that same year inspired vice investigations in twenty-seven cities and three states in the subsequent five years.[5] In the popular press, dozens of sanctimoniously sensational books appeared, excoriating (in lavish detail) the seamy underworld of commercial sex, and U.S. magazines published a veritable flood of articles on prostitution. *The Reader's Guide to Periodical Literature* lists 156 entries under the heading "prostitution" for the years between 1910 and 1914 (compared with 36 entries between 1890 and 1909 and 41 between 1915 and 1924).[6]

Amid all that loud discussion decrying the silence around sex and vice, Addams chimed in with her six chapters, in which she aligned herself with the vice crusaders of the day. Like them, she viewed prostitution as an unmitigated horror visited upon young, innocent victims caught up in a vicious commercialized net and in need of rescue by the state, acting in accord with a female code of chaste sexual conduct for all. Macmillan published the six chapters as a book in 1912, but Addams bargained to serialize them, in 1911, in the muckraking *McClure's Magazine* (rather than in the more staid, literary *American Magazine*, her publisher's preferred site).[7]

Addams, so often the mediator in other arenas, occupied a non-negotiable position on prostitution: only total abolition would suffice; not regulation, not segregation, only abolition. She stood solidly against those, including Chicago's mayor, Fred Busse, who sought to "regulate" the sex trade by segregating it into red light districts and then controlling for the age and health of prostitutes via registration and medical inspection. Complete abolition of sex slavery (for whites and nonwhites alike) was, she argued, the only moral position possible for the sons and daughters of Americans who had abolished race-based slave labor. To "ignore the multitudes of women who are held in literal bondage," declared Addams, would be a concession to the slaveholders' argument—and the brothel owners' argument—that the exploitation of one group by another is part of "human nature itself," that the "right of property" or the "supposed needs" of the male libido trumped the "rights of human life."[8]

Addams would have none of it. In the first chapter of *A New Conscience*, she aligned herself—and Abraham Lincoln—with the "extremists" who had called for abolition of race slavery. Adopting an uncharacteristically militaristic stance, America's first female recipient of the Nobel Peace Prize announced that "few righteous causes have escaped baptism with blood" and paraphrased Lincoln's second inaugural to claim: "If blood were exacted drop by drop in measure to the tears of anguished mothers and enslaved girls, the nation would still be obliged to go into the struggle" against prostitution.[9]

This was not just high-flying rhetoric for Addams, this was high-stakes reform advocacy. Her progressive ideology grounded social justice in sexual purity. The quasi-official tolerance of commercialized sex, she said, subverted all progressive efforts to "overcome the lusts of the flesh," which, for Addams, were regressively selfish and individualistic (47). The "obligations of race progress" required that human beings become more communal, more selfless, and more spiritual if they were going to build a world in which mutual care triumphed over the cash nexus (8). To achieve that goal, said Addams, Americans needed to face "the havoc wrought by the sexual instinct uncontrolled" and then realize that "when directed and spiritualized," when "transmuted to the highest ends," this "primal instinct" could do more than simply reproduce the race; it could become "an inspiration to the loftiest devotions and sacrifices" and, thus, "a fundamental factor in social progress" (46–47).

A critique of unregulated capitalism lay at the heart of *A New Conscience*. Addams believed that as long as the rules of laissez-faire capitalism operated on city streets, promoting a "sexual commerce" in which "the chastity of women is bought and sold," it would be impossible to raise up a new generation of Americans who could channel their sexual energies into the caring, communal work of progressive democracy (6). But while the book was unrelenting in its disdain for those who derived profit from trafficking in young, innocent females and for the crass materialism that fostered such trafficking, Addams did not align with those, such as Emma Goldman, who presaged today's socialist feminist stance on prostitution. That is to say, Addams did not argue that prostitution is simply one aspect of capitalism's exploitation of (female) workers, and it is this general economic exploitation that must be addressed. Although she identified materialism as the cause of the problem, Addams offered moral, not economic, reform as the solution. Abolition of prostitution was not, for her, an ultimate by-product of a general reordering of social and economic values; instead, it was a first step toward that moral reordering. As presented in *A New Conscience*, abolition of prostitution was to be a cause, not a result, of the progressive commitment to the spiritualized common good over sexualized individual selfishness.

While her book's title described prostitution as an "ancient evil," Addams's argument focused on the breakdown of "old types of social control" in the big, modern, anonymous city (95). Commercialized vice had increased in urban, industrial America for four reasons—two of them circumstantial, two of them causal. First, the circumstances of urban life meant that men could escape the "castigation and retribution" of village women's gossip, which had, for centuries, "performed a valuable function" in confining male sexuality "between the carefully clipped hedges . . . of conventional domesticity" (90, 94).[10] Second, the circumstances of urban life meant that young women were "almost as free from social control as . . . the traditional young man who comes up from the country to take care of himself in a great city" (14–15). But men's and women's modern freedom was not, by itself, the cause of commercialized vice, said Addams; prostitution was not the inevitable result of freedom but, rather, a social construct of the profiteering motive. Unregulated capitalism produced selfish, materialistic communities that, in turn, failed to foster higher ideals in business and social life. The result was a vicious cycle of low wages, delayed marriage and attendant male sexual frustration, female workers' exhaustion and emotional vulnerability to seduction, and the false—but highly profitable—notion that real masculinity was expressed through vice and that "personal development necessitates a rebellion against existing social laws" (48, 93).

Addams had read her G. Stanley Hall and had sensitively translated his findings from *Adolescence* into her own appreciation of youthful sexual urges when she wrote *Spirit of Youth and the City Streets*.[11] But while Addams would acknowledge the "molten forces" stirring in young people, especially in young men, she was not willing to indulge them. She wanted to divert them into productive social activity, such as labor organizing, not abandon them to the individual pursuit of crass pleasures that only fattened the coffers of vice profiteers (36).[12]

When Addams spoke of "a new conscience," she meant her progressive campaign for "a new form of social control" that challenged "the specious and illegitimate theories of freedom" that allowed for corrupting forms of entertainment on the city streets and challenged the civilizing authority of the family (93). When it came to sex, thought Addams, progressives simply had to convince their fellow citizens that "the old types of social control are powerless" against the salacious temptations of urban commerce, which enjoyed the perverse protection of "high-sounding" claims to "the great principle of liberty" (3, 93). The progressives' demand for social control of sexual conduct and urban recreation was, for Addams, consistent with demands for control of labor conditions and represented an optimistic, forward-looking insistence that the individual's sexual urge was not an uncontrollable force for private, profiteering evil but an impulse amenable to training for service to the common good. The community, acting through the government, had to assert "that it is in the interest of social progress itself that hard-won liberties must be restrained by the demonstrable needs of society" (94–95). Progress toward a more caring, humane, communal society rested on socializing sexual energy into selfless, spiritualized service to society and the family.

With *A New Conscience and an Ancient Evil,* Jane Addams issued a clear warning that progressives would not sit idly by while sex traffickers profited from "the loss of moral sensibility, the destruction of romantic love, the perversion of the longing for wife and child. The very stability and refinement of the social order," claimed Addams, depended upon "the preservation of these basic emotions" embedded in the traditional family structure (92). For Addams, public insistence on domesticated sexuality constituted a bold challenge to rapacious male materialism, and women's championing of that cause served as the vanguard of a progressive ethic of mutual care. She characterized her foe in this struggle as profit-crazed sex traffickers; she characterized Chicago's young working women as her friends—and as her maternal responsibility.

Read in the light of modern feminist debate over prostitution, *A New Conscience* stands in clear opposition to the liberal feminist view that prostitution should be legalized because legalization would allow for social regulation of coercive, abusive, and exploitive aspects of commercial sex while according adult women the right to choose their livelihood and to use their bodies as they wished. Liberal feminists argue, counter to Addams, that there is nothing inherently corrupting about selling sexual services; the corruption inheres in the context, and only legalized regulation, along with a general improvement in women's independent economic status, could address the context.[13]

Superficially, there is far more overlap between Addams's position and that of the modern "radical" feminist. They both oppose legalization and agree that legal prostitution is incompatible with freedom's insistence on consent, since it is inconceivable that any woman would freely consent to work as a prostitute.[14] But very different assumptions and motives brought Addams, in the early twentieth century, and radical feminists, in the late twentieth century, to this shared opposition to legalization and shared assumption of coercion in all cases of commercial sex. Modern radical feminists would not embrace Addams's assumption of coercion in all cases of nonmarital sex; they certainly could not sign on to her view that women would benefit if all sexual encounters were confined to traditional, patriarchal marriage. Modern radical feminists seek to liberate sexuality from the bonds of patriarchy, not set up women as moral guardians who would use political power not only to abolish the sex trade but to protect the male-headed family as well.[15]

More important for the purposes of this chapter is the fact that Addams would not be able to embrace the radical feminists' view that prostitutes represent all women's subordinate, exploited status in patriarchal society and that legalizing prostitution simply ratifies all women's oppression. Her book expressed an enormous amount of anger at men—those who organized, profited from, patronized, or simply tolerated prostitution—and that anger resonates with the radical feminist position. But Addams did not align with the key feature of the radical feminist analysis; she did not define the "social evil" as a function of categorical male domination and categorical female oppression. Unlike modern theorists such as Carole Pateman, Addams did not construct prostitution as a story of men using sex as a tool for asserting their power over all women. Hers was a story of profiteers exploiting men's corruptible sexual energy and enslaving vulnerable women to achieve that monetary goal. Women in Addams's story were collateral damage; their abuse was an effect of prostitution, not its motive. By contrast, for radical feminists, oppression of women is the primary motive in the sex trade.[16] Because Addams did not define prostitution as a function of all men's oppression of all women, she did not see everywoman in the "fallen" woman; indeed, her emphasis on the "ruin" of the female tainted by sexual corruption implied that loss of purity meant loss of identity as a female; having been deprived of her claim to purity, the "fallen" woman had lost her claim to womanhood—and the claim to moral and legal authority that came with it.[17] For radical feminists like Pateman, the sale of sex constitutes a sale of the self; for Addams, purity (not sexuality) constituted the female self that was stolen from women in the white slave trade.[18]

Modern feminist debate over prostitution often pivots on the question of "who" the prostitute is, what her circumstances are. Radicals tend to emphasize the prostitute as a victim of coercion in order to deny the possibility that choice is ever operating for women; liberals tend to emphasize the diversity of prostitute profiles in order to emphasize the possibility of choice.¹⁹ Turning to the evidence that Addams presented in *A New Conscience*, it is clear that her ideological commitment to the image of female victimhood in prostitution was so important to her that she stuck to that story even when her data suggested alternate interpretations of the situation.

Addams told her publisher that she wished to avoid "over-statement" in presenting the plight of the sexually exploited urban female, and, in *A New Conscience*, she referred dismissively to the era's "pamphleteering" on the subject.²⁰ To persuade her audience that she was a sober, reliable reporter on urban vice, Addams claimed personal knowledge drawn from "long residence in a crowded city quarter" and offered seemingly sociological accounts of the "unspeakable indignities" suffered by "unwilling," "virtuous," "lonely" girls, the details of which were just personal enough to be persuasive and just vague enough to preserve decorum (6, 11, 40, 27, 80).²¹

A book reviewer for the *Spectator*, a London magazine, admitted that "there are stories in [*A New Conscience*] extraordinary enough to make any reader rub his eyes," but he did "not doubt" that the stories were true. "Miss Addams is too well known in Chicago for her to trifle with her reputation for veracity," reasoned the British reviewer; "the ground of all her efforts would be cut from under her feet" were she to be found guilty of "foolish exaggeration." The *Literary Digest*, echoing a theme in several U.S. reviews, applauded the book's "frank and fearless statement of authentic facts," and in more than sixty surviving letters about the book, readers repeatedly thanked Addams for the "full frank discussion of all the essential facts," for "the scientific spirit in which you study social problems," and for presenting "the facts so straightforward and logically."²² Few readers at the time, or since, noted that Addams's factual reporting in *A New Conscience* lacked coherence or that her key assumption, the existence of a large, well-organized slave trade preying upon unwilling, sexually innocent victims, was not supported by the stories she narrated in the book.

So impressed were readers at the time with her literary ability to "look the hideous evil full in the face" but avoid sensational or salacious language that they believed that she had disciplined her presentation according to her stated principle that "nothing is gained by making the situation better or worse than it is, nor in any wise different from what it is."²³ So impressed have modern historians been that Addams did not demonize women as perverse or criminal for their role in the sex trade and never stereotyped immigrant nationalities as innately prone to sexual corruption that they, like Addams's fans, have missed opportunities to explore where—and why—*A New Conscience* offered up a flawed description of sexual conduct on the streets of her home city.[24]

There is, to begin with, the book's confused demographic profile of the prostitute. Addams, always intent on creating reader sympathy for the sex worker, always intent on casting that sex worker as a helpless victim, chose to exaggerate the numbers of immigrant women involved in prostitution. The report of the Chicago Vice Commission, which was published in the spring before Addams's summer of work on her book and was among her sources, made no mention of immigrant girls dominating the trade. Yet Addams put stories of immigrant women front and center in her book. The U.S. Immigration Commission, another of her sources, found that three-quarters of the women arrested for prostitution were American born. But at least three-quarters of the stories that Addams told in *A New Conscience* involved foreign-born females who appeared to be as virginal in their knowledge of the United States as they were of sex.[25] Readers were informed, in the fifth of the book's six chapters, that "more than half of the girls who have been recruited into a disreputable life in Chicago have come from the farms and smaller towns" surrounding the city. But the emphasis throughout the text was on the immigrant girl, who was, said Addams, "first in value to the white slave commerce" because she was "literally friendless and unable to speak the language" and so "discouraged she makes no effort to escape" (66, 9). To be sure, Addams crafted her immigrant profiles to elicit readers' sympathy, not their disdain, for foreign-born females, but the emotional emphasis on foreign girls' peasant innocence and vulnerability diverted readers' attention from the practical, economic reasons that even English-speaking, American-born daughters with nearby family wound up in the sex trade.

As part of her effort to show the cruelly exploitive nature of the commercial sex trade, Addams also emphasized the youth of those recruited into prostitution by conflating stories of child incest, child labor, and children's freedom on the streets with stories of female indenture in brothels. To demonstrate the "extreme youth of the victims of the white slave trade," she estimated that "the majority of the girls utilized by the trade" were under twenty years of age and that "most of them were procured when younger." Indeed, said Addams, who had access to data indicating that prostitutes were typically in their twenties, "the average age of the recruits to prostitution is between sixteen and eighteen years" (64,

57, 25). In one of the very few letters questioning her assertions in *A New Conscience*, John D. Rockefeller Jr., chair of New York's 1910 grand jury investigation into prostitution and someone familiar with prostitution data, asked Addams "on what facts" she based "this most astounding statement" about the youth of prostitutes. Her reply has not survived, but Addams might have explained that her book drew from the case files of the Juvenile Protective Association, with which Hull House and the Chicago juvenile court were both closely affiliated, and those files included only females below the age of nineteen.[26]

As with the nativity profile, this emphasis on prostitutes' youth served Addams's political desire to ignite readers' sympathy for females in the sex trade. She remarked in her first chapter that "one of the most obvious resources at our command," as reformers, "is the overwhelming pity and sense of protection which the recent revelations in the white slave traffic have aroused for the thousands of young girls, many of them still children, who are yearly sacrificed to the 'sins of the people.'" Later, while claiming that "many recent investigations have revealed the extreme youth of the victims of the white slave traffic," Addams noted that appeals for the "protection of minors . . . should make legislation on their behalf all the more feasible" (7, 62).[27]

The emphasis on youth accompanied Addams's repetition of the vice crusaders' frequent claim that the sex traffic needed constant infusions of new blood because prostitutes died within five years of enslavement. Again, evidence available at the time (and since reported by social historians) refuted that claim of early death by indicating that women floated in and out of the sex trade, typically choosing to leave the trade before five years to take up other lines of work or to get married.[28] While politically astute and certainly sensitive to the tragic lives of impoverished children, this dramatic emphasis on prostitutes' youth, confinement, and early death did more to advance Addams's position on the need for a dominant female ethic of sexual purity than it did to describe the actual situation on the streets.

Dorothy Ross argued elegantly, in her 1998 article, "Gendered Social Knowledge," that Jane Addams was not a trained social scientist and was not loyal to empiricism as a first principle. Rockford Female Seminary in the 1870s gave Addams a literary education and left her longing for an education in the scientific method, but her brief stint in medical school and her personal contacts with the sexism of her era's scientists persuaded her that science, after all, was not her bent.[29] Ross's analysis showed that

Addams's great talents as a storyteller and social theorist served her reform causes wonderfully well but did not make her a reliable reporter of sociological data. She was always most comfortable with and committed to "a view of knowledge as ideal truths," and she trusted her ideals of communal connection and female intuition to guide her application of information to a useful social purpose.[30] It was "sympathetic knowledge," Addams explained in *A New Conscience*, and not "only" the "information of the statistician," that would provide "a spur to action," and action, for Addams, was the goal of any study; applicability, not scientific accuracy, was her test of the value of information (7). Knowledge was not open ended, leading to any possible conclusion; information was a tool for achieving universal, unchanging social ideals. There is no particular scandal in finding that Jane Addams misinformed her readers about prostitution; this finding simply aids our understanding of Addams's particular variant of pragmatism and reminds us that Addams is best categorized among her Victorian generation's progressive social philosophers, not among its pioneering social scientists.[31]

So convincing were Addams's stories in *A New Conscience* that no one noticed, or cared about, the incompatible claims she made regarding the typical prostitute. Although the immigrant girl was "first in value to the white slave commerce," the American-born department store clerk and the downtown waitress were also in constant "danger," and "no young woman was more exposed to temptation" than the native-born office worker (30, 32, 97). While the innocent obedience of the foreign peasant made her an easy mark, according to Addams, the American girl's belief that "there is no ordinary limit to her ambition" made her equally vulnerable to "the allurements which are designedly placed around many young girls in order to draw them into an evil life" (31, 1). On one page, Addams pointed to the fact that 16 percent of Chicago's working women lived on their own, apart from family, and these women "without home ties," suffering from "loneliness" and "isolation" in their individual rooming-house flats, were more vulnerable to the slave traders than women living with their families. But two pages later, she argued that "all statistics of prostitution give the largest number of recruits for this life as coming from domestic service and the second largest number from girls who live at home with no definite occupation whatever" (41, 43). Addams insisted that factory girls were "much less open to direct inducement" from slave traders because they were under the "protection of working among plain people," but she offered numerous examples of factory girls whose families, presumably plain people, were responsible for their daughters' entrapment in the sex business (33, 37 40–43).[32]

The cumulative message of so many conflicting claims was that every young woman in Chicago—immigrant and native born, white collar and blue, living alone or with her family—was fair game for the "procurers and evil-minded" men who could be found "hovering" "wherever many girls are gathered together more or less unprotected and embroiled in the struggle for a livelihood" (30).[33]

It is as easy as it is incorrect to assume that Addams's whole purpose in *A New Conscience* was to put women's "struggle for a livelihood" at the heart of her campaign to abolish sexual slavery. Knowing how sympathetic Addams was to women's wage struggle, knowing how determined she was to draw the connections between unregulated capitalism and commercial vice, and knowing how unsentimental and commonsensical she could be in the face of social problems, it is naturally tempting to presume that Addams argued that women became prostitutes for rational economic reasons and that better wages for women was the obvious public policy needed to attack the sex trade. But as already noted, Addams did not align with Emma Goldman, who made that economic argument the year before Addams serialized her book, nor did Addams presage the modern liberal and socialist feminist interest in bettering all women's economic standing so that circumstances would not force women into prostitution.[34] Jane Addams's argument about the connection between poverty and prostitution was not quite so simple or straightforward.

If she had simply wanted to argue that prostitution was the direct result of unregulated capitalism and female poverty, Addams need not have organized her whole book around the existence of the white slave traffic. Lurid images of abduction by an organized syndicate were not necessary if her point was to show that exploitive employers forced destitute female workers to walk the streets for survival. Thus, it is noteworthy that Addams chose to frame her Chicago stories in the context of a "widespread commercial enterprise" designed to "procure a sufficient number of girls for the white slave market" even though that framing ignored the recent reports of the New York grand jury, the Chicago Vice Commission, and the Vice Commission of Minneapolis, all of which found no evidence of a well-organized, nationwide (much less worldwide) network of white slave traders.[35]

It was not her critical stance toward capitalism that dictated this emphasis on the white slave traffic; again, the simple argument that poverty forced women to choose prostitution would have sufficed. But that straight line of argument from impoverishment to prostitution was not one that Addams could pursue because she would not and could not concede that any female would ever "go out deliberately to find illicit methods of earning money" (36).

It is essential to pause over this point because it illuminates Addams's idealized and essentialized image of women as naturally chaste. This ideal did not simply influence Addams's discussion of prostitution; her discussion of prostitution was shaped by her conviction that women's devotion to their own chastity was the all-important signifier of women's moral fitness for leadership in moral and social uplift. Addams may not have subscribed to the radical feminist view that prostitutes represent all women's oppression, but she did believe that the solution to prostitution was the social and political empowerment of all women's selfless, communalistic commitment to chastity and marital sex. To the degree that her position on prostitution was feminist in seeking to alter women's status, that feminist agenda was about raising women's moral authority to protect other women from sex traders, not to free young working women from repressive sexual codes or exploitive capitalist employers.

Key to Addams's sympathetic analysis of the plight of the prostitute was the argument that girls' youthful longings and material needs operated as emotional vulnerabilities that a designing slave trader could exploit. Female longings and material needs were not presented in *A New Conscience* as conscious, calculated motives that might cause a young woman to make her own independent, albeit risky, decisions.

Addams reasoned that most working women were in economic trouble, but most did not become prostitutes. Therefore, impoverished women were not the agents driving prostitution. Men who preyed on impoverished women were the agents (see, for example, 11, 15, 17, 19–20, 26, 30, 65, 69). Addams drew "some small degree of comfort" from the fact that most women were not choosing, of their own free will, to ease their economic woes by turning tricks. "The chastity of women," declared Addams, referring to the female base on which she believed progressive social order would be built, was "holding its own" despite bad men's corrupting efforts. It was, in fact, women's virtuous resistance that necessitated the slave trade; vice criminals were forced to construct "large business enterprises . . . throughout the world in order to secure a sufficient number of victims for this modern market." Addams took heart from the notion that "white slave traders find it necessary" to "forcibly . . . detain their victims" because that meant both "chastity and self-restraint" were "firmly established in the modern city" and could be used in the battle against the lords of vice. At the same time, she chastised a complacent American public for depending "upon the inner restraint and training of this girlish multitude to protect it from disaster" (26, 28, 86).[36]

The image of the prostitute as helpless victim was standard in the white slave traffic literature of the day, and Addams's contribution to that image was not remarkable. She pointed to "piteous tales of girls who were thus easily deceived," spoke with great sympathy for the girl who was "least able to defend herself" and an "easy prey for the procurers," and she made her reader heave a sigh of relief for the "unsuspecting girl" who, with luck, "narrowly escaped a well-organized plot" to bind her to brothel life (14, 19). The innocent young Polish woman, "desperate with hunger," stopped men on the street "as she had seen other girls do" to ask for food, and only later realized "the price she was expected to pay." To elicit her reader's sympathy for this woman, Addams wrote, "Even in her shocked revolt she could not understand, of course, that she herself epitomized that hideous choice between starvation and vice which is perhaps the crowning disgrace of all civilization" (23).[37] The key to this sympathetic portrait was the young woman's shock and her inability to understand the economic bargain she was being forced to make.

Addams wound up contradicting this image of chaste, naive girlhood because she had competing aims and uncooperative data. She not only wanted to present girls as innocent, unwilling victims in the sex trade that materialism produced, she also wanted to show that the urban culture surrounding those girls was morally corrupted by materialism. To depict innocence, as we have seen, Addams emphasized the wide-eyed naïveté of the young girl lured into the trap of sin by men's trickery and then powerless to escape. To depict citywide moral decay, however, she described savvy young women who acquired their own tricks for economic survival on the wicked streets of Chicago.

In the thirty vignettes she included in A New Conscience, Addams recounted only three or four actual stories of the forcible abduction of an unknowing, unwilling young woman. The narrative thrust of the book emphasized immigrant female victimhood, but most of the actual vignettes were about worldly girls on Chicago's bawdy streets, girls who ran errands for the pretty whore down the hallway, spent darkened hours in cheap movies, frequented dance halls and their adjoining saloons, learned about all manner of illicit moneymaking from friends and neighbors, and found their own ways to survive the neglect of working mothers and the abuse of drunken fathers (see, for example, 23, 27–29, 31–32, 51–58, 61–63). Drawing on the lives surrounding her on Halsted Street, Addams told stories about working girls desperate for money, or hungry for a bit of fun, or pining for something pretty, or too physically or psychologically exhausted from unremitting work to resist a moneymaking proposition. These women were not captured or drugged or beaten or locked up; they were women who found a way to buy nice clothes by "filling regular appointments in a disreputable saloon," or kept their unemployment a secret from needy parents by coming home with earnings from noon-hour trysts in downtown hotels or "made the best bargain possible" with a male co-worker to get the travel money to visit a dying mother or rebelled against overly strict parents by escaping to the dance hall—and the intoxicating dangers therein (39, 29, 41; see also 14, 33, 37–38, 40–41, 49–50, 69, 73–75).

This was the world Jane Addams actually lived in, and it is the world Kathy Peiss, Joanne Meyerowitz, Nan Enstad, Elizabeth Clement, and other historians of the urban working class have been describing for the past two decades. It was a world in which, for better or worse, safely or not, young urban women were making their own way by making their own calculations about "treating," "charity," casual prostitution, and entering the life full time.[38] Indeed, on the second-to-last page of a book devoted to the organized white slave trade, Addams admitted that the whole trend was toward "clandestine prostitution," the casual, individual deals that females cut with men—in saloons, dance halls, and back alleys—to make extra money (98).

The difference between Addams and the social historians who have documented the subculture of these young urban working women is that Addams, for ideological reasons, chose to couch her stories of a vibrant streetwise culture within a desolate framework of isolated victimhood and international sex trafficking. Girls who cared more about clothes and fun than strict propriety and girls who turned tricks out of economic need were, on the pages of *A New Conscience*, just as powerless as the unwilling white slave. Social historians of these "women adrift" do not glamorize their struggles any more than Addams did, but they do regard the women as active players, not passive slaves, in the pursuit of "cheap amusements."[39] By conflating streetwise sexual play with prostitution and defining all female participants in sexualized recreation as tragically "ruined," Addams perpetuated the stigma associated with female sexual initiative and ignored the ways in which young women's small sexual rebellions were challenging the stigmatization of sexual women.[40]

In her autobiography, *Twenty Years at Hull-House*, Addams had famously cast her role as that of an interpreter, explaining the common sense of her neighbors' constrained choices to genteel citizens who had a limited understanding of life in Chicago's Nineteenth Ward. She played that role impressively well when it came to explaining her neighbors' labor grievances or ethnic customs or political conduct.[41] In the case of sexual behavior, however, Addams could describe the city's newly sexualized cultural terrain, but she could not interpret the logic or the benefit of that popular culture; she could not see it as anything but lonely, selfish, and dangerous. Addams wanted young women to have fun in the city, and she knew young people needed heterosexual recreation; integral to her reform project was recognition that "the great business of youth is securing a mate" (76). But the loose sexual conduct she observed around Chicago did not square with her notions of family creation or healthy communities. At age fifty-two, she looked upon the "purposely slow" dancing in the commercial halls and longed for the "jollity and bracing exercise of the peasant dance" and the "careful decorum of the formal dance" (49). In every other regard, Jane Addams was a forward-looking agent of urban social change, but on the subject of sexual expression, she longed for village mores. Her commitment to a sexuality of spiritual and marital sacrifice meant that she could never be as cosmopolitan about sex as she was about ethnicity; sexual pluralism was simply not in her gender vision.

This is not to say that Addams did not try to apply her talent for "affectionate interpretation" to her tale of female corruption.[42] "Because she is young and feminine," wrote Addams, a girl's "mind secretly dwells upon a future love, upon a home"; thus, a prostitute's unwavering love for her pimp was touching evidence of her unspoiled feminine nature (31, 20). So, too, there was logic in young women's longing for the "good times" and for the material luxuries that were on tempting display all around the city. Such longings were "not astonishing," Addams explained. Given the selfish materialism fostered in an unregulated, capitalist economy, no one should be shocked that "a swelling tide of self-pity" might "finally overcome" a young woman's "instincts for decency and righteousness." The whole society was drenched "with vicious practices designed to accelerate the demoralization of unwilling victims," explained Addams; it was hardly surprising that girls were lured into sin through the glitter of a pretty necklace or a night on the town (36, 11).

Addams even admitted at one point (but only at one point) in her text that "very often all that is necessary to effectively help the girl who is on the edge of wrongdoing is to lend her money for her board until she finds work. . . . Upon such simple economic needs does the tried virtue of a good girl sometimes depend." Those seeking evidence that Addams understood the prostitute's economic motives can find it in her generosity toward the girl who fought the good fight but finally "sold out for a pair of shoes" and her understanding of those who "yield to temptation only when hard pressed by debt incurred during illness or non-employment" (36). The argument posed here does not require denial that Addams made such comments about economic need. The point is that such comments were always accompanied by the reminder that, during hard times, "the immigrant girl is subjected to great dangers," liable to derangement and insanity and, thus, "easy to exploit." Poverty was always linked to an emotional, moral deficit in the female, not simply to cold, hard calculation (36, 29, 37, 32).

Like radical feminists who regard willing prostitutes as victims of false consciousness, Addams dismissed contemporary prostitutes' blunt testimonies that they knowingly entered the sex trade simply to make more money. "Although economic pressure as a reason for entering an illicit life has . . . been brought out in court," admitted Addams, "it is no doubt often exaggerated; a girl always prefers to think that economic pressure is the reason for her downfall, even when the immediate causes have been her love of pleasure, her desire for finery, or the influence of evil companions. It is easy for her, as for all of us, to be deceived as to real motives" (28). There it was: economic pressure was not the "real" motive; a breakdown of moral righteousness was. Addams understood how the city could turn a girl's head and make her vulnerable to a procurer's seduction, but she was not going to dismiss the transgression with a thoroughly economic, materialist explanation. Materialism had created the trouble in the first place. So while Addams was far too progressive to hold the individual girl personally responsible for her immorality, she was going to define the problem as a moral problem requiring moral solutions.

For anyone attempting to position Addams on the map of gender politics, the impressive finding here is not simply that she knew, and understood, that women were making their own individual, calculated bargains with a random population of male customers. The finding to note is that she knew this and still insisted on constructing a book about prostitution that depicted these women as naive victims captured by an organized white slave trade. In a stunningly candid discussion of the modern feminist debate over prostitution, Margaret Baldwin, a self-defined radical feminist on the subject, notes how all feminists present their own renditions of those "other" women's lives in ways that will merge with feminists' larger accounts of class and gender oppression. "In all of this," argues Baldwin, "we cast ourselves in the role of the john: It could be any way. This is how I want it."[43] Like johns, says Baldwin, feminists make prostitutes serve their ideological purposes. That is a harsh analysis of modern feminists' motives in their ideologically selective use of evidence on prostitution; it is certainly a harsh analysis of Addams. But it serves to underscore the point that *A New Conscience* was not a sociological study of prostitution or gender power; it was an ideological statement about the importance of sexual purity in a progressive society.

Walter Lippmann did not call Addams's book "hysterical" because she defined prostitution as a moral problem or because she wanted to channel youth's sexual energies away from carnal expression and into productive social activities. On the contrary, Lippmann applauded Addams's effort to make "ideals the goal of natural desire," agreed that "every lust is capable of some civilized expression," and thought it quite possible to "harness desire to many interests." He praised Addams for writing "brilliantly about sex and its 'sublimation'" in her "wisely sweet book" *Youth and the Spirit of the City Streets*, where, he noted, her "keen insight" and "fine sympathy" derived from an honest "interpretation of human character."[44]

It was Addams's demand for the abolition, instead of the regulation, of prostitution that rendered *A New Conscience* "hysterical" in Lippmann's judgment.[45] Arguing that "the merely negative law" was the "emptiest of all imposition from on top" and that politics is "irrelevant if the only method it knows is to ostracize the desires it cannot manage," Lippmann expressed honest surprise that Addams, a famous opponent of repression and militarism, would so confidently "put her faith in the policeman and the district attorney" as the agents of progressive uplift.[46] On the same page where Addams called for "a little less ruthlessness" in regard to those "wretched women" engaged in "street solicitation," she also applauded the "vigorous efforts" of a "former" Chicago police chief who "successfully cleared the streets" of all streetwalkers, claiming that his sweep "demonstrates that legal suppression is possible" (23). For Lippmann, such "distorted enthusiasm" and "moral fervor" suggested that, in the singular case of prostitution, Addams showed "very considerable willingness to gloss over human need in the interests of unanalyzed reform. To put it bluntly," concluded Lippmann, "Miss Addams let her impatience get the better of her wisdom."[47] Today's liberal feminists would agree with him. They argue that criminalization does nothing to help the woman trapped in prostitution and is irrelevant to those women who freely choose that work. All that criminalization accomplishes, according to liberal feminists, is the further degradation and marginalization of the very population of women whom feminists claim they wish to help. Criminalization may be a theoretically consistent response to the view that prostitution always entails enslavement, but it is not, say the liberals, a practical response to women's actual circumstances.[48]

Jane Addams was no stranger to strong state action when she turned her sights on prostitution in 1911. She had long advocated for laws dictating factory conditions, housing conditions, health conditions, child labor, women's labor, and compulsory education. She believed deeply in the power and duty of the state to create a social environment in which citizens could flourish. From that standpoint, her demand for strong laws and vigorous police action to abolish prostitution is not so very surprising. It is, however, surprising to hear America's then preeminent mediator proudly connect her "extremist" stance on the sex trade to her forefathers' radical abolitionism on race slavery. Neither Addams's father, John Addams, nor his colleague in the Republican Party Abraham Lincoln, had ever been radical abolitionists, and in an article published the same year as *A New Conscience*, Addams legitimized her own bent for moderation by admiring Lincoln's talent for "the best possible" solution.[49]

In the Progressive Era's debate over economic reform, Addams explicitly rejected socialism because she regarded it as unrealistic about human behavior; the economic legislation she endorsed was intended to regulate, not obliterate, capitalism. And in her all dealings with workers and employers, she counseled compromise and negotiation rather than street battles or court injunctions. Even in the case of alcohol, which she always placed at the nexus of sin and profit, she called on the state to "control and regulate" its sale in *A New Conscience*; she did not call for prohibition (86).[50] When it came to sex work, however, she embraced the strong-arm tactics of the vice crusader, aligning herself with zealous prosecutors like Clifford G. Roe and Edwin W. Sims, and applauding raids and arrests as part of a "determined, businesslike fight against the procuring of girls" (11–12).

One of the peculiarities in Addams's alignment with those who advocated a vigorous police role in combating vice is that she simultaneously blamed police corruption for allowing vice to thrive. *A New Conscience* was only one of many venues in which she denounced the close, profitable ties between elected officials, saloonkeepers, brothel owners, and the police. Writing in 1911, when Chicago still had a quasi-tolerated but wholly illegal red light district, Addams claimed that the city's system of payoff schemes and protection rackets was thriving "because the men engaged in an unlawful business expect to pay money for its protection." In that way, she said, "the corruption of the police department is firmly established" (18).

Addams never explained why or how the motives for this corruption would disappear under a strict abolition, and nowhere in *A New Conscience* did she consider the possibility that legalization of prostitution would eliminate the twin evils of police corruption and pimp protection that put women under male control in the sex business.[51] None of this is surprising in light of Addams's spiritualized ambitions for sexual expression, but it is surprising in light of her customary distrust of militaristic repression as a means of enacting social change.[52] As it turned out, the abolitionists' call was answered in Chicago in the fall of 1912, just months after *A New Conscience* appeared, and the brothels and streetwalkers were driven out of downtown. The result was a dramatic increase, among white women, in "clandestine prostitution," facilitated by pimps and telephones, along with the heightened concentration of brothels in the city's southside black neighborhoods, where police protection rackets thrived.[53] Addams had not sought that outcome; *A New Conscience* had included brief, but sensitive, remarks about the unique vulnerabilities of black women (55, 77). But the practical effect of the "abolition" methods that Addams endorsed was to increase the power of pimps and the burdens on black neighborhoods.[54]

In *A New Conscience*, Addams did not, of course, confine herself to police remedies for prostitution. She proposed a whole series of long-term communal reforms aimed at a spiritual transformation that would divert, if not annihilate, the lustful impulses that prostitution exploited. Although she claimed, at the start of the book, that "moral judgments concerning the entire group of questions centering about illicit affections between men and were are . . . not considered here," she treated all the city's opportunities for "illicit affections" as the staging area for prostitution. "Mere friendly propinquity may constitute a danger," warned Addams; "virtually every girl" who came to "grief" via the sex trade began by "accepting invitations to dinners and places of amusement" where "improprieties were deliberately fostered" for the sake of profit (32, 98, 49).

The focus of Addams's interest was on social reforms that could spiritualize lust by socializing young people to enjoy intellectual, athletic, and artistic outlets for their urges. Children's imaginations could be "kept free from sensuality," thought Addams, if the community would enact "protective legislation" (49, 57). Throughout the pages of her book on prostitution, Addams called on her community to take responsibility for providing the sort of public education, public rehabilitation, and public recreation that would divert young people's attention away from the cheap glitter of the streets.

A New Conscience repeatedly recommended expanded provision of the public playgrounds, public gymnasiums, parks with supervised dance halls, and other types of "innocent recreation" that Hull House had pioneered in establishing back in the 1890s. It called, as well, for classes in "sex hygiene" in the public schools, a controversial proposal that Addams softened by focusing entirely on boys' need to be trained away from a "purely selfish point of view." Naturally, given the close ties between Hull House, the Juvenile Protective Association, and the Chicago Juvenile Court, Addams also fully endorsed court efforts to provide wayward children with psychiatric services (49, 47, 55–57).[55]

In her approach to the rehabilitation of prostitutes, Addams made the basic assumption that once a female was lured into vice, the temptations of the flesh were "seared" into her "tender" mind "with red-hot irons" and incorporated "into every fibre of her being," rendering her "helpless" to break the commercial vice habit (57, 11). For that reason, Addams did not question the juvenile court practice of giving delinquent boys probation but putting delinquent girls—almost all of whom were arrested for "a loss of chastity"—into public or charitable "rescue homes" where their rehabilitation could be conducted in isolation from corrupting forces (50).[56] So intent was Addams on ensuring that young females not fall prey to the seductions of vice that she recommended that "the state" undertake a system of "oversight" of girls after they left school, monitoring their safety for six and a half years, "the average length of time that a working girl is employed" before marriage. Such a system, thought Addams, would allow the community to protect its investment in girls' education from the "utter loss" attendant upon contact with vice (60).[57]

Addams did not include the minimum wage in her list of social reforms needed to combat prostitution. Again, this is not surprising given her insistence on the moral, rather than material, causes of female vulnerability to the white slave traffic, but it is worth noting in the context of her gender politics. She certainly commented on female workers' low wages and on the myriad ways in which illness, industrial accidents, and family crises could put a working woman "up against it," but in contrast to her firm demands for immediate laws separating the saloon from the dance hall, she rather passively predicted that "low wages will doubtless in time be modified by Minimum Wage Boards" (35, 38).

So slight was Addams's attention to wages as a vice remedy that Rebecca Lose, a member of the State Federation of Pennsylvania Women, wrote to her after reading *A New Conscience* to say that she thought it was "a pity to neglect so logical a method and one so surely effective . . . since authorities agree that women and girls in general would far rather lead decent lives when they can." Lose thought it was "all very well to form societies for the suppression of the social evil and for the encouragement of social purity," but doubted that anyone's virtue, however aroused, "was of sufficiently stalwart character to withstand" the "onslaughts" of "hunger or cold or dullness or misery."[58] This was the sort of common sense about working-class reality that readers typically heard from Addams herself—in the pages of *Democracy and Social Ethics*, *Youth and the Spirit of the City Streets*, and *Twenty Years at Hull-House*. But when it came to prostitution, readers such as Lose had to provide this practical perspective.

The three most fundamental and intertwined remedies that Addams offered for prostitution went right to the heart of her gender politics and, thus, to the center of her idealized view of women's uniquely purifying role in creating a progressive society. *A New Conscience* endorsed woman suffrage; a single, feminine standard of sexuality for both males and females; and the reaffirmation of the male-provider family as the sole site for physical sexual expression. All three of these remedies represented Addams's heartfelt commitment to the traditional family structure, within which she envisioned the formalizing of modern women's moral and political authority. With these remedies in hand, American women would institute the caring, communal correctives that Addams envisioned when she spoke of "democracy and social ethics," "newer ideals of peace," and "a new conscience."

Jane Addams's commitment to woman suffrage was always fueled by her commitment to the social reforms that she believed enfranchised women would enact. Rather than emphasize women's "right" to vote, Addams focused on women's "duty" to exercise this privilege. She argued in *A New Conscience*, as she would elsewhere, that women denied the franchise were not trained to think about civic matters, but if they could be aroused to grasp the importance of such matters—including the white slave traffic—they would demand the franchise and take aggressive reform action. Addams's implied retort to women who thought she should not write about such nasty topics as prostitution was that men, even "good" men, were cynical about the social evil and doubted it could be abolished; a new conscience would have to come from women because women had a unique, personal investment in safeguarding—and advancing—female chastity.[59]

At the most basic level, argued Addams, "the primitive maternal instinct" prompted women to want to protect exploited children and naive young women (87). With the vote, women would raise the age of consent, would enact more humane ways of dealing with women arrested for prostitution, would help unwed mothers, and would insist on the social controls needed to eliminate corrupting cultural influences from the urban environment. Comparably basic was women's interest, as wives, in domesticating their husbands, channeling their masculine energies into productive, remunerative labor and away from alcohol and vice. Addams took it for granted that males had to "submit to control in spite of themselves" while women were readily inclined to embrace "the desirability of chastity . . . not only as a personal virtue indispensable in women and desirable in men, but as a great basic requirement which society has learned to demand because it has been proven necessary for human welfare" (92, 95). Theodore Roosevelt wrote a letter to Addams after reading the first excerpt from her book in *McClure's Magazine*. He applauded her vision of a society in which chastity was a value for men as well as women. "Some of our Socialist friends," he claimed, "wish to do away with the injustices of the double standard for the sexes by lowering that standard for women." Roosevelt, however, aligned himself with Addams—and with everyone else in the mainstream of reform—by arguing that the sexual standard "should be raised for men."[60] Addams scoffed at the popular notion that men's access to prostitutes left "virtuous women" more safe on the streets and in their homes. Nonsense, she said; social acceptance of men's use of prostitutes allowed men of "wretched private character," those who "have not submitted to self-control," to ascend to positions of public authority, where, inevitably, their corrupt sexual morals were manifest in equally corrupt business and political conduct (92, 96). This is as close as she came to the radical feminist position that prostitution is a function of general male dominance, but she did not go so far as to say that this rapacious ethic dominated all men's treatment of all women; as a reformer dedicated to the need for and possibility of change, she carefully stigmatized male behavior as both pervasive and aberrant.

Addams sought a single, female standard of sexuality because she wanted women to be "freer and nobler, less timid of reputation and more human." To achieve that, women needed to be able to move beyond the traditional system of "negative chastity" in which women were guarded and chaperoned. Addams's chaste, utopian vision—evocative of Charlotte Perkins Gilman's vision in *Herland*—was of a world in which women were free to engage in "self-directed activity and a varied circle of interests," working alongside "many men as well as women" because a "single standard" of sexual conduct meant no threat to her body or her reputation if she operated in a public space. In this world, where female standards of chastity were the rule, men and women would enjoy "virtue between equals."[61]

Nowhere in Addams's vision of gender equality and a single sexual standard did there exist the possibility of heterosexual contact, between consenting adults, outside of marriage. The year after Emma Goldman announced to her own, very small, audience that "stupid social customs" condemned unwed women to a "life of celibacy or prostitution," Addams was demanding that men agree to similarly confine themselves to the marriage bed. While Goldman mocked the "moralist" who approved of women marrying for economic support but disapproved of them engaging in unwed sex for the same purpose, Addams insisted that human beings had "always" regulated "the great primitive instinct" of sex through the instrument of marriage—and achieved great gains in the process.[62] Although Hull-House provided child care services for working mothers in the neighborhood, Addams had come around, by 1911, to endorsing a "family wage" for married men and a "mothers' pension" for women. She agreed with the novelist (and Fabian socialist) H. G. Wells that it was a "monstrous absurdity" to ask women "who are discharging the supreme social function" to also work for wages.⁶³ Full-time mothering and a father's family wage—not a system of unmarried mothers trying to work and care for children, not a system of unattached adults coming together for sensual pleasure—was the only system that could socialize all citizens into an ethic of mutual care. Even "the sordid marriages," observed Addams after twenty-two years in the Nineteenth Ward, "almost always end in some form of family affection. The young couple . . . after twenty years of hard work in meagre, unlovely surroundings, in spite of stupidity and many mistakes, in the face of failure and even wrongdoing [will have] unfolded lives of unassuming affection and family devotion to a group of children. They will have faithfully fulfilled that obligation which falls to the lot of the majority of men and women, with its high rewards and painful sacrifices" (92).

Coming at the end of a book in which she recounted all the dispiriting family influences that could make a girl vulnerable to vice, this sounds peculiarly romantic. But if we take seriously Jane Addams's belief that caring mutuality and individual sacrifice for the good of the whole are the chief aims of a progressive society, and take seriously her belief that women's chaste leadership is the obvious route to that goal, then her devotion to the family and her anger at commercialized vice for rendering females unfit for marriage and motherhood make sense. Addams's personal path of unmarried service was not a path she could—or would—recommend to the mass of young women in Chicago. Her recognition that most of those young women wanted to be with men, wanted to be married, wanted to be mothers was one of her most realistic positions. The difficulties she had understanding her young neighbors' new expressions of unwed sexuality violate our sense of Addams as an open, expansive social evolutionist, but they do not contradict our sense of her fundamental conviction that sexual purity was essential to the creation of a caring, progressive society. What remains to explore in the record of Addams's activism is the effect of her sexual convictions on her relations with the young women of her neighborhood. The fact that Addams was not liberal in regard to sexuality is simply that, a fact, a part of our understanding of who Jane Addams was and where she fit in her era. But it becomes a more complex fact if we find that her sexual attitudes interfered with who she meant to be: a useful, trusted neighbor for young people, especially young women. That story is yet to be told, but *A New Conscience* tells us that it is a story worth exploring.

In *Second Twenty Years at Hull-House*, published in 1930, Addams reaffirmed her belief that loose sexual morals were the cultural expression of the politics of individualism. Looking back over the gulf that widened between Addams and younger people in the 1920s, she argued that "reckless youth" had exploited the Freudian injunction against sexual repression, rejected the "value of self-criticism and self-denial," and become "abject followers of blind forces admittedly beyond their control." The result, she noted, was a generation that placed "the liberty of the individual" and the "new freedom in sex relations" ahead of campaigns for the political liberty of less-blessed peoples.[64] The sensuality, materialism, and narcissism she had feared in 1912 were in full bloom in the 1920s; Addams's "new conscience" had failed to take hold, but she still believed it was the best path to social justice.

Notes

1. Walter Lippmann, *A Preface to Politics* (New York: Mitchell Kennerley, 1913; repr., New York: Henry Holt, 1917), 79; Allen F. Davis, *American Heroine: The Life and Legend of Jane Addams* (New York: Oxford University Press, 1973), 183.

2. Charlene Haddock Seigfried, introduction to *Democracy and Social Ethics*, by Jane Addams (1902; Urbana: University of Illinois, 2002); Berenice A. Carroll and Clinton F. Fink, introduction to *Newer Ideals of Peace*, by Jane Addams (1907; Urbana: University of Illinois, 2007); Charlene Haddock Seigfried, introduction to *The Long Road of Woman's Memory* (1916; Urbana: University of Illinois, 2002); Katherine Joslin, introduction to *Peace and Bread in Time of War*, by Jane Addams (1922; Urbana: University of Illinois, 2002). Even Allen F. Davis's introduction to *The Spirit of Youth and the City Streets* (1909; Urbana: University of Illinois Press, 2001) refers to that volume as "one of Jane Addams's best books" (ix).

3. Katherine Joslin, introduction to *A New Conscience and an Ancient Evil*, by Jane Addams (1907; Urbana: University of Illinois Press, 2007), x, xvi, xxii. Joslin's claim derives from the argument she and Janet Beer made in "Diseases of the Body Politic: White Slavery and Jane Addams' *A New Conscience and an Ancient Evil* and Selected Short Stories by Charlotte Perkins Gilman," *Journal of American Studies* 33, no. 1 (1999): 1–18. While the argument presented herein agrees with Joslin's conclusion that *A New Conscience* is not a persuasive book, it does not agree with Joslin and Beers that Addams was making "an economic analysis closely paralleling Gilman's in *Women and Economics*" (3), since Gilman was arguing against female economic independence and, as I argue here, Addams was not.

4. Mark Thomas Connelly, *The Response to Prostitution in the Progressive Era* (Chapel Hill: University of North Carolina Press, 1980), 6. In describing the social anxiety that produced the prostitution panic of the day, Connelly further noted, "In the ideal world of civilized morality, all moral values were absolute and timeless, masculine and feminine roles were sharply defined and demarcated, sexuality was seen as a potentially destructive force, and life, in general, was conceived in terms of duty, service, and self-denial" (8–9).

5. Ibid., 16–17; Ruth Rosen, *The Lost Sisterhood: Prostitution in America, 1900–1918* (Baltimore: Johns Hopkins University Press, 1983), 14–15.

6. See, for example, Samuel Paynter Wilson, *Chicago and Its Cess-Pools of Infamy* (Chicago:

Samuel Paynter Wilson, 1910); O. Edward Janney, M.D., *White Slave Traffic in America* (Baltimore: Lord Baltimore Press, 1911); Clifford G. Roe, *The Great War on White Slavery or Fighting for the Protection of Our Girls* (Chicago: Clifford G. Roe and B. S. Steadwell, 1911). David Langum reported on the entries in the *Reader's Guide to Periodical Literature* in *Crossing Over the Line: Legislating Morality and the Mann Act* (Chicago: University of Chicago Press, 1994), 15.

7. Jane Addams to Edward C. Marsh, July 31, 1911, Macmillan Company Authors Collection, New York Public Library; George Brett to Jane Addams, August 2, 1911, Swarthmore College Peace Collection, Jane Addams Papers, Series 1; Edward C. Marsh to Jane Addams, August 17, 1911, Swarthmore College Peace Collection, Jane Addams Papers, Series 1. All included in Jane Addams Papers, 1860–1960, microfilm edition, reel 6, frames 368, 394, 423.

8. Chicago Vice Commission, *The Social Evil in Chicago: A Study of Existing Conditions with Recommendations* (Chicago: Vice Commission, 1911). Mayor Fred Busse's preface to the report makes clear his support for a regulatory approach (4). See also Eric Anderson, "Prostitution and Social Justice: Chicago, 1910–1915," *Social Service Review* 48 (June 1974): 207. Jane Addams, *A New Conscience and an Ancient Evil* (1907; Urbana: University of Illinois Press, 2007), 8, 99, 5, 98.

9. Addams, *A New Conscience*, 6. References to this work appear parenthetically in the text.

10. There is an unfortunate misprint in the 2002 edition of *A New Conscience* (90). There, instead of saying that "the village gossip with her vituperative tongue after all performs a valuable function both of castigation and retribution," the University of Illinois edition has Addams saying that the "village gossip" was "valuable" for the function of "castration." Addams certainly welcomed public disdain of men who violated their marriage vows, but she did not endorse castration.

11. G. Stanley Hall, *Adolescence: Its Psychology and Its Relation to Physiology, Anthropology, Sociology, Sex, Crime, Religion, and Education* (New York: D. Appleton, 1904); Addams, *Spirit of Youth and the City Streets*, 17–19, 27–30.

12. In her introduction to the 2002 edition of *A New Conscience*, Katherine Joslin suggested that Addams feared the "molten forces" as a powerful source for labor organizing, ethnic integration, sexual revolution, or radical change in domestic life. The argument presented here is that Addams wanted to harness those "molten forces" for such public enterprises as labor organizing and ethnic integration and hoped that this public activity would divert energies away from sexual or domestic change.

13. The literature detailing the modern liberal feminist position is far more rich and complex than can be captured here. For useful expressions of the liberal viewpoint, see Martha Nussbaum, "'Whether from Reason or Prejudice': Taking Money for Bodily Services," *Journal of Legal Studies* 27 (June 1998) and Sibyl Schwarzenbach, "Contractarians and Feminists Debate Prostitution," *NYU Review of Law and Social Change* 18 (1990–91): 103–30. Both the Nussbaum and Schwarzenbach articles are reprinted in *Prostitution and Pornography: Philosophical Debate about the Sex Industry*, ed. Jessica Spector (Stanford: Stanford University Press, 2006). See also Elizabeth Bernstein, *Temporarily Yours: Intimacy, Authenticity, and the Commerce of Sex* (Chicago: University of Chicago Press, 2007), especially chap. 7, "Sexuality Debates and Pleasure Wars."

14. As with the literature on liberal feminism and pornography, there is a vast, nuanced body of work on the radical feminist position, and this chapter attempts only to summarize the core tenets of that position. See Jessica Spector, "Introduction: Sex, Money, and Philosophy," in *Prostitution and Pornography*, ed. Spector, 1–13; Carole Pateman, "What's Wrong with Prostitution," reprinted from *The Sexual Contract* (Stanford: Stanford University Press, 1988), in *Prostitution and Pornography*, ed. Spector, 50–79. See also Sarah Bromberg, "Feminist Issues in Prostitution," in *Prostitution: On Whores, Hustlers, and Johns*, ed. James Elias, Vern L. Bullough, Veronica Elias, and Gwen Brewer (Amherst, N.Y.: Prometheus Books, 1998), 294–300.

15. See, for example, Margaret Baldwin, "Split at the Root: Prostitution and Feminist Discourses of Law Reform," in *Prostitution and Pornography*, ed. Spector, 106–45; Pateman, "What's Wrong with Prostitution," 60–65; Nussbaum, "'Whether from Reason or Prejudice,'" 183; Bernstein, *Temporarily Yours*, chap. 7. By contrast, see Addams, *A New Conscience*, 87.

16. For a clear articulation of this radical feminist position, see Pateman, "What's Wrong with Prostitution," 63–69.

17. Addams, *A New Conscience*, 24, 51, 78. Margaret Baldwin argues that modern feminists, even radicals who define the prostitute as emblematic of all women, typically talk about the prostitute as "the other woman," the woman whom they are not. Just as the prostitute psychologically distances herself from the john, so reformers distance themselves from the prostitute, and they do this as part of a bargain with the state to affirm—and protect—their own condition of "legal citizenship." Addams and other progressive female reformers certainly bid for the status of citizens and stewards by defining themselves as uniquely positioned to rescue the "fallen woman" and thus the community from corruption. Baldwin, "Split at the Root," in *Prostitution and Pornography*, ed. Spector, 142–44.

18. Pateman, "What's Wrong with Prostitution," 69.

19. Bernstein, *Temporarily Yours*, chaps. 1, 7; Nussbaum, "'Whether from Reason or Prejudice,'" 180–93; Baldwin, "Split at the Root," 140–44; Bromberg, "Feminist Issues in Prostitution," 295–99.

20. Jane Addams to George P. Brett, January 13, 1911, Macmillan Company Authors Collection, New York Public Library, included in Jane Addams Papers, 1860–1960, microfilm edition, reel 6, frame 47; Addams, *A New Conscience*, 7.

21. See, for example, "The White Slave Traffic in the United States," *Spectator* 108 (June 1912): 873. Addams's dear friend Dr. Alice Hamilton commended the manuscript for combining "evasion and frankness together" and for avoiding "ugly words" and "uglier" supposition. In what appears to be a gentle critique of the book's uncharacteristically dramatic tone, Hamilton wrote, "Every now and then I catch my breath and I listen and think, 'There now, that is really she,' but I do wish there were more of those passages." August 14, 1911, Swarthmore College Peace Collection, Jane Addams Papers, Series 1. Included in Jane Addams Papers, 1860–1960, microfilm edition, reel 6, frames 408–11.

For other letters praising Addams's deft handling of the topic, see John Graham Brooks to Jane Addams, December 23, 1911; Martha French to Jane Addams, April 22, 1912; Edwin Seligman to Jane Addams, April 25, 1912; George Lewis to Jane Addams, April 30, 1912; Henry Cochems to Jane Addams, November 4, 1912; and Julia Lathrop to Jane Addams, November 13, 1912. Lathrop's brief note quoted Hamlet, speaking of Ophelia, to describe Addams's achievement in *A New Conscience*: "Everything she turns to favor and to prettiness." All letters located in Swarthmore College Peace Collection, Jane Addams Papers, Series 1. All included in Jane Addams Papers, 1860–1960, microfilm edition, reel 6, frames 698, 947, 955, 962, and reel 7, frames 355 and 422.

22. "The White Slave Traffic in the United States," 873; *Literary Digest* 44 (May 18, 1912): 1066. Henry Metcalf to Jane Addams, January 18, 1912; Adela Isabel Coit to Jane Addams, October 14, 1912, Swarthmore College Peace Collection, Jane Addams Papers, Series 1. Included in Jane Addams Papers, 1860–1960, microfilm edition, reel 6, frame 776 and reel 7, frame 250.

23. Addams, *A New Conscience*, 64, 6; reviews in *Annals of the American Academy of Political and Social Sciences* 43 (September 1912): 327; *Nation* 94 (June 13, 1912): 594; *New York Times*, May 26, 1912, 321.

24. Barbara Meil Hobson, in *Uneasy Virtue: The Politics of Prostitution and the American Reform Tradition* (New York: Basic Books, 1987), identified Addams's "millennialist fervor" and observed that "hidden agendas" often shaped sociological studies of prostitution at the time (155), but Hobson did not explore the particular inaccuracies in Addams's text. In his excellent overview of the history of prostitution in the Progressive Era, *The Response to Prostitution*, Mark Connelly categorized Addams with the socialists in "causally" linking prostitution to low wages. Seven pages later, Connelly described Addams as "certainly one of the most advanced social thinkers of her time" whose book on prostitution "on the whole, was not advanced" because of its emphasis on "moral development" and "social control" (31, 38). Both his statements can be supported by evidence from *A New Conscience*. It was not Connelly's purpose to conduct a close textual analysis of the connection between Addams's economic and moralistic arguments. That is the purpose here and, for that reason,

my argument seeks to define more precisely the exact link Addams drew between economic and moral causes for prostitution.

The conclusions here do not agree with Brian Donovan's claims in *White Slave Crusaders: Race, Gender, and Anti-vice Activism, 1887–1917* (Urbana: University of Illinois Press, 2006). Donovan asserts that "Addams recognized prostitution as a choice that some women pursued, yet a choice often made under harsh circumstances. By not writing a scenario of abduction and trickery, Addams blamed employment conditions instead of individual men" (66–67). My analysis of *A New Conscience* took shape before I read Donovan. It was not designed to refute his claims but does aspire to offer a more nuanced, more persuasive interpretation of the complications and contradictions of the text.

25. Connelly, *The Response to Prostitution*, 62–63; Timothy J. Gilfoyle, *City of Eros: New York City, Prostitution, and the Commercialization of Sex, 1790–1920* (New York: Norton, 1992), 292; Rosen, *The Lost Sisterhood*, 44; Hobson, *Uneasy Virtue*, 142. The Vice Commission of Philadelphia reported that of the 1,201 prostitutes interviewed for the study, only 133 were foreign born. See Vice Commission of Philadelphia, *Report on Existing Conditions with Recommendations* (1913) in *The Prostitute and the Social Reformer: Commercial Vice in the Progressive Era* (New York: Arno Press, 1974), 17.

26. Connelly, for example, notes that the Chicago Vice Commission reported on one group of thirty prostitutes whose average age was 23.5. Timothy Gilfoyle found that the average age of prostitutes was actually increasing in the first decade of the twentieth century. Gilfoyle, *City of Eros*, 284–87. John D. Rockefeller Jr. to Jane Addams, February 14, 1912, Swarthmore College Peace Collection, Jane Addams Papers, Series 1. Included in Jane Addams Papers, 1860–1960, microfilm edition, reel 6, frame 824. Preface to Addams, *New Conscience and an Ancient Evil*.

27. Linda Gordon comments on the mix of conviction and strategy that went into maternalists' emphasis on the vulnerability of children. "Putting children first was not only a moral stance but also a posture in which, as I imagine it, women held up children in front of them, plump little legs and adorable wide eyes inducing a suspicious gatekeeper to open the door to the public treasury." Gordon, "Putting Children First: Women, Maternalism, and Welfare in the Early Twentieth Century," in *U.S. History as Women's History: New Feminist Essays*, ed. Linda K. Kerber, Alice Kessler-Harris, and Kathryn Kish Sklar (Chapel Hill: University of North Carolina Press, 1995).

28. Addams, *A New Conscience*, 28; Connelly, *The Response to Prostitution*, 22.

29. Ruth Rosen, in *The Lost Sisterhood*, discussed the medical dangers attendant upon prostitution, including venereal disease, drug addiction, and pregnancy. Doubt about claims that prostitutes were dead within five years does not take away from these very real heath risks; instead, it tries to consider those risks in the context of real women's lived experience, not in the context of melodramatic demise (98–100).

30. Dorothy Ross, "Gendered Social Knowledge: Domestic Discourse, Jane Addams, and the Possibilities of Social Science," in *Gender and American Social Science*, ed. Helene Silverberg (Princeton: Princeton University Press, 1998), 235–64; Victoria Bissell Brown, *The Education of Jane Addams* (Philadelphia: University of Pennsylvania Press, 2004), chaps. 4–6. Kathryn Kish Sklar's work on Florence Kelley demonstrates that she, unlike Addams, was trained as a social scientist and, with the leadership she provided in producing the neighborhood study *Hull-House Maps and Papers*, Kelley certainly introduced social science methods into Addams's endeavors. But while exposure to Kelley gave Addams an appreciation for the methods and the power of empiricism, it did not replace Addams's philosophical bent with an empirical one. Sklar, "*Hull-House Maps and Papers*: Social Science as Women's Work in the 1890s," in *Gender and American Social Science*, ed. Silverberg, 128–55; Sklar, *Florence Kelley and the Nation's Work* (New Haven: Yale University Press, 1995).

31. Ross, "Gendered Social Knowledge," 246.

32. Philosophers are more likely to view Addams as a social scientist than are social scientists. See, for example, Charlene Haddock Seigfried, introduction to *Democracy and Social Ethics*, xxii; Marilyn Fischer, *On Addams* (Toronto: Thomson Wadsworth, 2004), 68–69.

33. The data from empirical investigations on prostitutes in various cities indicated that domestic servants and factory girls were most likely to become prostitutes, if only because they represented the two largest groups of female workers. See, for example, Vice Commission of Philadelphia, *Report on Existing Conditions with Recommendations*, 86–87.

34. Addams put quotation marks around the text "Wherever many girls are gathered together more or less unprotected and embroiled in the struggle for a livelihood, near by will be hovering the procurers and evil-minded," but, as was so often true in her writings, she did not cite the source for the quote.

35. Addams, *A New Conscience*, 93; Emma Goldman, "The Traffic in Women," in *Anarchism and Other Essays with Biographic Sketch by Hippolyte Havel* (New York: Mother Earth, 1910), 177–94. Addams differentiated herself from the socialists: "The Socialists contend that commercialized vice is fundamentally a question of poverty, a by-product of despair, which will disappear only with the abolition of poverty itself" (93). She proceeded quickly to argue that "whether we are Socialists or not, we will all admit that every level of culture breeds its own particular brand of vice," making clear that she did not think poverty was the sole cause of prostitution. See Nussbaum, "'Whether from Reason or Prejudice,'" 200–207, and Baldwin, "Split at the Root," 134–35, where Baldwin discusses Rachel West and the socialist feminist view that prostitution is not about sex, but about profits. See also Laurie Shrage, "Prostitution and the Case for Decriminalization," in *Prostitution and Pornography*, ed. Spector, 240–46.

36. "White Slave Trade Is Not Organized: So Says the Rockefeller Grand Jury's Presentment," *New York Times*, June 29, 1910, 16; Chicago Vice Commission, *The Social Evil in Chicago*, 229–32, where the commission placed "white slave traffic" fifth on its five-point list of causes of prostitution and devoted virtually no space in the report to a vast vice business network. The Vice Commission of Minneapolis reported in 1911 that it had been "unable to secure any evidence of the existence of an organized system in Minneapolis for the supply of prostitutes for local use, nor to learn of more than one or two instances, covering many years, of forcible detention of girls for immoral purposes." In *The Prostitute and the Social Reformer*, 75. See Connelly, *The Response to Prostitution*, 55, 129–32; Rosen, *The Lost Sisterhood*, 113, 124–25.

37. In arguing that the existence of the white slave traffic proved the strength of female virtue, Addams was echoing the opinion of General Theodore A. Bingham, ex-police commissioner of New York City, who was quoted in the report of the Vice Commission of Minneapolis. Even though the Minneapolis commission found no evidence of an organized slave trade, it included Bingham's view that "if women, in large numbers, were willing to become prostitutes, it would not be necessary to have such an enormous machine (as that of the white slave traffic) to recruit the ranks." Report of the Vice Commission of Minneapolis, 93, in *The Prostitute and the Social Reformer*, 93.

38. Kathy Peiss, *Cheap Amusements: Working Women and Leisure in Turn-of-the-Century New York* (Philadelphia: Temple University Press, 1986); Joanne J. Meyerowitz, *Women Adrift: Independent Wage Earners in Chicago, 1880–1930* (Chicago: University of Chicago Press, 1988); Elizabeth Alice Clement, *Love for Sale: Courting, Treating, and Prostitution in New York City, 1900–1945* (Chapel Hill: University of North Carolina Press, 2006); Nan Enstad, *Ladies of Labor, Girls of Adventure: Working Women, Popular Culture, and Labor Politics at the Turn of the Century* (New York: Columbia University Press, 1999); Sharon E. Wood, *The Freedom of the Streets: Work, Citizenship, and Sexuality in a Gilded Age City* (Chapel Hill: University of North Carolina Press, 2005).

39. As Joanne Meyerowitz put it, "The 'women adrift' were neither liberated individuals nor isolated victims. On the one hand, prevailing institutions and ideologies shaped and circumscribed their choices. . . . On the other hand, jobs in the city enabled women to live, however poorly, outside of the family and explore new social networks." *Women Adrift*, xxii. As Kathy Peiss put it, "One could argue that this culture was primarily a product of the leisure industry's efforts to market entertainment and consumption to working-class women, who were lulled into a state of false consciousness. Without denying the importance of these points, I think it is necessary to understand

how women pushed at the boundaries of constrained lives and shaped cultural forms for their own purposes." *Cheap Amusements*, 6.

40. Schwarzenbach criticizes radical feminists for similarly resisting the notion that the meaning of particular sexual behaviors can change over time, especially when actors take initiative to alter their meaning. "Contractarians and Feminists Debate Prostitution," in *Prostitution and Pornography*, ed. Spector, 229–30.

41. Addams, *Twenty Years at Hull-House with Autobiographical Notes* (New York: Macmillan, 1910), 167. A superb example of Addams's talent for explaining the logic underlying her neighbors' perspective to readers of Addams's social class can be found in Addams, *Democracy and Social Ethics*, chap. 1, "Charitable Effort," 11–34.

42. Jane Addams, "A Modern Lear," *Survey* 29 (November 2, 1912): 136.

43. Baldwin, "Split at the Root," 140–41.

44. Lippmann, *Preface to Politics*, 77, 50, 79, 42, 78.

45. Ibid., 79.

46. Ibid., 45, 39, 79.

47. Ibid., 78–79.

48. The liberal feminist critique of criminalization is articulated in Norma Jean Almodovar, "Porn Stars, Radical Feminists, Cops, and Outlaw Whores," in *Prostitution and Pornography*, ed. Spector, 149–73; Nussbaum, "'Whether from Reason or Prejudice,'" 190–93; Schwarzenbach, "Contractarians and Feminists Debate Prostitution," 231–39; and Shrage, "Prostitution and the Case for Decriminalization," 240–46.

49. Addams, "A Modern Lear," 137.

50. Addams welcomed prohibition when it came, but she never campaigned for it as she did for abolition of prostitution.

51. Hobson, *Uneasy Virtue*, 143, 163–64.

52. For example, see Jane Addams, *Newer Ideals of Peace*, chap. 2, "Survival of Militarism in City Government" and chap. 4, "Militarism and Industrial Legislation."

53. Walter Reckless, *Vice in Chicago* (Chicago: University of Chicago Press, 1933). Reckless found that the result of more strict police enforcement after the brothel sweep of 1912 was the dispersal of prostitutes in "neighborhoods of declining respectability," meaning that vice activity was even more interlaced into the lives of children than before. Reckless also found that tight enforcement in the white downtown created an "enormous growth" in prostitution in black areas. In 1914, black women constituted 2 percent of the Chicago population and 16 percent of those arrested for prostitution; in 1929, they constituted 7 percent of the Chicago population and 70 percent of those arrested. For the actual police sweep of the downtown brothel districts, see "Fighting Vice Segregation in Chicago," *Literary Digest* 45 (November 9, 1912): 848. See also Anderson, "Prostitution and Social Justice," 214–15.

54. Bernstein explores a similar effect of modern criminalization in *Temporarily Yours*, chap. 2.

55. Addams was far more militant on the subject of sex hygiene in the schools than her colleagues in the anti-vice community. The Chicago Vice Commission, whose thirty members included Hull-House colleagues such as Ellen Henrotin and Graham Taylor, devoted considerable attention to "Child Protection and Education," but hesitated over providing a school curriculum in sex hygiene below college level, recommending, instead, that fathers teach their sons and that mothers, drawing on "maternal instinct . . . find a way" to teach their daughters the "dangers" of sex. Chicago Vice Commission, *The Social Evil in Chicago*, 37, 253.

56. See also Sophonisba P. Breckinridge and Edith Abbott, *The Delinquent Child* (New York: Charities Publication Committee, 1912), 37–42; Mary E. Odem, *Delinquent Daughters: Protecting and Policing Adolescent Female Sexuality in the United States, 1885–1920* (Chapel Hill: University of North Carolina Press, 1995); Steven Schlossman and Stephanie Wallach, "The Crime of Precocious Sexuality: Female Juvenile Delinquency in the Progressive Era," *Harvard Educational Review* 48 (February 1978): 65–95.

57. Julia Lathrop, Addams's great friend and colleague and, in 1912, the first head of the U.S. Children's Bureau, wrote in the *Hull-House Bulletin* in 1897 that "dependency would seem the natural right of every child." This concept had a powerful impact on redistribution of resources for children's benefit in the Progressive Era, but it spilled over into problematic control of young people's lives when applied to those in their late teens and early twenties who were seeking independence from paternalistic or maternalistic control. Lathrop quoted in Elizabeth J. Clapp, *Mothers of All Children: Women Reformers and the Rise of Juvenile Courts in Progressive Era America* (University Park: Pennsylvania State University Press, 1998), 60.

58. Rebecca Lose to Jane Addams, May 3, 1912, Swarthmore College Peace Collection, Jane Addams Papers, Series 1; Jane Addams Papers, 1860–1960, microfilm edition, reel 6, frames 967–69. See also George Weidenfeld to Jane Addams, January 25, 1912, Swarthmore College Peace Collection, Jane Addams Papers, Series 1; Jane Addams Papers, 1860–1960, microfilm edition, reel 6, frames 790–92. Weidenfeld praised the socialists for understanding that raising the standard of living was the only reform that would address prostitution, and he criticized Addams for thinking that repressive legislation would have any effect.

59. Addams, *A New Conscience*, 87–89; Jane Addams, "Why Women Should Vote," *Ladies' Home Journal* 27 (January 1910): 21–22.

60. Theodore Roosevelt to Jane Addams, October 31, 1911, Swarthmore College Peace Collection, Jane Addams Papers, Series 1; Jane Addams Papers, 1860–1960, microfilm edition, reel 6, frame 512.

61. Addams, *A New Conscience*, 96; Charlotte Perkins Gilman, *Herland* (New York: Pantheon Books, 1979), originally published in *Forerunner*, 1915.

62. Addams, *A New Conscience*, 94–95; Goldman, "The Traffic in Women," http://xroads .virginia.edu/~HYPER/Goldman/traffic.html. In *A New Conscience*, Addams referred approvingly to a hugely popular play, *Damaged Goods*, by the French playwright Eugene Brieux, which dealt candidly with the "social evil" and the effects of men's sexual exploits on the health of their wives and children. Although the play was not actually produced on an American stage until 1913, Addams read it while she was writing her prostitution book because Sophonisba Breckinridge sent it to her in Maine. The popularity of *Damaged Goods* has often been taken as evidence that American culture was becoming more liberated on the subject of sex, but an insightful analysis by Katie Johnson demonstrates that the play was more acceptable than others on the topic precisely because it mounted such an impassioned defense for traditional marriage against the threat of the diseased body of the prostitute. Like Addams, Brieux did not intend to demonize the prostitute, but the "pseudo-scientific, bourgeois, heteronormative framings" of the plot had the effect of turning the whore into the "flower of evil." Katie N. Johnson, "Damaged Goods: Sex Hysteria and the Prostitute Fatale," *Theatre Survey* 44 (May 2003): 61. Sophonisba Breckinridge to Jane Addams, August 2, 1911, Sophonisba Breckinridge Papers, Library of Congress, in Jane Addams Papers, 1860–1960, microfilm edition, reel 6, frame 393.

63. Sonya Michel, "The Limits of Maternalism: Policies Toward American Wage-Earning Mothers During the Progressive Era," in *Mothers of a New World: Maternalist Politics and the Origins of Welfare States* (New York: Routledge, 1993), 290–91; Addams, *A New Conscience*, 53.

64. Jane Addams, *Second Twenty Years at Hull-House* (New York: Macmillan, 1930), 193–95.

6

Toward a Queer Social Welfare Studies

Unsettling Jane Addams

Shannon Jackson

Just when our affection becomes large enough to care for the unworthy among the poor as we would care for the unworthy among our kin, is certainly a perplexing question.
—Jane Addams (1902)

If we understand kinship to be a set of practices that institutes relationships of various kinds that negotiate the reproduction of life and the demands of death, then kinship practices will be those that emerge to address fundamental forms of human dependency.
—Judith Butler (2002)

My task in this essay, located as it is in a volume that explores Jane Addams's relationship to contemporary theory, is to imagine a relationship between the legacies of Hull House and a body of thought that consolidated in the 1990s under the rubric of poststructuralist queer theory. To argue for that relationship is, to some degree, an improbable task. Many historians of social welfare place Jane Addams's Hull House settlement as an origin point in the invention of state welfare in the United

From *Jane Addams and the Practice of Democracy: Multidisciplinary Essays on Theory and Practice*, ed. Wendy Chmielewski, Marilyn Fischer, and Carol Nackenoff. Copyright 2009 by the Board of Trustees of the University of Illinois. Used with the permission of the University of Illinois Press.

States; meanwhile, many poststructuralist critics of sexual identity invoke the operations of state welfare as an insidiously dangerous source of social normalization. Similarly, many historians of the family position Addams's Hull House settlement as a central locus and activator of maternalist politics; meanwhile, many critics of gender and sexuality cite the rhetoric of the family and motherhood as an instantiator of gender and heteronormative inequity. Given the critical suspicion of the "maternal" "State" with which she has been allied, how could it be possible for Jane Addams and Hull House to converse transhistorically with contemporary theoretical paradigms? I will say at the outset of this short essay that any conversation will require a more heterogeneous view of the concept of state welfare and a more heterogeneous view of Hull House as a place of operation. As Licia Fiol-Matta demonstrates in her study of Latin American leader Gabriela Mistral in *A Queer Mother for the Nation*, the public and private practices of maternalism, sexuality, and the nation-state can intersect in complex and ambiguous ways.[1] It is only by recognizing the challenge of both state welfare and of Hull House to conventions of private and public that we can find an alternate way of connecting the dots between them. Indeed, whatever the limits of both of these spheres, I want to foreground the capacity of both state welfare and Hull House to imagine a sphere of obligation and kinship that exceeds biological ties, undoing conventions of publicity and privacy along the way. It is only with such an alternate emphasis that we can begin to conceptualize the legacy of Jane Addams and Hull House for poststructuralist critiques of sexual identity and social belonging. And it is only with such an alternate emphasis that we can begin to see queer politics as having something to do with the domestic politics that is state welfare.

In an earlier book on Hull House reform called *Lines of Activity*, I analyzed a variety of politically volatile Hull House performance spaces—social clubs, festivals, athletics, gymnastics, theater, living history museums, dance, and folklore—in connection to larger issues of immigration, juvenile justice, and urbanization.[2] Here, I want to develop the historiographic implications of another strain of settlement performance, specifically the everyday performances of "home," "family," "kinship," and "domesticity" developed by reformers themselves. My goal is to argue for a connection between what I called Hull House's "queer domesticity" and several contemporary concerns. Those concerns are various but related. At a time when theorists of sexuality are attempting to map a relation between the psychic and the social, that is, between the most intimate and the most abstract structures of social life, the discourse of and around Jane Addams offers a useful case study. Conversely, queer studies offers a particular opportunity for staging an investigation of Jane Addams. Queer theory's emergence within the discontinuous field of "gender studies" has revised feminisms of all varieties while also countering sexual essentialisms and sexual positivisms in gay and lesbian historiography; hence, queer theory also provides a way of reevaluating some of the ways that historians of gender and sexuality have made use of Jane Addams. More importantly, I want to use Jane Addams and Hull House to argue for a more considered and mutually galvanizing relationship between the field of feminist welfare studies and the field of queer theory. It is my sense that both of these domains possess reductive conceptions of the other, casting the first as unreflecting state functionalism and the second as an abstract form of groundless theoretical musing. To me, each of these domains only fits these stereotypes in their habits of stereotyping the other. And when that happens, the potential for creating a rigorous and mutually transforming interdisciplinary project goes unrealized as does the possibility for a vibrant, if internally bracing, political alliance.

Central to a concept of queer welfare studies is my interest in imagining a kind of progressive model of extended kinship in the state's attempt to encourage its members to "care" for those who are not biological kin. My hope is to argue for a connection between the necessity of reorganizing what Judith Butler calls "fundamental forms of human dependency" and Jane Addams's question—posed in the language of her time—about what it takes to care for all human beings as "we would the unworthy amongst our kin." I will want to suggest that Jane Addams's pursuit of social welfare within the context of state government is, along with its limits and unintended consequences, a queer imagining. Such a connection means reanimating another, older, left image of the state. It means figuring the state, not only as an insidious propeller of gender normalization, but also as a vehicle for instantiating and supporting publicly diffused forms of human attachment and obligation. Indeed, it is with such an emphasis that a notion of "queer welfare studies" can be conceived as a useful rather than oxymoronic phrase. The state, it is important to remember, has a history of being figured not only as the seat of paternal, disciplinary, or capitalist authority but also as the vehicle for actualizing a social contract based in human interdependency. Like the effort to imagine queer kinship in our contemporary moment, such a model of the state is also important for the as yet unrealized possibility of imagining human interdependency as something that exceeds biological ties and that surpasses the obligatory network of the private nuclear family. Intriguingly, and to some perversely, it is in this imagined network of nonbiological obligation and extrafamilial connection that the social impulses of state welfare can start to look provocatively, and progressively, queer.

We cannot resituate the state's pursuit (or the pursuit of the state), however, unless we also contend with the essentializing effects of the maternal politics with which Addams has been aligned in certain strains of feminism as well as with the normalizing effects of the state criticized by liberal, feminist, conservative, libertarian, queer radical, and radically right thinkers alike. To do so, I focus my attention on Jean Bethke Elshtain's recent book on Jane Addams, particularly as I see it refracted through Elshtain's earlier feminist scholarship in *Public Man, Private Woman*.[3] My interest here is to consider feminism's ability to foreground the intensely contingent, micro, affective, and (after Charlene Haddock Seigfried) "pragmatic" domains with which kinship and domestic knowledge is traditionally associated.[4] However, I am equally concerned to address the untoward consequences of certain deployments of categories such as "woman" or "family" or "mother" and to resist prescriptive assessments of how domestic lives, familial lives, parental lives, or women's lives should be instituted. In returning this doubled approach back to issues of the state, I will argue for a more situated understanding of state welfare, questioning liberal, conservative, and feminist critiques of its heartless institutionalization *and* antiessentialist critiques of its gendered normalization. Again, I think that an unsettled interpretation of Jane Addams's unsettled life elicits reflection on these conundrums, central as they are to the articulation of a relationship amongst queer theory, the legacies of feminism, and the socialized operations of public welfare.

Earlier, I suggested the need to reanimate an older left model of the state; however, the suggestion bears reflection about exactly why that model is less than animate in our contemporary moment. The suspiciousness of state involvement in matters of family and childhood are well known in a contemporary U.S. context where constituencies affiliated with the right argue against the intervention of "big government" in private matters. That critique is largely expressed as a concern for "taxpayers' money" and for what in the 1990s was called the "culture of dependency" that such programs ostensibly produce. The critique of state intrusion is not only a habit of the right, however, for other left-allied thinkers are also suspicious of state operations, though on quite different grounds. Feminist historians and theorists such as Mimi Abramovitz, Nancy Fraser, Linda Gordon, Wendy Brown, and Kathy Ferguson have been concerned with the way that the inherited liberal, capitalist, paternalist, and bureaucratic dimensions of the state carried gendered assumptions that actually hampered rather than enabled gender equity.[5] These and other scholars argued that, whether by naturalizing the concept of the private family, by instituting family wage policies that reinforced the notion of the male breadwinner, by construing reproductive labor as something other than productive, or by feminizing the bureaucratic implementations of state power, what Brown calls the "man in the state" could directly and indirectly neutralize the feminist possibilities of federal redress.[6] While the work of Michel Foucault influenced some of these feminist critiques, his intellectual histories have also galvanized the equally strong if somewhat differently inflected suspicions of the state that appear in poststructuralist queer theory. Spurred by Foucault's excavations of the state and prison apparatus, by his historical critiques of sexual normalization, and by his identification of the network of nonstate public operations he called "governmentality," a variety of critical theorists in the humanities and social sciences have become concerned with the "productive" effects of power. Scholars such as Michael Warner, Lauren Berlant, Lee Edelman, and Judith Butler particularly seek to understand the paradoxical ways that juridical and governmental systems can have the effect of standardizing the persons and experiences that they "help," requiring normative and normalizing discourses that define and delimit human categories in order to recognize, provide for, and evaluate them.[7] Wendy Brown, one of the figures whose work crosses the domains of both feminist political theory and queer theory, co-wrote an introduction to *Left Legalism/Left Critique* with Janet Halley that outlines the Foucaultian concern succinctly: "Whereas 'liberals' treat identities as mechanisms for voicing injustice that the state must recognize and repair, from [our] left perspective, identities are double-edged: they can be crucial sites of belonging and political mobilization, but they can also be important vehicles of domination through regulation."[8] This tacit and insidious form of domination, so central to a Foucaultian understanding of power, has been fundamental to a left-allied, poststructuralist critique of sexuality. In the strains of queer theory that have been particularly concerned with this question, the state is largely figured as a diffuse but pervasive force in sexual normalization. Its operations, therefore, should be resisted. In Judith Butler's discussion of kinship (reprinted also in Brown and Halley's collection), for example, she offers a strong argument in favor of this resistance by using the example of "gay marriage." Butler's concern is that gays and lesbians who seek state sanction for same-sex partnership under the marriage law are at risk of becoming newly vulnerable to the state's regulatory operations.

> The petition for marriage rights seeks to solicit state recognition for nonheterosexual unions, and so configures the state as withholding an entitlement that it really should distribute in a nondiscriminatory way, regardless of sexual orientation. That the state's offer might result in the intensification of normalization is not widely recognized as a problem within the mainstream lesbian and gay movement, typified by the Human Rights Campaign. The normalizing powers of the state are made especially clear, however, when we consider how continuing quandaries about kinship both condition and limit the marriage debates.... Variations on kinship that depart from normative, dyadic heterosexually based family forms secured through the marriage vow are figured not only as dangerous for the child, but perilous to the putative natural and cultural laws said to sustain human intelligibility.[9]

The danger here is that the privileges and recognition that might come from the state's involvement in same-sex marriage in turn come with varieties of prescription and standardization. A moment that might seem to open up conventional definitions of attachment and belonging will in fact enforce more conventions—based in "dyadic heterosexually based family forms"—into this space of alternate imagining.

Nearly one hundred years ago, Jane Addams and her coterie of Hull House activists began what contemporary theorists might retroactively construe as a similarly dangerous bargain with the state. Having worked to give discursive and structural power to a number of issues that pressed heavily on the lives of their neighbors, particularly those involving issues of immigration, labor, and women's rights, Hull House residents worked continuously on a number of overlapping fronts that affected the so-called private lives of children and their parents. From juvenile justice to public health to public child care, these activists sought ways of alleviating the stresses, economic deprivations, and health dangers that affected the lives of working parents and their children. The difficulty of addressing such issues in the United States, then as now, revolved around the appropriateness of governmental involvement in matters deemed "private." Jane Addams remembered with frustration the ideological resistances to federalization.

> It became clear that the Federal Government could interest itself in agriculture and fisheries, but not in childhood. There was evidently confusion in the minds of many of our fellow countrymen between self-government and local government. Americans have thought for a long time—perhaps the idea is inherited from town meetings—that unless government is localized they do not exercise self-government at all. Such a conception, if persisted in, must narrow our notion of government and circumscribe our national life. We forget that politics are largely a matter of adjusted human relations through any unit of government which best serves the purpose. More and more, social workers, with thousands of other persons throughout the nation had increasingly felt the need . . . [to] make social reform a political issue of national dimensions.[10]

It was the strong belief of many of these reformers that matters of childhood in all their variety warranted the "adjusted human relations" that governmental interest could provide. Many of these activists were in fact not biological mothers but deployed an expediently "maternalist" discourse, one that would sound essentialist a century later. Indeed, discourses of "city housekeeping" and "mother's politics" propelled various efforts in domestic democracy where activists sought recognition and aid to support the social labor of women. With such hopes in mind, reformers and researchers endeavored to reach state and federal levels of influence on a number of fronts. It was with no small degree of pride that Hull House resident Julia Lathrop completed a study of and recommendations for addressing maternity health and compensation, introducing the plan with the sardonic humor of an ironic Progressive. "This document has been compiled in the hope that the information might prove useful to the people of one of the few great countries which as yet have no system of state or national assistance in maternity—the United States."[11] Lathrop herself was, by this point, the first director of the Children's Bureau, saddled with the task of creating a federal social service network that would provide the care necessary for the health and welfare of children and working families.

Of course, it has become clear to a variety of historians of social welfare—and clear, from a different perspective, to a variety of post-Foucauldian theorists of identity—that the bargain struck by Jane Addams, Julia Lathrop, and so many other domestically inspired reformers was, to echo Brown and Halley, "double-edged." To some, the federal government's "interest" in childhood became a means of disseminating prescriptions and censorships about what proper childhood entailed. Similarly, the "adjusted human relations" provided by a governmental interest in maternity came with new ideals and normalizations about how the maternal should be performed. In many cases and from several vantage points, the governmental interest in caring for families came with the price of instituting bounded familial models, those dyadic forms whose restriction Judith Butler would critique at the end of the twentieth century. Brown and Halley turn to a familiar figure to dramatize the argument.

> Although Foucault helpfully drew our attention to the ways that powers of regulation operate and regulate in extralegal or legal domains, he may have underestimated the degree to which the modern liberal state itself can operate as micropower. . . . "The law" . . . has incorporated the managerial, normativizing, regularizing biopoweristic forms that he proposed were distinguishable from the juridical form . . . now also [taking] the form of the Department of Youth Services worker who inspects your personal life in minute detail to decide whether you are a fit person to adopt your lover's child. This underpaid and overworked functionary, laden with forms that standardize good parenting, has his or her effects on you and on parenting more broadly not through rules about it but through mobile, shifting, highly momentary assessments.[12]

The biopoweristic form of the Youth Services worker serves as an emblem of the indiscrete invasion of the state, one where even well-intentioned adoption laws create the grounds for uncomfortable assessments of sexuality, parenting, and kinship performance. The encounter with what is now the state's "underpaid and overworked functionary" may sound quite familiar to readers of Jane Addams, for the kind of untoward scrutiny that Brown and Halley find in the state's practice is quite similar to the one

Addams criticized in charity practice. Indeed, Addams's potent dramatization of the politics of "friendly-visiting" of poor families—and the conflicted mindset of the "friendly visitor"—is one of her most quoted.

> The daintily clad charity visitor who steps into the little house made untidy by the vigorous efforts of her hostess, the washerwoman, is no longer sure of her superiority to the latter. . . . She is often embarrassed to find herself obliged to lay all the stress of her teaching and advice upon the industrial virtues. . . . She insists that they must work and be self-supporting, that the most dangerous of all situations is idleness, that seeking one's pleasure, while ignoring claims and responsibilities, is the most ignoble of actions. . . . As she daily holds up these standards, it often occurs to the mind of the sensitive visitor, whose conscience has been made tender by much talk of brotherhood and equality, that she has no right to say these things; that her untrained hands are no more fitted to cope with actual conditions than those of her broken-down family.[13]

Even as a contemporary reader might be chagrined to find similar practices of assessment and judgment—whether of work ethic or of sexual normativity—across these historical moments, it is worth noting that Addams's involvement with Hull House was in part an attempt to take relations of "care" out of this kind of charity model. Hull House and the settlement movement were attempts to create a more reciprocal sphere of interpersonal engagement across class lines, one where life instruction and personal transformation happened in more than one direction. Addams and fellow settlers, however, soon felt that they needed to turn to civic and state power in order to actualize this goal, for settlers found that a highly local focus on interpersonal ethics could not compensate for systemic inequities of gender, ethnicity, age, and class. Addams's quest for a redefinition of government was thus based on the desire to institute provisions for all citizens and to do so without recourse to what she and others found to be the undemocratic "relation which obtains between benefactor and beneficiary." The turn to government occurred after she and fellow settlers realized that such "adjusted human relations" required intervention at the macrolevel of federal structure as much as the microlevel of private ethics. Indeed, the effects of poverty, prejudice, and gendered labor practices demonstrated again and again that so-called macro-

and microspheres, so-called public and private realms, were intimately entangled with each other. The contemporary paradox now is that such a well-intentioned progressive vision of the state has morphed to justify the insidious appearance of the "Youth Services worker" in the present. Is that appearance a sign of what remains of the United State's welfare state's progressive social contract? Or is that appearance of the State at Your Door a sign of state normalization in Halley and Brown's terms? In the different answers to these questions, we have an exemplary instance of mutual distrust between the domain of social welfare studies and the thought structures of poststructuralist queer theory. Hence, it is at such a moment that I want to suggest that an alternate remembering is in order. Without endorsing the practices of assessment or the standards used by this invasive state functionary, I think that it is equally important for left-allied thinkers in queer theory and poststructuralist political theory more generally to remember the broader systemic impulses that brought the Youth Services to our door as well as the feminist critique of public and private that she has the potential still to supply. A more capacious understanding of social welfare and domestic democracy is central to imagining a relational model of subjectivity and extended kinship for both critical welfare studies and queer theory; it is also central to countering the hyper-individualist impulses that currently and oddly appear in both right and left critiques of governmental intrusion.

I would like now to take this kind of reflection back to the historiography on Jane Addams and Hull House in order to see how an orientation toward queer welfare studies adjusts our view of Addams as well as certain habits of critical reflection in feminism, welfare history, and queer theory. Questions of history, theory, publicity, gender, and sexuality are at issue in the attempt to train one's attention on domestic life at Hull House, as Jane Addams indirectly elaborated it in her own writing but also as it was practiced in the highly encumbered, embodied, and spatially innovative life of the settlement. As most readers of this volume know, the settlement endeavor differed in method from other philanthropic efforts of the time in that its reformers moved into the neighborhoods it sought to help. Hull House residents and their colleagues throughout the nation followed an ethic of radical locality, choosing to spend all hours of work, living, and leisure within the spaces it sought to change. I think that there is a certain kind of theoretical opportunity—particularly an opportunity for theories of sexuality—in the attempt to analyze the settling processes of the settlement. While earlier sexual historiographical questions might have focused on "whether Jane Addams was a lesbian," recent scholarship on queer theory has focused its lens less on recovering bounded instances of gay and lesbian identity; instead, it investigates the structures by which subjectivity is provisionally constituted in order to isolate the instabilities of apparently "normal" and normalizing social spheres. Such a sensibility provides a useful starting point for interrogating Hull House practice, asking us to think about how what Beatrice Webb called its "higgledy-piggledy" social life created an alternate kind of social sphere.[14] As I have argued elsewhere, settling at Hull House was a daily lesson in undoing gendered and classed conventions of privacy and publicity, providing a material plane that actuated and was actuated by the movement of people who patently and tacitly redefined their lives. It is here that a queer theoretical approach to Hull House space proves useful, asking us to see something conceptually generative in its contradictions and its movement. Hull House's queer domesticity, fragile and provisional as it was, finds a suitably complicated analytic in the kind of frame that Judith Butler offers for the study of queer kinship and its less than intelligible manifestations.

> Even within the field of intelligible sexuality, one finds that the binaries that anchor its operations permit for middle zones. . . . These are not precisely places where one can choose to hang out, subject positions one might opt to occupy. These are nonplaces in which one finds oneself in spite of oneself. . . . They are not sites of enunciation, but shifts in the topography from which a questionably audible claim emerges: the claim of the not-yet-subject and the nearly recognizable. That there are such regions, and that they are not precisely options, suggest that what troubles the distinction between legitimacy and illegitimacy are social practices, specifically sexual practices, that do not appear immediately coherent in the available lexicon of legitimation.[15]

Indeed, the social and domestic practices of Hull House have not always been "immediately coherent in the available lexicon of legitimation." Contemporaneous outsiders called the settlement "unnatural," worrying that its women were "spinsters" or that its men were "mollycoddles." More recently, contemporary scholars have worked to make sense of the settlement within available normative terms such as *home, woman, family,* and *mother* or within available counter-normative terms such as *commune, feminist, lesbian*, or *activist*. By attending to the nonplace of the settlement as a "shift in the topography" of available subjectivities, however, we come instead to a better sense of the significance of its lived character. Rather than using available terms as critical barometers with which to measure deviation, we can conceive Hull House space as a generative region if not exactly a fixed "option," thereby allowing us to see the unsettling of terms such as *family, kinship, welfare*, and *the state*, even when such redefinition was not self-consciously foregrounded.

That redefinition, for instance, meant adapting to an alternate spatial style, allowing the inherited formality of the Hull mansion's parlors, dining rooms, and bedrooms to be disrupted by the continual reentry of children, adolescents, working women, immigrants, and varieties of neighbors.[16] Residents learned to write up urban reports in the middle of a house filled with children's social clubs. Bedroom spaces became receiving spaces with an addition of extra chairs; bedroom spaces became storage spaces when the settlement's theater director housed all of her costumes and props in her room. New social rituals were created to facilitate a public household; residents shared the responsibility of waiting at the door to receive expected but mostly unexpected visitors. Hull House's ongoing social redefinition also meant adapting or retreating when the disruption was too much, when it felt too crowded, or too loud, or, as one resident complained, when "the bell kept ringing." At these and other more discouraging moments, residents worried that the social claims of urban life were too overwhelming or that, as one resident lamented, "we were trying to sweep back the tide with a broom."[17] That spatial redefinition also supported and was supported by a redefinition of kinship that settling women and men performed in the hallways, kitchens, and gathering spaces of the settlement. Many who opted out of traditional heterosexual marriage formed same-sex bonds of attachment with fellow "Sister-Settlers" as well as bold, mutually supporting, and only occasionally romantic heterosexual attachments with sibling "Brothers."[18] It meant forming bonds of attachment to hundreds of children who were not biological offspring, whether in a children's health clinic, a children's art class, or in the free child care offered in the settlement living room. Settlers argued, shared meals, and distributed household tasks while juggling their commitments as labor leaders, teachers, club leaders, urban analysts, scientists, and policy writers. Indeed, this "plan of living which may be called cooperative," as Jane Addams roundaboutly phrased it, seemed necessary to act on the public mission of Hull House.[19] Such a realization comes when reckoning with the very public doings of this previously private house, in reading stories and letters of sensory disruption and transformation in the settlement's living rooms, dining rooms, bedrooms, bridges, and relocated front doors. Hull House's complexly shifting topography not only disrupts the available lexicons of publicity and privacy but threatens to expose the instability of that binary in apparently stable forms of family, home, kinship, and state welfare as well.

To bring this domain of Jane Addams's life back to a critique of feminist and queer studies, I would like now to turn to Jean Bethke Elshtain's recently published study of Jane Addams, *Jane Addams and the Dream of American Democracy: A Life*. Elshtain's work provides a useful place from which to link Jane Addams to debates within gender studies, for Elshtain has been a key figure in feminist political theory more generally. Elshtain's groundbreaking *Public Man, Private Woman* was intent upon articulating a feminist politics that acknowledged the limits placed upon women by their association with the private but took issue with a feminist politics that, in Elshtain's view, was in danger of forfeiting the pleasures and dismissing the importance of maintaining a bounded private sphere. For Elshtain, this was also an epistemological issue. It was about valuing knowledges of the particular and the concrete, rather than the "rational" and the "abstract" that were the traditional orientation of a Western, masculinist intellectual perspective. "Why should a personalized, localized, particular female subject be brought into the more abstract, rationalized, universal mode? . . . The private world also exudes its own values and imperatives in part because it is the theater of particularity and everyday concrete meaning. If that mode were suppressed altogether in favor of the exigencies and demands of abstract personhood and the pull towards rationalization, . . . who would tend to the little world, keeping alive its life-redeeming joys and tragedies?"[20] For her, feminist thinkers were in danger of remarginalizing the care of that "little world" in a way that perpetuated rather than challenged the perceptions of their male philosophical forebears. Hence, Simone de Beauvoir received as formidable a critique from Elshtain as did a canon of white male figures culled from the history of Western intellectual thought.

Interestingly, a very similar kind of analytic orientation can be found in Elshtain's 2002 biography of Jane Addams. In Elshtain's chapter titles, such as "The Family Claim and the Social Claim," "Compassion Without Condescension," and "Women's Remembering Heart," Addams's vocabulary mixes with Elshtain's earlier concepts to argue for the relevance of the so-called private realm in the upkeep of and reformation of the public. Addams's concepts of city housekeeping are invoked throughout these chapters. Within American feminist history, of course, Addams is recognized for her writings on city housekeeping where she defined women's involvement in public life as an extension rather than as a violation of their traditional domestic roles. This was Addams's strategic, and rhetorically deferential, contribution to the suffrage movement and to a longer tradition of domestic democracy, arguing for the vote as a means for women to sustain rather than to violate their traditional roles as nurturers of the health and cleanliness of the community. Indeed, along with her study of charity workers cited above, Addams's stories of the role of women in reforming the inequities of garbage collection, of contaminated milk supplies, and of unsanitary housing are some of her most memorable. Addams deploys such stories in her arguments for city housekeeping to rationalize women's public participation on behalf of issues that, because of their systemic dependence upon governmental operations, were improperly understood as stably private. Elshtain rechronicles many of these stories as well, though she is more interested in using those stories to celebrate the "private" world than she is in unsettling divisions between public and private. What is, I think, more uncertain is where Elshtain locates the discursive origin of Addams's thoughts on the relation between private and public. "What Addams insists upon is that the female body—most important, the maternal female body—is the central image of social generativity and fecundity. Clearly, one need not be a mother in the biological sense—although she found this the most vital of human activities—in order to locate oneself with this image."[21] This image, Elshtain argues, served as the foundation for Addams's imagining of a new body politic, a society of what Elshtain calls, quoting John O'Neill, "familied contexts" that held up the maternal body as the basis for their own social generativity. If there is a fixation on the maternal body in all its corporeality and "fecundity" in Addams's writing, Elshtain's book does not offer a quotation. The fact that this biography does not see the need to testifies, I think, to a slip in an argument that wants to foreground the world of contingency but ends up essentializing the bodies of the female figures who historically have managed it.

In part, my concern with this move is that Elshtain's argument ignores the rhetorical expediency of "city housekeeping" as an expediently self-deferential argument; by telling citizens that female publicity could be a continuation rather than a violation of gendered roles, city housekeepers made use of a strategic essentialism whose public incarnation actually involved behaviors that were far from traditional and that kept them outside of the walls of the "house." There is related concern, however, that to me is more urgent for my argument. I am concerned about the way that Elshtain's valuation of the private ends up fortifying its boundaries, indirectly normalizing its contents, and, moreover, standardizing proper conceptions of the feminine, the family, and the maternal along with it. Indeed, it seems that this is a place where Elshtain's analysis of Jane Addams bears the burden of reinforcing her earlier arguments in *Public Man, Private Woman*. That burden in turn produces blind spots around her analysis of Hull House's own domestic practices on the microscale as well as the involvement of Hull House in social welfare on the macroscale. Elshtain's caveat that one "need not be a biological mother" too cavalierly bypasses the limits placed on some people's full identification with this image. Indeed, a psychoanalytic frame joined to a social analysis would foreground the partiality of *anyone's* complete identification with such an image, note the politics of that partiality, and elaborate the dangers of its disavowal. While I would not suggest that queer theory has a purchase on this kind of analytic, I would suggest that it is that kind of question that theorists of sexuality would want to ask. Because Jane Addams was not a biological mother who simultaneously made use of a kind of maternal rhetoric, the partiality of her alignment seems particularly important. It is in that space between the regulating image and the daily practices of individuals—a "shift in the topography" that does "not appear immediately coherent in the available lexicon of legitimation"— that alternate conceptions of parenthood, family, and social formation can be gleaned, if not exactly legitimated. Indeed, Elshtain's invocation of the "maternal body" in Addams's thought (without a citation of the maternal body in Addams's thought) seems to be an exemplary instance of an "available lexicon" being imposed upon a practice and a person whose place in the topography of family and sexual politics is not as easily fixed.

It is with this sense of possibility in mind that we might return to the everyday practices of the settlement; here, Hull House's daily performances of domesticity become, not only methodological interesting, but also politically weighted. To examine the internals of Hull House is to see the spaces of public and private redefined in several directions and on different scales. As my brief account of the redefinition of spatial styles and cooperative living suggested, the "settling" process of the settlement reflected the need not simply for an extension beyond the domestic sphere (e.g., garbage collecting and suffrage) but also a reciprocal undoing of the domestic sphere (e.g., household duties and kinship bonding). That is, the externalized maternality of city housekeeping simultaneously required an internalized sociality within the household sphere. This undoing produced a space of everyday life that was intriguingly unsettled, with doors opening, bells ringing, and chairs moving as the push and pull of settlement practice dictated. As noted above, Hull House settlers cultivated relationships of various kinds—same-sex attachment and identification (Jane Addams and Mary Rozet Smith being the most famous), mixed-sex romantic attachment (amongst several male and female residents), fictive kinship between metaphoric "Sister-Settlers" and later "Brothers" (who called each other "Sister Kelley, Sister Lathrop, Brother Twose"), committed attachment between children and non-biological parental surrogates (Florence Kelley's children being an early example).[22] This kind of everyday life defused and rerouted intimate attachment onto an alternate familial plane, one that resisted heteronormativity without necessarily falling into the presentist categories of homosexual identity. My interest in the queerness of Hull House's queer domesticity thus has to do with how non-normative formations of what was often called a "family" by its inhabitants occurred in a space of varied intimate alignments between and amongst the sexes and between and amongst biological and nonbiological parents, children, and siblings.

To incorporate this provocative "region" into a discussion of city housekeeping is thus to expand the reach of the concept. It is to show domesticity as something that is both extended publicly but also reworked privately. It is also to allow the value of the epistemologically particular and concrete (Elshtain's "little world") to be shared by different domains and persons, not always biological mothers and not always women. While there might be several ways to explain the reluctance of Elshtain's biography to contend with the full history of the settlement, I want to address the oversight by pursuing another tack that further addresses tensions in gender studies. For if, as I suggested, the extension of the domestic sphere also requires its reciprocal undoing, then it is this latter part of the equation that Elshtain's feminist political theory cannot abide. It is precisely the ability of Hull House reformers to imagine systemic connection and obligation outside of blood family ties—i.e., social welfare—that Elshtain's analysis seems unwilling to track. Let me return to her earlier critiques of feminist theorizing in *Public Man, Private Woman*, where she writes, "The past fifteen years have seen a number of visions of family-less, asocial existence celebrated. These have taken several forms, including one in which, not having biological nuclear families, all individuals, including children, would be 'free' to look for the best contractual deal in living arrangements."[23] In an argument that defines feminism within a classically liberal distrust of the threat to private autonomy, she criticizes the contemporaneous commune experiments of the sixties and seventies as having a similarly flawed understanding of freedom. Additionally, "institutional" forms of child care—presumably those that occur in social service agencies—receive a blow. Modes of institutional child care that call themselves "familial," Elshtain writes, use only "hollow, sentimentalized repetition of terms for family relations—'brother,' 'sister' 'family.'"[24] She continues, "To call some abstract structure, or a loose collection of like-minded, unrelated peers 'families' is to treat our most basic human relationships frivolously."[25] Using the failure and exhaustion of social experiments on the fringes and on the federal level as proof against possible alternatives, she argues, "It is the family that constitutes our 'common humanity.'. . . This makes the family 'the universal basis of human culture. . . . As language constitutes the essence of man as a species, and not reason, so the family and not the social order is the setting that humanizes him.'"[26]

I would not myself want to oversentimentalize the practices of the like-minded peers who called themselves a family at a Hull House. Nor would I want to ignore the difficulty and exhaustion that they endured in the maintenance of this sphere. However, I do think that we need a more complex analytic in order to recognize and interpret the fullness of these peoples' very full lives. I think that we need to value the rituals by which biologically unrelated persons formed a relation, and I think that we need terms other than "hollow" and "frivolous" to characterize them. Elshtain's rhetoric provides little to help us understand, for instance, the expressions of emotion that can be found in the letters of settlers who tended to children who were not biological offspring, an attachment that is as clear in Dr. Alice Hamilton's descriptions of her work with settler and neighborhood children ("He stood the cauterizing in a way that made me feel like crying") as it is in Jane Addams and Mary Rozet Smith's poignant conversations around a Jane Club resident's decision to give up her child for adoption ("My heart quaked when I first had it definitely fixed in my mind").[27] Nor does it help us account for how the settlement as an institution provided hundreds of children with a sense of kinship. To recognize the affective world of this "institution" would not ignore the partiality—what Elshtain calls the "looseness"—of these relations but rather use that partiality to allow the family, the maternal, and the child to be the basis for our most complicated theorizing rather than the basis for our most unchallenged prescription. That kind of complexity has been a persistent goal in queer studies, where, before and after Kath Weston, same-sex partnerships have prompted a necessary investigation of the character, nature, reach, and limits of having "families we choose."[28] As such, it is one place where Jane Addams's life and career can help us reflect more generally on some key debates in the fields of gender studies. The supposed contradictions of her historical example can help us to think with more openness and precision about the principles of feminism and sexuality. They also help us to imagine a queer welfare studies based in shared systems for promoting an ethics of extended kinship.

A similar kind of blind spot can be turned to opportunity when it comes to Jane Addams's equivocal position in the formation of social welfare. Again, the fact that the precepts of city housekeeping also contributed to a discourse behind the formation of this large state apparatus is largely ignored in Elshtain's book. Given the tendency in Elshtain's earlier work to criticize such "institutional" formations for their erosion of the family, this is consistent. Once again, however, I think that those contemporary individuals who devote themselves to working within the field of social service—Brown and Halley's "overworked functionaries"—and those scholars who devote themselves to historicizing its predicament need a more complicated and hospitable analytic to make sense of their work. They need something more than accusations of "hollowness" from certain feminists, and they need more than unremarked indifference from the intellectual biography of one of social welfare's most pivotal historical figures. Jane Addams's original interest in the intensely local micropractices of neighborly interaction cannot neutralize the fact that Hull House played a role in the formation of a more diffuse, macro-oriented system of public welfare. Some of us—and I would include myself—are perhaps more interested and more skilled in interpreting the local and intimate practices of settling than the federal processes of social servicing. Nevertheless, it seems important that our shared paradigms allow a conversation between these scales rather than foster more defensiveness between them. Elshtain's earlier argument against the frivolous, institutional, and loose redefinition of the family only exemplifies Judith Butler's claim that "variations on kinship that depart from normative, dyadic heterosexually based family forms secured through the marriage vow are figured not only as dangerous for the child, but perilous to the putative natural and cultural laws said to sustain human intelligibility."[29] While Butler's critique is directed at "the normalizing powers of the state," the example of Elshtain's analysis shows that criticism of variation is also possible within certain strains of feminism. Placing them together forces attention on the fact that same-sex partnership might not be the only castigated "variation" but that the operations of public institutions of care—i.e. social welfare—often receive similar castigations of abnormality and unnatural violation. Indeed, as much as the state figures in left critique and queer theory as an insidious vehicle of familial normalization (as I noted in my opening paragraphs), it is just as likely to receive criticism from the right and from liberal feminists for being a violation of the family as "our most basic human relationship." It is the prevalence of a strangely similar argument from so many sides of the political spectrum that makes queer welfare studies so hard to sustain. From some quarters, social welfare is a scandalous vehicle of familial denormalization; from others, it is a scandalous vehicle of familial renormalization. The public institutionalization of care across nonbiological lines—my tax dollars for your children, my psychic allegiance for your regulating society—cannot quite get support from anywhere in the United States. Jane Addams and Hull House, however, occupy an intriguingly liminal position in this overdetermined critical topography. Her example is a reminder that the system of social welfare is part of a complicated genealogy that is associated as much with the denormalization of nuclear family bonding as it is with the family's oppressive renaturalization. By remembering that social welfare and queer studies both promote a model of extended kinship, we have the potential for an interdisciplinary allegiance that can not only do a better job of remembering the radicality of Jane Addams's life, but do a better job of promoting queer welfare studies as a generative space of social imagining.

My thoughts in this essay focused mostly upon how debates within feminism, sexuality, and queer theory help to unsettle Jane Addams. By way of conclusion, I would like also to reflect further in the reverse direction, that is, on how an unsettled Jane Addams speaks back to these fields. If Hull House and Jane Addams can elicit methodological innovation from queer theory, then the same goes for queer theory's political significance as well. What I find particularly significant is an undertheorized connection between Hull House's queer domesticity and the larger kinds of social unsettling for which it is better known. The conventional history of social welfare questions the role of such "abnormal" women in the history of social welfare. How could such women—most unmarried, most not biological parents—guide a system that attends explicitly to the cultivation of families and of children? A more generous answer to the question could suggest that there is a relation between micro redefinitions of family and the macroformation of state welfare. Given that queer theorists such as Lisa Duggan, Judith Butler, Wendy Brown, and others have worked recently to translate the psychoanalytic operations of queer subjectivity to larger public spheres, Hull House enables links to micro- and macrodomains. To take this connection seriously, however, would be to resist some convenient prejudices, to be willing to see, for instance, public welfare as something more than "a force of normalization" (from queer theorists) or just another "abstract structure" (from liberal feminists). Indeed, if the practitioners of social welfare are merely "functionaries"— whether "hollow" or "insidious"—in the work of Halley and Brown *and* in the work of Jean Bethke Elshtain, then we have an odd alignment that renders the important philosophical differences amongst and between these thinkers obscure. To take the possibility of queer welfare studies seriously would also require a more subtle analysis of what counts as "nonnormative" and a willingness to see it even in women who look, to presentist eyes, somewhat conventional. If queer theory has been somewhat ahistorical in its objects and in its approaches, then Jane Addams and Hull House offer the challenge of interpreting queer subjectivities that did not always overtly "resist," that rarely cross-dressed, and that spoke sentences that sounded the maternal discourses of their times. That these same individuals argued for care and nonphilanthropic obligation beyond blood ties, that they rarely had biological children but were never "childless," suggests that they occupied one of those less than legible topographies to which Judith Butler refers. A cautious approach to the understanding of this zone exposes similarly ambivalent zones within the history of families and the histories of state welfare, both of which are now too quickly bounded for easy celebration or easy vilification from several directions—some conservative, some liberal feminist, and some queer left. Through such methodological and conceptual experiments, however, we might come to a better understanding of a tacit, formative, and undertheorized connection between queer politics and domestic politics, between a queer critique of sexuality and a left imagining of social welfare.

Notes

1. Licia Fiol-Matta, *A Queer Mother for the Nation: The State and Gabriela Mistral* (Minneapolis: University of Minnesota Press, 2002).
2. Shannon Jackson, *Lines of Activity: Performance, Historiography, Hull House Domesticity* (Ann Arbor: University of Michigan Press, 2000).
3. Jean Bethke Elshtain, *Jane Addams and the Dream of American Democracy: A Life* (New York: Basic Books, 2002); Elshtain, *Public Man, Private Woman: Women in Social and Political Thought* (Princeton: Princeton University Press, 1981).
4. Charlene Haddock Seigfried, *Pragmatism and Feminism: Reweaving the Social Fabric* (Chicago: University of Chicago Press, 1996).
5. Mimi Abramovitz, *Regulating the Lives of Women: Social Welfare Policy from Colonial Times to the Present*, rev. ed. (Boston: South End Press, 1996); Nancy Fraser, *Justice Interruptus: Critical Reflections on the "Postsocialist" Condition* (New York: Routledge, 1997); Linda Gordon and Nancy Fraser, "A Genealogy of Dependency," *Signs* 19 (1994): 309–36; Wendy Brown, *States of Injury: Power and Freedom in Late Modernity* (Princeton: Princeton University Press, 1995); Kathy Ferguson, *The Feminist Case Against Bureaucracy* (Philadelphia: Temple University Press, 1984).
6. Brown, *States of Injury*, 166.
7. Judith Butler, *The Psychic Life of Power: Theories in Subjection* (Stanford, Calif.: Stanford University Press, 1997); Lauren Berlant, *The Queen of America Goes to Washington City: Essays on Sex and Citizenship* (Durham: Duke University Press, 1997); Michael Warner, ed., *Fear of a Queer Planet: Queer Politics and Social Theory* (Minneapolis: University of Minnesota Press, 1993); Lee Edelman, *No Future: Queer Theory and the Death Drive* (Durham: Duke University Press, 2004).
8. Wendy Brown and Janet Halley, "Introduction," in *Left Legalism/Left Critique*, ed. Wendy Brown and Janet Halley (Durham: Duke University Press, 2002), 7.
9. Judith Butler, "Is Kinship Always Already Heterosexual?" in *Left Legalism/Left Critique*, ed. Wendy Brown and Janet Halley (Durham: Duke University Press, 2002), 231.
10. Jane Addams, *The Second Twenty Years at Hull House, September 1909 to September 1929, with a Record of Growing World Consciousness* (New York: The Macmillan Company, 1930), 23.
11. Julia Lathrop, "Letter of Transmission," in H. Harris, *Maternity Benefits Systems in Certain Foreign Countries*, U.S. Children's Bureau Bulletin 57 (Washington, D.C., 1919), 2.
12. Brown and Halley, "Introduction," 13–14.
13. Jane Addams, *Democracy and Social Ethics* (Champaign: University of Illinois Press, 2002), 14, 16, 17–18.
14. Beatrice Webb, *Beatrice Webb's American Diary, 1898* (repr., Madison: University of Wisconsin Press, 1963), 107.
15. Butler, "Kinship?" 235.
16. Jackson, *Lines of Activity*, 37–94, 147–202.
17. Jackson, *Lines of Activity*, 186.
18. Jackson, *Lines of Activity*, 164–87.
19. Jackson, *Lines of Activity*, 187.
20. Elshtain, *Public Man, Private Woman*, 305.
21. Elshtain, *Jane Addams*, 160.
22. Jackson, *Lines of Activity*, 147–202.

23. Elshtain, *Public Man, Private Woman*, 325.
24. Elshtain, *Public Man, Private Woman*, 330.
25. Elshtain, *Public Man, Private Woman*, 331.
26. Elshtain, *Public Man, Private Woman*, 327.
27. Jackson, *Lines of Activity*, 163, 170.
28. Kath Weston, *Families We Choose: Lesbians, Gays, Kinship*, rev. ed. (New York: Columbia University Press, 1997).
29. Judith Butler, "Is Kinship Always Heterosexual?" *Difference: A Journal of Feminist Cultural Studies* 13, no. 1 (2002): 16.

7

Love on Halsted Street

A Contemplation on Jane Addams

Louise W. Knight

In 1980 lesbian poet Adrienne Rich looked at American history and saw a gaping hole. She wanted to know "how and why women's choice of women as passionate comrades, life partners, co-workers, lovers, tribe, has been crushed, invalidated, forced into hiding and disguised." She called for scholars to deal with lesbian experience as "[natural] and a reality, and as a source of knowledge and power available to women."[1]

During the past twenty-eight years, that gaping hole has begun to be filled. Historians Lillian Faderman, Carroll Smith-Rosenberg, Estelle Freedman, John D'Emilio, and Blanche Wiesen Cook, among others, have re-researched and reinterpreted the history and brought it into print. Some of their work deals with the white upper-middle-class women social reformers of the nineteenth and twentieth centuries who had romantic female life partners; those studied include Jane Addams, Anna Howard Shaw, Carrie Chapman Catt, Frances Willard, Frances Kellor, M. Carey Thomas, and Mary Emma Woolley. In her book *To Believe in Women*, Lillian Faderman tells their stories for a general audience.[2] The stories of working-class lesbians are also coming to the light, thanks to the fine work of Allan Bérubé, Madeline D. Davis, Elizabeth Lapovsky Kennedy, and, most recently, Anne Enke.[3]

And what of the physical side of these partnerships? In researching the intimate relations of late nineteenth-century upper-middle-class female reformers, historians have found plenty of evidence that they slept together and hugged and kissed, but often no unambiguous evidence survives of sexual contact. May we still call these women "lesbian"? Some say no, because the term and the identity did not exist during much of their lifetimes. If we set that historiographical issue aside, there are two benefits to including romantic nonsexual relations in definitions of lesbian relations. For one thing, the inclusive definition highlights the deeper dimensions of same-sex attachment and identity that lesbianism is also about. For another, it increases the honesty of society's conversation about the nature of intimate love. For is it not the case that heterosexual love, as many people live it, sometimes loses its sexual dimension? Yet that fact is hardly discussed and it is more or less taboo to do so. Perhaps the gay and lesbian communities can help the straight community, as they often have before, by speaking the truth that straight people do not want to hear.

Was Jane Addams a lesbian in either sense? I would like to take up that question in a broader context: what was the place of love in her life and thought? It seems to me that Addams thought about, and explored, three functions of love: intimate love; affectionate, cooperative love; and love of humanity, sometimes called love of the stranger. She experienced romantic intimate love with two woman partners—Ellen Gates Starr and Mary Rozet Smith. While the partnership with Starr lasted only six years, they may well have expected it to be a lifetime commitment. The partnership with Smith began just as the one with Starr was ending. Jane Addams was thirty-three and Smith twenty-four. The relationship lasted forty years, until Mary's death in 1934.[4] She experienced affectionate, cooperative love through her political activism. For decades she worked with men and women trade union leaders, union members, club members, social workers, clergy, and others to advance women's suffrage; end child labor; improve worker and immigrant rights; and promote civil rights, free speech, and peace. And she experienced love of humanity as the lesson of her life at Hull House and as the vital spur to her work for social justice. When she was a youth, it was an ideal that her imagination seized on; when she was a young woman, it was a seemingly impossible goal to achieve; and when she was a mature adult, it was a rule of living, a guide to her every human interaction.

With these diverse meanings in mind, I believe that love was Jane Addams's most absorbing passion. She was one of those rare people who were thinking about the importance of love all the time—not always succeeding in being loving, of course, but steadily trying. In this chapter I will address all three functions of love but spend the most time on the first. I will also consider how various postmodern feminist theories might apply to these observations; how biographers have dealt with her love life, intimate and otherwise; and the price that is paid when that story is not told.

Romantic, Intimate Love

In our times, sexuality is intertwined with intimate love. But it has not always been thus. As John D'Emilio and Estelle Freedman explain in their fine work, *Intimate Matters*, "The dominant meaning of sexuality has changed during our history from a primary association with reproduction within families to a primary association with emotional intimacy and physical pleasure for individuals."[5] At the same time, the meaning of intimate love has also changed. Addams's experiences and views illustrate the kind of intimate love—highly spiritualized, disembodied—that she and many others of her background aspired to.

Of course, the question of Addams's sexuality remains. Whether she ever had sexual contact with anyone must always remain unknowable; she may have. While no evidence survives to prove it, that does not mean she did not. As D'Emilio has noted, firsthand accounts of past sexual experiences are rare. But perhaps we can make an educated guess about her sexuality based on what we know about her most intimate relations and what her attitudes toward sexuality were in general. I take up this question because it is of interest at present. But I suspect that fifty years from now our curiosity will seem a bit prurient. I have yet to read a biography of a straight man that dwelt much on his married sex life. (His affairs, of course, are another subject entirely.)

The first thing to note is that when Jane Addams was in her teens and early twenties she was not romantically interested in boys, or men, or in the idea of falling in love, period. She read many novels and wrote about them in letters but never mentioned any stories of love affairs she encountered. Addams had one boyfriend in her life that we know about, boyfriend at least from his point of view. His name was Rollin Salisbury, and he was a student of Beloit College, the men's school down the road, when Addams was at Rockford Seminary. Like Jane, he was editor of his school's college paper, his college's best orator, and valedictorian of his class. Soon after they both graduated in 1881, he proposed marriage and she turned him down.[6]

Whatever Addams thought of Salisbury, she was not generally sanguine about the benefits of marriage for women like her, who wanted to pursue careers. Toward the end of her life she wrote about the difficult, forced choice women of her generation had faced between marriage and a career. Men either "did not want . . . to marry women of the new type . . . or thought that women could not do both." She wanted the freedom to challenge herself and grow. She added with a touch of pride that career women in those earlier days possessed "pioneer qualities of character and sometimes the divine urge of intellectual hunger."[7] All her imagination and determination were channeled into her ambition. Indeed, she might easily have avoided all partnerships, even with a woman, all her life. Many of her closest friends did. They put their careers first, over their emotional lives.

In college and for some years after, Addams felt the same way. While girls at Rockford Seminary, like girls at other schools, often formed intense, romantic friendships, Jane did not. She did not approve of them. To her cousin, also away at school, she explained that she thought such crushes demeaning and said that she admired cold people.[8] When Addams became friends with Ellen Gates Starr in their freshman year at Rockford Female Seminary, they formed no schoolgirl crush. Their bond was primarily intellectual. They shared a love of reading, inquisitive and restless minds, a puzzled curiosity about religion, and a determination to become cultured young women. Ellen had to leave college after one year to earn her living as a teacher at a girls' school in Chicago, but the two friends kept up a correspondence about books and God and sometimes visited each other. That pattern continued after Addams graduated from college in 1881.

Temperamentally, the friends were opposites. Addams was described by her cousin as "cool," and it was meant as a compliment. Starr was passionate and wore her emotions on her sleeve. She sometimes had crushes on other women and longed for emotional intimacy in a way that Addams did not. Throughout much of her life Starr often mentioned in her letters, playfully, that she was falling in love with someone, usually a woman. Yet by 1887 the two had become close friends, and by 1888 they had decided to live their lives together.

What caused Addams to partner with Ellen? First there was the utter loneliness of her twenties, and her need to break free of the restraints of her family. But she also had come to realize that she needed the friendship of someone who believed in her ideas if she were to overcome her self-doubts and accomplish her dreams. After suffering from depression for several years after graduating from college, she wrote her stepbrother from Europe, "[I am becoming] more convinced all the time . . . [that] there are certain feelings and conclusions which can never be reached except in an atmosphere of affection and congeniality." Soon after she wrote Starr, "I am more convinced every day that friendship . . . is the main thing in life." A few years later she would express her belief that close friendships were essential to her intellectual development. She wrote, "Intellectual life requires for its expansion . . . the influence of the affection of others."[9]

Her friendship with Ellen began to deepen in 1885, soon after Jane returned from Europe. They spent a week together, and afterward they were more openly loving and devoted to each other in their letters. Two years later, Ellen was the first person Jane Addams told about her vague dream to start a settlement house. They were traveling together with friends in Europe at the time, and Addams was feeling depressed that she had agreed to take the trip instead of acting upon her dream. Finally, she told Ellen, and to her great relief, Ellen's excitement about her idea made it seem, suddenly, "convincing and tangible."[10] Ellen agreed on the spot to join her in the adventure. They decided to lead this new settlement life together in the spirit of social Christianity, to which they were both devoted. We can hear that commitment in what Jane wrote to Ellen soon after: "Let us love each other through thick and thin and work out a salvation."[11] They had wanted to combine work and love, and now they had found a way to do it.

Jane moved to Chicago in early 1889. As they began the project, their feelings for each other amounted to a mutual admiration society. Ellen admired Jane's spiritual strength, writing to her cousin, "Jane strengthens the weak knees. I don't know how I should live my life without her." Jane admired Ellen's ebullient and impatient "zeal." Ellen gave Jane confidence and courage. Jane wrote to Ellen, speaking of her friend in the third person, "I think [often] . . . of the soul . . . without whom I get on so badly."[12] They thought of themselves as a couple and as each other's new family. They now began sending news of each other to their blood families.

They also shared a bed without the necessity to do so. And if they were sharing a bed, then we naturally ask: what about sex? That possibility—viewed as a dangerous temptation—was obvious to at least one person, Starr's cousin in Massachusetts, Mary Allen. Just when Starr and Addams were about to move into their new home on Halsted Street, Allen wrote to admonish Starr for failing to consider the physical temptations that would be hard to avoid in her new intimate life with Addams. Mary's letter does not survive, but Starr's reply does. She wrote, "About the weakness of the flesh, which you think I have not considered—probably I haven't. I don't quite know how to. Perhaps it's as well not to. I do know, however, the strength of the beautiful spiritual life beside me. . . . I couldn't do this [start a settlement house] without her."[13]

What kind of love was this? Addams and Starr and their contemporaries, drawing on classical Greek ideas, called it platonic love. When she was fifteen, Addams had written in a letter, " I am a great admirer of Platonic love or rather, sacred friendship. I think it is much higher than what is generally implied in the word love." By "higher" she meant more spiritual and less of the body. In platonic love, which was much admired in educated circles in Addams's day, two people aspired to elevate their sexual urges and sensual feelings to a higher plane, to love the beautiful and the excellent not in one body but in the beauty of the individual soul and in the wider world. As one advice book put it, the imagination "exalted the soul, instead of flaming the senses."[14] Plato called this "sublimation." It was considered a *good* thing.

In her forties, Addams still believed in platonic love. In 1909, she invoked Diotima's famous speech about love in Plato's *Symposium* to explain her hope that city youth find a way to avoid sensuality and sex. Following Diotima, she proposed that the "sex impulse," as she called it, be redirected, so that it could "awaken the imagination and the heart."

The sex impulse, she wrote, can "overflow into neighboring fields of consciousness."[15] She may have been further encouraged to believe this from reading German anthropologist Johann Bachofen's influential book, *Mother-Right* (1861), in which he argues that lesbianism, like monogamous marriage, required the conversion of lust into spiritual love.[16]

To us, in our times, the idea of aspiring to such spiritualized love is peculiar. We are convinced that nothing is more transcendent than sex. But we will not begin to understand Jane Addams's attitude toward intimate love if we do not grasp the kind of intimacy she most aspired to—the meeting of two souls, the connection of two spirits, what she sometimes called "the intercourse of two minds." Even in casual encounters, she sought this kind of connection. She wrote, "We go to social gatherings, hoping that somehow, with somebody, we can have the real intercourse of mind with mind."[17]

Jane Addams's romantic friendship with Mary Rozet Smith developed slowly. Mary was nine years younger than Jane. A former student of Ellen's, she volunteered in the Hull House kindergarten from the settlement house's first days. Wealthy by birth and unmarried, she became a regular visitor to Hull House, staying there for days at a time, although she never moved in permanently. She lived at home and was devoted to caring for her parents, but Hull House answered her longing for something else meaningful to do, as well as for a community of friends and intimate, romantic love.

Meanwhile, Jane's emotional partnership with Ellen was fading. Their mutual admiration society ended as, over time, close proximity revealed to each the human side of the other. The differences that had once made the other intriguing began to grate. Jane now found Ellen's willingness to criticize, which she had once appreciated, simply wearing. Ellen found Jane's willingness to find goodness in everyone and everything, which she had once found wonderfully generous, simply foolish.[18]

When Jane fell seriously ill in 1895, she went to stay at Mary's house to recover. The long, quiet days together showed them both what Mary may have known long before Jane did—that they were joined together by an abiding love. Addams was stunned by the discovery and regretful that she had not realized what was possible sooner. She wrote a poignant poem about how she had "lost unnumbered days" because she "did not know" that Mary was ready to give her "the miracle" of "delivering love."[19]

In Mary Rozet Smith, Addams had found the love of her life. In their partnership she took her platonic love life to a new level. Mary was beautiful in a way that Ellen was not, both physically and spiritually. (Addams did love beauty.) And though both Ellen and Mary had deep souls, Mary's was more truly embodied in her daily presence. She was described by many as a gentle, generous, loving person, someone to whom people at Hull House often turned for help. Mary was also devoted to Hull House in a wholehearted way, while Ellen, with her high standards, was the settlement's sharp-tongued critic. Mary's wealth funded many settlement projects, and she was a lifetime member of the board of directors.[20]

In all the years that followed, Jane and Mary tried to be together as much as they could. They often traveled together when Jane was on a lecture tour, and they took vacations together. When apart, Jane wrote Mary how much she missed her and thought about her. She told her sister, Alice, once how much Mary meant to her. "She is so good to me that I would find life a different thing without her." And Mary felt the same. She wrote to Jane, "You can never know what it is to me to have had you and to have you now." Once when Mary was away traveling with her parents in Europe, Jane wrote her, "You must know, dear, how I long for you all the time. . . . There is reason in the habit of married folk keeping together."[21] Mary loved Jane Addams for who she was, accepted her, flaws and all, listened to her and believed in her. She also brought out the gentleness in Addams.[22] They both found life impossible without each other. After Mary died, Jane told her nephew, "I thought over everything. I suppose I could have willed my heart to stop beating, and I longed to relax into doing that, but the thought of what she had been to me for so long kept me from being cowardly."[23] She survived Mary a year; it was the most she could manage.

Although Addams and Smith were clearly devoted to each other, we might ask whether they could have deepened their love if they had had sexual relations. But again that question probably tells us more about our times and our ideas than theirs. If someone had told Addams that her life partnership with Mary was incomplete or less than devoted because sex was not part of it, she would have smiled and disagreed. She thought that platonic love was the highest form of love. And she aimed to practice it. We cannot know if she and Mary succeeded all the time, but there is an observation Addams makes in her passage about Diotima that hints that she at least knew firsthand of the difficulties involved. She wrote, "It is neither a short nor easy undertaking to substitute the love of beauty for mere desire, to place the mind above the senses."[24] For us, in the twenty-first century, this perspective is worth contemplating, especially because many couples today, both gay and straight, eventually arrive at this same place—a place where the intercourse of souls is considered the highest form of love.

Affectionate, Cooperative Love

Intimate love was just one of three kinds of love that Jane Addams treasured and nurtured in her life. The second kind was affectionate, cooperative love, the love among those joined in a common effort, whether they were fellow citizens, fellow workers, or fellow social activists. Addams thought love was part of cooperation because she thought affection was an essential part of any human relationship. She liked to quote Leo Tolstoy, Russian novelist and Christian apologist, on the subject: "We constantly think that there are circumstances in which human beings can be treated without affection, and there are no such circumstances."[25]

From her first days at Hull House, Addams sought to practice this sort of love by cooperating with the people who lived in the neighborhood. In 1892 she wrote that she and Ellen had begun the settlement with the conviction that "it would be a foolish and unwarranted expenditure of force to oppose or to antagonize any individual or set of people in the neighborhood." They intended, she explained, to live "with opposition to no man, [and] with recognition of the good in every man, even the meanest." A few years later she wrote that the settlement was "designed" to promote "co-operation with all [the] good which it finds in its neighborhood."[26]

Addams thought of cooperation not just as a good thing to do but also as a social reform theory. She had read about it in the writings of Auguste Comte, the French social philosopher; in essays about the social utopian theorist Robert Owen; and in the writings of the British social Christians, particularly the founders of the world settlement movement, Samuel and Henrietta Barnett, whose settlement house, Toynbee Hall in London, she also visited.[27]

Embracing cooperation as a social reform theory, Addams set out to embed it in her work. The cooperative projects she undertook with neighbors included the Jane Club, a residential club for single working women; the Coal Cooperative, which sold coal wholesale to its members;

and the Working People's Social Science Club, which hosted a weekly lecture series at Hull House. Hull House itself was a cooperative effort at many levels. She and the other residents set policies for the house as voting members of the Residents Committee; they set up the settlement's clubs as self-governing; and their daily life at the settlement involved endless moments of spontaneous cooperation. Addams and the other residents even wrote a book cooperatively, *Hull-House Maps and Papers*. In Chicago, Addams cooperated with trade unions on legislation to reform working conditions, and with women's clubs to create the city's first homeless shelter for women and children and to create one of the nation's first juvenile county courts.[28]

In the opening years of the twentieth century, Addams began to work cooperatively with new national coalitions on issues such as child labor, women's trade union organizing, and racial justice. When others had the idea, she would join and help. She was not the kind of leader who decided to start something new and then rallied supporters to her cause. That may have been why it was so difficult for her to start Hull House. She took leadership responsibilities on occasion—most notably as president of the Woman's Peace Party and of the Women's International League for Peace and Freedom—when she thought she could make a strategic difference in that role, but much of the time she was just part of the team, albeit the most famous part.[29] All her closest friends—Florence Kelley, Lillian Wald, Alice Hamilton, Louise de Koven Bowen, and Mary Rozet Smith—were also her colleagues in reform efforts.

Love of Humanity

Jane Addams is perhaps best known for being a lover of humanity, an idea that dominated her age in a way that it does not dominate the twenty-first century. Addams's unusual achievement was to translate a cold ideal, with all its implicit condescension and blind eagerness to erase human difference, into a way of life that involved affectionate respect for people in all their diversity, and an appreciation that she belonged among them as no better or worse than their equal.

When she was young, like all people whose ethics are shaped by reading, she understood the idea abstractly, having absorbed it through her Christian upbringing and the humanitarian and Christian writings of

Matthew Arnold, John Ruskin, George Eliot, and Leo Tolstoy, among others. And the idea was still abstract to her when she went to live on Halsted Street among the kinds of people she and others of her class thought of as "humanity"—immigrants and the working people. Although she intended to, and would, treat them with respect, putting into practice a social democracy of manners, she also saw them as the Other and felt herself superior because of her education, her culture, the great number of books she had read, and her exposure to the high culture of Europe through travel.

But her new chosen life would not let her stay uneducated. People who lived around Hull House talked with her about what they had been through and their hopes and fears, and asked her to sit with them when they were ill or to care for their children. She came to know people of many races and ethnicities and of every level of education and economic condition, type of personality, and state of cleanliness. Her admiration for their best human traits—their courage, generosity of spirit, and understanding of the foibles of human nature—grew daily, but she was also always looking to discover who they were in their individuality, to know what they had experienced and what they had learned. She observed, "It is impossible that you should live in a neighborhood and constantly meet people with certain ideas and notions without modifying your own."[30]

Her thinking changed in two ways. One was that she arrived at a new definition of being cultured. The cultivated person, she wrote in *Twenty Years at Hull-House*, is "a citizen of the world because of his growing understanding of all kinds of people and their varying experiences."[31] In addition, she began to trust "the people" in a new way. Her belief in the ideal of democracy had always required it, but now it became a real feeling, grounded in her experience and knowledge. She came to see that possessing a wide range of affectionate personal relations was what loving humanity meant and was the only way to strengthen democracy. Our first task as citizens, Addams believed, was to get to know one another. "When we consciously limit our intercourse to certain kinds of people whom we have previously decided to respect, we grow contemptuous of our fellow human beings."[32] She wrote, "The men who know the people best are the best democrats. That is the test."[33] The greatest menace to democracy is a "lack of faith in the people, [a] lack of faith in all kinds of people."[34] Although Addams is often charged with believing that everyone was alike, with being a "universalist," nothing could have been further from the truth. Her respect for diversity was profound and grounded in a far greater breadth of experience than that possessed by many who have criticized her on this point.

Life on Halsted Street informed Jane Addams's political consciousness and shaped her soul. Slowly and in the wake of many mistakes, she connected to her own humanity through her broadened affections. She wrote, "Love is the creative force of the universe, the principle which binds men together and by their interdependence on each other makes them human."[35] Or as Archbishop Desmond Tutu once put it, "My humanity is bound up in yours, for we can only be human together."

Theorizing Jane Addams and Hull House

As the chapters in this volume illustrate, one of the more fascinating aspects of studying Jane Addams in the late twentieth and early twenty-first centuries is to discover the ways that her life confirms and casts light on postmodern feminist theory and vice versa. Although she was apparently—judging from her reputation as presented in the newspapers—a staid, even old-fashioned Victorian woman, she was actually something far more complicated and interesting. Postmodern theory is well equipped to tease out some of her more startling and radical aspects.

For example, theorists argue persuasively that the category "lesbian" is generally inadequate when interpreted narrowly, and the history of Jane Addams's same-sex partnerships supports their case. Yet abandoning the concept of "lesbian," with its rich history of challenging mainstream heterosexual society, does not seem wise either. For example, lesbian theory insists on the possibility of androgyny, and Addams fulfills that possibility in interesting ways. Carolyn Heilbrun has defined androgyny as "a condition under which the characteristics of the sexes and the human impulses expressed by men and women are not rigidly assigned. Androgyny seeks to liberate the individual from the confines of the appropriate."[36]

This perfectly sums up Addams's ability, which grew over her lifetime, to release herself from the need to conform to gender roles. While her public image as a female saint allowed the media to insist she was a familiar kind of acceptable woman, while she certainly dressed with appropriate feminine style and maintained a suitably feminine demeanor, and while she was happy to remind her female audiences of the ways their domestic responsibilities might motivate their willingness to participate in social reform, her actions were matter-of-factly ungendered. She cofounded and built through impressive fund-raising a large institution, lectured, lobbied, published books, engaged in partisan politics, seconded the party nomination of a presidential candidate, advised presidents, founded national and international peace organizations, and even attempted to bring the violence of World War I to a halt. Criticism for breaking with female traditions often rained down upon her head, but never once did she trim her sails or limit her ambition because she was a woman. She simply proceeded.

Informing her actions was a philosophy to match. Like John Stuart Mill, whose book *Subjection of Women* stretched her mind when she was in her twenties, and like Margaret Fuller, whose *Woman in the Nineteenth Century* stretched her mind in college, Addams understood that gender stereotypes wasted talent that the world badly needed. She wrote, "Our hope [of social achievement] . . . lies in the complete mobilization of the human spirit, using all our unrealized and unevoked capacity."[37] Nonconfrontational by temperament, Addams did not challenge gender roles by debating them. But she knew exactly what she was doing.

Similarly, theories that explode old stereotypes about the nature of family are illustrated in Addams's own experience. When she was born, there was no stigma associated with upper-middle-class women who lived together as lifelong partners, but that changed over her lifetime. And when she and Ellen cofounded Hull House in 1889, such arrangements, which included sexual relations in some cases, were still not viewed as sexual. They were common enough that they had a name—they were called Boston marriages.[38] Interestingly enough, a shift in attitude, which began in the late 1890s, coincided with a broader backlash against women in general. Contributing to this hostility toward same-sex partnerships was the work of social scientists, including Freud. As we know, they were busy in the early 1900s establishing homosexuality, whether male or female, as a disease, and devising a new scientific terminology to convey these views as science.

By the 1920s, women who had established Boston marriages in the earlier balmy times were lying low, even as younger women began to develop closeted lesbian identities. Things were not so difficult for Jane Addams, because she lived as part of a group at Hull House, but prominent women leaders of institutions who lived alone with their lovers now found that arrangement a political liability. The most obvious case was that of Mary Woolley, president of Mount Holyoke College, whose partnership with an English professor at the school had become increasingly controversial.[39] Thus it was that in the twentieth century lesbian women—and of course gay men as well—lost what gay playwright Terrence McNally has called the final civil right: the right to love as anyone else loves.

Addams's choice to live at Hull House, that is, among friends who were her colleagues in reform work, also challenged conventions about family life. When it first opened in 1889, the settlement was a radical way for single women to live at a time when few single women, other than those in Boston marriages, lived outside their family of origin or the family created by their marriage. And within its walls even more radical things were going on. Shannon Jackson notes that domestic relations within Hull House included not only same-sex attachment and identification, but also sibling attachments (residents called each other "sister" and "brother"), mixed-sex attachment (married couples lived there and others fell in love there), mothers and aunts with children (Florence Kelley's often visited, and Jane Addams raised a niece and nephew there after her sister died). Jackson argues that "this kind of everyday life diffused and rerouted intimate attachment onto an alternative familial plane, one that resisted heteronormativity without necessarily falling into the presentist categories of homosexual identity." Struck by the example Hull House offers, Jackson calls for "a more complex analytic in order to recognize and interpret the fullness of these people's very full lives," one that would "value the rituals by which biologically unrelated persons formed a relation."[40]

Theorists have also noted the intimate bond that shared work creates. Poet bell hooks writes that the erotic means demanding "the most from ourselves, from our lives, from our work."[41] This summarizes well the spirit that Addams and Starr created at Hull House. And Addams treasured sharing in that spirit. She writes, "But more gratifying than any understanding or response from without could possibly be was the consciousness that a growing group of residents was gathering at Hull-House, held together in that soundest of all social bonds, the companionship of mutual interests."[42] Although Addams would never herself have called the deep pleasure she felt "erotic," hooks could have been writing about Hull House and Addams's life there, but especially about her life with Mary Rozet Smith, when she said that the erotic provides "the power which comes from sharing deeply any pursuit with another person."[43]

How Heroes Are Hidden

The long silence about the historical significance of Addams's intimate love life, with its obvious implication, to modern eyes, of lesbianism, is not surprising. It is linked to the changing history of sexuality during the years biographers have been writing. Historians writing about Addams in the 1960s and 1970s for the most part reflected their times. They all acknowledged that she had close friendships with Ellen Gates Starr and Mary Rozet Smith, and several noted how emotionally dependent she was on Smith for love and support. But they ignored the depth and nature of the two single-sex partnerships, even though evidence survived in these women's personal papers. That which was taboo was not discussed. Similarly, while historians in those years often noted that Hull House offered single women a new kind of place in which to live, few noticed the depth of challenge that Hull House posed to heterosexual norms and the nuclear family. As Adrienne Rich's frustration indicates, in 1980 the scales had yet to fall from society's eyes.

Since then gay and lesbian historians have led the way in unearthing these relationships and new patterns of affectionate commitment; straight historians have gradually followed. It has been a revelation and a joy to learn about the remarkable contributions gay men and lesbian women have made to the United States. We all want to see ourselves reflected in the great accomplishments of history; now, finally, the gay and lesbian communities are beginning to have that deeply human satisfaction. Jane Addams, too, belongs to lesbian history.

Notes

1. Adrienne Rich, "Compulsory Heterosexuality and Lesbian Existence," in "Women, Sex, and Sexuality" theme issue, *Signs* 5, no. 4 (1980): 632, 633.
2. Lillian Faderman, *To Believe in Women: What Lesbians Have Done for America—A History* (Boston: Houghton Mifflin, 1999). See also her *Odd Girls and Twilight Lovers: A History of Lesbian Life in Twentieth-Century America* (New York: Penguin, 1991).
3. Allan Bérubé, *Coming Out Under Fire: The History of Gay Men and Women in World War II* (New York: Free Press, 1990); Madeline D. Davis and Elizabeth Lapovsky Kennedy, *Boots of Leather, Slippers of Gold: The History of a Lesbian Community* (New York: Routledge, 1993); Anne Enke, *Finding the Movement: Sexuality, Contested Space, and Feminist Activism* (Durham: Duke University Press, 2007).
4. Louise W. Knight, *Citizen: Jane Addams and the Struggle for Democracy* (Chicago: University of Chicago Press, 2005), 249–52, 351–52, 359–62.

5. John D'Emilio and Estelle B. Freedman, *Intimate Matters: A History of Sexuality in America*, 2nd ed. (Chicago: University of Chicago Press, 1997), xv.

6. Knight, *Citizen*, 123–24.

7. Jane Addams, *Second Twenty Years at Hull-House* (New York: Macmillan, 1930), 196.

8. Addams's letter to her cousin Vallie Beck does not survive, but Vallie's reply, which does, supplies the content of Addams's letter because of how she answered it. Vallie Beck to Jane Addams, November 4, 1877. See also Knight, *Citizen*, 82.

9. Jane Addams to George Haldeman, January 4, 1884; Jane Addams to Ellen Gates Starr, November 3, 1883. Jane Addams Papers Microfilm (JAPM). The third quotation is from Jane Addams, "Outgrowths," TS, December1890 [dated erroneously 1891 in the JAPM microfilm], 9. JAPM, reel 46: frame 0480. Regarding evidence for 1890 date, see Knight, *Citizen*, 472n66.

10. Addams, *Twenty Years*, 87.

11. Jane Addams to Ellen Gates Starr, January 24, 1889.

12. Ellen Gates Starr to Mary Allen, September 1/15, 1889, Ellen Gates Starr Papers, Sophia Smith Collection, Smith College, Northampton, Mass.; Jane Addams to Ellen Gates Starr, June 4, 1889.

13. Ellen Gates Starr to Mary Allen, September 15, 1889. Ellen Gates Starr Papers. Ellen Gates Starr mentions in another letter that they shared a bed. See Ellen Gates Starr to Mary Allen, December 7 [1890], and Ellen Gates Starr to Mary Allen, "Xmas Eve" [December 24, 1890], Ellen Gates Starr Papers.

14. Quoted in Knight, *Citizen*, 74.

15. Jane Addams, *The Spirit of Youth and the City Streets* (New York: Macmillan, 1909), 16.

16. Sharon Marcus, *Between Women: Friendship, Desire, and Marriage in Victorian England* (Princeton: Princeton University Press, 2007), 225.

17. Jane Addams, "Social Settlements," in *Proceedings of the National Conference of Charities and Correction, Twenty-Fourth Conference, July 7–14, 1897* (Boston: n.p., 1898), 341.

18. Knight, *Citizen*, 249–50.

19. For the complete poem, see JAPM, 45:1599. James Weber Linn reprints part of the poem in *Jane Addams: A Biography* (New York: D. Appleton-Century, 1935), 289.

20. For gifts, see Knight, *Citizen*, 252, 334, 368; for the board, see 334.

21. Jane Addams to Alice Addams Haldeman, December 4, 1896, JAPM, 3:518; Mary Rozet Smith to Jane Addams, [December? 1896], JAPM, 3:512; Jane Addams to Mary Rozet Smith, May 26, 1902, JAPM, 4:391.

22. Linn, *Jane Addams*, 150.

23. Ibid., 407–8.

24. Addams, *Spirit of Youth and the City Streets*, 30.

25. Quoted in Jane Addams, *A New Conscience and an Ancient Evil* (New York: Macmillan, 1912), 178.

26. Jane Addams, "The Subjective Necessity for Social Settlements," in *Philanthropy and Social Progress*, ed. Henry C. Adams (New York: Crowell, 1893), 20, 23; Jane Addams, "The Settlement as a Factor in the Labor Movement," in *Hull-House Maps and Papers*, by Residents of Hull House (New York: Crowell, 1895), 187.

27. Louise W. Knight, "Jane Addams's Theory of Cooperation," in *Jane Addams and the Practice of Democracy*, ed. Marilyn Fischer, Carol Nackenoff, and Wendy Chmielewski (Urbana: University of Illinois Press, 2009), 65–69.

28. Jane Addams, *Twenty Years at Hull-House with Autobiographical Notes* (New York: Macmillan, 1910), 136, 134–35, 179; Knight, "Jane Addams's Theory of Cooperation," 69–72; the Residents of Hull House, *Hull-House Maps and Papers*. For another conceptualization of Hull House's cooperative practices, see Shannon Jackson, "Toward a Queer Social Welfare Studies: Unsettling Jane Addams," in *Jane Addams and the Practice of Democracy*, ed. Fischer, Nackenoff, and Chmielewski, 143–61.

29. Louise W. Knight, *Jane Addams: Spirit in Action* (New York: Norton, 2010), chaps. 4–6.

30. Addams, "Social Settlements," 343. For more about what she learned, see Knight, *Citizen*, chap. 9.

31. Addams, *Twenty Years*, 359.

32. Addams, *Democracy and Social Ethics* (New York: Macmillan, 1902), 10.

33. Jane Addams, "Address at the Civic Dedication of the Abraham Lincoln Center," *Unity* 55 (July 27, 1905): 365.

34. Jane Addams, "What Is the Greatest Menace to the Century's Progress?" [assigned toast topic], *Report of the Sunset Club, February 14, 1901*, 339. JAPM, 46:1034.

35. Addams, "Subjective Necessity," 19–20.

36. Carolyn Heilbrun, *Toward a Recognition of Androgyny* (New York: Norton, 1982), x.

37. Addams, *Second Twenty Years*, 2. For Mill and Fuller, see Knight, *Citizen*, 148–49, 86.

38. Lillian Faderman, *Surpassing the Love of Men: Romantic Friendship and Love Between Women from the Renaissance to the Present* (New York: William Morris, 1981), chap. 4, "Boston Marriages."

39. Faderman, *To Believe in Women*, 229–30, 232–33.

40. Jackson, "Toward a Queer Social Welfare Studies," 158.

41. Audre Lorde, "The Uses of the Erotic: The Erotics of Power," in *Sister Outsider* (Berkeley: Ten Speed Press, 1984), 54.

42. Addams, *Twenty Years*, 151.

43. Lorde, "The Uses of the Erotic," 56.

Part Three

Religion and Politics

8

The Theology of Jane Addams

Religion "Seeking Its Own Adjustment"

Eleanor J. Stebner

A stained-glass chancel window at Third Presbyterian Church in Rochester, New York, holds a medallion of Jane Addams, who is depicted as helping a child. She is among ten individuals (in addition to biblical figures such as Jesus, Luke, Paul, and various personifications of Christian mercy and kindness) who are highlighted as representing Christian service. Addams's medallion is grouped with those of Wilfred Grenfell, depicted as working as a missionary in Labrador; Florence Nightingale, caring for the wounded during the Crimean War; Albert Schweitzer, attending to a sick African; and Walter Rauschenbusch, professing the social gospel.[1] Across the continent in Berkeley, California, Addams is depicted in another church's stained-glass window. The Northbrae Community Church (a nondenominational congregation with Presbyterian roots) shows Addams with what appears to be two children and an adult before the facade of Hull House. In this creation, Addams is grouped with Walter Rauschenbusch, again; George W. Carver; and one of her great heroes, Abraham Lincoln. The purpose of this specific row of windows is to show individuals engaged in social action within their particular historical and social contexts.[2]

One can only speculate if other sanctuaries scattered between upstate New York and the West Coast hold similar depictions of Jane Addams. Such representations point to the enduring religious aura of Addams as a role model, a do-gooder, a humanitarian who helped the poor and the needy. Such representations also uphold maternal or feminine gender stereotypes; they do not show Addams before congressional hearings or lecturing before packed audiences or as an able administrator or social thinker, but rather, as a humble incarnation of religious virtue.

The irony of such depictions is that Addams's religious beliefs are a matter of debate among scholars. While general consensus exists about her early religious struggles and influences, there is little consensus on her adult theological views. Scholars speculate on whether she was a Christian and whether she based her actions and beliefs on Christian teachings or traditions. Numerous questions arise when considering Addams's religious views: What did she think about Christianity and the role of religion within culture and society? Did she see religion as a private source of comfort for individuals or as a source for social change or social amelioration? Was she aware of late nineteenth- and early twentieth-century feminist critiques of Christianity and religion, and, if so, what did she think about such ideas, which agitated many religious people of her day?

Jane Addams's second-to-last book, *The Excellent Becomes the Permanent*, was published in 1932. It consists of ten memorial addresses or eulogies that Addams had given through the decades and also an introductory chapter and a final essay (excerpts of which were published earlier) on her childhood "reactions to death." She wrote that she had two purposes for this book. The first was to answer the questions that she had been asked countless times, namely, "What do you believe? What is your attitude toward the future life?" The second purpose was to memorialize some of the people associated with Hull House, so that their lives and actions might be "made immortal in the life which they worthily had and used."³

While the book does preserve the memory of some of the Hull House friends and associates, it does not provide a particularly useful insight into Addams's beliefs or theology. Indeed, other sources better illuminate her religious perspectives. Addams did, however, discuss the topic of immortality and suggested that "her own generation [was] much less interested in a future life" than were previous generations.⁴ While perhaps "deplor[ing] that [their] assurance is less" than that of their forebears, Addams wrote that religion was itself adapting to new conditions; it was, she said, "seeking its own adjustment."⁵

This chapter discusses Addams's religious formation and theology. It identifies the spectrum of scholarly debate surrounding her religious perspectives and compares her thought to social gospel and feminist theologies of the late nineteenth and early twentieth century. Finally, it suggests how some of Addams's ideas connect with insights of feminist theology and spirituality as they emerged in the mid- to later part of the twentieth century.

First, it is important to state that Jane Addams had a theology, which is to say that she had a way of thinking and talking about God.⁶ Her theology, however, was not orthodox or conventional when compared with the mainstream Christian denominations and traditions of her day. Like many of her contemporaries, Addams was biblically literate, but she was not a biblical literalist. She initially fit best into the tradition of liberal evangelical Protestantism, especially the social gospel stream of her day, and by the end of her life she embraced more Unitarian and Universalist perspectives. While she knew that particular beliefs provided individuals with a sense of personal comfort, she herself did not find solace in religious doctrines that were unprovable, and she never viewed the churches, denominations, or traditions as other than human institutions. Although she lacked an overt feminist critique of religion and its teachings, her theology upheld the centrality of praxis and the empowerment of women as moral agents. She embraced a Christology that focused on the life and teachings of Jesus; the Jewish prophets; and other humans (such as Tolstoy and Gandhi) who called for a just, nurturing, and peaceful world. Such perspectives are not unusual when compared to the feminist theological movements as they emerged decades after her death.

While it can be said that Addams had a theology, it must also be noted that she was not a theologian. She was not particularly interested in pursuing questions of scriptural authority or interpretation or ecclesiastical power and privilege. She neither saw the power of patriarchal structures in influencing cultural mores nor—as did her contemporary, Charlotte Perkins Gilman—viewed religion as the "strongest cultural influence affecting humanity."[7] Yet two years before her death, Addams addressed the 1933 World Fellowship of Faiths convention, where she talked about the religions of the world being like the "colours of the prism." She speculated that all religions see the "truth in different colours." Humanity's purpose is to aim toward "win[ning] the good life," obtainable when religious people "know the truth and attempt to live up to it and die for it if need be."[8] Addams pointed toward a spirituality of human interdependence and mutuality, an eschatological hope that could be realized on earth by people willing to work for—and suffer for—its fulfillment; this vision was not reliant on the mercy or transcendent power of a deity, but rather, on humans learning to live together beyond their differences. She wanted religion to focus on the known historical present and not the unknown ahistorical future, and she called on the religions of the world to exalt a shared common humanity. Some of these ideas resonate with later twentieth-century theologies, as expressed within feminist theology, feminist spirituality, and interreligious (or interfaith) movements.

Addams's early religious formation was shaped by the culture in which she came of age, her father, and her struggles with the human experience of death.[9] Addams grew up in a culture prominently shaped by a Christian worldview and what were believed to be Christian moral values. Her childhood community regularly hosted Christian revival services and, although Addams was not allowed to attend these religious and social events, she heard about their passionate preaching on heaven and hell and their use of the so-called mourner's bench as a tool to lead sinners into a state of repentance.[10] In contrast with the emotional and popular revival culture, Addams also related how she and her stepbrother, George, having learned the Lord's Prayer from the Latin Vulgate, would repeat it every night because it "seemed to [them] more religious than 'plain English.'" She also confessed to holding in her head an "outrageous picture" of "the Lord upon His throne surrounded by tiers and tiers of saints and angels" for many years, a product of a sketch on the songbook used in her Sunday school.[11]

Although she was fascinated by the revivals and religious ritual, Addams's father most influenced her religious views as a child and young adult. John Addams had Quaker roots but did not belong officially to any meetinghouse or Christian denomination. As a leader in their small midwestern community, however, he taught Sunday school in a union church and attended either the Methodist or Presbyterian churches.[12] Jane, an inquisitive child, asked her father one day about the doctrine of foreordination (or predestination), a theological principle asserting that God knew—or had determined—which humans would be damned and which would be saved.[13] Addams was perplexed by this idea. Her father replied by saying, first, that neither his nor her mind could ever understand such theological tenets, and second, that it did not matter if they understood them. What mattered, he said, was not pretending to comprehend what was incomprehensible and being honest with one's self about it. Addams said that this insight was as "valuable a lesson as the shorter catechism itself contains."[14]

Addams was not only intrigued and perplexed as a child by religious practices and ideas; she was also disturbed by death. She had no recollections of the death of her mother (which occurred when Jane was only two years old), but she recounts the death of a relative when Jane was six years old and the burial of a schoolgirl's mother.[15] In both instances, death terrified her. Later, as a fifteen-year-old, she was at the bedside of Polly, who had been her mother's nurse and had lived in the family home, when Polly died. The "riddle of life and death pressed hard" on Addams, and she again sought the acumen of her father, who was "much too wise to grow dogmatic upon the great theme of death."[16]

Addams's theological questions on the nature of humans (as sinners or saved) and how to reconcile the reality of death with life were outweighed by the overwhelming emphasis put on her to live a moral, responsible, and other-person-focused life. Her angst about telling lies, her insecurities about being ugly, and her awe at her father for being so upright as never to be offered a bribe, speak of her focus on moral conduct.[17] She was taught, by her father and the dominant middle-class culture, to think about the needs and feelings of others and place these before her own. Addams related how excited she was as an eight-year-old when she had a new coat to wear to Sunday school. She put it on, delighting at how "gorgeous" it was, and then sought her father's approval. To her great disappointment he told her that it was a "very pretty cloak" but that she should not wear it because doing so would only make the "other little girls feel bad."[18] Perhaps her father was simply upholding the Quaker tradition of modest dress, but the result was that moral conduct was emphasized over theological beliefs: she was to be a good girl, which meant that she was to think about others before herself.

It was at Rockford Female Seminary and through her friendship with Ellen Gates Starr that Addams began to struggle explicitly with religious adherence and commitment. Rockford Seminary was an evangelical Christian school that aimed to prepare women not only for their future roles as wives and mothers, but also for their possible roles as Christian missionaries. Addams withstood the pressures to experience an emotional conversion to an evangelical Christianity even when students and faculty were praying over her and the few other "unconverted" students.[19] While she enjoyed reading the Greek New Testament every Sunday for two years with Rockford professor Sarah Anderson (she also read many of the classics), conversion did not interest her. She later reflected that withstanding such peer pressure—"clinging to an individual conviction"—was the "best moral training" she received from the seminary.[20] Her education at Rockford, however, also introduced her to the writings and ideas of numerous thinkers who influenced her theological and ethical questions: John Ruskin, Matthew Arnold, Alfred Tennyson, and Horace Bushnell, these writers adding to her previous reading of Thomas Carlyle and Ralph Waldo Emerson.

Correspondence with her college friend Ellen Gates Starr portrays a less intellectual and more personal searching. Unlike Starr, who would join the Episcopal Church (and eventually convert to Roman Catholicism), Addams was not drawn to theological doctrine or ecclesiastical traditions. In an 1879 exchange of letters between Addams and Starr, the former wrote that she was intrigued by the "idea of a female god," "a Primal Cause, not Nature exactly, but a fostering mother, a necessity, brooding and watching over all things, not passive, the mystery of creation."[21] In 1880 Addams conducted a covert religious experiment, so to speak, when she decided not to pray for three months; she observed no noticeable difference in her life as a consequence of omitting actions of personal piety from her daily schedule.[22] In correspondence between Addams and Starr in 1880, Addams wrote that she needed religion in a "practical sense," as a way to improve herself; she viewed this use of religion as ultimately selfish.[23]

Addams's young adult ponderings on religion were irrevocably changed with the sudden death of her father in 1881; her subsequent depression, illness, and withdrawal (a form of failure) from medical school in Philadelphia; and her years of searching for a purpose beyond meeting the trivial expectations of a woman of her age and generation.[24] She eventually made her way through these trying years. She read profusely and was greatly influenced by Leo Tolstoy's *What to Do Then* in the late 1880s, which she experienced as addressing the "widespread moral malaise" of her generation and which profoundly "modified" not only her personal views, but also the "religious convictions" of her generation.[25] Such writings appealed to what she called her generation's *Weltschmerz*, the "sense of futility, of misdirected energy, the belief that the pursuit of cultivation would not in the end bring either solace or relief."[26] She took two extended trips to Europe, where she viewed religious art and visited cathedrals. She became acquainted with Christian socialism and the experiment of Toynbee Hall, under the leadership of Canon Samuel and Henrietta Barnett. Inspired by the nascent settlement house movement, she and Starr decided to found a settlement house in Chicago; it was to be a "cathedral of humanity," a concept similar to that of the "religion of humanity" of Auguste Comte, the founder of positivism.[27] She wore a Chi-Rho cross brooch, a symbol to her of pre-Constantinian Christianity.[28]

At the age of twenty-five, Addams joined the Presbyterian Church in her hometown of Cedarville, Illinois. She wrote that the minister was open enough to not make her assent to theological tenets and that she experienced no "emotional" conversion; she joined, however, to "take on the outward expressions of the religious life in all humility and sincerity." Christian church membership was for Addams an "outward symbol of fellowship." It was based on her understanding that the early Christian movement was one that expressed devotion to the earliest "ideals of democracy," where "fisherman" and "slave" were joined in "universal fellowship." "Who was I," she asked rhetorically, "with my dreams of universal fellowship, that I did not identify myself with the institutional statement of this belief, as it stood in the little village in which I was born, and without which testimony in each remote hamlet of Christendom it would be so easy for the world to slip back into the doctrines of selection and aristocracy?"[29] Upon moving to Chicago, where she and Starr began what they called their little scheme, Addams transferred her membership to the Ewing Congregational Church, a small evangelical church in the Hull House neighborhood.[30]

Addams understood her Hull House undertaking to be an outlet for young women especially to connect their ideals with their actions. In her essay "The Subjective Necessity for Social Settlements," she wrote that settlement houses were expressions of democratic ideals, a way to "socialize democracy," and were based on the premise that the "good we secure for ourselves is precarious and uncertain . . . until it is secured for all of us."[31] They also provided a space where individuals may "share the race life," meaning that they provided opportunities for middle- and upper-middle-class residents to know of the experiences of neighborhood people (that is, poor and immigrant individuals) and thereby extend their humanity by broadening their experiences. But Addams also believed that the movement showed a "certain renaissance going forward in Christianity." "The impulse to share the lives of the poor, the desire to make social service, irrespective of propaganda, express the spirit of Christ, is as old as Christianity itself," she wrote.[32] Addams believed that the teachings of Jesus were not dogmatic and that his revelation was dependent upon his followers' ability to implement it in action, to show "love as a cosmic force."[33] She believed that the early Christian movement became exemplified in Jesus's followers having a "deep enthusiasm for humanity" that could be realized only in fellowship with one another. Christianity for the young people of her day—and for her as well—was not a "set of ideas" that could be "proclaimed and instituted apart from the social life of the community." As a manifestation of a "wider humanitarian movement," settlement houses, she suggested, were part of a "spiritual force" claiming early Christian humanitarianism.[34] In 1892 Addams wrote that the settlement house was "a new impulse to an old gospel" and that the "church we are looking for is to be known as the Humanitarian church."[35]

Addams was most explicit about Christianity in the early years of her work at Hull House and was perhaps the most personally religious during these years.[36] She and Starr used the Christian churches as key locales for networking and building the financial and community support of the financially fledging Hull House, as well.[37] After they attempted to hold religious household services among residents of various or no religious beliefs, Hull House did not organize religious programming and therefore was labeled, mostly critically, as an irreligious institution.[38] Although Addams continued to talk to and with Christian leaders throughout her lifetime, establishing relationships with social gospel leaders, such as Walter Rauschenbusch, and liberal Christian ministers, such as David Swing—her explicit words on Christianity lessened with time. In an ironic twist—and one that may have indeed occurred as a way to reinforce a "feminine spirituality"—Addams herself came to be viewed as a most "spiritual" person. Allen F. Davis reflected that it was difficult to ascertain why this happened, for Addams was "hardly spiritual, certainly not nearly as concerned with the spirit as Ellen [Gates Starr]."[39] Yet stained-glass immortalizations of Addams point to the enduring perception that Addams was herself an incarnation of spirituality in its compassionate exemplification.

While scholars agree basically with the factors influencing Addams's early religious formation and her young adult theological perspectives, they disagree on how to interpret her mature religious perspectives. Christopher Lasch wrote in 1965 that Addams came to "reject an intellectual theology based on the rationalism of her day." In 1973 Allen F. Davis noted that while Addams was religious when she started Hull House and thought of herself as doing a form of Christian service, she became agnostic. According to Amanda Porterfield, writing in 1980, Addams "translated Christian idealism into the secularized practice of social activism." In 1988 Mary Jo Deegan claimed that Addams, like the men she associated with at the University of Chicago school of applied sociology, "abandoned . . . religious answers for secular ones." Kathryn Kish Sklar said in 1989 that Addams and "her cohort patched together a religion of their own making. . . . It lacked institutional and theological moorings. In reality theirs was not a religion at all." Eleanor J. Stebner suggested in 1997 that Addams, in her calling for a "new religious expression" based on the humanitarian aspects of Christianity, emphasized the spiritual roots of Christianity and not its religious doctrine. Doing this enabled Addams to navigate over the divisive chasms of opposing religious doctrines and beliefs. In 2002 Jean Bethke Elshtain noted that Addams saw Jesus as "a proto-democrat bearing a saving message with egalitarianism at its heart." She suggested that Addams sought a "truly useful Christianity" and therefore "[pared] away the belief in the mystical and the miraculous." R. A. R. Edwards critiqued the arguments made by Stebner and Elshtain, saying that while they "both wish to recover Addams as a reformer with a distinctly Christian sensibility . . . Addams's faith can best be described as the reduction of Christianity to a therapeutic faith in human potential." Edwards (not unlike Lasch, Davis, and Porterfield) argued that Addams's "liberal Protestantism [was transformed] by secular assumptions and commitments."[40]

In light of these positions, it is interesting to examine in detail the interpretations of Addams's theology by two scholars, Georgia Harkness and James B. Hunt. Harkness (1891–1974), a Methodist theologian who was one of the first women to teach in a denominational theological school, addressed the topic of Addams's religion in an article commemorating the hundredth anniversary of Addams's birth.[41] Harkness praised the work Addams did in founding Hull House, her prolificacy as a writer, her role in the Women's Peace Party and then the Women's International League for Peace and Freedom, and her overall humanitarianism. She then asked, "What of her religion?" and pondered if Addams had any church connection. Harkness concluded, after a "diligent search of her writings," that Addams was "a theist and a liberal Christian whose motivation came primarily from the ethical teachings of Jesus." She said that although Addams's "religious insight" was "not ecclesiastical or fully evangelical . . . what she drew from the Gospels motivated her both to a faith in God and to works of love far in excess of those of the many who looked on Hull House as an irreligious institution."[42] Harkness then reviewed Addams's religious upbringing, her reverence for Jesus, and his emphasis on service to human need. A pioneering, staunch ecumenist herself, Harkness attributed Addams's relative silence on religion to the "persistent problem posed by the plurality of religious forms within what one hopes to see become a common democratic culture" and applauded her attempts to transform charity from a morally based incentive to a "corrective action."[43] She had great respect for Addams's moral courage regarding pacifism in the face of vehement opposition.

Hunt, in his essay exploring Addams's connection with the Presbyterian denomination, suggested that Addams's "religious struggle and faith were crucial in [her] vocational choice."[44] After reviewing her initial religious commitments, her later association with social gospel leaders such as Walter Rauschenbusch, and her increasing associations with Roman Catholic and socialist immigrants, Hunt argued that she "minimize[d] an orthodox Christian commitment and became increasingly secular and pragmatic in her outlook."[45] She did not receive the support she desired from the pastor or members of the evangelical Moody Church and became slowly alienated from her Presbyterian connection. Indeed, Hunt suggested that by the early 1900s, Addams, through her writing in the *Unity* magazine, declared her Unitarian theological views.[46] Key friends and associates of Hull House, such as Florence Kelley and Alice Hamilton, also "urged greater attention to economic analysis and urged a secular socialism as the basis for reform."[47] Hunt reiterated the point made by

Allen F. Davis, namely, that Kelley "hooted at the evening prayer sessions" and was more responsible than anyone else for politicizing Hull House.[48] In conclusion, Hunt declared that although Addams's vocation was shaped by her short formal association with Presbyterianism it "would be extravagant to claim Jane Addams for Presbyterianism."[49]

Jane Addams's theology was not markedly different from that of some of her associates who are linked to the social gospel, liberal evangelical, or Christian socialist movements. People such as Walter Rauschenbusch (1861–1918), Father James Huntington (1854–1935), and Vida Scudder (1861–1954) attempted to "apply the Christian gospel to particular social problems of the day."[50] Addams kept in contact with such folks, especially those who were also part of the settlement house movement. Take her thirty-plus-year association with the Reverend Graham Taylor (1851–1938), for example. Taylor, after teaching at Hartford Theological Seminary, moved in 1892 to a position at the Chicago Theological Seminary (CTS), where he founded a department of Christian sociology and in 1894 opened the Chicago Commons. Taylor and Addams had great respect for each other. At the 1928 dedication of Graham Taylor Hall at CTS, Addams was one of the individuals to give a tribute. While she focused on Taylor as a Christian sociologist, she upheld the contribution he made not only to sociology, but also to the field of theology. In her mind, his achievement was in his attempt to make a "satisfactory synthesis" between the problems associated with personality, social ethics, and the philosophy of religion.[51] Taylor responded by speaking of Addams as embodying "spiritual ideals and motives," and he also uplifted their "kindred faith."[52]

As with other individuals who became identified as social gospelers, Addams was critical of the institutional churches in their emphasis on theological doctrine and dogma over ethical practice and concerns; like those critics, she advocated temperance and a society based on cooperation. The social gospel movement, however, was largely associated with clergymen. While women, such as Vida Scudder, are now being considered as part of the social gospel movement, Addams cannot be considered a full-fledged one. Walter Rauschenbusch published what became the seminal work of the movement, *Christianizing the Social Order*, in 1912. The tripartite emphasis on the "fatherhood of God," the "brotherhood of man," and the "kingdom of God" on earth were too theologically anchored for Addams. Indeed, her mature theology might better be compared with that of liberal Christian missionary and humanitarian Albert

Schweitzer (1875–1965), who, in 1915, introduced his theological concept *Ehrfurcht vor dem Leben*—reverence for life—a philosophy based less in a Christian mindset than in a general religious mystical understanding of interdependence and respect for all life. Her theology might also reflect the thought of Roman Catholic theologian Friedrich von Hügel (1852–1925), who, in his 1908 classic *The Mystical Element of Religion*, suggested that all religions exist in tension between three components, the institutional, the intellectual, and the mystical.[53] Addams, unlike Schweitzer and von Hügel, did not advocate a personal mystical experience with the divine. She did, however, call on the institutional aspects of religious expression to respond and adapt to society, even though she did not address their theological (or what von Hügel calls the intellectual) components.

Comparing Addams's theology with social gospel and other theologies of her day is useful in broadening its interpretations. If one compares her theology with only traditional, orthodox, and sectarian theologies, she would certainly be rendered an agnostic, a secularist, or a nonbeliever. Christian theology, however, was not monolithic and has always involved a spectrum of emphases and spokespersons. Addams believed that the new emphasis some churches were putting on social methods and social reform was a necessary adjustment being made on the part of the churches. She praised the 1908 formation of the Federal Council of Churches, for example, as a "going forward," as a way in which Christians of differing creeds could join together in addressing "social maladjustments."[54] Addams believed that the early twentieth-century ecumenical movement, which joined together different denominations and traditions in actions—not in beliefs—was a way in which the churches could retain its tradition of prophecy and "cast its lot with the poor." She believed, in fact, that the churches were obligated to "leave the temples" so that they could "minister without ceremony or ritual, directly to the needs of the sinner and the outcast."[55] The 1908 Social Creed, written principally by Methodist Episcopal church leader Frank Mason North (1850–1935), in its emphasis on addressing problems associated with labor, living wage, mediation, and arbitration, and the application of the Golden Rule as the highest law possible in society, could easily have been penned by Addams herself. Addams was not the only one who desired what they called a social Christianity.

Addams was often critical of the Christian churches in their lack of applying their teachings to the larger social world, in their harsh moral judgments of others, and in their own sense of self-righteousness. She expressed these views by drawing upon the prophetic tradition that she found in the person of Jesus and in the Hebrew prophets. In critiquing the hypocrisy of church people in how they treated the "so-called 'fallen' women," for example, Addams used Jesus as the primary example of how such women were not beyond being "drawn into the radius of that wondrous affection He promulgated." She said that Jesus himself was "most severe" when he encountered "two sins—contempt for a human creature and self-righteousness." She called contemptuous and self-righteous churchgoers "irreligious" because of their attitude toward prostitutes and declared that the "brothel, the saloon, and the gambling hall" were an unholy trinity financially benefiting some men while loathing women.[56] In reflecting on the practice of charity, Addams dismissed the moralistic connections made between poverty and "vice and laziness" and expressed the need to reform the system scientifically so that it would become more humane; she evoked the Hebrew prophet Micah's words for "those who would join the great forward-moving process led by Jehovah," namely, that we are "to love mercy . . . to do justly . . . [and] to walk humbly with God."[57] Addams wanted Christianity to direct its energies toward establishing just human relationships in the broadest sense of the word. Social salvation was her concern. While she understood the need for people to have a personal faith or an individual sense of assurance, especially in the face of death, she did not dare to articulate a doctrine in light of what is ultimately unknown to humans.

The theology of Addams needs also to be compared with the scant feminist theological voices of her day. Matilda Joslyn Gage (1826–1898), Elizabeth Cady Stanton (1815–1902), and Charlotte Perkins Gilman (1860–1935) were outspoken in their feminist critiques of Christianity in particular and of the connections between the oppression of women and the authority of religious texts and traditional doctrines. Gage became increasingly concerned about the connections between religion and women as she aged. In 1893 she published *Women, Church, and the State*, in which she provided a sweeping historical examination of Western Christian society in regard to women and state authority.[58] Gage and Stanton were friends and colleagues. The controversial publication of Stanton's *The Woman's Bible* in 1895 and 1898 is often identified with the nineteenth-century (sometimes called the "first wave") feminist theology movement. Critical of the way churchmen and society at large interpreted particular biblical texts as a way to enforce patriarchal cultural structures, Stanton boldly wrote that the Bible was key in preventing "woman's emancipation" and "hold[ing] her in [a] 'divinely ordained sphere.'"[59] The attempt to revise and interpret particular biblical passages proved to be a highly contentious undertaking, and, in 1896, the Woman Suffrage Association "repudiated" it as not in any way reflecting an official or theological position of their organization.[60] Gage (among others) wrote a letter of support that stated that the "Christian theory of the sacredness of the Bible has been at the cost of the world's civilization" and that the "Christian Church is not based upon Christ as a saviour but upon its own teachings that woman brought sin into the world, a theory in direct contradiction . . . to spiritual truth."[61]

Both Gage and Stanton were more than a generation older than Addams, and it is difficult to link directly their feminist theological critiques with her. Yet Addams was aware of the gist of such critiques. In her lecture on prostitution and the church, she stated that with Augustine the "heart of a woman [became linked] with the gate of hell." "The very word woman in the writings of the church fathers," she said, came to stand for the "basest temptations."[62] The theological association between *woman* and *tempter* was ridiculous to Addams, and she called upon the Christian Church to "forget its ecclesiastical traditions . . . [and] go back to the method advocated by Jesus himself for dealing with all sinners," namely, forgiveness.[63]

Addams's words reflected awareness of feminist theological critique and she used it in her social reform agenda. But might Addams's beliefs be better compared with the feminist theological critique of her contemporary Charlotte Perkins Gilman? Gilman, a radical feminist, was also a friend of Hull House. Indeed, she had lived there for one summer in the 1890s, and its residents, including Addams, read with great anticipation her 1898 book, *Women and Economics*.[64] In 1928 Gilman published her last book, *His Religion and Hers*, in which she asserted the centrality of religion in forming and modifying human behavior and values and its role in making women slaves of men. She argued that "by its primitive preoccupation with death and after-death, [religion] still fails in its application to life."[65] Gilman believed that women, whose central experiences focused on the giving of life rather than the taking of it, would promote a "birth-based" religion rather than a "death-based" one.[66] She believed that religion was "of no consequence" at all unless it was "applied" to addressing the present and future life of the planet.[67] Highly critical of her day's fundamentalist Christian movement, Gilman said it consisted of "quaint reactionaries" who desired a "death-based theoretical 'faith' as apart from a system of living" and who therefore emphasized "miracles and legends and not teachings of Jesus."[68]

Addams's mature theology was different from that of Gilman's theology in two major ways. First, Addams did not grant such a significant role to religion within a society or in the forming of cultural values, and second, she did not have such a pronounced feminist lens in which to interpret the power of institutionalized religion or its understanding of women, their roles, and their lot in life. Just as Addams was slow to take on women's suffrage, it is perhaps true, as Mary Jo Deegan suggested, that she never fully "understood patriarchal power."[69] Realizing this, however, does not eliminate some of the similarities that she had with a feminist theologian such as Gilman. These similarities include her upholding teachings that emphasize living in the here and now over beliefs that promise a heavenly future. Like Gilman, Addams was critical of established Christian churches for emphasizing personal morals over social engagement. A religion without a social ethic was anathema to Addams, as was quietism in the face of social problems. Addams called on Christianity in particular and on the religions of the world in general to adapt to a democratic ideal where followers of varying religious perspectives would be able to work together toward social amelioration. She did not advocate that people give up their religious traditions and views, but she thought that people of differing creeds could unite in common actions. Such a perspective was based on her theology. Addams held the person and work of Jesus in high regard; she emphasized his humanity (with no indication of what she thought of his divinity), his compassion toward the outcast, and his teachings. She thought that the institutional churches had distorted his central message by uplifting adherence to church doctrine rather than application to life. As she wrote in her 1924 Christmas message, she wanted humanity to reach a new level in "human understanding," in claiming a "moral energy adequate to repair the ravages of a world war, in a fellowship warm enough to melt down national animosities."[70] In the final estimate, Addams wanted religion to be practical and useful in contributing to a better world. Like Gilman, she wanted a religion that was life giving. While not explicit in offering a feminist critique of religion, she did speak to its potential in transforming life. For her, this transformation was ultimately a collective endeavor.

Addams liked to tell a story that she first heard at the 1893 Congress of Religions about a woman dying and finding herself in a pit.[71] The woman desired very much to escape this hellhole, and one day she heard a voice asking her to identify one selfless act in which she had participated while she was alive. After much thought, she remembered that she had once given a rotten carrot to a beggar. She then saw a rotten carrot descend into the pit. She grabbed hold of it and it started to pull her up. How relieved she was. But then she noticed that a person was grabbing hold of her ankles and another person to the ankles of that person. A chain was formed that would eventually pull everyone out of the pit. And the woman said, "This is my carrot; let go at once; it is not strong enough for so many, and it will surely break if you all take hold."[72] As soon as the words were out of her mouth, the carrot broke and everyone dropped back down into the pit. Addams told this story as a myth to communicate the ultimate interdependence of all people. She believed that the religions of the world needed to recognize that "no one is going to get up by himself; we must all go up together if we go up at all."[73]

The late nineteenth- and early twentieth-century feminist theology movement did not make much of an impact on either the Christian churches or religion in general. Since the 1970s, however, it has flourished.[74] Feminist theologians have published works in biblical, historical, systematic, ethical or moral, pastoral, and philosophical areas.[75] While initially dominated by the voices of white privileged women, since the 1980s especially, women of color, lesbians, and women from the Two-Thirds World have vocalized their critiques of religion and its linkage with patriarchal social systems, violence, and oppression. In 1985 Rosemary Radford Ruether presented what is now considered a classic interpretation of the goals of feminist theology, namely, it is to be "consciously pluralistic," involve "network[s] of solidarity," and identify texts and practices that are not only male centered but also misogynist.[76] She identified three stages of feminist theology: first, to critique the "masculine bias of theology"; second, to seek "alternative traditions which support the autonomous personhood of women"; and third, to "restate the norms and methods of theology itself in light of this critique and alternative tradition."[77]

While Addams's theology cannot be directly linked with the feminist theology movements that emerged more than three decades after her death, some similarities are striking. Addams's emphasis, for example, on vocalizing the varying experiences of women—from the young, white, educated woman who is told by her pastor that she could contribute to society by taking care of the chancel flowers, to immigrant women sewing pieces in badly lit rooms, to lonely and despairing elderly women being sent to poorhouses, to women being beaten by their men—is similar to the central emphasis given by later twentieth-century feminist theologians on the realities of women's lives. Her desire for religions to adjust and recognize their culpability in supporting systems of injustice is similar to the emphases of later twentieth-century feminist theologians and the connections they identified between traditional religious teachings and systems of sexism, racism, classism, and heterosexism. Even Addams's assumption that the early Christian movement was markedly different from its later historical and institutional developments resonates with the work of some feminist theologians who reconstruct the early Jesus movement as a "discipleship of equals," for example.[78] Contemporary critiques of the religious traditions, and the desire to present alternatives to established (and mostly male-dominated) religions—as in goddess or Gaia theology movements—is not too far from Addams's young ponderings of a "fostering mother."[79] Addams believed that religious institutions could be mobilized as agents for social change, and she wanted religious adherents to set aside their differences and recognize their common bond of humanity. Even the mantra of the global ethic as advocated by hundreds of theologians and religious leaders around the world—"No world peace without peace between the religions"—picks up on Addams's desire for the religions of the world to see themselves as particular colors of a prism.[80] For the most part, feminist theologians have attempted to foster religious change from within their respected traditions, and Addams would have, at the very least, applauded such actions.

Perhaps if Addams had been born in 1960 rather than 1860, she may have better recognized the importance of religion in forming peoples, cultures, and ideals. Given her early religious quests, she may even have become a feminist theologian.[81] In the meantime, stained-glass depictions of her remain for contemporary religious people to view; whether they see her as a meek and mild do-gooder or as an intelligent theological critic has more to do with themselves than with Addams.

Notes

1. See www.thirdpresbyterian.org/music/windows/windows00.html.
2. Northbrae's windows depict not only Christian religious and historical figures, but also reli-

gious leaders such as the Buddha, Mohammed, and Gandhi (see www.northbrae.org/adams.html). St. John's Episcopal Church in Stamford, Connecticut (see www.stjohns-stamford.org/parishlife/glass/socialaction/), and Grace (Episcopal) Cathedral in San Francisco, California (see www.gracecathedral.org/enrichment/crypt/cry_20030129b.shtml) also feature Jane Addams in their stained-glass windows.

3. Jane Addams, *The Excellent Becomes the Permanent* (1932; Freeport: Books for Libraries Press, 1970), 3, 10.

4. Ibid., 5.

5. Ibid., 5.

6. The word *theology* comes from the Latin *theologia*. See Dorothee Solle, *Thinking About God: An Introduction to Theology* (Philadelphia: Trinity Press International, 1991).

7. Charlotte Perkins Gilman, *His Religion and Hers: A Study of the Faith of Our Fathers and the Work of Our Mothers* (1923), intro. Michael S. Kimmel (Walnut Creek, Calif.: AltaMira Press, 2003), 188.

8. Jane Addams, "Opening of the First Session, June 18, 1933," in *Jane Addams' Essays and Speeches*, ed. and intro. Marilyn Fischer and Judy D. Whipps (London: Continuum International, 2005).

9. Most of these young and youthful experiences are filtered through Addams's adult interpretations as contained in her *Twenty Years at Hull-House* (1910), foreword by Henry Steele Commager (New York: Signet Classic, 1981). For an excellent discussion on Addams's religious development into young adulthood, see Victoria Bissell Brown, "The Sermon of the Deed: Jane Addams's Spiritual Evolution," in *Jane Addams and the Practice of Democracy*, ed. Marilyn Fischer, Carol Nackenoff, and Wendy Chmielewski (Urbana: University of Illinois Press, 2009), 21–39.

10. Jane Addams, "A Personal Experience in Interpreting Memory," in *The Jane Addams Reader*, ed. Jean Bethke Elshtain (New York: Basic Books, 2002), 408.

11. Addams, *Twenty Years*, 30.

12. Ibid., 22–23; James B. Hunt, "Jane Addams: The Presbyterian Connection," *American Presbyterians* 68, no. 4 (1990): 231.

13. Several different theological strands exist regarding this theological principle that scholars trace back to the debate between Augustine and Pelagius. Followers of reformed theology (identified with John Calvin) debated between supralapsarianism, sublapsarianism (or infralapsarianism), double predestination, and so on. It was—and remains—a complicated theological debate within some Christian circles.

14. Addams, *Twenty Years*, 27. "The shorter catechism" refers to the Presbyterian (Westminster, 1648) document, a reformed statement of faith similar to that of the Heidelberg 1563 catechism. The shorter catechism begins with the question "What is the chief aim of man?" The response is "Man's chief end is to glorify God and to enjoy him forever." While the question and answer point to key theological assumptions and doctrine, they aim at a more mystical or spiritual relationship between a human being and deity. The shorter catechism ought not be confused with the small (Lutheran, 1529) catechism, which begins with the Ten Commandments.

15. Addams, "A Personal Experience in Interpreting Memory," 406, 409–10.

16. Addams, *Twenty Years*, 30–31.

17. Ibid., 19–20, 39.

18. Ibid., 27.

19. Ibid., 50.

20. Ibid., 54.

21. Jane Addams to Ellen Gates Starr, August 11, 1879, in *The Selected Papers of Jane Addams*, ed. Mary Lynn McCree Bryan, Barbara Bair, and Maree De Angury, vol. 1, *Preparing to Lead, 1860–1881* (Urbana: University of Illinois Press, 2003), 286. Quoted at length in Hunt, "The Presbyterian Connection," 234. See also Louise W. Knight, *Citizen: Jane Addams and the Struggle for Democracy*

The Theology of Jane Addams   219

(Chicago: University of Chicago Press, 2005), 93–94; Victoria Bissell Brown, *The Education of Jane Addams* (Philadelphia: University of Pennsylvania Press, 2004), 87, 89. For a sketch and comparison of Addams's and Starr's lives and religious perspectives, see Eleanor J. Stebner, *The Women of Hull House: A Study in Spirituality, Vocation, and Friendship* (Albany: State University of New York Press, 1997), chap. 4.

22. Hunt, "The Presbyterian Connection," 235. This experiment is reminiscent of one that Addams said she and her friends conducted over their ingestion of opium (Addams, *Twenty Years*, 48).

23. Jane Addams to Ellen Gates Starr, January 29, 1880, in *Selected Papers*, ed. Bryan, Bair, and De Angury, 334; Hunt, "The Presbyterian Connection," 30. See also Jean Bethke Elshtain, "Jane Addams: A Pilgrim's Progress," *Journal of Religion* 78, no. 3 (1998): 340.

24. Addams came to eventually use Tolstoy's term "the snare of preparation" to talk about the young women especially who were imprisoned by familial and social constraints resulting in a "curious inactivity" during the very years they longed to be active in engaging and changing their world (Addams, *Twenty Years*, 74). She also wrote much on what she called the "family claim," weighing heavily on women who desired to contribute to the larger society beyond their "filial relations." See Addams, *Democracy and Social Ethics* (New York: Macmillan, 1902), especially chaps. 3, 4.

25. See "A Book That Changed My Life," *Christian Century Magazine*, October 13, 1927, www.christiancentury.org/article.lasso?id=1189.

26. Addams, *Twenty Years*, 64.

27. Ibid., 71, 114. Refer also to Maurice Hamington, "Jane Addams," *The Stanford Encyclopedia of Philosophy* (Summer 2007 edition), ed. Edward N. Zalta; see http://plato.stanford.edu/archives/sum2007/entries/addams-jane/.

28. Brown, *The Education of Jane Addams*, 264. Historical theologians—especially in Anabaptist and Protestant traditions—often make a distinction between pre- and post-Constantine Christianity; in doing so, they uphold early Christianity in utopian terms and criticize the later synthesis of state power and religion in the forming of a medieval Christendom.

29. Addams, *Twenty Years*, 68–69.

30. Hull House Association—Scrapbooks, Ewing Street Church Membership Survey, 1894–1895 (dated February 1895), UIC-Special Collections. See also Hunt, "The Presbyterian Connection," 240; Stebner, *Women of Hull House*, 77. Louise Knight, in *Citizen* (223), acknowledges Addams's transfer to this neighborhood church, although other scholars continue to say that Addams transferred her membership to the prestigious Fourth Presbyterian Church in downtown Chicago. See, for example, Gioia Diliberto, *A Useful Woman: The Early Life of Jane Addams* (New York: Lisa Drew Book/Scribner, 1999), 144. Addams was part of this congregation at least through 1925; see Stebner, *Women of Hull House*, 206n31.

31. Addams, *Twenty Years*, 92. Addams's essay was originally published in Henry C. Adams, ed., *Philanthropy and Social Progress: Seven Essays* (New York: Thomas Y. Crowell, 1893). It is also reprinted in *The Jane Addams Reader*, ed. Elshtain, 14–28. For a recent overview of the settlement house movement, see Eleanor J. Stebner, "The Settlement House Movement," in *Encyclopedia of Women and Religion in North America*, ed. Rosemary Skinner Keller and Rosemary Radford Ruether (Bloomington: Indiana University Press, 2006), vol. 3, 1059–69.

32. Addams, *Twenty Years*, 95.

33. Ibid., 96.

34. Ibid., 96–97.

35. *Chicago Unity* (November 1892). Hull-House Scrapbook, vol. 1, UI-C Special Collections Library.

36. Knight, in *Citizen*, suggests that during the years 1890–91 Addams's "faith may have been closest to traditional dogma" (223).

37. Diliberto, in *A Useful Woman*, argues that it is "hard not to see a hint of opportunism in [Addams's] decision to join a church" (135–36).

38. Addams, *Twenty Years*, 307–8, 109. Addams was also dropped from teaching a course at the Deaconess Training School because she did not overtly proselytize through Hull House.

39. Allen F. Davis, *American Heroine: The Life and Legend of Jane Addams* (London: Oxford University Press, 1973), 61. See also Amanda Porterfield, *Feminine Spirituality in America: From Sarah Edwards to Martha Graham* (Philadelphia: Temple University, 1980), who argued that Addams's popularity as a religious "saint" linked "Victorian and progressive values" (166); and Jill Conway, "Women Reformers and American Culture, 1870–1930," *Journal of Social History* 5, no. 2 (1971–72): 164–77, who argued that women such as Addams were seen as embodying a form of innate femininity.

40. Christopher Lasch, *The New Radicalism in America, 1889–1963* (New York: Norton, 1965), 29; Davis, *American Heroine*, 74; Porterfield, *Feminine Spirituality in America*, 162; Mary Jo Deegan, *Jane Addams and the Men of the Chicago School, 1892–1918* (New Brunswick, N.J.: Transaction Books, 1988), 71–72; Kathryn Kish Sklar, "Religious and Moral Authority as Factors Shaping the Balance of Power for Women's Political Culture in the Twentieth Century," paper presented at the hundredth anniversary of the Founding of Hull House, Rockford, Illinois, October 1989; Stebner, *Women of Hull House*, 80–83, 102–3; Jean Bethke Elstain, *Jane Addams and the Dream of American Democracy: A Life* (New York: Basic Books, 2002). See also Elstain, "Jane Addams: A Pilgrim's Progress," *Journal of Religion* 78, no. 3 (1998), 339–60; R. A. R. Edwards, "Jane Addams, Walter Rauschenbusch, and Dorothy Day: A Comparative Study of Settlement Theology," in *Gender and the Social Gospel*, ed. Wendy J. Deichmann Edwards and Carolyn De Swarte Gifford (Urbana: University of Illinois Press, 2003), 157, 151.

41. Georgia Harkness, "Jane Addams in Retrospect," *Christian Century* 77 (January 1960), 39–41. For a biography on Harkness, see Rosemary Skinner Keller, *Georgia Harkness: For Such a Time as This* (Nashville: Abingdon Press, 1992).

42. Harkness, "Jane Addams in Retrospect," 39.

43. Ibid., 40, 41.

44. Hunt, "The Presbyterian Connection," 232.

45. Ibid., 240–41.

46. Ibid., 241.

47. Ibid., 242.

48. Davis, *American Heroine*, 77.

49. Hunt, "The Presbyterian Connection," 242.

50. Susan Hill Lindley, "The Social Gospel," in *Encyclopedia of Women and Religion in North America*, ed. Keller and Ruether, vol. 3, 1069. For recent publications on the social gospel movement, see Wendy J. Deichmann Edwards and Carolyn De Swarte Gifford, eds., *Gender and the Social Gospel* (Urbana: University of Illinois Press, 2003); Christopher H. Evans, *The Social Gospel Today* (Louisville, Tenn.: Westminster John Knox Press, 2001). For a recent biography on Rauschenbusch, see Christopher H. Evans, *The Kingdom Is Always but Coming* (Grand Rapids, Mich.: Wm. B. Eerdmans, 2004); on Scudder, see Elizabeth L. Hinson-Hasty, *Beyond the Social Maze: Exploring Vida Dutton Scudder's Theological Ethics* (New York: T & T Clark International, 2006).

51. Jane Addams, "Graham Taylor—Pioneer in Sociology," *Chicago Theological Seminary Register* 17, no. 4 (1928): 22.

52. Graham Taylor, "Response," *Chicago Theological Seminary Register* 17, no. 4 (1928): 25.

53. Walter Rauschenbusch, *Christianizing the Social Order* (New York: Macmillan, 1912); *Albert Schweitzer: Essential Writings*, ed. James Brabazon (Maryknoll, N.Y.: Orbis Books, 2005); Friedrich von Hügel, *The Mystical Element of Religion* (1908; 2nd ed., 1923; New York: Crossroad, 1999).

54. Jane Addams, "Religious Education and Contemporary Social Conditions," in *The Jane Addams Reader*, ed. Elshtain, 203.

55. Ibid., 203.

56. Jane Addams, "A Challenge to the Contemporary Church," *Survey* 28 (May 4, 1912): 195,

196. See also Jane Addams, "The Church and the Social Evil: Christian Responsibility for a Terrible Modern Scourge," *Methodist Review Quarterly* 61, no. 4 (1912): 665.

57. Jane Addams, "The Subtle Problems of Charity," in *The Jane Addams Reader*, ed. Elshtain, 63, 72, 75.

58. Matilda Joslyn Gage, *Woman, Church, and State*, intro. Sally Roesch Wagner (Amherst, N.Y.: Humanity Books, 2002).

59. Elizabeth Cady Stanton, *The Woman's Bible* (1895; Boston: Northeastern University Press, 1993), 7.

60. Stanton, *Woman's Bible*, 215.

61. Ibid., 208–9.

62. Addams, "A Challenge to the Contemporary Church," 195.

63. Ibid., 196, 198.

64. Deegan, *Jane Addams and the Men of the Chicago School*, 229.

65. Charlotte Perkins Gilman, *His Religion and Hers: A Study of the Faith of Our Fathers and the Work of Our Mothers* (1923), intro. Michael S. Kimmel (Walnut Creek, Calif.: AltaMira Press, 2003), ix–x.

66. Gilman, *His Religion and Hers*, 45–46.

67. Ibid., 283.

68. Ibid., 226. The so-called fundamentalist movement emerged in the 1910s from a cohort of theologians mostly based at Princeton Theological Seminary and came to a crisis when Harry Emerson Fosdick preached his famous 1922 sermon titled "Shall the Fundamentalists Win?" followed by the 1925 Scopes trial.

69. Deegan, *Jane Addams and the Men of the Chicago School*, 242–43.

70. Jane Addams, "'Whoso Liveth to Himself': A Message to Believers in Peace and Freedom," in *Jane Addams' Essays and Speeches*, ed. Fischer and Whipps, 263–65.

71. Jane Addams, "The Sheltered Woman and the Magdalen," in *The Jane Addams Reader*, ed. Elshtain, 266. Addams wrote this article in 1913 and said that the speaker was a "man from India." The speaker was not from India, but was Prince Serge Wolkonsky, who identified the tale as a Russian legend. See Minot Judson Savage, ed., *World's Congress of Religions* (Chicago: 1893), 31–32.

72. Addams, "The Sheltered Woman and the Magdalen," 266.

73. Addams, "Opening of the First Session, June 18, 1933," in *Jane Addams' Essays and Speeches*, ed. Fischer and Whipps, 366. Addams correctly identified Serge Wolkonsky as the source of the tale in this address.

74. The essay by Valerie Saiving, "The Human Situation: A Feminine View," *Journal of Religion* 40, no. 2 (1960): 100–112, is usually pointed to as a beginning of the feminist theology movement in the mid-twentieth century.

75. It is impossible to list the contributions of feminist theologians since the 1960s. See several anthologies: Carol P. Christ and Judith Plaskow, eds., *Womanspirit Rising: A Feminist Reader in Religion* (1979; reissue, San Francisco: Harper, 1992); Ann Loades, ed., *Feminist Theology: A Reader* (Louisville, Tenn: Westminster John Knox Press, 1990); Letty M. Russell, ed., *Inheriting Our Mothers' Gardens: Feminist Theology in Third World Perspective* (Louisville, Tenn.: Westminster John Knox Press, 1988).

76. Rosemary Radford Ruether, "The Future of Feminist Theology in the Academy," *Journal of the American Academy of Religion* 53, no. 4 (1985): 704.

77. Ruether, "Future of Feminist Theology in the Academy," 706, 707, 709. Ruether stated that these stages are interrelated and are not lineal.

78. See Elizabeth Schüssler Fiorenza, *Discipleship of Equals: A Critical Feminist Ekklesia-logy of Liberation* (New York: Herder and Herder, 1993).

79. For examples, see Naomi Goldenberg, *The Changing of the Gods* (Boston: Beacon, 1979); Charlotte Caron, *To Make and Make Again: Feminist Ritual Thealogy* (New York: Crossroad, 1993).

80. For examples, see Hans Küng, *A Global Ethic for Global Politics and Economics* (London: SCM Press, 1997); Gerrie ter Haar and James J. Busuttil, *Bridges or Barrier: Religion, Violence, and Visions for Peace* (Leiden: Brill, 2005).

81. This is a play on Jill Conway's comment: Conway, in critiquing the post-Freud generation of women, said that had Addams been "born into this generation [she] would have sought psychiatric assistance instead of founding Hull-House; she would have sought the answers to her problems in self-awareness rather than in activism; and she would have expected to find their resolution in personal relationships." Jill Conway, "Jane Addams: An American Heroine," *Daedalus* 93 (Spring 1964): 778.

9

Social Democracy, Cosmopolitan Hospitality, and Intercivilizational Peace

Lessons from Jane Addams

Judith M. Green

> The Hebrew prophet made three requirements from those who would join the great forward-moving procession led by Jehovah. "To love mercy" and at the same time "to do justly" is the difficult task; to fulfill the first requirement alone is to fall into the error of indiscriminate giving with all its disastrous results; to fulfill the second solely is to obtain the stern policy of withholding, and it results in such a dreary lack of sympathy and understanding that the establishment of justice is impossible. It may be that the combination of the two can never be attained save as we fulfill still the third requirement—"to walk humbly with God," which may mean to walk for many dreary miles beside the lowliest of His creatures . . . with the pangs and throes to which the poor human understanding is subjected whenever it attempts to comprehend the meaning of life.
> —Jane Addams, "Charitable Effort," *Democracy and Social Ethics* (1902)

The great pragmatist-feminist philosopher Jane Addams had two major practical causes during her lifetime: hospitality and peace, both of them rooted in and expressed in terms of the meaning and the obligations of social democracy. These practical causes and the complex political, economic, cultural, religious, and existential issues they frame and grow out of are as important now as they were for Addams, a century and more ago. Her writings and her life example offer valuable insights about these interlinked causes, issues, and ideals from which we can learn important lessons for transforming the problem-situation of our own times, suggesting critical correctives of important recent work on these subjects by Samuel P. Huntington, Seyla Benhabib, and others.[1]

From the beginnings of the modern feminist movement in the late eighteenth century, moral concern about human welfare motivated the efforts of many of the movement's most influential thinkers—Marie-Olympe de Gouges, Mary Wollstonecraft, Elizabeth Cady Stanton, Frederick Douglass, Sojourner Truth, John Stuart Mill, Harriet Taylor Mill—to transform traditional cultural practices and political institutions in ways that would develop women's capabilities and include their voices and lived experience in public discourse, not only for women's sake but also for the wider benefit of their nations and civilizations. Jane Addams was an inheritor of the world changes their ideas and efforts helped to bring about by the late nineteenth century, a member of the first generation of highly educated women who had the intellectual, economic, social, and psychological resources to live independent lives and to act as public figures seeking to bring about progressive social changes. Addams's contributions as a creative social theorist and institutional experimenter brought her international influence during her lifetime, and her living example served as a model for other feminist thinkers and activists in the rising generations who knew her. However, the long historical delay before women were admitted to graduate study of philosophy and feminist theory was taken seriously in the academy has led to a contemporary situation in which many influential feminist thinkers whose work focuses on Addams's cultural and political issues—Seyla Benhabib, Alison Jaggar, Iris Marion Young, Judith Butler, Julia Kristeva, and others—show no awareness of the importance and continuing usefulness of Addams's contributions, including her effective linkage of the public and the personal; her pragmatist critique of Kant; her war-chastened evolutionary analysis; her insights about nationalism; her experimental cooperative method; and her specific suggestions about how empowering women can promote social democracy, cosmopolitan hospitality, and intercivilizational peace.

My purpose in this chapter is to show how Addams's contributions can advance our philosophical understanding of these three great social ideals as well as the practical effectiveness of our efforts to actualize them. Because these and related aspects of Addams's work are understood and appreciated by very few contemporary thinkers, feminist or nonfeminist, I will explain them in relation to both her lived context and our own. Finally, I will show why Addams's pragmatist-feminist cosmopolitanism offers important correctives both to Huntington's nonfeminist, anticosmopolitan prescription for intercivilizational peace and to Benhabib's more promising, largely congenial feminist cosmopolitan alternative.

Addams's Pragmatist-Feminist Framework: Social Democracy, Renascent Christianity, Experienced Truth, and the Obligations of Hospitality

For Jane Addams, democracy is an evolving ideal whose fuller meaning we as individuals, as social groups, and as civilizations come to appreciate and instantiate more fully as our growth of understanding evolves.[2] At the time she and Ellen Gates Starr founded Hull House, Addams understood democracy as an increasingly world-attractive public and political ideal with implications and prerequisites of opportunities for human development and dignified living for all. At the same time, she felt called as a "renascent Christian" to play an active role in ensuring that those opportunities and their material bases were actually available to poor and culturally marginalized new immigrants to one of the United States' great "receiving cities"—Chicago, the city she claimed as her home, in which her father's valued accomplishments and example had equipped her with wealth, social standing, education, and moral vision.[3]

The founding of Hull House in 1889 met both "subjective" and "objective" needs that Addams felt and acted upon at the time. Her "subjective" need was to serve the poor, prompted by a "sense of humanity" she believed to be widely shared among privileged, idealistic young people.[4] The "objective" needs of the newcomers included acknowledgment, welcome, information, social and educational opportunities, and advocacy on their behalf with wealthy and powerful political and economic actors and institutions, in addition to basic needs of some of them for health care, decent housing, and nutritional support. Addams believed that these "objective" needs also were shared by the receiving city, the receiving nation, and the international community of nations, as well as the immigrant cultural groups, families, and individuals Hull House most directly and obviously served.[5]

Her "renascent Christianity," which Addams claimed for herself at the age of twenty-five, was not narrow and doctrinal, but rather focused on simplicity, a life of joyful service to others, and a belief that the truth that Jesus of Nazareth shared was not a proposition or a compendium of specific teachings, but rather a performative demonstration of the meaning and power of love as the ultimate, world-transforming cosmic force. Even before she witnessed how the first social settlement, London's Toynbee Hall, was effectively serving the needs of poor East Enders, Addams had been searching for some time for a way to live a contributive, meaningful, joyful life modeled on the lifestyle of the early Christians, yet put into action in modern industrial contexts. Addams saw one evening in a moment of vision how the Toynbee Hall example could be modified to serve Chicago's poor and diverse new immigrants. With some hesitation, she shared her vision the next day with Starr, her college friend and traveling companion, who immediately affirmed it and promised her partnership in the project.[6]

These two friends, with the support of a growing circle of idealistic, educated American women and men (eventually including William James, John Dewey, and George Herbert Mead), used Addams's inheritance from her father to purchase a mansion on Chicago's West Side that was now surrounded by poor communities of new immigrants. Addams, Starr, and a group of similarly educated women friends took up residence there, founded social and educational clubs with and for their new neighbors, consulted with them about what other collaborative efforts might be most valuable as well as which occasions called for personal advocacy and more direct forms of aid, and raised funds from wealthy American idealists to expand Hull House's physical plant and its outreach to the community.[7] Addams was very clear in her letters, speeches, essays, and memoirs that this work was in no way "benevolence" or "philanthropy," but rather the fulfillment of democratic obligations to neighbors in need, as well as a project of scholarly research to understand those needs and the best process of meeting them, and finally, an effective way to satisfy her own and others' need for meaning and joy in living.[8]

In her *Democracy and Social Ethics* (1902), which was celebrated in a letter to her from William James as "one of the great books of our time" and quoted by John Dewey in the 1932 revised edition of *Ethics* as expressing the key insight he proposed to develop there, Addams argued that democracy has always been more than a form of government or even a political ideal. Democracy is a *social* ideal, without which democratic political institutions are empty and ineffective. As a social ideal, Addams argued, democracy has practical meanings of freedom as empowerment, equality as effective opportunities for growth and contribution, and community as fellow feeling and ongoing collaboration, both in mutually determining how to advance the common good and in bringing such plans into active achievement. Democracy so understood had not yet been fully actualized in America, she assessed, but it must be and it could be, drawing on the energies and the creative imaginations of many idealistic, educated young people who harbor a secret, unnamed dream of participating actively in the hard work of America's social transformation toward the democratic ideal.

As an ethical ideal, Addams's social democracy has implications for both "normal" and "emergency" times of community living. In normal times, it implies contributing one's talents to the common good, whether by growing and preparing nutritious foods and drinks for others, by manufacturing necessary goods, by building healthy and inspiring cities, by teaching the young, by healing the sick, or by caring for the elderly, while always discussing and learning with one's neighbors how to meet the community's needs—and at the same time, participating in the life of one's nation and contributing to the advancement of world civilizations. In emergency times, when floods, or wars, or great needs and longings bring newcomers to a community, the democratic ideal requires participating according to one's capabilities in the community's combined response of hospitable concern. Thus, Addams's conception of the social obligation of citizenship in a democratic community to practice hospitality in normal as well as emergency times is distinguishable from, yet personally motivated and energized by, both a widely shared "sense of humanity" and her "renascent Christian" call to love and joyful service to others.

In her essay "Charitable Effort" in *Democracy and Social Ethics*, Addams demonstrates the transformative ethical meaning of the democratic ideal by narrating an anecdote about a young, idealistic "charitable" worker's efforts to teach her own middle-class values and virtues of planning and saving to the strikingly generous and hardworking poor women she seeks to assist. Exemplifying Addams's favored philosophical method, this story shows rather than argues that the learning in such transactions is profoundly mutual, leading to a higher moral standard and a deeper understanding of the social situation than either differently located party could achieve alone. The openness to receive from as well as share with the other in mutual hospitality transforms the situation and leads all involved to moral as well as intellectual growth that does not depend upon some mediating step of considering and adopting a proposition about a new belief to be affirmed as true. For the reader, the new truth comes from understanding the story and imaginatively undergoing the experience, with the shifts in feeling and perspective involved on all sides. Retrospectively, one may be motivated to distill or sum up this experienced truth as a proposition or an aphorism to carry along for guidance on one's journey into new situations, which in turn will verify or modify it. However, its meaning as well as its warrant will never be fully separable from its initial context and its narrative expression as these are linked to other experiences with which it shares family resemblances. Nonetheless, such a truth can carry a kind of illuminating power for memory and imagination that can help to stabilize its lessons and guide new perceptions linked with actions.

Social Evolution, Cosmopolitanism, and the Process of Peace-Building

In contrast with her daily experience-based understanding of the meaning, value, and processes of active, mutual hospitality across lines of cultural and economic differences, Addams's initial understanding of peace was more abstract, tightly interwoven with and perhaps misled by her pragmatist worldview, her renascent Christian hopes, and her democratic ideal commitments. In *Newer Ideals of Peace* (1907), Addams writes of an eventual substitution of the progressive change-making ways of peace for the abrupt, inefficient, and horrifying ways of war as the result of an evolutionary process she believed to be well under way and soon to achieve the great good of all humanity living together in mutual cosmopolitan hospitality across lines of national and civilizational differences. The outbreak of World War I a few years later dramatically challenged, if not falsified, this initial hypothesis, dividing the well-known leaders of the Progressive movement between those who saw America's entry into this war as a necessary and therefore justifiable means to end all wars (Dewey and Mead), and those who saw it as retrogressive in the evolutionary history of civilization, morally unjustifiable, and an impassable route to the desired end of peace (Addams alone). In spite of her "saint-like" national and international reputation for her effective work with the poor at Hull House, Addams was both patronized as naive and vilified as unpatriotic for her opposition to America's entry into the Great War, which already was destroying Western civilization's major cities, in Europe, and surrounding agricultural lands, as well as the ideals of its young people for which she still held such great hopes. All these were well known to her from travels and reading that had led by a kind of mirroring to her vision of Hull House as welcoming immigrants from these places, to which she would later return on their behalf to tell their stories and share their lessons of journeying across the world's great divides.

Perhaps because her commitment to the "new neighbors" of Hull House and to the places from which they came was deep and personal, and perhaps because her "renascent Christianity" supported her expansive social interpretation of the democratic ideal, Addams never gave up on the cause of peace, in spite of World War I's great blow to her hopes and those of countless others. Instead, she revised her hypothesis about the *evolutionary inevitability* of peace into one of *higher evolutionary possibility*—*if* the attitudes and active collaborative methods of mutual cosmopolitan hospitality could be brought to bear across lines of difference by creative activists committed to the cause whose personal reservoirs of hope could sustain them in working together to advance the work of peace, even in the midst of mind-numbing horror. Thus, the still-living Women's International League for Peace and Freedom was born as an active collaboration to gather and share "objective" information about the realities of the war, to inquire into its causes, to think together about what could be done to transform those causes and to meet the needs of the suffering, and to bring warring peoples and their leaders into social and educational relationships that would critically challenge their beliefs and widen their embrace of others within a motivating "sense of humanity." This peace-building process was designed to work by stimulating personal growth, new habits of cooperative action, and the creation of new institutions of social democracy worldwide.

In *Peace and Bread in Time of War* (1922), Addams reflected on the lessons about this active evolutionary process of building the attitudes, understandings, and institutions for a peaceful new world order that she and her fellow feminist activists learned during World War I through their collective efforts under the banner of the Women's International League for Peace and Freedom, which coordinated women's efforts in various war-torn countries to document the costs of the war to noncombatants and to advocate for the replacement of militaristic values with those that reflected the more humanistic longings of all peoples. Unlike

Woodrow Wilson, who was no social democrat, Addams did not envision the world's future democracies as narrowly political and cast in an already-achieved American mold. Instead, she foresaw each example of democracy as ultimately social, context specific, and forged out of painful as well as hope-spurring past experiences and imaginative, hypothetical reframings of more ideal possibilities, which could be tried and improved on the basis of future experiences that would allow the nations and civilizations of the world to learn from and with each other. Addams also speculated in *Peace and Bread in Time of War* about the evolutionary contribution of individuals who were willing and able to think and act in ways that advanced the social morality of their culture, even though the costs of dissent may be great in times of collective danger. Although daunted by the horror and the practical difficulties of the work, Addams remained determined to give her lifetime, her social capital, and her always fragile health to standing up for the progressive possibilities of peace, which she hoped would be greatly advanced by institutionalization of the peace-building process in the League of Nations.

However, ten years later, in "Later Reflections on Peace" (1932), which was transcribed from a radio interview, Addams criticized the continuing belief among many international analysts that military force was necessary to peace even after the creation of the League of Nations, arguing that it can be achieved only through a "gradual moralization of international relations" that substituted law for violence.[9] She suggested that a substitution of more peaceful habits and expectations was actually occurring through a three-stage process:

1. creation of mechanisms through the League of Nations for international arbitration and adjudication;
2. a sense of security arising from their use; and
3. gradual disarmament as weapons were no longer seen as necessary, but rather as threats to security.[10]

Addams criticized the armaments industry as a hindrance to war and called for its nationalization. She also called for the promotion of world trade by the removal of tariffs, because "unrestricted intercourse between nations must in the long run make for better understanding and goodwill."[11]

Again, Addams was insightful in her analysis of many of the requirements for peace, but wildly wrong about its progress, perhaps because she failed to take due account of the three kinds of nationalist "creeds" she had acknowledged in *Peace and Bread in Time of War*. When Addams died three years later on May 21, 1935, after sharing the Nobel Peace Prize with an advocate of the Great War who once had called her unpatriotic, she had not yet completed her inquiries about peace-building and crystallized her truths to the level of clarity that she had achieved earlier concerning the intertwined meanings and processes of social democracy and cosmopolitan hospitality. However, we who are her inheritors may be able to carry her lessons further by critically and imaginatively combining them with the lessons of later generations' struggles for peace in the midst of a continuing history of war, including the Holocaust, World War II, countless postcolonial struggles, the Vietnam War, the Gulf War, the Balkans War, 9/11 and the emergence of global terrorism, and current international conflicts both licensed and unlicensed by the United Nations. More clearly understanding the strengths and weaknesses of Addams's philosophy of evolutionary peace-building amid emerging nationalisms will help us to identify related insights and mistakes in recent work by nonfeminists like Huntington and feminists like Benhabib, and to improve our efforts accordingly.

Addams's Evolutionary Peace-Building amid Emerging Nationalisms

In *Newer Ideals of Peace* (1907), Addams reframed earlier philosophies of peace and various campaigns for its achievement in evolutionary pragmatist terms that still offer valuable insights for us today, *if* we critically correct her analysis in light of her own subsequent experience as well as later developments she could not have anticipated. Her greatest mistake in *Newer Ideals* was to hypothesize that permanent intercivilizational peace was rapidly blooming forth worldwide on the basis of promising international trends at the end of the nineteenth century, failing to take adequate account of what she later called the "new nationalism" that gave rise to what some called the Great War only a few years later, as well as to World War II and the countless other bloody struggles that have followed it. Nonetheless, her pragmatist critique of "older ideals of peace," including Tolstoy's, and of key aspects of Kant's approach to building a cosmopolitan peace that Benhabib and other twenty-first-century thinkers still employ, is a helpful tool for realistically reframing how we think about peace and the actions we can take to promote it, especially when we clarify the air of evolutionary inevitability that clouds Addams's otherwise promising analysis and take serious account of her later analysis of emerging nationalisms.

In *Newer Ideals of Peace*, Addams contrasts the "more aggressive," "active," and "dynamic" ideals that she and William James were advancing with "the older dove-like ideal" of Tolstoy and others, suggesting that if the social forces of the newer ideals "were made really operative upon society, they would, in the end, quite as a natural process, do away with war."[12] The older ideal is problematic in many ways, Addams suggests, calling it "a creed" advocated by "a small body of men" either in terms of "higher imaginative pity" aroused through identification with portrayals of the unglorious life and death of the common soldier in the midst of war's cruelty and squalor, or in terms of "an appeal to the sense of prudence," focusing on the high social cost of remaining armed for war as well as actually conducting it. By calling the older ideal a creed to which its evangelists must continually attract new adherents, Addams evokes a dogmatic propositional structure of truth claims with an otherworldly character, including a complete rejection of this world's habits of living and its existing social institutions, as well as a prescription for peace through all-at-once *individual* conversions, instead of through a more complex *social* process of remembering, recentering, redirecting, and rebuilding. Whether framed in terms of either "pity" or "prudence," Addams argues, the older approaches to peacemaking have been unrealistic about the background of war and ineffective in their efforts to persuade modern empires to give up its practice.

In contrast, Addams's newer "humanistic" ideals aim to guide transformations of those social sentiments, habits of action, ideas, and institutional structures that lead to and sustain the practice of war. While expressing concern that she will be misunderstood, Addams offers the phrases "readjusting moral values" and "forming new centers of spiritual energy"—wording that might have emerged in interchanges with Dewey and James—to suggest the depth and character of the personal and cultural reorientations she has in mind. Responding to anticipated criticisms that war is an unchangeable part of human nature and that thus peace is impossible, Addams invokes equally ancient "impulses and energies" toward hospitality, calling these socially resurgent in the early years of the twentieth century and becoming international for the first time. "For it is not merely the desire for a conscience at rest, for a sense of justice no longer outraged, that would pull us into new paths where there would be no more war nor preparations for war. . . . That 'ancient kindliness which sat beside the cradle of the race,' and which is ever ready to assert itself against ambition and greed and the desire for achievement, is manifesting itself now with unusual force, and for the first time presents international aspects."[13] The fact that World War I broke out less than ten years after Addams wrote these lines does not prove that she was wrong in this claim; after all, she acknowledged that struggle was an equally "primitive and profound" impulse and experience as hospitable kindliness. Moreover, various kinds of internationalist thinking and organizations clearly had been emerging in the foregoing decades, including in the influential writings of Kant, Marx, and James, as well as the founding of the International Red Cross, Toynbee Hall, and Hull House itself, with all the evidence it made available to her and others about the changing thinking and lifeways of some of Chicago's first-generation immigrants.

It was to these recent immigrants that Addams turned for examples of the kinds of profound personal and cultural shifts that made hospitable urban living possible for them under conditions of great social and existential pressure, working and living as they were with neighbors of different national origins, languages, religions, and daily customs. With Hull House support, these newcomers worked to retain and to share the best of their cultures of origin, at the same time as they sought membership in a new nation-state. Their success in achieving both these goals depended upon their ability to adapt their thinking and habits of action to those of a diverse cosmopolitan city in which they shared only "fundamental equalities and universal necessities" with others (225).

Addams wrote, "As their hopes and dreams are a prophecy of the future development in city government, in charity, in education, so their daily lives are a forecast of coming international relations" (226). Although she had written only a few lines earlier of these first-generation immigrants in terms of kindliness, peace, even holiness, she meant by this later comment only that the *cosmopolitan urban transformations* required by the challenges of meeting their common basic needs and represented by various adjustments in public aspects of their cultural habits of living indicate *the path of progress* that others' personal, cultural, and institutional developments, guided by the ideal of social democracy, must take in the United States and worldwide.

Addams reasoned in terms of a contextual logic of development in conditions of urban diversity: "Because of their difference in all external matters, in all of the non-essentials of life, the people in a cosmopolitan city are forced to found their community of interests upon the basic and essential likenesses of their common human nature; for, after all, the things that make men alike are stronger and more primitive than the things that separate them" (227).

In contrast to Huntington's analysis in terms of a "clash of civilizations," Addams's analysis here suggests that cultural and even civilizational differences are real, important, and valuable, but that they do not go "all the way down" with us—that there is an *evolving* "*common human nature*" that includes some shared fundamental impulses and energies toward sociality, as well some universal basic needs. Although her immigrant neighbors were not "shouting for peace" at that time—in fact, they still shared the habits of war of both their nations of origin and their new nation—Addams believed that this was less important than the practical conditions of their cosmopolitan living experience, in which their evolving "common human nature" was combining with a shared situation, close acquaintance, and daily acts of kindness to transform ignorance-based biases and inherited enmities.

Clearly, Addams regarded these first-generation immigrants as exemplars for others in the creation of the conditions for a future cosmopolitan peace, including in their development of a "cosmopolitan patriotism" that she hoped would spread to their more established neighbors, eventually making war impossible for them: "There arises the hope that when this newer patriotism becomes large enough, it will overcome arbitrary boundaries and soak up the notion of nationalism. We may then give up war, because we shall find it as difficult to make war upon a nation at the other side of the globe as upon our next-door neighbor" (228). Addams is right to point hopefully to multiple loyalties as well as to boundaries on aggressive behavior that come from recognition of fellow human beings as our neighbors, and even more so from consciously valuing our cooperative daily interchanges. However, as will be discussed below, she did not emphasize sufficiently how ideology and nationalism can destroy such neighborly loyalties and practices, as witness the Holocaust, the United States' incarceration of Japanese American citizens during World War II, Cambodia's "killing fields," genocides in Rwanda and Darfur, "ethnic cleansing" in the Balkans, deadly gang warfare in the United States' poor urban neighborhoods, daily suicide bombings in the Middle East, Bush-era incarcerations of alleged terrorists without trial at the U.S. facility at Guantánamo Bay in Cuba, and dramatic attacks on public places worldwide that demonstrate that since 9/11, no one is safe.

Interwoven in *Newer Ideals of Peace* with critical comments about the ideas and practical efforts of Tolstoy, Verestchagin, Bloch, Bentham, Buckle, and others, Addams's largely indirect critique of Kant's approach to building a cosmopolitan peace focuses on four broad aspects of his view:

1. overreliance on appeal to conscience,
2. distancing of reason from sentiment and habit,
3. theoretical ahistoricism, and
4. separation of law from social morality.

Important as it is, Addams argues, conscience grows and changes with one's experience and surrounding milieu. Thus, an appeal to conscience may be meaningless at one point in a person's life and at a later point unnecessary, because one's whole way of living and situated sense of self now makes the morally preferable course of action seem natural and necessary.

As an example of this, Addams imagines the pointlessness of calling on the mature William Shakespeare to desist from his youthful, pre-London life of folly, a life that would no longer have held any appeal for the London-dwelling actor and playwright. An even more resonant example is her account of the role of practical necessity in driving moral developments in the lives of Hull House's immigrant neighbors: "The individual, under such pressure, must shape his life with some reference to the demands of social justice, not only to avoid crushing the little folk about him, but in order to save himself from death by crushing. It is an instance of the irresistible coalescing of the altruistic and egoistic impulse which is the strength of social morality . . . anyone who lives with them knows that they are sentimental and compassionate" (227).

Reason may later ratify what it once ignored or rejected, Addams suggests, because it works within a course of experience in which one at first responds to necessity and prevailing social sentiments by initiating a series of actions that eventually becomes a habit of dealing with one's current situation. Later, one can reflect on the meaning, consequences, and implications of that habit for future situations. Only then can one create moral theories, as well as laws and other institutions that actually support it or limit its range.

Social sentiments, however, are the key to this process; and fortunately, social sentiments can be guided by knowledge through education and active inquiry. This is how progressive moral change has occurred over the course of human history, Addams argues—led not by abstract moral theorizing or by antecedent legislation, but by a complex flow of experience in which social sentiments play a leading role, derivative habits of action are formed and reflectively adjusted, and only later the lessons are harvested in moral theorizing, and the laws and other social institutions are adjusted accordingly. The good news, in Addams's view, was that such cosmopolitan, socially democratic, peace-seeking sentiments and habits were already emerging early in the twentieth century. Always an honest scholar, however, Addams noted that history also shows that experience can flow in a retrogressive direction, changing course in a moment of violent reaction: "Reversion to that brute struggle may at any moment cost the destruction of the painfully acquired bonds of equity, the ties of mutual principle, which are wrought with such effort and loosed with such ease" (228). Thus, the bad news of Addams's post-Kantian theory of the processes of cosmopolitan peace is that it suggests that effective laws and lasting institutions of peace will emerge only when a wide social consensus supporting them evolves worldwide out of a complex set of cosmopolitan social sentiments and reflectively adjusted, culture-transforming habits of integrated living that can be damaged at any time by reversion to war.

After offering this prophetic caution, Addams surprisingly offered an unrealistically hopeful prognosis for the twentieth century as an era in which the sentiments, habits, beliefs, and institutions of war would permanently evolve into international neighborliness and the lifeways of peace.

> An American philosopher [William James] has lately reminded us of the need to "discover in the social realm the moral equivalent for war.". . . Perhaps our very hope that these substitutes may be discovered has become the custodian of a secret change that is going on all about us. We care less each day for the heroism connected with warfare and destruction, and constantly admire more that which pertains to labor and the nourishing of human life. The new heroism manifests itself at the present moment in a universal determination to abolish poverty and dis-

ease, a manifestation so widespread that it may justly be called international. (228–29)

Although she expressed these hopes with some caution, Addams clearly believed that this newer spirit of humanitarianism was rapidly replacing the spirit of warfare, though still in need of active, even "aggressive" encouragement, because its multitudinous new adjustments must be worked into actuality through daily experience.

Addams and James were right to call for new kinds of heroes and new visions of engaged, energetic living that would evoke the best in us, and the twentieth and twenty-first centuries have produced many inspiring heroes and hopeful visions—and yet wars continue and people continue to call their sons and daughters who die in these bloody conflicts "heroes" because they gave their lives for causes that they believed required such a sacrifice. The problem is that while some have worked heroically to banish poverty, disease, racism, and other threats to human dignity, others have worked equally hard to cultivate the "new kinds of nationalism" Addams later recognized in *Peace and Bread in Time of War*. Their efforts have led to a series of ever-more-brutal wars, damaging though never destroying our evolving cosmopolitan social sentiments and our increasingly integrated habits of global living in a process of dialectical struggle whose future course is still unclear.

It is instructive that Addams took nationalism seriously even when she wrote *Newer Ideals of Peace*, but her analysis of its tendencies was unrealistically hopeful because she relied on a conception of social evolution that she always expected to be progressive, even when acknowledging that it could be retrogressive. Based on the examples of Italy, Germany, and other new nations she visited in 1885, which had come into existence out of smaller regional units, she regarded nationalism as working toward practical integrations that stress similarities and common interests over differences; thus, she was foreseeing the kind of development that eventually led to the European Community, though only after two world wars. Addams's analysis of integrative historical tendencies gained further support from her experiences at Hull House, working with new immigrants who gave up some of their age-old habits and lifeways in order to frame new ones that allowed them to express fellow feeling in dealings with their new neighbors within a shared dehumanizing context of poverty and demanding industrial labor. International humanitarian movements and recent philosophical currents also seemed to verify her analysis.

Therefore, in 1907 Addams—echoed by Benhabib a century later—interpreted nationalism as inevitably evolving into internationalism, just as she speculated that tribalism had evolved into intertribalism out of a need to satisfy a sentiment of experience-based compassion for the other who once was enemy. Even in 1922, Addams argued that war against one's own natural kind serves no evolutionary purpose, being practiced elsewhere in the animal world only by ants. It is not ties of blood that bind, Addams argued, but ties of common feeling. Like Benhabib, Addams argued that these can change, have changed, and are changing.

Chastened by the experience of the Great War and its aftermath, however, in *Peace and Bread in Time of War,* Addams rightly revised her earlier analysis of nationalism, treating it as the major obstacle to cosmopolitan hospitality and peace-building it still is: "Whereas nationalism thirty years earlier had seemed generous and inclusive, stressing likenesses, it now appeared dogmatic and ruthless, insisting upon historic prerogatives quite independent of the popular will."[14] Nonetheless, she reaffirmed her evolutionary thinking by labeling such nationalism "curiously anachronistic" in "its blind intolerance," but any suggestion of peace's inevitability is gone. If we would actualize this higher evolutionary possibility, Addams argues, we must work for it against multiple opponents who seek to advance their ends through war.

Claiming to offer not a timeless and unchanging analysis, but rather a paradigm that would help to explain events of the post–World War I era, Addams analyzed this "new nationalism" in terms of three kinds of "creeds" related to specific kinds of contexts and differing ideological objectives:

1. "hypernationalism" of suppressed groups seeking independence, as in Ireland and Poland;
2. "imperialistic nationalism" of world powers, such as Great Britain and the United States, that sought to stabilize and protect their domains as matters of unchallenged national policy; and
3. "revolutionary" nationalism of groups seeking to found a new world order, as in Russia.[15]

Remembering the meanings we connected with "creed" in Addams's 1907 critique of "older ideals of peace" will help us to understand what she might mean by calling these new kinds of nationalism "creeds." They are expressed in a set of dogmatic propositions associated with social sentiments with a quasi-religious quality; in their all-or-nothing form and fervor, they deny or reject important aspects of current reality, including the weight and merits of rival nationalisms; and they obscure what actually must be done in their suggestion that victory will come in all-at-once conversion of their enemies, perhaps through humiliating defeat in battle, instead of guiding a more complex, mutually beneficial social process of remembering, recentering, redirecting, and rebuilding.

These three kinds of nationalism are still with us today, and still expressed in creedlike forms. It is not *civilizations per se* that clash, as Huntington argues, but rather *rival nationalisms of these multiple kinds*. Noting Addams's distinctions between them and her criticism of their common creedlike form may help us to understand them in order to transform their social sentiments, habits of action, ideas, and institutions in ways that make them more compatible with social democracy, cosmopolitan hospitality, and intercivilizational peace.

Addams suggested that if leaders of these differing kinds of nationalist movements could meet in a kind of "ecumenical council" to confer with one another, they might find that all the world's nations showed traces of all three kinds of nationalism, all of which are objects of sincere devotion. Perhaps, she suggested, the founding of the League of Nations signaled the beginning of a time when rival nationalisms might find some kind of common ground to limit the damage and perhaps transform the character of their struggle, "when the differing types will no longer suppress each other but live together in a fuller and richer comity than has ever before been possible."[16] However, this would require that they find a "universal motive"—not universal values, or a universal civilization, or even universal interests—that could overcome the "overstimulated nationalism" that followed World War I.[17]

If we can find such a universal motive, cosmopolitan peace is still possible, Addams argued, though its terms must be negotiated among the leaders of rival nationalist groups—which would mean including revolutionary movements at the table with new nations and old imperial powers—and it must be made actual in daily cross-difference interchanges. To advance this process today, we, like Addams, must work to create opportunities for cross-difference sociality and education, employ public rhetoric that engages realistically with contemporary experience while stimulating democratic and hospitable social sentiments, and collaborate with others in forms of humanitarian service that expand love of nation in more international directions. We will be helped in this process by taking seriously Dewey's theoretical addendum that nations as social formations still fill important human needs for identity, history, and culture that are both more distinctive and more interconnected than the broader, civilizational "forms of life" that Wittgenstein, Rorty, and Huntington have treated as ultimate and disjunctive human frames of meaning.[18]

Addams's Lessons, Critical Corrections, and Suggestions for the Future

Reflecting on these lessons from Addams as well as Dewey's addendum can help us to understand why Huntington's "clash of civilizations" paradigm for framing international developments since the end of the Cold War both helps and hinders our efforts to advance present possibilities of building social democracy, cosmopolitan hospitality, and intercivilizational peace. Such reflections also can help us to see what is insightful and what is unrealistic in Seyla Benhabib's recent work on the evolution of transnationally portable democratic rights and obligations of hospitality. Finally, reflecting on Addams's life witness and her sustaining practice of "renascent Christianity" can help us to see the promise in current efforts by a diverse group of religious leaders to form a progressive spiritual coalition to challenge religious fundamentalists and nationalists, as well as democratic decision makers and ordinary citizens, to join a peacebuilding global process of democratically transforming the urgent problems of our times.

Thinking about how desirable developments in Addams's philosophy reflected adjustments in both "thick" and "thin" norms during an earlier historical period of struggle shows us how certain aspects of Huntington's analysis can advance our understanding of the challenges and opportunities for peace-building in the coming years.[19] Instead of focusing on the once-standard level of the clash of interests of rival nation-states during the earlier "Westphalian" era of international relations, which was regulated by a "hands off" norm concerning one another's "internal affairs" that guided most nations' political and diplomatic policies, Huntington rightly directs our attention to the level of culture that underlies this political surface.[20] As Royce, Dewey, Mead, and other classical pragmatists taught, this is the level at which social selves are formed, deep loyalties are forged, and the world and its time-process are framed in terms of an inherited language, history, common sense, religious sensibility, moral code, and a schema for meaningful living.[21] Cultures and the larger civilizations of which they form contributive and derivative parts can and do clash as they seek to advance and protect both material and nonmaterial interests, including cultural autonomy, linguistic viability, preservation of traditional lands and distinctive forms of beauty, faithfulness to their spiritual inheritance, and fulfillment of intergenerational ideal-guided hopes. While most Americans still see such cultural and civilizational interests as identical with or inseparable from the United States' international political interests as a nation-state, Huntington's analysis can help us to distinguish these in ways that are more common in Europe, Africa, and other parts of the world. To citizens of other nations who resent the United States' role in recent history, our national motto, "One out of many," which Huntington analyzes in cultural terms, expresses neither reality nor a desirable guiding ideal for this post-Westphalian era of economics-focused globalization that has been so costly to so many peoples' material and nonmaterial interests.

However, in spite of its usefulness in directing our attention to the level of differing cultures and civilizations, Huntington's analysis involves at least two distortions that block its usefulness as a guide to advancing social democracy, cosmopolitan hospitality, and intercivilizational peace in these troubled times. The first distortion is Huntington's suggestion that we cannot hope to understand other civilizations, to share some of their nonmaterial as well as material interests, and to find or forge a common ground of shared interests and concerns of both kinds that we could advance together as what Addams called a "universal motive"—a third alternative to both clash and noninterference. This is a significant distortion, both because globalization as we now experience it means positively that some basis for cross-civilizational mutuality already exists, and negatively in that we must do more to acknowledge and tend to the combination of material and nonmaterial interests that this process is currently ill guided to positively transform and advance for most peoples.

Practical separatism along civilizational lines is not actual, feasible, or desirable in such a closely interlinked world. Without an abrupt end to trade, worker flows, and scholarly exchange, as well as an immediate imposition of a communications "wall" to block the infusion of alien ideas and cultural values, the process of intercivilizational exchange will continue. Moreover, for wealthy Western nations and Japan to attempt to ignore the needs and the internal cultural dynamics of Huntington's other major civilizations (Islamic, Hindu, Orthodox, Buddhist, Sinic, African, and Latin American) would simply ratify the unjust distributions of wealth and opportunity that were put in motion during the colonial era and carried forward by economic globalization. Contrary to Huntington's underlying assumption as well as the hopes of the inheritors of all three kinds of nationalists Addams identified, there are no pure and unchanging cultures. Thus, there is no way to protect imperial cultures and civilizations from multiculturalism, or to restore postcolonial cultures and civilizations to precolonial forms and preserve them from future external influences. Instead, cultural change is an ongoing historical process that always reflects the influences of other cultures, though it may be possible for these to become more consciously chosen and more restrained, instead of imperially imposed and thoughtlessly adopted.[22]

The second distortion is that Huntington's analysis ignores real and important cultural, religious, regional, postcolonial, and economic *clashes within civilizations*, and even *within nation-states* such as the United States of America, Canada, Mexico, Italy, France, the United Kingdom, Nigeria, Botswana, and South Africa. Instead, he treats both nations and civilizations as blocs, constituting these along lines of recent and ongoing international clashes in a way that is both theoretically arbitrary and methodically circular. Just what constitutes a civilization in this age of globalization is unclear, especially after three centuries of colonization that exported and imported cultural, religious, artistic, and linguistic elements as well as trade goods and whole families between subordinate nations and imperial centers. Either "civilization" is a troublemaking, anachronistic concept; or it is covertly normative; or it is radically ambiguous in our present historical period. For example, if Islam and Christianity mark two different civilizations, as Huntington suggests, then most of or all the nation-states listed above incorporate clashes of cultures and civilizations within them. This would make Huntington's recommended strategy of noninterference neither feasible nor democratically desirable. Alternatively, if the traditionally Islamic civilizational line of demarcation between "peoples of the Book" (the Bible) and infidels is taken seriously, then followers of Islam, Judaism, and Christianity should stand together against all others—potentially if not yet actually—and their clashes with each other must be caused at other levels or locations of differences.

Thus, where to locate present causes of what Huntington calls "a clash of civilizations" is an empirical as well as a conceptual and aspirational question. Where are the deep and active lines of our divisions? What ways of framing these help most to clarify current dynamics while acknowledging the most significant commonalities as well as the most significant differences that are actually in play? What may we reasonably and respectfully hope for as the guiding basis for our individual and intergroup efforts to ameliorate injustices, exclusions, misunderstandings, and unmet needs; for the adjustments in our personal habits and cultural traditions that living amid diversity requires; and for our efforts to influence national, regional, and international policies to redirect globalization?

As did Addams before her, Benhabib anticipates a cosmopolitan future in which nations have voluntarily recognized their responsibilities of hospitality to immigrants who arrive in need from zones of war and other emergencies. Like Dewey, Benhabib sees the continuing reality and perhaps the human need for "bounded communities." Unlike Dewey, however, she defines these in term of "insiders" who have a voice in democratic decisions and "outsiders" who do not, seeing this aspect of democratic law and politics as permanently in tension with the imperative to hospitality. With Kant, Benhabib unrealistically treats this hospitality imperative as rationally universal in character, rather than as a family-resemblant set of cultural products growing out of the evolution of human experience in diverse locations that date back to ancient times in their motivating roots and specific characters.[23]

Thus, Benhabib has too much confidence in the clarity and reliability of hospitality's call, which Addams eventually came to realize could be perverted and outshouted by nationalism. Moreover, unlike Addams's vision of democracy as fundamentally and eventually social, democracy for Benhabib is solely a Kantian political concept limited to institutions and decision processes for "insiders" within "bounded communities" of particular nations and localities. They alone have legitimate authority to decide what rights and opportunities "outsiders" shall have, although the post-Westphalian regime of international human rights now lures many democratic insiders to voluntarily expand outsiders' rights and opportunities with its siren song of hospitality they experience as both deep within them and beyond them as citizens of nation-states.[24]

In *Another Cosmopolitanism*, Benhabib writes, as did Addams elsewhere a hundred years before her, about norms of hospitality as somehow evolving on their own toward a future time when they will be almost universally acknowledged. "It will be my thesis," she states early on in this short work, "that since the UN Declaration of Human Rights in 1948, we have entered into a phase in the evolution of global civil society, which is characterized by a transition from *international* to *cosmopolitan* norms of justice."[25] Later, in a startling comment on "the ontological status of cosmopolitan norms in a post-metaphysical universe," Benhabib implies that their evolution is independent of history, related resentments, and the continuing struggles of inheritor generations.

> Such norms and principles are morally constructive: they create a universe of meaning, values, and social relations that had not existed before by changing the normative constituents and evaluative principles of the world of "objective spirit," to use Hegelian language. They found a new order—a *novo ordo saeculorum*. They are thus subject to all the paradoxes of revolutionary beginnings. Their legitimacy cannot be justified by appeal to antecedents or to consequents: it is the fact that there was no precedent for them that makes them unprecedented; equally, we can only know their consequences once they have been adopted and enacted.[26]

The goal of this evolutionary process of cosmopolitan norms and principles will be achieved, Benhabib suggests, when the electorates of the various "bounded communities" freely acknowledge so many rights of outsiders—including rights to vote in their community of residence and to publicly manifest diverse religious commitments, as well as rights to education, health care, fair wages, and so on—as to make these democratic rights within nations functionally portable across national boundaries. Such cosmopolitan norms would then operate even if someone's reasons for seeking reception in a new nation did not involve the kinds of emergency conditions that ground her conception and Kant's of the transnational ethical obligations of hospitality.

Writing in a post-9/11 historical context of global fear of terrorism, war, backlash, and nostalgia for simpler times, Benhabib does acknowledge the possibility that a conservative electorate may refuse to acknowledge even emergency-based duties of hospitality while rejecting entirely more extensive participation and welfare rights for outsiders as well as opportunities for them to become insiders; for example, "I do not want to underestimate ... the extent of public dissatisfaction with and significant xenophobic resentment toward France's Muslim population."[27] However, like Addams before World War I, Benhabib does not expect that such evolutionarily retrogressive views will long stand unchanged. Benhabib's examples of actual democratic adjustments to the evolving hospitality imperative and the expansion of transnational human rights within Europe are well chosen and encouraging. Unfortunately, as Addams learned, there is a powerful set of rival forces and factions in play, working against the kind of cause Benhabib now champions. Even in reasonable Germany, opponents from various political and religious backgrounds have worked to block the construction of a beautifully designed mosque in the heart of Cologne, sometimes called "the Rome of the North" and the site of a great medieval cathedral. In the United States of America, where ignorance of others' histories, languages, and cultures is the norm, and our previous president prosecuted wars to advance international "democracy" while actively fostering the belief that others oppose us because they envy us, the struggle over the status and rights of the millions of illegal immigrants who reside, work, and pay taxes in our midst has evoked such deep hostility and revulsion among some "insiders" as to provoke more hate mail—both letters and e-mails—than members of Congress supporting "immigration liberalization" have ever received on any other subject, including war and peace. Meanwhile, "ethnic cleansing" as a technique and even a motive for civil wars has become common in the Balkans, Africa, and the Middle East. Such fierce opposition to hospitality and human rights must be taken seriously—these norms will not just "evolve" without negotiation, education, and daily effort by influential leaders and ordinary people who feel their call.

Therefore, in these matters of social democracy and hospitality, Benhabib would be wise to learn hard lessons from Addams and Dewey: especially since 9/11, nationalism and xenophobia are virulently alive in many parts of the world, perhaps as much in the United States as anywhere else, combining fear, anger, protectiveness toward evolved lifeways, and refusal to share what we have, even with needy claimants during a time of war. This is the dark side of membership in Benhabib's "bounded communities" that Addams and Dewey and their younger "critical pragmatist" colleague Alain Locke recognized and sought to transform through a combination of education and cross-difference collaboration, guided by a social and international reframing of the democratic ideal.[28]

Without such a social expansion of the meaning and practices of democracy to include daily obligations of hospitality as well as those that arise in times of emergency, a "bounded community" of angry and frightened individuals has no motive and no intellectual resources for opening its doors to outsiders at all, much less for treating them as new neighbors. Moreover, unless various older cultural traditions of hospitality survive within it or the ideal of social democracy somehow invades it, a postmodern "bounded community" has no basis for offering hospitality to strangers and wayfarers in the twenty-first century, other than short-sighted pursuit of the majority's convergent self-interest or that of dominant elites like that which guides the United States' current policies about legal immigration and the awarding of "green cards" (resident alien work permits) on the basis of bringing special skills or blood ties to already-valued citizens. Fortunately, the ideal of social democracy is still what James called a "live option" for many individuals and whole peoples who may be able to bring some of the positive communicative resources of globalization to bear in showing resistant Americans and other nationalists what can and must be done to promote peace and provide for all in a shared world.[29]

The good side of globalization, and of the related formation of regional international entities such as the European Community, is that, without advance notice or publicity, it has opened up windows and doors in the old "bounded communities" of which Benhabib writes. People everywhere are becoming more familiar with one another's languages, looks, and lifeways through television, movies, music, trade goods, and the Internet, as well as travel, international study, and experiences of work and volunteer service in other countries. Thus, many of us find it easier now to be open to mutually educative transactions with others of differing nations, cultures, and religions than did any generation before us. Speaking together and learning from one another, we can develop better-informed perspectives, both appreciative and critical, on our own and others' nations.

Moreover, the growing popularity of Addams's social democratic ideal explains the deeper meaning of the widespread adoption since World War II of democratic politics and institutions worldwide that Robert Dahl documented in *On Democracy* (1998). Many people in newly democratic places seek not only the franchise and the standard assurances of government nonintrusion in their lives that Benhabib suggests by associating democracy with "bounded communities," but also post-traditional opportunities to participate in shaping the future and to be acknowledged and appreciated across lines of difference, as individuals as well as members of their cultures, religions, and nation-states. They seek to meet the basic needs of those they care for and to enjoy some leisure, to form their own views and to be taken seriously in their expression as they interact with others in pursuit of common truths as well as common goods, and to participate in an energetic global common life that includes but exceeds their families' localities, cultures, and nation-states. This is not to suggest that these newly democratic peoples' homeplaces and cultures no longer matter to them, but rather that the "bounds" that may once have characterized them no longer apply in their minds and ways of living; it is rather those who oppose democracy who seek to reinstitute the old "bounds." Thus, there is something that seems retrogressive in Benhabib's association of democracy with the more limited meanings and the old "bounds" that Jane Addams was already challenging a century ago, a century after Kant.

Benhabib hints at but fails to explain this post-"bounded," transnational aspect of the emergent patterns of democratic social living as well as the individual aspirations and efforts that fuel that emergence. However, a growing commitment to the ideal of social democracy already bridges her "inevitable and necessary tension" between evolving transnational ethical norms of hospitality and democratic decision processes among many twenty-first-century European "insiders," helping to explain both France's "scarf affair" and Germany's struggles over resident aliens' status as "neighbors" that recently led to opportunities for them to vote in local elections.[30] Just as Addams theorized in *Democracy and Social Ethics* (1902) and *Twenty Years at Hull-House* (1910), the ideal of democracy is developing ever wider social meanings beyond the institutions and practices of political self-governance. As nation-states, cultures, localities, and individuals wrestle with one another over the implications of this and other ideals for daily living, over access to opportunities, and over the possibilities for nontraditional life plans that these represent, a whole range of future scenarios filled with new meanings and causes are emerging and rapidly being conveyed to global audiences.

These new "plays" receive mixed reviews from the actors as well as their audiences. The rapid pace of change exhilarates a few, but provokes adverse reaction among many who would prefer continuity in their previous roles and scripts, or who simply find the rapidity of change frightening and exhausting. Some find that the terms of engagement and even the larger subject have been changed in centuries-old inherited struggles for intergroup justice, perhaps originating during the centuries when their countries were colonized by imperial powers that transformed their cultures, their landscapes, and their built infrastructures as well as their forms of politics and economic life. The course of suffering of many once colonized and enslaved peoples continues into the present after the age of empires ended without redress, being simply replaced by a new set of rules of the game that allowed everyone to begin again with whatever they had or lacked, including education, wealth, hard forms of power, allies, and internationally recognized cultural capital.

In this suddenly emerging new world order, many find their most cherished values ignored, affronted, or deferred by dominant or insurgent cultures, religions, or economic elites. Television, movies, and the Internet bring information and outright fantasies about how others live into cities, villages, and family homes worldwide, including to those who struggle to care for their families when others live in luxury. Those who find their way of life mocked or demonized through these media may be motivated to band together with others to demand resources or recognition from those who they believe deny them unjustly.

Thus, the powerful "formal" democracies that fail to practice cosmopolitan hospitality—and even to pay their just debts from the past—are threatened by various "nationalisms" within and without their borders, some mapping existing nation-states, others demanding new ones; some seeking "purer" religious and cultural forms, others demanding unquestioning patriotism in support of violent confrontations with real and imagined enemies; some seeking specific programs of changes, other simply seeking fewer or slower changes.

Cosmopolitan norms of hospitality will not continue to evolve in transnational, socially democratic, peace-building ways, as both Addams and Benhabib hoped, unless we who believe in them effectively confront these rival nationalisms. Formally democratic institutions and practices will continue to be used to block the emergence of the attitudes, habits, and shared lifeways of a deeper social and international democracy unless significant numbers of brave, fallibilistic inquirers like Jane Addams, John Dewey, and Alain Locke employ education, advocacy, legal challenges, the arts, economic experiments, and new communications media to open up the minds and hearts of those who can learn to live together in peace and mutual growth amid differences, and also to marginalize the influence of recalcitrant nationalists of various antidemocratic kinds. Peace is not inevitable, nor is the widespread embrace of a deep and transnational social democracy, including the normalization of practices of hospitality on a daily basis as well as in times of emergency.

Fortunately, however, no fixed human nature or counterprocess of history bars the possibility of fuller actualization of Addams's three interlinked ideals of social democracy, cosmopolitan hospitality, and intercivilizational peace. Therefore, with Viktor Frankl's Holocaust-born spirit of "tragic optimism" expressed in a Jamesian fallibilistic yet renewable "will to believe," we can reasonably and meaningfully follow Jane Addams's "renascent Christian" example of joyful living in service to others, as well as some of her still-useful strategies for transforming the problem-situation of our times: active, lifelong engagement in listening to and learning from others, inquiring together how we can improve a problem-situation we share, multiplying opportunities for sociality and education amid diversity, finding our greatest lived interest in personal growth and our life meaning in melioristic patterns of advocacy and service that advance and evolve our culturally shared yet not exclusive ideals while meeting our neighbors' needs.[31] In a spirit of pragmatic piety, we can appreciatively and critically adapt Jane Addams's lessons within twenty-first-century inquiries to advance social democracy, hospitality, and peace, employing some of her methods and creatively imagining new ones that combine our own specific locations, gifts, and senses of calling to address the great issues and needs of our time: educating about and redressing postcolonial economic and cultural injustices that are inseparable from present patterns of immigration worldwide, transforming globalization in ways that respect and advance diverse peoples' material and nonmaterial interests, challenging various kinds of terrorisms while rejecting war as our only or best response, reversing global warming within the next twenty-five years, and reframing or effectively marginalizing the various narrow religious fundamentalisms and nationalisms that make all these other projects so much more difficult.

On this last religious challenge, too, Jane Addams's writings and life witness offer valuable guidance for us today. Although this aspect of her contribution is seldom commented on by contemporary admirers, Addams's understanding and active deployment of her religious inheritance and personal convictions offer key insights for these times when religious clashes constitute one of the main lines of struggle, as well as an important barrier to many locally and regionally contextualized peace-building efforts. Addams's minimally propositional, antidogmatic take on Christianity that locates its truth in a love-centered way of life finds echoes in the writings and activism of the Vietnamese Buddhist thinker Thich Nhat Hanh and those of the Dalai Lama. It finds American inheritors in

Rabbi Michael Lerner, Protestant "lay preacher" Cornel West, Christian evangelical pastor and writer Jim Wallis, Benedictine nun Joan Chittister, and others who are working to build a progressive spiritual network that can take on together many of the theoretical, political, and practical challenges of justice-doing and peace-building. If such efforts can expand to include more Buddhist, Jewish, Christian, Hindu, and Muslim thinkers, leaders, and activists, they can become the correlate on the religious level of the Women's International League for Peace and Freedom: documenting conditions, inquiring together to find causes and solutions, supporting one another's efforts to influence their own specific religious and cultural constituencies, and working together to reach wider publics and decision makers on local, national, regional, and international levels.

To stay grounded in the suffering and hopes of those they aim to liberate, these broad, cross-cultural, and interreligious efforts must be paired with the kind of personal engagement in direct service to "neighbors" that Addams, Starr, and the other women of Hull House pioneered by offering acknowledgment and welcome, and by creating context-specific social and educational opportunities for those who need them worldwide, in addition to meeting their many basic human needs. Such faith-based initiatives must be replicated at local levels globally to help individual people who are also members of shared cultures and religions to listen to one another, to deliberate, and to learn together while working on projects of mutual concern that make justice-doing and peace-building real, important, and possible for them. Actively participating in such grounding engagements in mutual cosmopolitan hospitality will keep their leaders sober, yet inspired by the real situation they experience with others, even if they, like Addams, discover that their hours for service are better spent listening, speaking, and writing than in baking bread. Such service-grounded, future-guiding, democratic cosmopolitan leaders may come to share Addams's vision of a thousand voices singing the Hallelujah Chorus together, taking pleasure with her that "the leading voices [can] still be distinguished, but that the differences of training and cultivation between them and the voices of the chorus [are] lost in the fact that they are all human voices lifted by a high motive."[32]

Notes

1. In *The Clash of Civilizations and the Remaking of World Order* (New York: Simon and Schuster, 1996), Samuel P. Huntington argued that "culture and cultural identities, which at the broadest

level are civilization identities, are shaping the patterns of cohesion, disintegration, and conflict in the post-Cold War world" (20). Four of Huntington's corollaries of this thesis are descriptive. Instead of "a universal civilization in any meaningful sense," he says, a seven- to nine-sector "multipolar and multicivilizational" world order is emerging; the West's (Europe and North America's) civilizational power is declining as Asian and Muslim civilizational powers are expanding; specific cultures are reaffirming themselves and cooperating along civilizational lines; and Western universalist claims are leading to conflict with other civilizations. Huntington's fifth corollary is prescriptive: "the survival of the West" requires that Americans reaffirm a Western cultural identity instead of a multicultural one, and that all Westerners reframe our understanding of our civilization's place in the world as unique, rather than universal, and vulnerable to challenges from others that require us to unite in order to renew and protect it. In his view, three rules for avoiding major intercivilizational wars in the coming years (316, 320) follow from this analysis: (1) all states must refrain from intervening in conflicts within other civilizations (the *abstention rule*); (2) core states must negotiate with one another to limit or stop "fault line wars" within their civilizations (the *mediation rule*); and (3) people in all civilizations must search for and work to expand the values, institutions, and practices they share with people of other civilizations (the *commonalities rule*).

Building on Huntington's insights about the importance of cultural differences in international relations while avoiding his distortions about the ultimately disjunctive demarcation of civilizations, Seyla Benhabib has highlighted in *Another Cosmopolitanism* (Oxford: Oxford University Press, 2006) the emergence since World War II of an intercivilizational and intercultural as well as international human rights regime that already has greatly influenced local communities as well as national political conversations within virtually all nation-states. Although her focus is on law because of her concern about enforceability, Benhabib's analysis offers clear evidence of intercivilizational learning and of cross-difference collaboration in building justice-based peace, suggesting that virulent dissents from this growing body of human rights principles and practices in both the United States and the Middle East reflect other, noncivilizational levels and locations of clash. However, Benhabib is overconfident in the capability of the evolving human rights regime to do the work of mutual hospitality and peace-building on its own. She fails to take seriously enough the "dark side" of human potentials that Jane Addams experienced as manifested in the three kinds of exclusive and aggressive nationalism that are still with us, as well as in the determined, culpable ignorance of many of the world's most fortunate citizens that still sustains quietism concerning their neighbors' needs, which are being exacerbated by economic and cultural globalization as we presently know it.

2. See Jane Addams, "The Subjective Necessity of Social Settlements," in *Philanthropy and Social Progress: Seven Essays*, by Jane Addams, Robert A. Woods, J. O. S. Huntington, Franklin H. Giddings, and Bernard Bosanquet (Thomas Crowell, 1893); 1–26, and Jane Addams, *Democracy and Social Ethics* (New York: Macmillan, 1902); Jane Addams, *Twenty Years at Hull-House* (1910).

3. My phrase "renascent Christian" refers to Addams's self-association with a "renaissance of Christianity" focusing on a cosmic principle of love, a life of joyful service, and a nonpropositional analysis of the truth of the life of Jesus of Nazareth, as distinguished from particular words and teachings associated with him in the canonical biblical texts. See "The Subjective Necessity for Social Settlements" (1892) and *Twenty Years at Hull-House* (1910).

4. See "The Subjective Necessity for Social Settlements."

5. See Jane Addams, "The Objective Value of a Social Settlement" (1892), in *Philanthropy and Social Progress*, by Addams, Woods, Huntington, Giddings, and Bosanquet, 27–56.

6. Addams's moment of vision occurred during the evening after she had witnessed a bullfight in which not only the bull but also several horses had died, an event she continued to watch in total fascination after her friends had departed in disgust. See *Twenty Years*.

7. See "The Objective Value of a Social Settlement" and *Twenty Years*.

8. See "The Subjective Necessity of Social Settlements."

9. Addams, "Later Reflections on Peace" (1932), in Christopher Lasch, *The Social Thought of Jane Addams* (New York: Macmillan, 1965), 253.

10. Ibid., 255–56.
11. Ibid., 257.
12. See Jane Addams's introduction to *Newer Ideals of Peace* (New York: Macmillan, 1907).
13. Addams, *Newer Ideals of Peace*, in Lasch, *The Social Thought of Jane Addams*, 221. References to this work are found parenthetically in the text.
14. Addams, *Peace and Bread in Time of War* (1922), in Lasch, *The Social Thought of Jane Addams*, 247.
15. Ibid., 248.
16. Ibid., 248–49.
17. Ibid., 249.
18. See John Dewey, "Nationalizing Education," in *National Education Association of the United States: Addresses and Proceedings of the Fifty-fourth Annual Meeting* 54 (1916): 183–89; Ludwig Wittgenstein, *Philosophical Investigations* (Blackwell, 1953); Richard Rorty, *Achieving Our Country: Leftist Thought in Twentieth-Century America* (Cambridge: Harvard University Press, 1998); and Huntington, *The Clash of Civilizations*.
19. Following Michael Walzer, Huntington argues that cultures in their specificity are generally "thick" in how they offer moral guidance in daily living, and yet some related "thin" ethical elements that derive from common aspects of the human condition and "universal dispositions" are shared within and between cultures. Instead of propounding and seeking to advance supposedly culture-free or culturally superior universal norms, we should "accept diversity," Huntington advises, while seeking to discover and advance such "thin" cross-cultural norms (318; see Walzer, *Thick and Thin: Moral Argument at Home and Abroad* [Notre Dame, Ind.: University of Notre Dame Press, 1994], 1–11).
20. In *Another Cosmopolitanism*, Seyla Benhabib explains the "Westphalian" international world order that guided international relations for hundreds of years after the signing of the Treaty of Westphalia in 1648: "In the classical Westphalian regime of sovereignty states are free and equal; they enjoy ultimate authority over all objects and subjects within a circumscribed territory; relations with other sovereigns are voluntary and contingent; these relations are limited in kind and scope to transitory military and economic alliances as well as cultural and religious affinities; above all states 'regard cross-border processes as a "private matter" concerning only those immediately affected'" (23; quoting David Held, "Law of States, Law of Peoples: Three Models of Sovereignty," *Legal Theory* 8 [2002]: 4). Benhabib's purpose is to contrast this "Westphalian" world order with a globalized world order ruled by shared, universal values, which, she argues, has been emerging since the nineteenth century out of a new ethical vision signaled by Kant's essay "Perpetual Peace." For a different take on the wisdom of replacing the Westphalian world order entirely, see Huntington, *The Clash of Civilizations*, 35, 52, 54. See also David Brooks, "The Human Community," *New York Times*, May 11, 2007, A27, in which he traces Tony Blair's national and international politics of enforceable, universal values during Blair's many years as prime minister of the United Kingdom to the communitarian theology of John Macmurray.
21. See Josiah Royce, *The Problem of Christianity* (New York: Macmillan, 1914) and *The Philosophy of Loyalty* (New York: Macmillan, 1920); John Dewey, *Human Nature and Conduct* (New York: Henry Holt, 1922) and *The Public and Its Problems* (New York: Henry Holt, 1927); and George Herbert Mead, *Mind, Self, and Society* (Chicago: Chicago of University Press, 1934).
22. See Alain Locke on the impossibility of pure cultures in *Race Contacts and Interracial Relations*, ed. Jeffrey C. Stewart (Washington, D.C.: Howard University Press, 1992).
23. For a more detailed discussion of my own views on this question of the roots of hospitality norms and traditions, see Judith Green, "Building a Cosmopolitan World Future Through Pragmatist Mutual Hospitality," in *Pragmatism and the Problem of Race*, ed. Donald Koch and Bill E. Lawson (Indianapolis: Indiana University Press, 2004), 203–24.
24. On "Westphalian" and "post-Westphalian" world orders, see note 20 above.

25. Benhabib, *Another Cosmopolitanism*, 16.

26. She adds: "Cosmopolitan norms, of which 'crimes against humanity' is the most significant, create such new moral facts by opening novel spaces for signification, meaning, and rearticulation in human relations" (Benhabib, *Another Cosmopolitanism*, 72–73).

27. Benhabib, *Another Cosmopolitanism*, 61.

28. For contemporary analyses of the implications of Locke's approach to promoting cosmopolitan unity amidst diversity, see Leonard Harris, ed., *The Critical Pragmatism of Alain Locke* (Lanham, Md.: Rowman and Littlefield, 1999). See also my *Deep Democracy: Community, Diversity, and Transformation* (Lanham, Md.: Rowman and Littlefield, 1999), especially chap. 4, "Cosmopolitan Unity Amidst Valued Diversity: Alain Locke's Vision of Deeply Democratic Transformation." See also my "Building a Cosmopolitan World Future."

29. See James's influential and controversial essay, "The Will to Believe," in *The Will to Believe and Other Essays in Popular Philosophy* (New York: Longmans, Green, 1897) and widely reprinted.

30. Benhabib, *Another Cosmopolitanism*, 18, 51–61, 62–67.

31. See Viktor Frankl, *Man's Search for Meaning* (New York: Pocket Books, 1984).

32. Addams, "The Subjective Necessity of Social Settlements," 43.

10

Community Organizing

Addams and Alinsky

Maurice Hamington

A settlement constantly endeavors to make its neighborhood realize that it belongs to the city as a whole, and can only improve as the city improves.

—Jane Addams

The job of the organizer is to maneuver and bait the establishment so that it will publicly attack him as the "dangerous enemy." The word "enemy" is sufficient to put the organizer on the side of the people.

—Saul Alinsky

It is not a coincidence that Chicago produced two of the most important figures in community organizing of the twentieth century: Jane Addams and Saul Alinsky (1909–1972). Chicago was a center of social upheaval, as exhibited by the Haymarket riots of 1888, the Pullman strike of 1894, and the race riots of 1919 (as well as race riots in the 1940s, 1950s, and 1960s). This city's social unrest existed in dynamic relationship to ideas about social change and reform fomented in Chicago, as witnessed in the settlement work of Addams's Hull House, the socialist work of Eugene Debs's American Railway Union, the urban research and social theorizing of the Chicago School, and the Back of the Yards organization, founded by Alinsky.[1] Addams was the visible leader of one reform effort, the social settlement movement, and Alinsky's name is synonymous with the community organizing movement. As activist Heather Booth describes, "Alinsky is to community organizing as Freud is to psychoanalysis."[2]

In this chapter, I challenge the notion that the genealogy and influence of community organizing originates with Alinsky and suggest that the innovation of Jane Addams's work and philosophy is being overlooked. The settlement movement has been characterized as well meaning but paternalistic and patronizing, while the community organizing movement is described as a grassroots effort that was tough minded and effective.[3] These characterizations have gender overtones fomented by Alinsky's personal sexism and frequent attacks on the methods of the settlement workers. Alinsky and his organization reinforced gender stereotypes and held to traditional notions of separate spheres. Theorist and activist Jo Freeman recounts an exchange with Alinsky:

> While I worked for the TORCH [a community newspaper] I looked for support to organize women. After hearing Saul Alinsky at a UTC [Urban Training Center] workshop I asked if I could enroll in his Industrial Areas Foundation to learn how to organize. Women don't make good organizers, he told me. We might let you in, but you'll have to pay your own tuition of $10,000 per year. In July 1967 I applied to the Institute for Policy Studies, a New Left thinktank in Washington, D.C. which sponsored students who wanted to do political research and organizing. "I want to organize women," I told [Alinsky organizers] Art Waskow and Robb Burlage. "There's no future in that," they replied. My application was denied.[4]

This chapter focuses on the comparative community-organizing philosophies of Addams and Alinsky. I wish to dispel some of the misconceptions about the differences between the two leaders, while highlighting other crucial dichotomies. I claim that although Addams and Alinsky differed in regard to how to leverage power and in their social vision, in many ways Alinsky (through the Chicago School) was an unwitting protégé of Addams when it came to social epistemology and participative democracy.

The Addams Model of Community Organizing

In the late nineteenth century and early twentieth, Addams authored a series of articles that served to define the social settlement movement and established Addams as the spokesperson for the movement. Addams viewed social settlements as experiments in learning that cut across culture and class: "Hull-House endeavors to make social intercourse express the growing sense of the economic unity of society, and may be described as an effort to add the social function to democracy."[5] Her ultimate goal was social advancement, and she felt it was possible only if citizens were highly invested in one another. This "social democracy" required what she described as "sympathetic knowledge," or a duty to learn about others in society, no matter how unfamiliar those others were, with an openness to caring for and acting on behalf of those others. For Addams, sympathetic knowledge was the connective understanding necessary for a robust democracy.[6] Social settlements were physical manifestations of her democratic philosophy. The settlement was a multifaceted educational conduit that existed to facilitate social knowledge across boundaries of identity such as class and culture. Those in the neighborhood had an opportunity to learn about one another as well as about how to navigate and succeed in the United States through settlement programs. Simultaneously, settlement workers learned from the various cultures around them. Addams reflected upon and thematized what she learned through her writing and speeches, thus allowing those not involved in settlements to learn about the experiences as well. The social settlements were intentionally not charity organizations, and Addams was quick to criticize that label: "I am always sorry to have Hull House regarded as philanthropy."[7] Starting from the feminist ontological view that humans are fundamentally connected in a web of relationships rather than being atomistic agents, the social settlements facilitated self-sufficiency by supporting community ties and promoting lifelong learning. Addams analogized social settlements as good neighbors, and as such, modeled the behavior of members in a healthy democracy. Good neighbors listen carefully, respect community members, and respond to their needs. If garbage needed to be collected, the settlement workers found a way to get it picked up. If working parents needed day care, the settlement workers organized to offer it.

One example of Addams's concern for women and the development of self-sufficiency in the neighborhood can be seen in the creation of the Jane Club, described in *Twenty Years at Hull-House*. At a time when collective bargaining did not enjoy the legal protections that it does today, Addams observed that single-women labor union members were particularly vulnerable when it came to periods of unemployment created by strikes or lockouts. During labor actions single working women could no longer afford rent money. Such vulnerability reduced the power of the bargaining unit and the influence of women within that unit. Collaborating with labor leaders such as Mary Kenney, Addams established a workingwoman's cooperative, subsequently named the Jane Club. This cooperative ensured that all members' rent was paid in the event of labor interruptions. Addams secured funding to provide housing for the Jane Club, but it operated as an independent entity, as described in the *Hull-House Year Book* (1934): "The club has been, from the beginning, self-governing, the officers being elected by the members from their own number."[8] This report came after the Jane Club's twenty-seventh year of continuous operation. The Jane Club allowed individual members to flourish through the power of communal enterprise. Addams's organizational vision made this project possible.

As seen in the example of the Jane Club, Addams's philosophy of community organizing was responsive, anti-ideological, fluid, and methodologically anti-antagonistic. Hull House residents did not preplan their exchanges with the community but listened and responded to the needs of the neighborhood. Addams and the residents demonstrated their non-ideological nature by avoiding affiliation with established advocacy groups, despite opportunities to make such connections. Although socialists and anarchists were invited to speak at Hull House, there were no formal associations. Many residents held religious beliefs, but no settlement ties to organized religion were made. Furthermore, Addams's lack of ideology meant that she was open to many different paths to achieving success. For example, she was willing to collaborate with government agencies to advance societal interests. Finally, Addams's philosophy of community organizing was anti-antagonistic, which should not be confused with being nonconfrontational. On many occasions, Addams confronted entrenched others in her struggles to advance the interests of the neighborhood. She did so without engaging in personal rancor. For example, on three occasions she organized unsuccessful opposition campaigns to unseat the local and corrupt alderman, Johnny Powers. However, Addams avoided personal antagonism. Although disagreeing with

Powers's backroom deals and cronyism, she was objective enough to admire his ability to form close ties with the community.[9] She refused to villainize others, although she was not afraid of pointing out their errors. In her account of the 1894 Pullman strike, she delineates the mistakes in leadership that George Pullman made, including a lack of connection to his workers and a blind paternalism.[10] Despite her support for labor organizing, she also recounted the errors of the workers. Pullman was not characterized as inherently evil, but rather as an all-too-human man gone astray. In community organizing, Addams attempted to keep all people in the conversation and avoided alienating individuals through unnecessary personal antagonism.

In summary, Addams's community organizing supported her political philosophy, which emphasized social democracy, widespread participation, and the development of connected/sympathetic knowledge. Although her philosophy came alive through the work of Hull House, it did not reflect the entire settlement movement. The settlement movement was a very disparate amalgamation of efforts. The more than four hundred settlements that existed at the movement's peak had no formal ties to one another. For example, although Hull House avoided religious affiliation, many other settlement communities overtly embraced religion.[11] The movement also underwent drastic changes through its decline in the 1930s, the largest of which being the use of professional social workers. After World War I, fewer volunteers were forthcoming, resulting in the settlements employing more contracted professionals, who did not reside at the settlement. These settlements became increasingly bureaucratic and institutionalized and thus less like the fluid and responsive Hull House that Addams had managed. Addams viewed proximal relations as paramount. She overcame her outsider status in the Hull House neighborhood by treating her neighbors with dignity and respect, as well as by living in the area for almost fifty years. Subsequent settlement workers had more specialized education, as described by Judith Ann Trolander: "In place of residents, the post World War II settlement house hired increasing numbers of M.S.W.s, changed its methods and image, enlarged its professional organizations, and attracted different kinds of people as settlement house works. Professionalization was the underlying cause of these changes."[12] These professional social workers were more clearly marked as outsiders to the community. Settlement houses continued to work for the improvement of impoverished communities, but the philosophy of community organizing moved away from Addams's vision of a highly connected and engaged good neighbor. I mention this evolution because the settlement movement that Alinsky confronted and criticized was not the same one that Addams had created in the early decades at Hull House. Karl Marx once famously declared, "I am not a Marxist," in response to the many unsavory manifestations of his work. If Addams had confronted the professionalized settlement movement of the second half of the twentieth century, she might have similarly declared, "I am not a settlement worker."

The Alinsky Model of Community Organizing

In 1889, Addams (with Ellen Gates Starr) opened Hull House in West Chicago, on Halsted Street. A half century later, in 1939, Saul Alinsky and Joseph Meeghan organized the Back of the Yards community, located behind Chicago's Union Stock Yards, the subject of Upton Sinclair's *The Jungle*. As early as 1906, Addams described the "sickening stench and scum" in the Chicago stockyards as "unendurable."[13] The inhabitants of the neighborhood that Alinsky confronted were largely foreign born, suffered from high rates of unemployment, and resided amid the environmental nightmare of the stockyards, with its pervasive putrid odor. Alinsky led the formation of the Back of the Yards Neighborhood Council (BYNC), a confederation of numerous local groups, brought together to collectively address issues in the neighborhood. Many of the local ethnic communities were at odds with one another, but Alinsky and Meeghan negotiated a major public meeting at which churches, fraternal clubs, athletic clubs, local businesses, and labor unions were represented. Alinsky did a great deal of behind-the-scenes work to bring the parties together, and he coordinated a highly effective public campaign for the event. The local newspapers immediately hailed him as the architect of a new movement for community justice.[14] The Alinsky-led coalition successfully leveraged public outrage to bring expanded city services and political power to the Back of the Yards community. This effort launched his almost thirty-five-year career in community organizing, which found him replicating the model in other beleaguered urban areas through the Industrial Area Foundation (IAF). In 1940, after securing funding from philanthropist Marshall Field and progressive Catholics in Chicago, Alinsky created the IAF to systematize his community-organizing efforts. The IAF took the Alinsky method to impoverished areas in Baltimore, Detroit, Little Rock, Rochester, San Antonio, and Toledo. Meeghan stayed to work in the BYNC, while Alinsky moved from battleground to battleground.

Alinsky's philosophy of community organizing is based on power relations. He built grassroots organizations that democratically leveraged power to address social inequities. It begins with understanding the community. Alinsky, drawing upon his roots in social science, advocated social research as a means to thoroughly understand a neighborhood and its problems. As Robert Bailey Jr. describes it, "Organizers seek to mobilize a community's residents to attack problems affecting their community."[15] Social research is followed by the identification and development of local leadership, which Alinsky characterized as "native" or "indigenous" leadership.[16] Alinsky viewed contacting and fostering native leadership as crucial to the process of understanding the neighborhood and rallying the community around a cause. Professional organizers provide the skills, but the community gains its power through participation and coordination in a manner analogous to labor union organizing. Alinsky's approach was to create an overarching "community organization" made up of representatives of local groups. Invitations are extended to these community groups rather than to individuals. The strategy is one of strength in numbers that parallels the solidarity crucial for effective collective bargaining. Ultimately, Alinsky viewed community organizing as a power struggle to gain rights and privileges for marginalized communities: "The present power age denies and evaluates everything in terms of power. To this common and accepted view, the field of organization has been no exception. It is universally assumed that the function of a People's Organization is similar to that of any other kind of organization, which is to become so strong, so powerful, that it can achieve its ends."[17] For Alinsky, the operant metaphor for community organizing was that of a battle or game to be won.

The BYNC applied Alinsky's organizing philosophy successfully to bring tangible and intangible benefits to the community.[18] Tangible benefits included improved services to the neighborhood, and among the intangible benefits was a new sense of pride. One incident that reveals how Alinsky valorized the leveraging of power occurred in 1944. The event also serves to contrast Alinsky's approach with that of Addams. An opportunity arose to bring a branch station of the Infant Welfare Society (a children's health clinic) to the Back of the Yards community. Two local organizations, BYNC and the University of Chicago Settlement, vied to house the station. To win the battle, Alinsky told the Infant Welfare Society's president that if the University of Chicago Settlement housed the infant station, the priests of the largely Catholic neighborhood would initiate a boycott from the pulpit. Alinsky viewed this conflict as an opportunity to gain status for BYNC as the voice of the community, and he was determined not to lose. He escalated the antagonism by accusing the Chicago Settlement of being anti-Catholic because it gave out birth control information. Alinsky made this accusation despite his own pro–birth control beliefs.[19] In a public struggle, he backed the Chicago Settlement into a corner and rebuffed their efforts at conciliation until it was clear that BYNC was victorious. Alinsky had once again demonstrated how effective his methods were, but at what cost? As a result of the confrontation, the Chicago Settlement never fully regained its stature in the community.[20] The BYNC used its newfound status to fight for increasing benefits for the community.

Common Themes

Superficially, Addams and Alinsky appear to have had very different organizing philosophies. However, a delineation between style and philosophical commitments reveals more commonality than is usually attributed to them. Part of the challenge of making this separation is that Alinsky and members of his organization intentionally and forcefully depicted themselves as differing strongly from social settlements. Sidney Hyman, whose sister had been a resident of Hull House, became an activist for Alinsky in the BYNC. In a 1983 interview describing his enthusiasm for working with Alinsky, Hyman contrasted Addams's philosophy with that of Alinsky:

> The good Episcopalian ladies with the good-bad conscience did everything for Hull House. These were the so-called hellfare workers, the Lady Bountifuls. Going to work for Jane Addams at Hull-House was a romantic thing to do for a young, sensitive woman. [Their noble purpose was] to help, but it was always the Lady Bountifuls who were *doing* the helping. Now Saul comes along and turns it around and sort of sets the whole Hull-House idea on its head. He says he doesn't want the hellfare worker, he

doesn't want the Lady Bountiful; he wants people to help themselves and *that* became a very romantic idea. A lot of people wanted to get in on that one, just like an earlier generation a lot of people wanted to get in on the Hull-House idea.[21]

Besides the blatant condescension and sexism in this quote, Hyman made the error of associating Addams with unreflective charity work; however, the real target of his critique should have been what the settlements evolved into during the post-Addams era rather than Addams's philosophy. Addams would likely have been aghast at such an association with charity work because she vehemently contended that settlements were intended to facilitate education and connection, not charity. In *Democracy and Social Ethics*, she devotes an entire chapter to criticizing well-meaning, but ineffective charity workers who fail to understand the communities that they attempt to serve. Addams's criticism of charity workers is strikingly similar to Hyman and Alinsky's criticism of social settlement workers. Addams challenges the class structure of charity, for example, when she criticizes the charity worker who judges the cleanliness of the neighborhood home "over against her own parasitic cleanliness and a social standing only attained through status."[22] The notion that Addams stood for charity, in opposition to Alinsky, who stood for collective action, is not borne out by historical examination. It can be demonstrated that Addams and Alinsky shared much in terms of their philosophy of community organizing, with some important exceptions.

Addams and Alinsky shared a concern for listening to and learning the needs of the community, employing both quantitative and qualitative means to gain perspective. When asked how to organize people, Alinsky responded, "You find out what they care about, what they are worried about, and you organize them around these issues."[23] Addams began her settlement with the simple plan of being a good neighbor, but within five years of opening Hull House, she and her cohort were engaging in systematic research to understand the community. In 1895, Addams coauthored *Hull-House Maps and Papers*, a groundbreaking social study on the ethnicity and conditions surrounding the settlement. Historian Kathryn Kish Sklar refers to this study as "the single most important work by American women social scientists before 1900."[24] In the introduction, Addams makes it clear that *Hull-House Maps and Papers* is not in the interest of science, but part of a connection to the community that will serve to facilitate progress: "The residents of Hull-House offer these maps and papers to the public, not as exhaustive treatises, but as recorded observations, which may possibly be of value, because they are immediate, and the result of long acquaintance. All the writers have been in actual residence in Hull-House, some of them for five years; their energies however, have been chiefly directed not towards sociological investigation, but to constructive work."[25] In this manner, both Addams and Alinsky demonstrated a respect for the knowledge generated by social science and the scientific method, and each understood the need for presence and responsiveness beyond quantitative analysis.

Both Alinsky and Addams advocated for the active participation of community members in the organizing of social efforts. Addams recognized that when existing social institutions do not provide a reasonable means for citizen participation, those citizens will organize to resist. For example, according to Addams, an unresponsive government "forces the most patriotic citizens to ignore the Government and to embody their scruples and hopes of progress in voluntary organizations."[26] Hull House afforded numerous opportunities for local groups to organize, particularly as clubs or labor unions. The settlement acted as an incubator for such groups, providing meeting space and expertise without formal affiliations. Similarly, Alinsky viewed his organizations as fully democratic: "This kind of organization can be built only if people are working together for real, attainable objectives."[27] Alinsky's community groups were democratic to the point that he regretted some of the directions chosen by local groups he helped found.[28]

Both Addams and Alinsky were committed to giving the disenfranchised a voice. Addams may have held paternalistic ideas when she opened Hull House, but she soon realized that the community needed to speak for itself: "The residents at Hull House find in themselves a constantly increasing tendency to consult their neighbors on the advisability of each new undertaking."[29] Addams came to view the active participation of the marginalized as essential to the success of the settlement. For Addams, settlements "draw into participation in our culture large numbers of persons who would otherwise have to remain outside."[30] In the same way, Alinsky was very concerned that the United States was facing a crisis of disenfranchisement: "It is a grave situation when a people resign their citizenship or when a resident of a great city, though he may desire to take a hand, lacks the means to participate."[31] Both community organizations provided citizens with a means to reengage themselves with political processes. In this trajectory, Alinsky and Addams held an expansive view of democracy that entailed a citizen's duty for active involvement. Correspondingly, both had an abiding faith in humanity. Alinsky describes the community organizer as having "a complete commitment to the belief that if people have the power, the opportunity to act, in the long run they will, most of the time, reach the right decisions."[32]

The resonance between the social philosophies of Addams and Alinsky is not surprising if the Chicago School connection is taken into account. Addams and Hull House helped shape the sociology department of the University of Chicago, which in turn influenced Alinsky's approach to community organizing. Mary Jo Deegan documents the strong ties between Addams and the early sociologists of the Chicago School, George Herbert Mead and William I. Thomas. During this early period, the sociologists collaborated with Addams often and were frequent visitors to Hull House, just as Addams visited and lectured at the University of Chicago. The academics hailed the publication of *Hull-House Maps and Papers* as a landmark work in urban sociology. The next generation of sociologists, including Robert Ezra Park and Ernest W. Burgess, were also interested in social settlements, but were more concerned with professionalizing the discipline of sociology in a manner that distanced itself from social work. An implicit gender divide emerged, as social workers were largely female and the academic sociologists were almost exclusively male. Alinsky attended the University of Chicago from 1926 to 1932, by which time most of the first generation of sociologists had left. Park and Burgess likely mentioned Addams only sparingly in the classroom, but this did not diminish her influence upon them. As Lawrence J. Engel puts it, "Although these male sociologists failed to acknowledge the significance of Addams, their work was nevertheless influenced by Hull House: its community-mapping techniques, its emphasis upon the social dimensions of democratic neighborhood life, and its institutional relationships within the community (labor churches, city agencies, etc.)."[33] Even though Alinsky was loath to credit his academic roots in forming his philosophy of community organizing, Engel identifies clear evidence of connection. Equally compelling is Deegan's evidence for Addams's influencing the Chicago School. This genealogy places Addams as an indirect and unacknowledged mentor of Alinsky and explains much of their philosophical convergence.

Divergence

Where Addams and Alinsky differed was in methodology and long-range vision. Addams emphasized cooperation devoid of antagonism. Her interest was in widening the circle of those actively engaged in any particular issue, and thus she avoided unnecessary alienation. Addams believed in the power of rational argument to sway the views of her opponents. She was not naive about conflict and recognized that it occurred, but she had faith in the ability of people to make common cause. Addams recognized the role of power and the ability that Hull House had to leverage its power. For example, Addams describes one function of the social settlement as being a "big brother whose mere presence on the play ground protects the little ones from bullies."[34] Nevertheless, their rhetorical methods diverged widely. Addams was guarded in her remarks in order to keep people engaged in the conversation. Alinsky was flamboyantly bombastic to intentionally provoke opponents. For example, in describing the difference between social workers and his organizers, Alinsky declared, "They organize to get rid of four-legged rats and stop there; we organize to get rid of four-legged rats so we can get on to removing two-legged rats."[35] He enjoyed a good battle, and he particularly enjoyed winning. Alinsky's organizations viewed each effort at social justice as a contest: "We are concerned with how to create mass organization to seize power and give it to the people."[36] Alinsky's *Rules for Radicals* maintains numerous war metaphors that describe community organizing as "warfare" with the "enemy," requiring "tactics" to gain and redistribute power. Accordingly, Alinsky's abrasiveness elicited numerous critics. Addams had her detractors as well, but they were for the positions that she took, not because of her rhetorical demeanor.

Methodology was not the only difference between the two. Perhaps more substantially, Addams and Alinsky had different approaches to the scope and long-range goals of community organizing. Alinsky was vague about the broad social changes he was attempting to institute and made little effort to thematize across the individual battles for social justice that he was waging. Joseph Heathcott claims that Alinsky's "lack of broader political vision" made his philosophy of community organizing less serviceable in an environment where large, stable organizational constituencies such as unions and churches were not there to support his planned confrontations. By contrast, Addams viewed social progress as the overarching goal to which all efforts are connected. For example, she found no contradiction in arguing for labor rights at the local level and advocating for peace at the international level. Both advanced the cause of social democracy. For Addams, war was regressive and wasteful and thus a threat to society. The success of labor unions brought greater quality of work life for all citizens and was thus a boon to society as well. Addams's philosophy also envisioned ongoing efforts at community organizing. For Addams, the social settlements were intended to be lasting good neighbors. She led the effort to convert the settlement workers' outsider status to insider status by living in proximity and reciprocity with oppressed peoples. Alinsky's organizations developed leadership talent within the community, and intended it to be strong enough to last, but there was no effort at a long-term presence by the organizer. Once the community organized, it was on its own with occasional consulting from the outside. These differences in method and vision cannot be directly correlated to success. Both Addams and Alinsky had their successes, and their failures.

An interesting example of the stylistic difference between Addams and Alinsky has to do with their approach to higher education. They both were college educated and benefited tremendously from the skills, knowledge, and mentors of their academic experience. Both found fault with abstract scholarship that found no basis in social advancement. Alinsky was explicit: "I never appealed to people based on abstract values."[37] Addams also recognized the limitations of abstract ideals. When it came to organizing social efforts around an issue such as prostitution or child labor, Addams thought it was crucial to use tangible examples that resonated with the audience in order to fuel interest and passion for the subject. Nevertheless, she maintained a commitment to scholarly reflection to help characterize and give meaning to social issues. In regard to a holistic notion of peace that was more than the absence of war and required local and international effort, Addams proposed that "it requires the philosopher to unify these spiritual efforts of the common man into the internationalism of good will."[38] Addams did have her criticism of scholarship that became too academic, as reflected in her falling out with the University of Chicago. Comparatively, Alinsky appears almost bitter in his anti-intellectual tirades. In a 1965 interview, Alinsky mused, "In college I took a lot of sociology courses too, but I can't say they made a deep impression on me. . . . Today the University of Chicago sociology department is just a tribe of head counters."[39] The professionalized social settlement workers of the era constituted one of the educated groups that

Alinsky railed against; he referred to their training as "formalized garbage they learned in school."[40]

Gender Mapping

Ultimately, Alinsky and his followers emphasized that they were engaging in a new brand of community organizing. Note that Alinsky reveled in the word *radical*. Alinsky's two most important works are *Rules for Radicals* and *Reveille for Radicals*. Sanford D. Horwitt's biography of Alinsky is titled *Let Them Call Me Radical*, and Marion K. Sanders's published interview with Alinsky is titled *The Professional Radical*. Alinsky defines a radical as "that unique person who actually believes what he says. He is that person to whom the common good is the greatest personal value. He is that person who genuinely and completely believes in mankind. The radical is so completely identified with mankind that he personally shares the pain, the injustices, and the sufferings of all his fellow men."[41] Despite this fixation with the term, was Alinsky a radical? Alinsky advocated for social reform and change using tactics designed to provoke and gain attention, but he did not question fundamental institutions of U.S. society such as capitalism. By many standards, including those of feminist theorists, Alinsky was a mild radical at best. Sociologists Donald C. Reitzes and Dietrich C. Reitzes claim that despite self-description to the contrary, Alinsky's philosophy of community organizing was not "radical and revolutionary."[42] During the civil rights movement in the United States, the Student Nonviolent Coordinating Committee (SNCC) held dialogues with Alinsky and his organizers, but the organization became frustrated because he was only advocating reform. Mike Miller, who worked for both SNCC and, later, an Alinsky organization, notes: "A common label attached to Alinsky was that he was only 'local,' failing to understand that major decisions were made at a national level."[43] I suggest that Alinsky was using the term *radical* not in the sense of challenging existing institutions and structures, but as describing a curmudgeon with integrity. Furthermore, the term is clearly gendered masculine in Alinsky's mind. Sexist in both language and style, Alinsky described a radical as a man who does not use methods traditionally described as "feminine." Further, in his writings, all Alinsky's examples of radicals—John P. Altgeld, Edward Bellamy, John Brown, Patrick Henry, Thomas

Jefferson, Henry Lloyd, Horace Mann, Thomas Paine, Upton Sinclair, and Lincoln Steffens—are male.

What is intriguing about the difference in methodology between Addams and Alinsky is how well it maps onto gender stereotypes. Addams was cooperative and caring in fostering lifelong learning and relationships. Alinsky was competitive and abrasive in trying to achieve victories in the name of social justice. Alinsky's organizing did not exclude women (although it did put up challenges for them, as Jo Freeman attests), but its demands and style favored men, and this was borne out demographically.[44] Kenneth Boulding describes Alinsky's community organizing as requiring "behavior more typically identified as male; activism, aggression, self assertion, and organizing more frequently associated with the 'managerial sex.'"[45] Perhaps not surprisingly, the "masculine" approach has been considered realistic and efficacious while the "feminine" approach has been thought of as naive and simplistic. Accordingly, for decades Alinsky has been assigned the title "father of community organizing," while Addams's community organizing legacy through social settlements has been overshadowed. Until recently, Addams has been excluded from serious consideration in philosophy and sociology as well as from association with community organizing or radicalism.[46] Given the breadth of her social theorizing, the volume of her publications, and her impact on local communities and international policies and institutions, one has to wonder if implicit sexism is not at the heart of her exclusion.

Susan Stall and Randy Stoecker authored one of the few comparative studies of gender and community organizing. They compare the "Alinsky approach" to a "women-centered approach" in community organizing; thus Addams is not a direct target of comparison, but she is a leading figure in their women-centered approach. This insightful and comprehensive study divides the two approaches along a split of public/private spheres. According to Stall and Stoecker, Alinsky's methods assume working within the public sphere, while a women-centered approach must traverse the private to the public. The assumptions of the two approaches are very different, with the Alinsky model assuming the self-interested agent and the women-centered approach assuming a caring model. Accordingly, Alinsky's organizers must find the issues that resonate with people's individual self-interest. The women-centered model seeks to foster connections between community members to facilitate caring.

Although this is a useful and well-documented analysis, a few of the assumptions found in Stall and Stoecker's discussion appear to belie the gender biases that they wished to highlight. Comparing an individual's community-organizing approach (Alinsky's) to an amalgamation of approaches (women centered) appears unbalanced. Stall and Stoecker claim, "Unlike the Alinsky model, the women-centered model of community organizing cannot be attributed to a single person or movement."[47] The implication of this statement is that Alinsky was solely responsible for his philosophy of community organizing, an approach that feminists have long criticized: the myth of the heroic male. Such a decontextualized claim ignores Alinsky's training and acknowledged mentors such as labor organizer John L. Lewis, as well as the aforementioned Park and Burgess. Furthermore, such an approach assumes that what Alinsky did was novel. His tactics may have been unique in the context of community organizing, but much of his philosophy, a social epistemology of participative and proximal relations, can be found in Addams's theories of the settlement movement.

Stall and Stoecker also seem to implicitly denigrate the ability of a women-centered approach to structure large-scale projects: "The presence, and partial restriction, of women in the private sphere leads the women-centered organizing model to emphasize a very different organizing process formed around creating an ideal private-sphere-like setting rather than a large public sphere organization."[48] Just because women were restricted from the public sphere did not mean that they did not enter or manipulate it. Addams's Hull House was very much an entrée into the public sphere that Addams and her cohort leveraged to become more widely influential. For example, Robyn Muncy documents how Hull House residents were responsible for creating the Women's Bureau, the first government agency headed by a woman, longtime Hull House resident Julia Lathrop. The Women's Bureau was not only a women-centered organization, but it also integrated numerous feminist principles of operation.[49] To be fair, Stall and Stoecker are not alone in assuming the primacy of Alinsky's community organizing, but it is intriguing that gender bias runs so deep that even those attending to it cannot escape it.[50]

Alinsky accomplished a great deal in his lifetime, and modern-day activists do well to study his philosophy and methods, but his legacy is perhaps generally overstated and inflated to match his larger-than-life personality. Judith Ann Trolander notes that Alinsky was a powerful spokesperson for community organizing and a brilliant self-promoter, which served to advance his cause.[51] Alinsky appears to have influenced the extent of his own legacy.

Conclusion: Addams as a Model of Feminist Community Organizing

In her study of community organizing, Marie Weil lists various U.S. social movements with significant female leadership, and no one is associated with more movements than Addams. Despite this delineation, Weil falls prey to gender perceptions, claiming:

> Despite a rich and proud heritage of female organizers and movement leaders, the field of community organization, in both its teaching models and its major exponents, has been a male-dominated preserve, where, even though values are expressed in terms of participatory democracy, much of the focus within the dominant practice methods has been nonsupportive or antithetical to feminism. Strategies have largely been based on "macho-power" models, manipulativeness, and zero-sum gamesmanship.[52]

I would qualify Weil's largely accurate description by suggesting not that the field has been male dominated, but that the portrayal of it has been. Much like Alinsky's effort to depict himself as using necessary masculine methods over and against inferior feminine methods, history has masked the successful communitarian and cooperative efforts of women organizers as anachronistic. In this manner, feminist community organizing is hidden behind the acclaim heaped upon male organizing. The feminist process of reassessing given historical truths reveals more grassroots organizing and theorizing about community building than is commonly assumed.

Addams develops a feminist philosophy of community organizing emphasizing proximal relations and sympathetic knowledge that in some ways resonates more with modern feminist sensibilities than it did with first or second wave feminism. In 1990, Patricia Yancey Martin explored the dimensions of a feminist organization. She offered numerous definitions, one of which was that a feminist organization is "pro-woman, political, and socially transformational."[53] Accordingly, Addams's approach to community organizing was inclusive, providing new and unique opportunities to empower women, including athletic expression, the dissemination of reproductive information, and economic independence. Hull House residents often found themselves engaged in political conflicts.

Ultimately, it was a women-centered community that modeled what women could accomplish in the public sphere. This form of community organizing has a modern quality in its fluidity and cosmopolitanism, and yet it sought to create lasting social relationships. Addams's settlement community was not bogged down in layers of bureaucracy or institutional rules and was therefore capable of responding quickly to the needs of the neighborhood. Addams embraced diversity in a manner that was ahead of her time. She believed that cultural and intellectual pluralism were crucial for the success of a democracy. Finally, her approach to community organizing supported the notion of setting down lasting roots in the community to provide ongoing service. This quality might particularly appeal to modern feminists in a world dominated by truncated social transactions and by technology that facilitates long-distance and transitory interactions. Hull House, and Addams's reflections upon society and social settlements, remains a fascinating example of feminist community organizing that has not been fully mined for its ongoing significance.

Notes

1. The Chicago School is associated with scholars at the University of Chicago in the very late nineteenth century and early twentieth century in the fields of economics, philosophy, psychology, religion, and sociology; however, the meaning of the term has evolved differently in the various disciplines. Addams was associated with early influential members of the Chicago School, including philosophers John Dewey and George Herbert Mead, while the later sociologists Robert Ezra Park and Ernest W. Burgess influenced Alinsky.

2. Robert A. Slayton, *Back of the Yards: The Making of a Local Democracy* (Chicago: University of Chicago Press, 1988), 198; Allen F. Davis, *Spearheads for Reform: The Social Settlements and the Progressive Movement, 1890–1914* (New York: Oxford University Press, 1967), 17, 20.

3. See, for example, Donald C. Reitzes and Dietrich C. Reitzes, "Saul D. Alinsky: A Neglected Source but Promising Resource," *American Sociologist* 17 (February 1982): 47–56.

4. Jo Freeman (aka Joreen), "On the Origins of the Women's Liberation Movement from a Strictly Personal Perspective," http://www.jofreeman.com/aboutjo/persorg.htm#footnote1 (accessed May 16, 2008).

5. Jane Addams, "Hull House (Chicago)," in *Encyclopedia of Social Reform*, ed. William D. P. Bliss (New York: Funk and Wagnalls, 1908), 587–90.

6. For a discussion of sympathetic knowledge, see Maurice Hamington, *The Social Philosophy of Jane Addams* (Urbana: University of Illinois Press, 2009).

7. Jane Addams, "The Objective Value of a Social Settlement," in *The Jane Addams Reader*, ed. Jean Bethke Elshtain (New York: Basic Books, 2002), 45.

8. The Women of Hull House, *Hull-House Year Book: Forty-fifth Year* (Chicago: Fred Klein, 1934?), 57.

9. Jane Addams, *Democracy and Social Ethics* (Urbana: University of Illinois Press, 2002), 99.

10. Jane Addams, "A Modern Lear," *Survey* 29 (November 2, 1912), 131–37.

11. Mina Carson, *Settlement Folk* (Chicago: University of Chicago Press, 1990), 219n38.

12. Judith Ann Trolander, *Professionalism and Social Change: From the Settlement House Movement to Neighborhood Centers, 1886 to the Present* (New York: Columbia University Press, 1987), 31–32.

13. Addams identifies the problems in the Chicago stockyards as a failure of the local government to adhere to the will of the local inhabitants, foreshadowing what Alinsky would confront more than thirty years later. Jane Addams, *Newer Ideals of Peace* (Urbana: University of Illinois Press, 2007), 58.

14. Sanford D. Horwitt, *Let Them Call Me Rebel* (New York: Vintage Books, 1992), 75.

15. Robert Bailey Jr., *Radicals in Urban Politics: The Alinsky Approach* (Chicago: University of Chicago Press, 1972), 49.

16. Saul Alinsky, *Reveille for Radicals* (New York: Vintage Books, 1969), 64.

17. Ibid., 53.

18. The BYNC Web site lists dozens of accomplishments enacted since its inception. http://www.bync.org/site/information/bync

19. Saul Alinsky, *Rules for Radicals: A Pragmatic Primer for Realistic Radicals* (New York: Vintage Books, 1971), 94.

20. Horwitt, *Let Them Call Me Rebel*, 138–43.

21. Sidney Hyman, quoted in Horwitt, *Let Them Call Me Rebel*, 127.

22. Addams, *Democracy and Social Ethics*, 12.

23. Saul Alinsky in Marion K. Sanders, *The Professional Radical: Conversations with Saul Alinsky* (New York: Harper and Row, 1970),

24. Kathryn Kish Sklar, "Hull-House Maps and Papers: Social Science as Women's Work in the 1890s," in *Gender and American Social Science: The Formative Years*, ed. Helene Silverberg (Princeton: Princeton University Press, 1998), 127.

25. Jane Addams, "Prefatory Note," in *Hull-House Maps and Papers: A Presentation of Nationalities and Wages in a Congested District of Chicago, Together with Comments and Essays on Problems Growing out of the Social Conditions by the Residents of Hull House* (Urbana: University of Illinois Press, 2007), 45.

26. Addams, *Newer Ideals of Peace*, 62.

27. Alinsky in Sanders, *The Professional Radical*, 48.

28. Bailey, *Radicals in Urban Politics*, 49.

29. Addams, "The Objective Value of a Social Settlement," 41.

30. Jane Addams, "Widening the Circle of Enlightenment," *Journal of Adult Education* 2, no. 3 (1930): 279.

31. Alinsky, *Rules for Radicals*, xxvi.

32. Alinsky, *Reveille for Radicals*, xiv.

33. Lawrence J. Engel, "Saul D. Alinsky and the Chicago School," *Journal of Speculative Philosophy* 16, no. 1 (2002): 63.

34. Addams, "The Objective Value of a Social Settlement," 43.

35. Alinsky, *Rules for Radicals*, 68.

36. Ibid., 3.

37. Alinsky in Sanders, *The Professional Radical*, 31.

38. Addams, *Newer Ideals of Peace*, 15.

39. Ibid., 14–15.

40. Alinsky, *Rules for Radicals*, 68.

41. Alinsky, *Reveille for Radicals*, 15.

42. Reitzes and Reitzes, "Saul D. Alinsky," 54.

43. Mike Miller, "The 60s Student Movement and Saul Alinsky: An Alliance That Never Happened," *Social Policy* 34 (Winter 2003–Spring 2004): 106.

44. Susan Stall and Randy Stoecker, "Community Organizing or Organizing Community? Gender and the Crafts of Empowerment," *Gender and Society* 12, no. 6 (1998): 735; Trolander, *Professionalism and Social Change*, 65.

45. Kenneth Boulding, "Alienation and Economic Development: The Larger Background of the Settlement Movement," in *Neighborhood Goals in a Rapidly Changing World* (New York: NFS, 1958), 62–63.

46. In their pioneering work, Mary Jo Deegan and Charlene Haddock Seigfried have asserted Addams's intellectual significance in sociology and philosophy, respectively. Deegan, *Jane Addams and the Men of the Chicago School, 1892–1918* (New Brunswick, N.J.: Transaction Books, 1988); Charlene Haddock Seigfried, *Pragmatism and Feminism: Reweaving the Social Fabric* (Chicago: University of Chicago Press, 1996).

47. Stall and Stoecker, "Community Organizing or Organizing Community?" 736.

48. Ibid., 746.

49. Robyn Muncy, *Creating a Female Dominion in American Reform, 1890–1935* (New York: Oxford University Press, 1991).

50. Joan Acker has observed that men, without challenging implicit assumptions about masculine primacy, dominate organizational theory. Joan Acker, "Hierarchies, Jobs, Bodies: A Theory of Gendered Organizations," *Gender and Society* 4, no. 2 (1990): 139–58.

51. Trolander, *Professionalism and Social Change*, 144.

52. Marie Weil, "Women, Community, and Organizing," in *Feminist Visions for Social Work*, ed. Nan Van Den Bergh and Lynn B. Cooper (Silver Spring, Md.: National Association of Social Workers, 1986), 192.

53. Patricia Yancey Martin, "Rethinking Feminist Organizations," *Gender and Society* 4, no. 2 (1990): 182.

11

Examining Addams's Democratic Theory Through a Postcolonial Feminist Lens

Judy D. Whipps

American military missions throughout the twentieth century and into the twenty-first have often been described by the U.S. government as attempts to "bring democracy" to the world or to make the world safe for democracy. Yet a clear articulation of what the term *democracy* means, beyond merely the process of voting, has not been offered by those who advocate such policies. In attempting to export American democracy

Thanks to Sor-hoon Tan and John Whalen-Bridge of the National University of Singapore for organizing a 2007 conference on Deweyan Pragmatism, where some of the ideas in this chapter were first discussed. The papers from that conference are published in Tan and Whalen-Bridge, *Democracy as Culture: Deweyan Pragmatism in a Globalizing World* (Albany: State University of New York, 2008).

through military means, U.S. officials, it appears, often expect to impose a Western view of democracy on other cultures, violating the democratic ideal of self-governance. Global activists and American thinkers have critiqued the "close association of democracy promotion with military intervention and regime change" (Carothers 2007, v) and have identified the military mission of "democracy" as a type of imperialism. In a similar way, many feminist thinkers and activists have critiqued the concept of Western democracy as a type of cultural and philosophical colonialism. A significant part of the life work of Jane Addams, as that of a visionary American thinker, centered around the mission of democracy. Given that her philosophy is an early model of feminist thought, it is informative to reexamine her vision of social democracy in light of these critiques. The first part of this chapter will briefly summarize how Addams's ideal of democracy developed and matured during her life experiences; the second part will examine whether her pragmatist philosophy of democracy holds up under a postcolonial feminist critique.

Addams's aspiration for a democratic society evolved with her as she continually reflected on her ideals in light of her experiences.[1] When she moved to Halsted Street in 1889, Addams had a desire to engage life as a participant rather than an observer, to "live in a really living world" rather than a "shadowy intellectual or aesthetic reflection of it" (1910/1990, 39). In the early years at Hull House, she tried out various philosophical lenses in order to understand and communicate her work. In 1892, in her earliest published articles, she framed her work in a Christian context, albeit in a form of humanitarian Christianity that could only be expressed in action. Taking Toynbee Hall as a model in the first years of Hull House, Addams led the residents in evening prayer and Bible reading, yet refused to allow Hull House to be considered mission work.[2] She also looked to art, literature, and other forms of culture as possible avenues of social change. But by the time she published her first book, *Democracy and Social Ethics*, she had found a theoretical grounding for her work, a conceptual framework that was large enough to keep growing as she went from neighborhood to global engagement, and that was aspirational enough to call others to join with her in this vision. Social democracy had become her central conceptual framework. This ideal of democracy informed her work with the labor unions, her activism in the women's movement, her reform work in education, and her leadership in the global peace movement. Democracy had become a concept large enough to serve as a beacon to Addams in the many re-creations of her career.

Growing up in Illinois in a prosperous family, Addams absorbed the liberal democracy that she learned from her father, a state senator, who was influenced by the rhetoric of the Civil War and Lincoln's presidency. The democracy that she learned at home and in college was for most part the Enlightenment era democracy of equality and human rights, focused on heroic individualism. As a child, her father paid her nickels or quarters to read the lives of Plutarch, which reinforced her sense of the heroic. Although her father was successful by the time Jane was born, she would have been aware that he built his wealth from the ground up in what was considered a frontier town, so she grew up also immersed in the culture of capitalistic achievement, with the understanding that success came through individual effort.

Yet by the early 1890s, Addams also had developed a conception of organic community, which in some ways conflicted with and moderated an articulation of liberal democratic individualism. In her earliest writings, she speaks of community as an organism, with all segments of society reliant on others, a living entity composed of individuals as organic elements of a whole.[3] As part of a social organization, she positioned the good of the individual or the group as ultimately dependent on the good of the whole and relationally dependent on others in the group.[4] This interdependent model of society is dramatically different from Lockean individualism, in which each individual is pitted against all others in a fight for goods and survival.

Addams came to critique earlier formulations of liberty and democracy that were not developed out of experience and interaction and that did not embrace the whole of society. She did not reject outright the liberal concepts of rights and autonomy, but rather believed that society had moved beyond political liberal democracy to a social democracy built on dialogue, joint experiences, and social equality. By 1902, when she wrote *Democracy and Social Ethics*, Addams theorized democracy as a continually evolving form of social association that must be redeveloped in each generation and in each locality. She reframed democracy as an ethical system, in which those who aspired to it were "under a moral obligation in choosing our experiences" and those experiences must lead to "mixing on the thronged and common road," where we can "at least see the size of one another's burdens" (1902/2002, 8, 7). Addams believed that social democracy as an ethical system represented evolutionary progress beyond individual ethics or family-based ethics, to an ethic that required one to think of good for the whole. Although she had been influenced by utilitarian thinkers such as John Stuart Mill, she did not portray this community ethic in utilitarian terms, as the good of the many outweighing the good of the individual, but rather as a requirement that each person and social institution prioritize the development of social goods that were integral to an organic social whole.

As Addams's experiential pragmatism developed, she moved theoretical democratic idealism to an understanding that democracy can exist only as a living principle, in particular localities and times. One of her critiques of the democratic vision of the American founders was that "their idealism was the type that is afraid of experience" (1907/2003, 32). Working with many different immigrant cultures, and working with European counterparts on social issues (see Sklar 1998), helped her understand that a democracy must grow out of local context and experience. As such, she argued against expanding American boundaries in the name of democracy and was opposed to the Spanish-American War in 1898 and the annexing of the Philippines shortly thereafter, on the grounds that it constituted imperialism. Addams was member of the Central Anti-Imperialist League of Chicago, which published one of her early essays on peace, "Democracy or Militarism." This essay criticized Americans' desire for colonies, warning that "with the success of imperialism the decadence of our republic will have already set in" (1899/2003, 2).

Democracy and Social Ethics was followed by *Newer Ideals of Peace* (1907). Here she argued that the cooperative ethic of democracy was threatened by the hierarchy and competition inherent in militarism. Writing long before the threat of World War I materialized, she conceptualized peace as much more than the absence of war and argued that peace required a reversal of militaristic and competitive practices in everyday life. She critiqued the classism exhibited by the founders of U.S. democracy, finding them militaristic in that "they founded their new government by an involuntary reference to a lower social state . . . [and] . . . depended upon penalties, coercion, compulsion, remnants of military codes to hold the community together" (1907/2003, 22). They relied on these traditional tactics of force, Addams thought, because they did not fully trust the people (23). That these hierarchies led to cultural and political imperialism, even in relations with immigrant groups, was apparent to Addams. "This attitude of contempt, of provincialism, this survival of the spirit of the conqueror toward an inferior people, has many manifestations" (29), extending to local civil governments, and even into family relationships.

Addams warned of equating democracy with nationalism as early as 1901 (1901/2003, 11). When democracy later became synonymous with American nationalism during and after the World War I era, Addams nearly stopped using the term. Wilson had used democracy as a rationale to call the United States to join the war, telling Americans that this was a war to "safeguard the world for democracy." In her later book *Peace and Bread*, published in 1922, the only time she uses the word *democracy* is when she is quoting war slogans; not once does she use it to describe her own efforts.

In the last decade of her life, she devoted her time to global peace work. She occasionally talked about democracy as an aspiration, but not with the same sense of hope as in her earlier years. On the rare occasions when she used the term, it was often with some nostalgia, as in 1934, when recalling the nineteenth-century vigor for "self-government and democracy," which had been replaced, she says, by a "demand for economic security" (1934/2003, 361). Yet the concept remained an inspiration for her. In a WILPF presidential address in 1929, she quotes Czech president Tomás Masaryk's statement that "democracy is a system of life," a phrase that could accurately describe Addams's continuing belief in democracy (1929/2003, 295).

Postcolonial Feminist Critique

Given that Addams was a formative thinker in the late nineteenth-century reconstruction of democracy beyond classical liberalism, and that she became a global figure in the women's peace movement, considering her democracy in a postcolonial feminist light illustrates both its problems and its strengths.

Since the second wave feminist movement of the 1960s and 1970s, women of color have critiqued Western feminist thought for its privileging of white women's experience as normative. Third world women and global feminists have continued this critique by illustrating similarities between the economic and political imperialism of globalization and the cultural hegemony of Western political thought. Chandra Talpade Mohanty's 1984 essay "Under Western Eyes: Feminist Scholarship and Colonial Discourse" was a beginning step toward a larger dialogue about the hegemony of Western feminist thought. Drawing a parallel to economic and political national exploitation, Mohanty named "the assumption of 'the West' as the primary referent in feminist theory and practice" as cultural imperialism. She critiqued positioning "Western/white women as the norm," noting that such a norm essentializes third world women as "other" and thus reenacts colonization (1991, 52). She examines how individuals and women in third world cultures are represented in theories of democracy, as well as noting that Western political and economic assumptions about democratic values are necessarily connected to capitalism. Mohanty's later work *Feminism Without Borders* expands this critique of feminist cultural colonization as well as considers how the stories and voices of women from diverse backgrounds could be included in feminist political and activist discussions. (A fuller examination of Addams's work in light of postcolonial critiques could be made; however, this chapter considers only those areas that apply to Addams's articulation of democracy.)

Democracy and Human Rights

Understanding the feminist critique of democracy requires examining the feminist critique of liberalism. The liberal Enlightenment concept of the "citizen" in a liberal democracy has been critiqued by many feminists, particularly Carole Pateman, Susan Moller Okin, and Chantal Mouffe.[5] As conceived in liberal democratic theory, the citizen is a nonparticularized ideal assumed to be blind to race, class, gender, and ethnicity, yet too often is normed as white, male, and privileged. Okin points out that the foundational concept of liberal human rights as articulated by Locke and his contemporaries was intentionally "formulated with male household heads in mind" (2000, 28). For example, Lockean human rights included the right of privacy within the family against outside intrusion, which for him encompassed "not interfering with a father's decision about whom his daughter should marry," without consideration of the daughter's rights (28). The late twentieth-century global human rights movement reformulated early liberal equality as inclusive of women's rights, as exhibited in the 1994 United Nations Human Rights Congress in Vienna, which equated women's rights with human rights. Yet these declarations have not been sufficient to end the oppression of women. In particular, the connections between global capitalism and democratization have resulted in Western political and economic support for economics that deny equal rights for women (Bayes, Hawkesworth, and Kelly 2001, 7–8).

Given that a vibrant liberal democracy is founded upon civic dialogue and deliberation, feminists have also pointed out that social equality is necessary for effective engagement in deliberation.[6] It is not sufficient to presume a political equality of representation that is necessarily separate from inequality in private lives. Such imbalance of power in our private and social lives necessarily affects the nature of political deliberation, which in turn shapes the laws that govern rights and equality. Addams lived in an era and in a community that was profoundly divided by economic class and racial divisions, yet she was able to conceive a democracy that was inclusive of differences.

The history of American exclusionary politics has demonstrated that a political democracy is not sufficient to ensure equality or human rights and therefore is insufficient to ensure women's rights. As Seyla Benhabib points out, the participants of a democratic discourse are limited within sovereign boundaries and by the ways that nations define citizenship, thereby often reifying traditional inclusions and exclusions. A global discussion of rights requires that social and human rights have been "disassociated from shared identity and political membership" (2006, 45). Because Addams reappropriated and reconfigured democracy as an ethic of social equality, rather than merely political governance, her theory of social democracy supports Benhabib's vision of rights disaggregated from political membership.

Although Addams does not clearly explicate the tension between individualistic liberalism and social equality, she is clear that the liberal rights described by the founders of American democracy are not sufficient for the democratic community she envisions. In "Addams's Radical Democracy: Moving Beyond Rights," Maurice Hamington draws out the ways that Addams critiqued the "elitist standpoint" of eighteenth-century democratic theory as unable to engage with and adapt to the real experiences of a diverse society (2004, 220). Addams does not develop an explicit philosophical feminist critique of the gender exclusions in liberal theory; however, in her use of women's experiences as the referent for thinking about rights and democracy, she breaks from the early founders of American democracy and most philosophical thinkers of her era. For example, in *Democracy and Social Ethics*, she uses women's experiences primarily throughout the book to analyze the changing nature of rights and responsibilities in a democratic state. In doing so, she reconfigures democratic human rights as necessarily inclusive of women's rights.

Privilege and Global "Other"-ness

Postcolonial feminism shares with previous feminisms a critical identification of positions of privilege—but whereas earlier feminists identified the location of privilege as white, male, and heterosexual, the insight of postcolonial feminism positions the locus of privilege in the categories of capitalist, Western, and northern. Contemporary feminists call for what Ann Ferguson describes as "a process of self-interrogation" as a step toward "reconstituting our given social identities" in order to begin building bridges to women in other cultures (2000, 190). If Addams were a contemporary feminist, we would expect her to identify herself as a member of a privileged class, as white, upper class, and American and a member of a dominant (victorious) Allied nation, and to reflect that consciousness of privilege in her work. We do not see this type of self-reflection or self-identification in Addams's work, yet we cannot necessarily conclude that Addams was unaware of her privilege. For a person who lived in the public gaze, she spoke very little about herself or her private life; even *Twenty Years at Hull-House*, her "autobiography," is fairly impersonal, with only a few chapters dealing with her childhood and personal experiences. As such, it is difficult to make any judgments about the extent to which she understood her own privileged position. One exception would be after her visit to Tolstoy—when he criticized her for owning land that she did not work and for not doing physical labor, Addams does question her own position as a person of a particular economic class. However, although she was certainly critical of U.S. imperialism, there is no evidence that she understood herself, as an American, to be speaking in a role of privilege and dominance in relationship to women from other cultures.

Lack of critical self-reflection of one's privilege and lack of cultural knowledge through diverse relationships can lead first world feminists to categorize third world (or "Two-Thirds World" per Mohanty) women as "other," although that is not necessarily the case for Addams. As Mohanty says, "It is in the production of this 'third-world difference' that Western feminisms appropriate and colonize the constitutive complexities which characterize the lives of women in these countries" (1991, 54). Creating otherness is a form of essentializing or speaking for women in various third world countries. According to Mohanty, "It is when 'women of Africa' becomes a homogeneous sociological grouping characterized by common dependencies or powerlessness (or even strengths) that problems arise—we say too little and too much at the same time" (59). Although Western feminists may have thought they were being inclusive by assuming commonality with global women based on gender, lack of attention to differences diminishes the pluralism needed for democracy. As Chantal Mouffe says, the "insistence on a substantive notion of the common good and shared moral values is incompatible with the pluralism" that she says is necessary for radical democratic politics (1997, 540). Addams does imagine a common good and shared values, yet the creation of the good for Addams must come from inclusive dialogue with diverse voices.

Another aspect of cultural colonization is the assumption that Westernization defines progress and that Western norms can be held as standards for other cultures. Addams's record in this area is more problematic. Early in her work she could be accused of holding Western ideals as the model for the rest of the world, which is reflective certainly of her education at a Christian seminary college. Traveling in Europe, she remembers with admiration Caird's *Evolution of Religion* (Addams 1910/1990, 24) and Comte's concept of a religion of humanity, a final synthesis of all religions in a "cathedral of humanity" (Addams 1910/1990, 50). Yet for both these philosophers, the evolution moves from and through a Christian context. Addams was looking for commonality while trying to understand her immigrant neighbors, wondering "how far it was possible to expect the same qualities of virtue and a similar standard of conduct from these diverse peoples" (24). One gets the sense from this that early in her work she was trying to understand her neighbors by attempting to position immigrant groups on an evolutionary framework. Attempting to find ways to connect or identify with others was fundamental to Addams's entire lifework, and she worked toward establishing those connections rather than focusing on difference. Yet in some of the ways that she did this she risked simplifying and essentializing female nature. An example of this is in *Peace and Bread*, when she finds the nature of the feminine in Fraser's stories of the "corn mother" (or "rice mother"), connecting her work with food rations to "woman's traditional activity" across cultures and throughout histories (1922/2002, 45). One of the dangers of this type of essentialism is that one may think that he or she can speak for others, assuming that the speaker's experience is true for other women in very different situations. Feminists have accurately named this taking of someone else's voice as a form of colonization. Yet even in the early years at Hull House, Addams was aware of the dangers of speaking for others. She made a point to bring a neighborhood resident with her whenever possible when she went on speaking engagements in Chicago.

Working on a global scale, Addams became aware of the dangers of essentialism when it came to European immigrant cultures, but did not seem to be conscious of the hegemony of Western thought in terms of wider global cultures. In that way she perhaps could be held to the same critique of essentialism as other Euro-American feminists of her era (and much of second wave feminism). Addams traveled extensively in Europe and had close connections of mostly European immigrants in the Hull House neighborhood as well as maintaining a thirty-year dialogue with feminists in Germany (Sklar 1998). She understood as "particularly stupid" the act of essentializing immigrants with a "collective judgment" about their culture. She argued that Americans should understand immigrants as "diversified" and "highly differentiated from each other by race, tradition, religion and European background," urging instead an understanding of the immigrants' particular "past history and experiences" (1919/2003, 192–94).

Addams was much less familiar with Asian and African cultures. She traveled to Asia in the 1920s, stopping briefly in India but spending much of her time in China and Japan. In her writing about Asia later in her life, she at times falls into what Martha Nussbaum calls "descriptive chauvinism"—looking at other cultures through the lens of Western standards, "recreating the other in the image of oneself" (1997, 138). Addams does this often in her attempts to find a common space with Asian women in their concerns for housing, education, and social conditions (1923/2003, 251–52).

In *Globalization and Feminist Activism*, Mary Hawkesworth identifies the "hierarchy of civilizations" as a common theme in late nineteenth-century Western thought, particularly following Darwin and Hegel. Early feminist activists often assimilated this hierarchical model of global cultures, such that "claims concerning a 'civilizing mission' shaped a good deal of this second strand of transnational feminist activism, marking it as an imperial project" (Hawkesworth 2006, 46). Examples of this privileging of Western culture show up in Addams's writing; for instance, in 1923 when she writes about women's right to vote in Asian cultures, she notes that "one finds in Japan that the women, although they do not vote, are much more westernized because they have had much wider educational facilities," equating Western education with progress. In this same article, she also wonders how Indian women will handle the right to vote, given that they have "lived in seclusion" and have "seldom discussed political affairs" (1923/2003, 251).

Yet Addams was at least partially aware of the problems of Western cultural hegemony. In 1930, after chairing the First Pan-Pacific Women's Conference in Hawaii, she criticized those who thought of "the advance of Western civilization as a sort of a game, an effort to make one type of culture predominate, which . . . may break down other cultures." Yet merely two paragraphs later, in praising Japanese social workers, she returns to her 1923 positive assessment of Japanese women, complimenting them because they were "bringing to [social work] the best training the West can give them . . . with an understanding of the situation all their own" (1930, 100–101), once again identifying Western education with progress.

Pragmatist Contextualization

Contemporary postcolonial feminists argue against universalized concepts of democracy or feminist rights that are applied without awareness of the specificity of location, culture, and time. As Mohanty says, "Historicizing and locating political agency is a necessary alternative to the formulations of the 'universality' of gendered oppression" (2004, 107). In this, postcolonial feminism shares with pragmatist feminism a critique of all universals in favor of situated, embodied, and particularized ways of knowing. As a pragmatist philosopher, Addams understood that political theory without relational particulars was meaningless, and in her work at Hull House came to see her community as a thickly associated group of cultural traditions. In one of her earliest essays on democracy and peace, she points out the necessity of the concrete and particular: "The political code, as well as the moral law, has no meaning and becomes absolutely emptied of its contents if we take out of it all relation to the world and concrete cases" (1899/2003, 1). Addams understood that social progress, either through governing models or reform models, needed to grow from the particular place and history wherein it worked. In 1904, she hypothesized a situation in which a government could enter a foreign land with the goal of creating self-government, but in doing so forcefully could destroy the "precious germ" of a novel idea of governing that may have been taking root. As she said then, "All progress must come from the native soil" (1904/2003, 32), articulating a pragmatist understanding of the necessity of historical and cultural rootedness of all social and political movements.

Because she was a pragmatist, Addams's philosophy was always in dialogue with practical experience, and she often used her own experiences and others' stories as fertile ground from which to start her philosophical thinking. She subjected her cherished ideals to practical testing and was willing to adapt or drop ideals when they did not work. She tells of an early example when, after visiting Tolstoy in Russia in 1896, she came back from Europe with the intent to make bread for two hours every day, but quickly realized that there were other demands on her time that made such "bread labor" impractical (1910/1990, 161). Understanding that Tolstoy's ideas of dress or his commitment to physical labor was impractical and even selfish in the context of the practicalities of her own life may have helped Addams to develop the pragmatist understanding that ideas are rooted in a particular social and historical context, growing out of experience and subsequently being tested in experience.[7]

Democratization: Capitalism Posing as Democracy

A feminist democracy requires disconnecting democracy from global capitalism (Mohanty 2004, 236), countering the media and politicians who often blur these concepts together. Western nations may say they are promoting democracy in other parts of the world, yet often the method used to promote that goal is the advancement of capitalism. This is a process of "democratization" or globalization in the belief that global capitalism will lead to democracy and human rights. However, instead of promoting equality, this type of democratization often has harmful effects on women's lives, perpetuating gendered inequalities and often creating new gendered hierarchies, instead of promoting equalities and rights for women. According to Mohanty, "The interests of contemporary transnational capital and the strategies employed enable it to draw upon indigenous social hierarchies and to construct and maintain ideologies of masculinity/femininity, technological superiority, appropriate development, skilled/unskilled labor, and so on" (167). Significantly for feminists, Mohanty points out that "it is especially on the bodies and lives of women and girls from the Third World/South—the Two-Thirds World— that global capitalism writes its script and it's by paying attention to and theorizing the experiences of these communities of women and girls that we demystify capitalism as a system" (235).[8] Hawkesworth took a close look at the social, political, and economic effects of democratization in the lives of women globally, concluding that the Euro-American style of democratization has "produced gendered redistribution of resources and responsibilities that make women worse off" (2001, 224). She discovered that in countries in Eastern and Central Europe, Latin America, and South Africa, democratization has resulted in increased violence toward women, skyrocketing unemployment among women, and less participation of women in the civil and political dialogue.

Addams's understanding of capitalism and democracy gradually but dramatically veered away from idealizing her father's frontier capitalism. Living among factory workers, working with the labor movement, Addams began to see the inconsistencies between democratic ethics and capitalism. By 1912, after two decades in the Hull House neighborhood, during which she became increasingly critical of the inequalities of capitalism, she was able to say that "the great principle of liberty has been translated . . . into the unlovely doctrine of commercial capitalism" (1912/2002, 93). In her support of labor unions and governmental regulations such as restrictions on child labor, her conception of democracy conflicted with the top-down hierarchies of traditional capitalism. She saw in her community that capitalism carried with it the aggressive hierarchies that set the tone for larger governmental violence; as she said, "Unrestricted commercialism is an excellent preparation for governmental aggression" (1907/2003, 109). Addams believed that the ideal of democracy, brought to the workplace, required that the workers have a voice regarding the conditions of their industrial jobs. Labor unions, for Addams, were an expression of democracy that grew out of the natural interdependence between workers and owners and became a way that workers could take some control over their work lives as well as their social and political lives. Addams moved toward a more socialist economy as a result of participating in and supporting the struggles of the labor movement to address the unchecked inequalities of laissez-faire capitalism. But she never identified herself as a socialist, as she rejected the Marxist ideology of revolution, believing instead in gradual social change.

Consistent with contemporary feminism, Addams wrote about how the economic inequalities created by industrial capitalism were particularly damaging to women and children, who, at the bottom of the social hierarchy, were the most vulnerable. Then, as now, women and girls suffered disproportionately. In the industrial culture of Chicago, women were left without their traditional roles in their communities; they "no longer work in the fields, nor milk the goats," and instead of spinning and weaving, the mother "buys all of the clothing already spun" (1902/2002, 82). This made women completely dependent on industrial goods and wages. Instead of being able to produce household goods on their own, they either worked long hours in factories or were entirely dependent on the wages that their husbands brought home. Married women and their children would sink into destitute poverty if their husbands were injured or if they left them, since women had little chance to earn a similar wage to men's if they did get work.

When she talked about social inequality, Addams highlighted the stories of the women and girls who were affected, and it was with these stories that she advocated for change in nearly every area of social, work, and domestic life. In *Democracy and Social Ethics*, she examines the life of the upper-class educated woman who is expected by her family to do nothing with her education, and later discusses another relational issue between women—that of hired domestic servants and the woman of the house who employs her. She wrote of the effect of unemployment when men who felt powerless in their work lives often turned to alcohol and violence toward women, who had no outside means of social or economic support. Younger women turned to prostitution to survive. Older women without children to support them were often forced into the county poorhouse. Addams points out that although men also were put in the poorhouse, women's lives were particularly tragic, as they did not have the option of leaving and tramping around the country looking for work as men did (1910/1990, 93). In writing about prostitution in Chicago, Addams comes to the same conclusions as contemporary postcolonial feminists when she says, "When the solidarity of human interest is actually realized, it will become unthinkable that one class of human beings should be sacrificed to the supposed needs of another" (1912/2002, 98).

As she was able to demonstrate, considering capitalism and democracy from the viewpoint of women's lives can dramatically change the discussion.

Feminist thinkers have, like Addams, criticized militarism as being antithetical to social equality and women's rights. Similar to other global feminist thinkers, Mohanty finds the link between "increasing militarization" and "masculinization" problematic in many arenas of social life, not only in actual war (2004, 229). Religious fundamentalism has become "deeply masculine" in its aggressive and competitive tactics as well as its gendered policies that prevent women from full participation. As discussed earlier, Addams also took a negative view toward the aggressive competitive spirit that Western cultures actively instilled in its young, particularly in boys. While Addams pointed to competitive hierarchical practice as a form of militarism, she stopped short of developing an explicitly feminist argument that linked cultural militarism with patriarchy.

Transnational democracy may be the only acceptable form of postcolonial feminist democracy (see Alexander and Mohanty 1996; Gould 2004). Such cross-border regional and global forms of democratic activism often address particular issues such as social justice and human rights and influence governmental policy making or have an impact on global governance such as in the United Nations. When these organizations are formed out of inclusive dialogue and activism, they illustrate the form of democracy that Addams advocated. Addams's international work, particularly in founding the Women's International League for Peace and Freedom (WILPF), was and is a forerunner of feminist transnational democracy. Although WILPF originated out of antiwar activism and as such was originally dominated by Western cultures (European and American), it has grown to be an influential international nongovernmental organization, with branches in thirty-seven countries and in every continent. WILPF continues to be one of Addams's enduring legacies.

As we have seen, there are many similarities between Addams's social democracy and postcolonial feminist writing, particularly in her active opposition to colonialism and imperialism. Although liberal democracy was a starting point for Addams, she broke from liberal individualism in her pragmatist conception of the individual as socially constructed and interwoven ontologically with community, rather than concerned primarily with self-interest. Her critique that the early liberal architects of democratic governments did not trust the people is still valid today, illustrated by the use of fear tactics and slogans instead of a deep deliberative democracy. While at times her essentializing of "woman" and of some non-Western countries is problematic, in her reflective and experiential engagement with and learning from many types of people, she avoided most of the imperialism of her time. And as Chantal Mouffe points out, the aim of any feminist radical democratic politics should be "the articulation of various different struggles against oppression" (1997, 543). Articulating struggles against oppression was without a doubt one of Addams's central goals, and those struggles necessitated the active participation of all those who were part of the community. The pragmatist inclusiveness, critique of hierarchies, and insistence on social equality in Addams's democracy remains valid today and can be seen as a support for the continuing work of postcolonial feminist thinkers.

Notes

1. Recent scholarship has highlighted how Addams's philosophy of democracy evolved and was radicalized. In particular, Louise Knight's (2005) biography *Citizen: Jane Addams and the Struggle for Democracy* traces the ways that Addams's search for democracy informed her early years. Maurice Hamington's (2004) essay "Addams's Radical Democracy: Moving Beyond Rights" demonstrates that Addams's writings on democracy broke away from liberalism of early American founders.

2. From the Residents Meeting Minute Book, 1893. Her letters to family at this time also were full of Christian references. Farrell traces how Addams's religious enthusiasm had become "muted" by the late 1890s. See Farrell 1967, 62.

3. Addams's 1892 articles on organic community were published in *Philanthropy and Social Progress* (1892/1970); portions were reprinted in *Twenty Years at Hull-House* (1910/1990).

4. In a different essay I have agued that Addams's conception of community could be a model for a feminist communitarianism, avoiding the problems with communitarian philosophies that feminist thinkers have articulated (Whipps 2004, 118–33).

5. In *The Democratic Paradox*, Chantal Mouffe (2000) makes the distinction between traditional rights-based liberalism and democracy. She points to the possibility that democracy can interfere with liberal individual rights given a majority vote that limits those rights.

6. See, for example, Watson 2007.

7. Tolstoy was critical of Addams's fashionable large sleeves on her dress and thought that Addams should wear peasant clothes, as he did. As Addams pointed out, that would alienate her from her neighbors, not make her one of them. Addams 1910/1990, 157.

8. In her analysis of the effect of global capitalism, Mohanty (2008) prefers the term "Two-Thirds World" rather than "third world" to talk about those in poverty who are the victims of global capitalism, acknowledging that every industrial country contains "Two-Thirds" populations (2003, 227). Using Mohanty's definition, the industrial immigrant populations of Chicago in the 1890s were in the "two-thirds" population within a first world, or "one-third" nation.

References

Addams, Jane. 1892/1970. *Philanthropy and Social Progress*. Montclair, N.J.: Patterson Smith.
———. 1899/2003. "Democracy or Militarism." *Liberty Tracts: Central Anti-Imperialist League of Chicago*. In *Jane Addams's Writings on Peace*, ed. Marilyn Fischer and Judy Whipps, vol. 4. Bristol, U.K.: Thoemmes Press.
———. 1901/2003. "One Menace to the Century's Progress." In *Jane Addams's Writings on Peace*, ed. Marilyn Fischer and Judy Whipps, vol. 4. Bristol, U.K.: Thoemmes Press.
———. 1902/2002. *Democracy and Social Ethics*. Ed. Charlene Haddock Seigfried. Urbana: University of Illinois Press.
———. 1904/2003. "Addresses of Miss Jane Addams." In *Jane Addams's Writings on Peace*, ed. Marilyn Fischer and Judy Whipps, vol. 4. Bristol, U.K.: Thoemmes Press.
———. 1907/2003. *Newer Ideals of Peace*. In *Jane Addams's Writings on Peace*, ed. Marilyn Fischer and Judy Whipps, vol. 1. Bristol, U.K.: Thoemmes Press.
———. 1909/1972. *The Spirit of Youth and the City Streets*. Urbana: University of Illinois Press.
———. 1910/1990. *Twenty Years at Hull-House with Autobiographical Notes*. Urbana: University of Illinois Press.
———. 1912/2002. *A New Conscience and an Ancient Evil*. Urbana: University of Illinois Press.
———. 1919/2003. "Americanization." *The Publications of the American Sociological Society* 14. In *Jane Addams's Writings on Peace*, ed. Marilyn Fischer and Judy Whipps, vol. 4. Bristol, U.K.: Thoemmes Press.
———. 1922/2002. *Peace and Bread in Time of War*. Urbana: University of Illinois Press.
———. 1923/2003. "A New Political Method Emerging in the Orient." In *Jane Addams's Writings on Peace*, ed. Marilyn Fischer and Judy Whipps, vol. 4. Bristol, U.K.: Thoemmes Press.
———. 1928/2003. "Presidential Address: Pan-Pacific Union." In *Jane Addams's Writings on Peace*, ed. Marilyn Fischer and Judy Whipps, vol. 4. Bristol, U.K.: Thoemmes Press.
———. 1929/2003. "Presidential Address." In *Jane Addams's Writings on Peace*, ed. Marilyn Fischer and Judy Whipps, vol. 4. Bristol, U.K.: Thoemmes Press.
———. 1930. *The Second Twenty Years at Hull-House*. New York: Macmillan.
———. 1934/2003. "Exaggerated Nationalism and International Comity." In *Jane Addams's Writings on Peace*, ed. Marilyn Fischer and Judy Whipps, vol. 4. Bristol, U.K.: Thoemmes Press.
Alexander, M. Jacqui, and Chandra T. Mohanty, eds. 1997. *Feminist Genealogies, Colonial Legacies, Democratic Futures*. New York: Routledge.
Bayes, Jane H., Mary E. Hawkesworth, and Rita Mae Kelly. 2001. "Globalization, Democratization, and Gender Regimes." In *Gender, Globalization, and Democratization*, ed. Rita Mae Kelly et al. Lanham, Md.: Rowman and Littlefield.
Benhabib, Seyla. 2006. *Another Cosmopolitanism*. Oxford: Oxford University Press.
Brooks, Ann. 2000. "Citizenship, Identity, and Social Justice: The Intersection of Feminist and Post-colonial Discourses." In *Challenging Democracy: International Perspec-

tives on Gender, Education, and Citizenship, ed. Madeleine Arnot and Jo-Ann Dillabough. New York: Routledge, 2000.
Carothers, Thomas. 2007. *U.S. Democracy Promotion During and After Bush*. Washington, D.C.: Carnegie Endowment for International Peace. http:www.carnegieendowment.org/files/democracy_promotion_after_bush_final.pdf.
Farrell, John. 1967. *Beloved Lady: A History of Jane Addams's Ideas on Reform and Peace*. Baltimore: Johns Hopkins University Press.
Ferguson, Ann. 2000. "Resisting the Veil of Privilege: Building Bridge Identities as an Ethico-Politics of Global Feminisms." In *Decentering the Center: Philosophy for a Multicultural, Post-colonial, and Feminist World*, ed. Uma Narayan and Sandra Harding. Bloomington: Indiana University Press.
Fischer, Marilyn. "Introduction to *Newer Ideals of Peace*." In *Jane Addams's Writings on Peace*, ed. Marilyn Fischer and Judy Whipps, vol. 1. Bristol, U.K.: Thoemmes Press.
Gould, Carol. 2004. *Globalizing Democracy and Human Rights*. Cambridge: Cambridge University Press.
Hamington, Maurice. 2004. "Addams's Radical Democracy: Moving Beyond Rights." *Journal of Speculative Philosophy* 18, no. 3: 216–23.
Hawkesworth, Mary E. 2001. "Democratization: Reflections on Gendered Dislocations in the Public Sphere." In *Gender, Globalization, and Democratization*, ed. Rita Mae Kelly et al. Lanham: Rowman and Littlefield.
———. 2006. *Globalization and Feminist Activism*. Lanham, Md.: Rowman and Littlefield.
Knight, Louise W. 2005. *Citizen: Jane Addams and the Struggle for Democracy*. Chicago: University of Chicago Press.
Mohanty, Chandra Talpade. 1991. "Under Western Eyes: Feminist Scholarship and Colonial Discourses." In *Third World Women and the Politics of Feminism*, ed. Chandra Talpade Mohanty, Ann Russo, and Lourdes Torres. Bloomington: Indiana University Press.
———. 2004. *Feminism Without Borders: Decolonizing Theory, Practicing Solidarity*. Durham: Duke University Press.
Mouffe, Chantal. 1997. "Feminism, Citizenship, and Radical Democratic Politics." In *Feminist Social Thought: A Reader*, ed. Diana Tietjens Meyers. New York: Routledge.
———. 2000. *The Democratic Paradox*. London: Verso Press.
Nussbaum, Martha. 1997. *Cultivating Humanity*. Cambridge: Harvard University Press.
Okin, Susan Moller. 2000. "Feminism, Women's Human Rights, and Cultural Differences." In *Decentering the Center: Philosophy for a Multicultural, Post-colonial and Feminist World*, ed. Uma Narayan and Sandra Harding. Bloomington: Indiana University Press.
Seigfried, Charlene Haddock. 1996. *Pragmatism and Feminism: Reweaving the Social Fabric*. Chicago: University of Chicago Press.
Sklar, Kathryn Kish. 1998. *Social Justice Feminists in the United States and Germany*. Ithaca: Cornell University Press.
Tan, Sor-hoon, and John Whalen-Bridge, eds. 2008. *Democracy as Culture: Deweyan Pragmatism in a Globalizing World*. Albany: State University of New York.
Watson, Lori. 2007. "Constituting Politics: Power, Reciprocity, and Identity." *Hypatia* 22, no. 4: 96–112.
Whipps, Judy. "Jane Addams's Social Thought as a Model for a Pragmatist-Feminist Communitarianism." *Hypatia* 19, no. 2: 118–33.

12

Engendering Democracy by Socializing It

Jane Addams's Contribution to Feminist Political Theorizing

Wendy Sarvasy

At the core of Jane Addams's democratic theory was the feminist problem of how to undo the gendered private/public split that blocked women's full incorporation into collective self-government. She observed that even after the subject matter of politics opened up to include the social problems generated by crowded industrial cities, women did not automatically bring forward their expertise to manage the new public sector programs. The pull of the privatized family claim held back affluent household managers from embracing a new public role. Their college-educated daughters dreamed of working to achieve a new world of social equality, but they were not trained in how to actualize this goal. Addams concluded that what was required was a gendered path into a new type of democratic citizenship for social justice.

To create this path, she reconfigured the relationship between the family and the state through the medium of the social. It was a third woman-friendly space of participatory politics, where the required socializing of democracy or tying it to social justice could proceed. Centered at Hull House, the social combined two processes of socializing democracy: the actualization of new relational foundations, characterized by vibrant cross-class alliances of women, and the extension of the social welfare responsibilities of the state through state feminism, whereby women carve out a power base within the administrative side of the state to advance substantive gender equality. Through her participation in these processes and her theorizing about her activism, I argue, Addams engendered democracy by socializing it.

To demonstrate this argument, I explain her method as a theory/activist dynamic. To establish that she found the theories of democratic citizenship inadequate from a feminist perspective, I outline Addams's explanation of why a gendered path was required to alter the theory. Then I present a notion of a multidimensional gendered path into democratic citizenship, capable of sustaining cross-class alliances of women. To illustrate how this path led to the founding of a new social space of democratic participation, I present her ideal type of feminist social politics, based on her analysis of the campaign for and enforcement of the 1893 Illinois Labor Law. Finally, while the notion of a gendered path would seem to be relevant only up to the point where women were incorporated into political citizenship in 1920, it is my contention that her theorizing has lasting significance, both for its feminist method and for current feminist discussions of how to combine care, citizenship, and democracy.

Theory/Activism Dynamic

The best way to characterize what I mean by Addams's theory/activist dynamic is to situate it within the context of how Lasch, Elshtain, and Seigfried have interpreted Addams as a theorist. Unlike Lasch, I do not separate her activism from her theorizing to make the case that she was an original feminist thinker. Yet in connecting the two, I do not, as Elshtain does, reduce her method of theorizing to the telling of autobiographical stories.[1] By writing a political biography instead of a systematic analysis of Addams's political theory, Elshtain denies a distinction that Addams herself made between a form of popular communication and a method of theorizing new concepts through practice.[2] In sharp contrast to Elshtain's approach, Seigfried uncovers the systematic nature of Addams's method of theorizing by placing her within the pragmatist philosophical tradition that grounded theory in experience and that rested on an epistemological assumption that theorizing advances through experimentation.[3] Persuaded by Seigfried's forceful interpretation, I approach Addams's work as fitting within feminist traditions of linking women's experiences and practices with theorizing. Specifically, the aim is to show how she generated new feminist theories through activism.

By focusing on activism, I narrow the range of relevant experiences or practices to what I call feminist social politics. This type of activism was supported by women's political culture at the turn of the twentieth century. It evolved *outside* women's direct electoral participation and paved the way for a defense of women's political citizenship. Women, engaged in feminist social politics, assumed the centrality of the administrative state as a site for exercising power to alleviate the inequalities in women's daily lives.[4] Yet this vibrant activism was not top down; it was embedded in gendered cross-class alliances.

In terms of presenting Addams's method as distinctly feminist, I depart from Lasch, who does not show how Addams's gendered analysis shaped her theorizing. For him, she was a powerful critic of industrialization and in addition a supporter of women's rights. In contrast to Seigfried, who concludes that outside her suffrage and peace writings, Addams did not develop an explicitly feminist theory and that such a theory has to be created from her actions by the interpreter, I am able to demonstrate a feminist method, because my focus is narrower: her contribution to feminist democratic theorizing.[5] In using the term *feminist*, I do not adopt Elshtain's maternalist or social feminist framing, because it constricts Addams to a brand of difference feminism that did not exist until the 1920s disagreement over the equal rights amendment and sex-based labor laws.[6] Also as we shall see, the gendered path into public life was not rooted in maternalism.

My analysis of the gendered path illustrates how Addams intertwined theorizing and activism. She began by uncovering the gender-biased theory of democratic citizenship. To discredit the assumption of this theory that women were not by nature suited for self-government, Addams participated in experiments with feminist social politics. As a theorist, she molded these experiments into ideal types that could be used to rethink democratic theory. Through this theory/activist dynamic, Addams showed how women in all their diversity were capable of self-government. Indeed they were political innovators. Through their socializing democracy project, they devised new woman-friendly modes of democratic participation.[7]

Justification for a Gendered Path

For Addams, democratic citizenship entailed fulfilling the duty to work for the common good. In her analysis of the place of middle-class daughters in the emerging social democracy, she drew on the political theory tradition of civic republicanism to demonstrate how its notion of citizenship rested on the gendered family-state relationship that supported men's civic engagement and blocked women's social activism. As she explained, middle-class sons had the duty to defend the country at a time of war. It was expected that when the state called, the families would release "sons and husbands and even the fathers of little children." Therefore, the sons, unlike their sisters, did not experience a debilitating tension between the claims of the family and those of the state. According to Addams, "The grown-up son has so long been considered a citizen with well-defined duties" that once he became a citizen-earner and took on his public identity, the family claim "cease[d] gradually to be made at all."[8]

In sharp contrast, the state did not require civic duties, even the exercise of the franchise in most states, from middle-class daughters. When Addams invented a new civic duty—the social claim—the practice of which did not require state authorization, she gave theoretical significance to the new activism directed at reshaping the state, so that it would call middle-class daughters out to serve the social welfare common good. When she characterized this new claim as "higher" than the claim of the privatized family, she intended to provoke middle-class parents into revising their gender-differentiated expectations for their children. Sons were not pulled back from civic engagement by the family claim, but it was "a constant difficulty in the way of those experiments and advances depending upon the initiative of women."[9] Until the family claim was embedded within the new social welfare common good, the daughters would not feel psychologically free to act.

Addams could have resolved the conflict between the two claims by adopting Wollstonecraft's feminist version of the civic republican tradition. She proposed a theory of gendered citizenship that turned the family into a space of civic engagement for citizen-mothers. According to Wollstonecraft, while the husband would perform his civic duties as a citizen-soldier or a political representative, "his wife, also an active citizen, should be equally intent to manage her family, educate her children, and assist her neighbors."[10] To ensure the equivalency of the two practices of civic virtue, Wollstonecraft stipulated the necessity of women sharing in the full range of civil and political rights, including within marriage. Yet Addams did not even raise the citizen-mother option for the daughters. They had actualized Wollstonecraft's dream of higher education for women; now they aspired to act in the larger world.

According to Addams, the college-educated daughter had learned to view herself "as a citizen of the world."[11] By using this framing, Addams showed how the political theory tradition of cosmopolitan thought molded the political expectations of her generation, as its members tried to turn into political action what they had learned in college courses about "the claims of human brotherhood."[12] The advantages of the cosmopolitan notion of citizenship were that it included women in a gender-neutral human identity based on "the essential dignity and equality of all men" and it did not require nation-state citizenship.[13] As Kant's version made clear, while women were not economically independent enough to have political nation-state citizenship, they definitely had standing as citizens of the world.[14] Thus, the cosmopolitan tradition offered Addams a starting point for a feminist rethinking of democratic citizenship that went beyond Wollstonecraft and honored her insight that gender difference, properly conceptualized, could drive the engendering of democracy.

Addams proposed to reshape the notion of citizen of the world through her theory/activist dynamic. Ultimately the strength of the notion that it included women was also its weakness. Its abstract understanding of equal moral worth did not help the daughters figure out after college how to address their very specific gendered problem: "a constant and totally unnecessary conflict between the social and family claims." They tried to defend their public aspirations by appealing to "the claims of human brotherhood," but this "vague and unformulated" sentiment was not sufficiently robust to rival the psychological pull of the "concrete and definitely asserted" family claim. The daughters suffered mental duress, as they "repressed" their world citizen aspirations. Sapped of her energy, according to Addams, the educated daughter "look[ed] out into the world, longing that some demand be made upon her powers, for they [were] too untrained to furnish the initiative."[15] Addams responded by practicing a new type of democratic citizenship shaped by a gendered path.

Gendered Path

The path was gendered, because it engaged middle-class daughters and mothers during a time of "reconstruction" in processes that redesigned the relationship between the family and the state. First, it directed the daughters to form relations with the working class, so that they could make tangible their social ethic and prove to their parents that they were not "restless" and "self-indulgent," but genuinely dedicated to advancing the common good. Through these new cross-class relations, the daughters would also gain experience with how to become "kindly citizens of the world through the pressure of a cosmopolitan neighborhood." Second, it forced the daughters to learn how to live with the contradictions of their intersectional location that both made possible the forging of relations with working-class women and reminded them of the structural inequalities that sustained their privileged position. Third, it provided opportunities for the daughters to bring their families of origin, especially their mothers, with them into the new social space of action. Through this path, both daughters and mothers would learn how "the larger life . . . surrounds and completes the individual and family life."[16]

To show why the middle-class daughter must "be brought in contact with the moral experiences of the many in order to procure an adequate social motive," Addams presented an ideal type of a charity worker. Through her education, she acquired a commitment to work for humanity, but she was oriented in an "individualistic" direction. The college experience had "fostered ambitions for personal distinction, and [had] trained [her] faculties almost exclusively in the direction of intellectual accumulation." The only way for her to socialize her ethics and to concretize her notion of cosmopolitan citizenship, so that she could work for a genuine common good, was "by a social process." This process started with her "reducing her social scruples to action." Through consistent contact with "her humble beneficiaries," she reaches an unexpected insight: they "are far in advance of her, not in charity or singleness of purpose, but in self-sacrificing."[17]

Their numerous acts of putting their neighbors' needs before their own, according to Addams, was the result of shared precarious material conditions and the intense intimacy that resulted. Mutual aid, not charity, characterized caring relations in the neighborhood. In political theory terms, the immigrant working class integrated the civic republican notion of civic virtue, as putting the good of the community before the individual's self-interest, with a very tangible cosmopolitan love of humanity. As Addams observed, her neighbors were "really attaining cosmopolitan relations through daily experience." For example, one woman missed a job opportunity that Addams arranged for her, because when a neighbor became sick, "the children ran for the family friend," who sacrificed improving her economic situation to care for the neighbor.[18] As the charity worker observed practices of solidarity, she learned how to socialize her ethics through an embodied cosmopolitan citizenship.

Underlying this argument was Addams's relational or experiential approach to ethics. As she explained, the charity worker's "moral concepts constantly tend[ed] to float away from her, unless they [had] a basis in the concrete relation of life." Significantly, Addams assumed that family ethics and social ethics were quite distinct, because each derived from qualitatively *different* sets of relations. Therefore social ethics were not an extension of family ethics. Daughters would grasp the nature of social justice only by joining social reform movements. As the theorist, Addams insisted that "the ideal itself must be a rational development of life." This phrase meant that the intertwining of democracy with social justice would have to come out of "a rule of living," applied within contexts of diversity.[19]

This interpretation challenges Elshtain's insistence that maternalism or the fact "that women's lives revolved around responsibility, care, and obligation" was "the rock-bottom of [Addams's] civic philosophy and her social feminism."[20] The first aspect of the gendered path showed that the educated daughters did not learn social ethics from their mothers or from privatized family responsibilities. As Addams explained, "Thus the identification with the common lot which is the essential idea of Democracy becomes the source and expression of social ethics."[21] This interpretation emerges once we recognize how Addams was bringing a pragmatist method to the problem of how to engender democracy by establishing a guiding social ethic. To make concrete the new social ethic, Addams called on the daughters to abandon the unequal paternalistic charity relationship and to engage in cross-class cooperation, as the context for a new combination of cosmopolitan citizenship and democratic activism for social justice.

At the heart of their effectiveness, according to Addams, was the second aspect of the gendered path: the ability to construct what feminists today call an intersectional location.[22] For the educated daughters, this location called for the sharing with their working-class sisters a critique of male privilege, while maintaining a critical posture toward their own privileged class and race position. The success of their activism for social justice hinged on their capacity to live with the "perplexity" or "contradiction" of their social position. For the residents of Hull House, according to Addams, "there was always present the harrowing consciousness of the differences in economic condition between ourselves and our neighbors." This difference could not be eradicated by taking some sort of vow of poverty, because, in the end, the affluent daughter had "two securities" denied the poor: resources for medical and elderly care. Therefore, Addams included in the characteristics of her ideal type of the charity worker, the capacity to live with the discomfort felt from her traveling back and forth from the homes of the families she visited to her home. As Addams concluded, she was "never free from perplexities which our growing democracy forces upon her."[23] To be the new type of democratic citizen working for social justice, Addams suggested, was to be confronted on a daily basis with the problem of structural inequalities.

Embracing this democratic pressure, Addams proposed to build into the intersectional location a method to help the affluent daughter learn *how* to socialize her aims: sympathetic understanding. The practice of this method required a consciousness of two distinct standpoints: her own class-based, race-based outlook and the outlook of her working-class allies and neighbors. Addams gave the example of how Julia Lathrop acted when she participated on the Illinois State Board of Charities in 1893. "[T]hrough her intimate knowledge of the beneficiaries" gained "through long residence among the poor," Lathrop "learned to view public institutions as she did, from the standpoint of the inmates rather than from that of the managers."[24]

The standard interpretation of Addams's notion of sympathetic understanding emphasizes her generosity of spirit and capacity to put herself inside the perspectives of others and to generalize the method to all classes.[25] My interpretation stresses that her notion was particularly relevant to affluent daughters trying on the shoes of working-class women. I cannot find any evidence that Addams expected the working-class daughter to practice sympathetic understanding toward her well-off sisters. In my interpretation, the practice of sympathetic understanding was critical for middle-class women, so that they would never forget their position of privilege.

Through activism, the daughters tested their adeptness at using their contradictory position to energize an alliance for social justice. Addams described how Hull House residents played a supportive role to several women's labor unions. The shirtmakers and the cloakmakers were organized at Hull House, the first in 1891 and the second in 1892. The 1892 organizing meeting brought together unionized Russian Jewish men and Irish American girls. The men were concerned that the girl workers were depressing wages. Because the two groups of cloakmakers needed each other, according to Addams, they were "being forced into a social democracy" that required them to form new social relations across gender, language, cultural, and religious differences. She also observed: "There was much less difference of any sort between the residents and working-girls than between the men and girls of the same trade." For Addams, the meeting illustrated how "the cultivated girl who consciously, and sometime heroically, crosses the 'chasm' [of class] to join hands with her working sisters" could advance the labor union movement for social justice.[26]

To engage in these processes of socializing democracy, daughters would have to be relieved of the debilitating narrowly defined family claim. Consequently, the notion of the gendered path included a third dimension: the creation of democratic experiences that would lead the household managers to "recognize and acknowledge the validity of the social obligation." Here Addams was applying her pragmatist assumption of "the impossibility of substituting a higher ethical standard for a lower one without similarity of experience." To facilitate the required radical shift, Addams argued, "the family in its entirety must be carried out into the larger life."[27]

Addams's use of the term "city housekeeping" sheds light on how she envisioned restructuring the relationship between the family and the state through the activism of middle-class women.[28] Usually this phrase is interpreted to reinforce a maternalist framing of Addams's theory, according to which women are called on in the least threatening terms to join the suffrage movement, so that they can take their nurturing activities from the home into public life, in order to protect their private families. While this use of the phrase was certainly part of the suffrage rhetoric, I want to suggest an additional interpretation by applying the notion of the gendered path. Within this conceptual framework, "city housekeeping" represented new experiences and the creation of new democratic relationships that were essential to sustain the new social ethic.

According to this interpretation, middle-class household managers needed to end the undemocratic mistress-servant relationship.[29] Then they had to turn their energies to creating connections with working-class immigrant mothers and daughters. Addams proposed one way to achieve this aim, through the Hull-House Labor Museum. It was a space where nonimmigrant women could come to meet immigrant women, as the latter demonstrated what added up to a common history of household labor directed at producing clothing. "When American women come to visit them," according to Addams, "the quickest method, in fact almost the only one of establishing a genuine companionship with them, is through this same industry, unless we except the still older occupation, the care of little children." This passage and her entire presentation of "city housekeeping" pointed to the centrality of labor, as a key common experience that would allow household managers to align with immigrant working-class women.[30] This alliance, Addams hoped, would lead the household managers to become activists for new labor laws that would protect working women. Such activism would in turn realign relations between middle-class mothers and daughters. As their experiences "become larger and more identical," Addams argued, "the clash of two codes of morals must drop away."[31] This socialization of ethics, through the privileging of working-class women's experiences with labor, was a necessary condition for engendering democracy, because it justified women's inclusion into public life.

The Social as a Space for Practicing Common Good Politics

The gendered path demonstrated the capacity of women to shape a new cross-class relational foundation for redirecting the common good. Yet they still needed extensive practice with how to reconfigure the family and the state, by putting the social welfare common good before individualistic interest or privatized family claims. Addams's solution was to activate and to theorize a third space, in which they could learn to formulate, defend, and administer specific labor and social welfare laws as instruments of the new common good. The center of this new space was the settlement house. In an 1892 formulation, Addams labeled Hull House "an effort toward social democracy."[32]

For the purposes of this chapter, I prefer the term *the social*, because it is used within the field of political theory, to define a negative force that undermines participatory democracy.[33] As I will suggest, Addams's formulation of the social challenges this dominant viewpoint. Like Aristotle's ideal polis, Addams's social was a space of collective self-determination that combined formulating and administering the law. Unlike Aristotle's influential ideal, the social began as a woman-friendly space for second-class citizens. Through Addams's application of a theory/activist dynamic, it evolved into a necessary participatory component of a healthy enlarged public sector.

Addams illustrated her ideal type of the social in her presentation of the politics surrounding the 1893 Illinois Labor Law. She asserted that its "inception" and "ministration" were "centered" at Hull House. She characterized the law as the "first modification of the undisturbed control of the aggressive captains of industry."[34] It banned labor by children under fourteen years of age, mandated an eight-hour day or forty-eight-hour week for women and minors (ages fourteen to eighteen), and set up a rigorous factory inspector system. According to Tax, Addams exaggerated the centrality of Hull House residents in the entire antisweatshop campaign that led up to the passage of the law. Addams also left out a key role she played in facilitating the private provision of school scholarships for children of widows.[35] These "distortions" of the historical record only strengthen my case that Addams's aim was theoretical: the distilling of the social as the space for tying feminist social politics to "the ideal development of the democratic state."[36]

The first part of the "ideal development" was turning "the method of public agitation" into "legislative enactment."[37] With the 1893 law, Addams emphasized the roles Hull House women activists played as they observed the working conditions of their neighbors; collected supportive empirical data; and mobilized different segments of the community, including "well-known Chicago women," to pull together a cross-class alliance to lobby for the Hull House–sponsored bill.[38] Even Tax acknowledged that it created a stronger system of government regulation than the proposal originally supported by the male-dominated Chicago Trade and Labor Assembly. According to Sklar, the activists innovated a style of gendered grassroots organizing, and they succeeded in passing their bill, because male-dominated partisan politics had produced "one of the most radical governors and state legislatures in Illinois history."[39] The new law innovated especially in the area of gender equality, both in the eight-hour-day provision and the quota for women factory inspectors.

Addams specifically pointed to the gendered issues the law addressed and ignored; therefore she showed how the law affected different segments of women and the prospects for tying social justice to gender equality. In contrast to men who worked at night and slept undisturbed during the day, working-class daughters were suffering from the combination of long hours, especially night work, and home management responsibilities. Enforcing an eight-hour day certainly would help them renegotiate their dual role. By banning labor by children under the age of fourteen, the legislation could hurt widows, who kept their children out of school to contribute to the family's financial needs. So the economic conditions of mother-headed families raised the need to experiment with income supplements to support child labor laws and mandatory school attendance. Addams also pointed to the new employment opportunities for women that the law established. While it set up ten deputy inspectors, five of whom *had* to be women, it also established a chief inspector and an assistant to the chief, both of whom turned out to be women.[40] In effect, the 1893 law suggested that women's incorporation into public life required a new notion of gender equality, generated by playing out the tension between gender equality, as identical treatment, and gender difference, as the recognition of substantive inequalities. The new women factory inspectors gained gender equality in professional employment, as they enforced a law that treated factory women's hours of work differently from men's.

The second part of the "ideal development" was not anticipated by Addams in her first formulations of settlement house citizenship, where embodied citizenship of the world entailed getting social legislation enacted.[41] The second part was truly a result of the activist/theory dynamic. It offered the vision of how a community could learn to engender a new social justice common good by vigilantly following the effects of enforcing a new law. Addams described how Hull House was at the center of practicing what we call today state feminism, whereby feminists take on state responsibilities to advance substantive gender equality. For contemporary analysts, state feminism raises the problem of how to keep feminists in the state true to the women's movements outside the state.[42] In Addams's vision, based on chief factory inspector Florence Kelley's innovations, the settlement house space merged the state and the social movement. Presumably, this approach to enforcing the law blocked the possibility of co-opting the inspectors, which had been the Chicago tradition.[43]

Kelley and her assistant, Alzina Parsons Stevens, lived at Hull House, and their official state office was just across the street. A "vigorous" deputy lived close by in the Jane Club, the cooperative living arrangement for working-class women that Addams had helped to found. The Eight-Hour Club, made up of working-class women who were affected by the law, met regularly at Hull House.[44] Presumably also at Hull House, Addams met with groups of working widows who were negatively affected by the child labor prohibition. All this activity dedicated to enforcement of the law turned family members into factory inspectors. Widows kept their children in school. Working-class families made sure their daughters worked only eight hours. Working-class daughters documented violations of the law and learned to speak publicly about the benefits of the law to the community.

By turning the enforcement of the law into a thick participatory experience, the activists showed how "the administration of an advanced law acts somewhat as a referendum." Over a period of two years, "the people" had become informed sufficiently on the workings of the law, so that they could pass judgment on whether it was a valuable tool for achieving social justice. Since the sex-based eight-hour day was declared unconstitutional by the Illinois Supreme Court in 1895, Addams pointed to the possible workings of this "referendum" influencing the formulation of future labor legislation.[45] By using a term usually applied to electoral politics, as in the case of the successful 1893 woman's suffrage campaign in Colorado, Addams was consciously enlarging the methods of registering the will of the people, both voters and nonvoters, to include one that was specifically applicable to acting in the social space.

To show how the referendum represented the acceptance of the social ethic, as embodied in government regulation of the workplace, Addams left out of her presentation of the enforcement of the 1893 law the privately funded school scholarships that middle-class club women provided to selected widows, so their children would attend school.[46] Addams's silence on the scholarships can be explained by her distinction between an individualistic ethic and a social ethic that she applied in her criticism of patronage politics. The alderman serviced individual fathers and mothers, but did not create public-sector programs that would benefit the common good.[47] Addams's ideal type of the social was centrally about how all sections of the community could be brought to understand that the social welfare common good should take precedence over individual interests. Therefore, she depicted the widows not as individually motivated to gain income supplements, but as strong supporters of a law that would advance the education of all children in the community.[48]

To further clarify her ideal type of the social, Addams drew a sharp distinction between two types of experiments, each of which created the conditions for a referendum: one innovated by philanthropists guided by an individualistic ethic and the other coming out of " a line of social experiment involving social righteousness." Experiments with privately funded libraries and kindergartens made it possible for the public to discuss "whether or not it is wise to incorporate [them] into the functions of government."[49] While a case could be made that some of the experiments at Hull House fit within this type of referendum process, Addams certainly recognized the limitations of the philanthropic version.

Employers and wealthy people were not going to champion factory labor legislation that required shorter hours and higher wages. Here the initiative had to come from social movements, with the labor movement, understood as representing, not class struggle, but a new social welfare common good, playing a key role. As Addams concluded: "If the method of public agitation could find quiet and orderly expression in legislative enactment and if labor measures could be submitted to the examination and judgment of the whole without a sense of division or of warfare, we should have the ideal development of the democratic state."[50] Addams used the 1893 law and the central role Hull House activists played to demonstrate how feminist social politics contributed to the advancement of this development.

Thus, within Addams's theory of how to socialize democracy, the settlement house as a space of practicing self-government was not a transitory institution that became obsolete once its experimental programs were adopted by the state. Instead it represented a space where women across classes could learn to work together to achieve social justice, especially in the area of actively carrying out the law. Because the settlement house interconnected the social and the state, the notion of civil society as associational life and antagonistic to the state does not capture the innovative aspects of Addams's democratic theory. Invented as a gendered social space of activism in response to the need for a gendered path to citizenship, the feminist settlement house perhaps is best viewed as a necessary participatory space for a modern citizenry that aims to link democracy and social justice, locally and globally.[51]

Implications

This chapter has presented a systematic application of Jane Addams's theory/activism dynamic to recover a usable Addams for contemporary feminist democratic theorizing. Instead of constructing her as fundamentally a maternalist, which creates distance between us and her, I have stressed the centrality of gendered social justice activism. Out of her activism in a new social space, Addams retheorized the relationship between the family and the state, so that both institutions could support the full incorporation of women as democratic citizens.

While I have stressed how Addams developed her analysis of the gendered path into public life by focusing on the perplexities of women of her own class, this acknowledgment should not limit the applicability of her methodology. Her understanding of her own intersectional location has important implications for the emerging interdisciplinary study of intersectionality, a theoretical and empirical framework of analysis. Usually this concept is seen as only relevant to the less powerful or oppressed. Addams's theory suggests otherwise.[52]

Finally, within the field of feminist political theory, the problem of how to combine care, citizenship, and democracy could advance tremendously by using Addams's distinction between the family ethic and the social ethic. This distinction provides a critique of privatized solutions to care needs and points the way for how to develop a new socialized care ethic through cross-class activism in social politics. With her deeply participatory vision, Addams's theory/activist approach to formulating and enforcing social welfare policy challenges feminist democratic theorists to rethink their negative view of the social as a bureaucratic structure of control. Only by incorporating the full Addams, not the truncated maternalist version, will feminist political theorists begin to build on her key insight: the engendering of democracy rests on socializing it.

Notes

1. Christopher Lasch, ed., *The Social Thought of Jane Addams* (New York: Irvington, 1982), xv; Jean Bethke Elshtain, *Jane Addams and the Dream of American Democracy: A Life* (New York: Basic Books, 2002).

2. Jane Addams, *Democracy and Social Ethics* (Urbana: University of Illinois Press, 2002), 101.

3. Charlene Haddock Seigfried, introduction to Addams, *Democracy and Social Ethics*, ix–xxxviii.

4. Kathryn Kish Sklar, "The Historical Foundations of Women's Power in the Creation of the American Welfare State, 1830–1930," in *Mothers of a New World: Maternalist Politics and the Origins of Welfare States*, ed. Seth Koven and Sonya Michel (New York: Routledge, 1993), 68. On the centrality of acting through the state, Sklar concludes, "Despite, or perhaps because of, their limited political rights, they [groups of working-class and middle-class women] viewed the expansion of state responsibility as a means of enhancing their own powers." Sklar, *Florence Kelley and the Nation's Work: The Rise of Women's Political Culture, 1830–1900* (New Haven: Yale University Press, 1995), 233.

5. Lasch, *The Social Thought of Jane Addams*; Charlene Haddock Seigfried, "Socializing Democracy: Jane Addams and John Dewey," *Philosophy of the Social Sciences* 29 (June 1999): 207–30.

6. Elshtain, *Jane Addams and the Dream of American Democracy*, 139; Nancy Cott, "What's in a Name? The Limits of 'Social Feminism'; or, Expanding the Vocabulary of Women's History," *Journal of American History* 76, no. 3 (1989): 816; Wendy Sarvasy, "Beyond the Difference Versus Equality Policy Debate: Postsuffrage Feminism, Citizenship, and the Quest for a Feminist Welfare State," *Signs* 17, no. 2 (1992): 330–31.

7. Wendy Sarvasy, "Social Citizenship from a Feminist Perspective," *Hypatia* 12, no. 4 (1997): 57–60.

8. Addams, *Democracy and Social Ethics*, 37, 39.

9. Ibid., 35.

10. Mary Wollstonecraft, *A Vindication of the Rights of Woman* (New York: Penguin Books, 1992), 264.

11. Addams, *Democracy and Social Ethics*, 40.

12. For a survey of the cosmopolitan tradition of political thought, see April Carter, *The Political Theory of Global Citizenship* (New York: Routledge, 2001). For an interpretation of Addams's contribution to this tradition, see Wendy Sarvasy, "A Global 'Common Table': Jane Addams's Theory of Democratic Cosmopolitanism and World Social Citizenship," in *Jane Addams and the Practice of Democracy*, ed. Marilyn Fischer, Carol Nackenoff, and Wendy Chmielewski (Urbana: University of Illinois Press, 2009), 183–202.

13. Addams, *Democracy and Social Ethics*, 42, 7.

14. Wendy Sarvasy and Patrizia Longo, "The Globalization of Care," *International Feminist Journal of Politics* 6, no. 3 (2004): 399–400.

15. Addams, *Democracy and Social Ethics*, 40, 42, 41, 40, 41.

16. Ibid., 38, 36, 41; Jane Addams, *Newer Ideals of Peace* (Urbana: University of Illinois Press, 2007), 13.

17. Addams, *Democracy and Social Ethics*, 6, 42, 33.

18. Ibid., 14; Jane Addams, *Newer Ideals of Peace*, 13.

19. Addams, *Democracy and Social Elites*, 33, 6–7.

20. Elshtain, *Jane Addams and the Dream of American Democracy*, 157.
21. Addams, *Democracy and Social Ethics*, 9.
22. Patricia Hill Collins, *Black Feminist Thought: Knowledge, Consciousness, and the Politics of Empowerment* (New York: Routledge, 1991), chap. 11.
23. Jane Addams, *Twenty Years at Hull-House* (New York: New American Library, 1961), 104; Addams, *Democracy and Social Ethics*, 31.
24. Addams, *Twenty Years at Hull-House*, 220.
25. Elshtain, *Jane Addams and the Dream of American Democracy*, 122; Seigfried, "Socializing Democracy: Jane Addams and John Dewey."
26. Jane Addams, "The Settlement as a Factor in the Labor Movement," in *Hull-House Maps and Papers* (New York: Arno Press, 1970), 188–90.
27. Addams, *Democracy and Social Ethics*, 38, 29, 38.
28. Addams, *Newer Ideals of Peace*, 101.
29. Addams, *Democracy and Social Ethics*, chap. 3.
30. Addams, *Newer Ideals of Peace*, 112. On the centrality of labor, Sklar observes, "Work (and its obverse—unemployment) set the framework within which they [large numbers of middle-class women] viewed social problems and posed solutions. Family life and motherhood were part, but only part, of that framework." Sklar, "The Historical Foundations of Women's Power," 45.
31. Addams, *Democracy and Social Ethics*, 44.
32. Jane Addams, "Hull-House, Chicago: An Effort Toward Social Democracy," *Forum* 14 (October 1892): 226–41.
33. Hannah Arendt, *The Human Condition* (Chicago: University of Chicago Press, 1998); Hanna Fenichel Pitkin, *The Attack of the Blob: Hannah Arendt's Concept of the Social* (Chicago: University of Chicago Press, 1998).
34. Addams, *Twenty Years at Hull-House*, 154.
35. Meredith Tax, *The Rising of the Women* (New York: Monthly Review Press, 1980), 302–3n40; Sklar, *Florence Kelley and the Nation's Work*, 240.
36. Addams, *Democracy and Social Ethics*, 76.
37. Ibid.
38. Addams, *Twenty Years at Hull-House*, 148–51.
39. Tax, *The Rising of the Women*, 82; Sklar, *Florence Kelley and the Nation's Work*, 233–35.
40. Addams, *Twenty Years at Hull-House*, 151–54.
41. Ibid., 98–99.
42. For the Scandinavian context of state feminism, see Helga Maria Hernes, *Welfare State and Woman Power: Essays in State Feminism* (Oslo: Norwegian University Press, 1987); for the Latin American context of state feminism as part of the transition to democracy, see Sonia E. Alvarez, *Engendering Democracy in Brazil: Women's Movements in Transition Politics* (Princeton: Princeton University Press, 1990), chap. 9.
43. Addams, *Twenty Years at Hull-House*, 154; Tax, *The Rising of the Women*, 73–74.
44. Addams, *Twenty Years at Hull-House*, 154, 152.
45. Ibid.
46. Sklar, *Florence Kelley and the Nation's Work*, 240. The provision of these scholarships turned members of the Illinois Federation of Women's Clubs into active enforcers of the law.
47. Addams, *Democracy and Social Ethics*, 116.
48. As Addams observed, "There was always a willingness, even among the poorest women, to keep on with the hard night scrubbing or the long days of washing for the children's sake." Addams, *Twenty Years at Hull-House*, 153.
49. Addams, *Democracy and Social Ethics*, 74.
50. Ibid., 76.
51. Addams specifically connected the early efforts at labor legislation and enforcement to "a

movement of world-wide significance and manifold manifestation." In effect, the 1893 effort showed how she envisioned turning the daughter's vague commitment to universal brotherhood into a tangible practice of democratic global citizenship for social justice. Addams, *Twenty Years at Hull-House,* 168, 153.

52. Cf. Collins, *Black Feminist Thought,* 225.

Selected Bibliography

Books by Jane Addams

Addams, Jane. *Democracy and Social Ethics*. 1902. Urbana: University of Illinois Press, 2002.
———. *The Excellent Becomes the Permanent*. 1932. Freeport, N.Y.: Books for Libraries Press, 1970.
———. *The Long Road of Woman's Memory*. 1916. Urbana: University of Illinois Press, 2002.
———. *My Friend, Julia Lathrop*. 1935. Urbana: University of Illinois Press, 2004.
———. *A New Conscience and an Ancient Evil*. 1912. Urbana: University of Illinois Press, 2002.
———. *Newer Ideals of Peace*. 1907. Urbana: University of Illinois Press, 2007.
———. *Peace and Bread in Time of War*. 1922. Urbana: University of Illinois Press, 2002.
———. *Second Twenty Years at Hull-House*. New York: Macmillan, 1930.
———. *The Spirit of Youth and the City Streets*. 1909. Urbana: University of Illinois Press, 1972.
———. *Twenty Years at Hull-House*. 1910. Urbana: University of Illinois Press, 1990.
Addams, Jane, Emily G. Balch, and Alice Hamilton. *Women at The Hague: The International Congress of Women and Its Results*. 1915. Urbana: University of Illinois Press, 2003.
Addams, Jane, et al. *The Child, the Clinic, and the Court*. Introduction by Jane Addams. New York: New Republic, 1925.
Residents of Hull House. *Hull-House Maps and Papers*. 1895. Urbana: University of Illinois Press, 2007.

Selected Articles by Jane Addams

Addams, Jane. "Americanization." 1919. In *The Jane Addams Reader*, ed. Jean Bethke Elshtain, 240–47. New York: Basic Books, 2002.

———. "Art Work." 1895. In *Eighty Years at Hull House*, ed. Mary Lynn McCree Bryan and Allen F. Davis, 50. Chicago: Quadrangle Books, 1969.
———. "As I See Women: In an Informal Talk with a Friend." *Ladies Home Journal* 32, no. 8 (1915): 11, 54.
———. "A Belated Industry." *American Journal of Sociology* 1, no. 5 (1896): 536–50.
———. "A Book That Changed My Life." *Christian Century* 44 (October 13, 1927): 1196–98.
———. "A Challenge to the Contemporary Church." *Survey* 28 (May 4, 1912): 195–98.
———. "The Child at the Point of Greatest Pressure." *National Conference of Charities and Correction Proceedings* (1912): 26–30. JAMC (reel 47-0279–0283), Special Collections, The University Library, The University of Illinois at Chicago.
———. "Child Labor and Education." *National Conference of Charities and Correction Proceedings* (1908): 364–68.
———. "Child Labor Legislation—A Requisite for Industrial Efficiency." 1905. In *On Education*, ed. Ellen Condliffe Lagemann, 124–35. New Brunswick, N.J.: Transaction Books, 1994.
———. "The Church and the Social Evil: Christian Responsibility for a Terrible Modern Scourge." *Methodist Review Quarterly* 61, no. 4 (1912): 665.
———. "The College Woman and Christianity." *Independent* 53 (August 8, 1901): 1852–55.
———. "Democracy or Militarism." 1899. *Liberty Tracts: Central Anti-Imperialist League of Chicago*, 35–39. In *Jane Addams's Writings on Peace*, ed. Marilyn Fischer and Judy D. Whipps. Vol. 4. Bristol, U.K.: Thoemmes Press, 2003.
———. "Devil Baby at Hull-House." *Atlantic Monthly* 118 (1916): 441–51.
———. "Exaggerated Nationalism and International Comity." 1934. In *Jane Addams's Writings on Peace*, ed. Marilyn Fischer and Judy D. Whipps, 168–70. Vol. 4. Bristol, U.K.: Thoemmes Press, 2003.
———. *First Report of the Labor Museum at Hull-House, Chicago, 1901–1902.* Pamphlet. Chicago, 1902.
———. "Foreign-Born Children in the Primary Grades." In *Journal of Proceedings and Addresses* (National Education Association) 36 (1897): 104–12.
———. "A Function of the Social Settlement." 1899. In *On Education*, ed. Ellen Condliffe Lagemann, 74–97. New Brunswick, N.J.: Transaction Books, 1994.
———. "Graham Taylor—Pioneer in Sociology." *Chicago Theological Seminary Register* 17, no. 4 (1928): 22.
———. "Has the Emancipation Act Been Nullified by National Indifference?" *Survey* 29, no. 18 (1913): 565–66.
———. "How to Build a Peace Program?" 1932. In *Jane Addams' Essays and Speeches*, ed. Marilyn Fischer and Judy D. Whipps, 329–38. London: Continuum International, 2005.
———. "Hull House (Chicago)." *Encyclopedia of Social Reform*, ed. William D. P. Bliss, 587–90. New York: Funk and Wagnalls, 1908.
———. "Hull House, Chicago: An Effort Toward Social Democracy." *Forum* 14 (October 1892): 226–41.
———. "The Humanizing Tendency of Industrial Education." 1904. In *On Education*, ed. Ellen Condliffe Lagemann, 120–23. New Brunswick, N.J.: Transaction Books, 1994.

———. "If Men Were Seeking the Elective Franchise." 1913. In *The Jane Addams Reader*, ed. Jean Bethke Elshtain, 229–34. New York: Basic Books, 2002.
———. "Immigrant Woman as She Adjusts Herself to American Life." *Biennial Convention Official Report* (General Federation of Women's Clubs, 1914), 370–74. JAPM 47:902–7.
———. "Immigration: A Field Neglected by the Scholar." *Commons* 10 (January 1905): 9–19.
———. "A Modern Devil-Baby." *American Journal of Sociology* 20 (1914): 117–18.
———. "A Modern Lear." 1912. In *Jane Addams and the Dream of American Democracy*, ed. Jean Bethke Elshtain, 163–76. New York: Basic Books, 2002.
———. "My Experiences as a Progressive Delegate." *McClure's Magazine* 40 (November 12, 1912): 12–14.
———. "National Protection for Children." *Annals of the American Academy of Political and Social Science* 29 (January–June 1907): 327–30.
———. "The Newer Ideals of Peace." 1902. In *Jane Addams' Essays and Speeches*, ed. Marilyn Fischer and Judy D. Whipps, 13–18. London: Continuum International, 2005.
———. "A New Impulse to an Old Gospel." *Forum* 14 (November 1892): 345–58.
———. "The New Internationalism." 1907. In *Jane Addams' Essays and Speeches*, ed. Marilyn Fischer and Judy D. Whipps, 43–45. New York: Continuum International, 2005.
———. "A New Political Method Emerging in the Orient." 1923. In *Jane Addams's Writings on Peace*, ed. Marilyn Fischer and Judy D. Whipps. Vol. 4. Bristol, U.K.: Thoemmes Press, 2003.
———. "The Objective Value of the Social Settlement." 1893. In *The Jane Addams Reader*, ed. Jean Bethke Elshtain, 29–45. New York: Basic Books, 2002.
———. "One Menace to the Century's Progress." 1901. In *Jane Addams' Essays and Speeches*, ed. Marilyn Fischer and Judy D. Whipps, 9–12. New York: Continuum International, 2005.
———. "Opening of the First Session, June 18, 1933." 1933. In *Jane Addams' Essays and Speeches*, ed. Marilyn Fischer and Judy D. Whipps, 365–66. London: Continuum International, 2005.
———. "Our National Self-Righteousness." 1933. In *The Jane Addams Reader*, ed. Jean Bethke Elshtain, 442–48. New York: Basic Books, 2002.
———. "Patriots and Pacifists in War Time." 1917. In *Jane Addams' Essays and Speeches*, ed. Marilyn Fischer and Judy D. Whipps, 153–64. London: Continuum International, 2005.
———. "Presidential Address." 1919. In *Jane Addams' Essays and Speeches*, ed. Marilyn Fischer and Judy D. Whipps, 197–202. London: Continuum International, 2005.
———. "Presidential Address: Pan-Pacific Union." 1928. In *Jane Addams's Writings on Peace*, ed. Marilyn Fischer and Judy D. Whipps. Vol. 4. Bristol, U.K.: Thoemmes Press, 2003.
———. "The Progressive Party and the Negro." 1912. In *Jane Addams' Essays and Speeches*, ed. Marilyn Fischer and Judy D. Whipps, 49–52. London: Continuum International, 2005.
———. "The Reaction of Modern Life upon Religious Education." *Religious Education* 4 (April 1909): 23–33.

———. "Religious Education and Contemporary Social Conditions." 1911. In *The Jane Addams Reader*, ed. Jean Bethke Elshtain, 196–204. New York: Basic Books, 2002.

———. "Respect for Law." 1901. In *Lynching and Rape: An Exchange of Views*, by Bettina Apthecker, 22–27. New York: American Institute for Marxist Studies, 1977.

———. "The Revolt Against War." 1915. In *Addams's Essays and Speeches on Peace (1899–1935)*, ed. Marilyn Fischer and Judy D. Whipps, 83–95. Bristol, U.K.: Thoemmes Press, 2003.

———. "The Sheltered Woman and the Magdalen." 1913. In *The Jane Addams Reader*, ed. Jean Bethke Elshtain, 264–69. New York: Basic Books, 2002.

———. "Social Control." *Crisis: A Record of the Darker Races* 1, no. 3 (1911): 22–23.

———. "The Subjective Necessity for Social Settlements." 1893. In *The Jane Addams Reader*, ed. Jean Bethke Elshtain, 14–28. New York: Basic Books, 2002.

———. "The Subtle Problems of Charity." 1899. In *The Jane Addams Reader*, ed. Jean Bethke Elshtain, 62–75. New York: Basic Books, 2002.

———. "Statement of Miss Jane Addams, of Chicago, Illinois, Representing the Woman's Peace Party." 1916. In *Jane Addams' Essays and Speeches*, ed. Marilyn Fischer and Judy D. Whipps, 121–34. London: Continuum International, 2005.

———. "Tolstoy and Gandhi." 1931. In *The Jane Addams Reader*, ed. Jean Bethke Elshtain, 436–41. New York: Basic Books, 2002.

———. "Trade Unions and Public Duty." *Annals of the Journal of Sociology* 4, no. 4 (1899): 33–55.

———. "Unexpected Reactions of a Traveler in Egypt." *Atlantic Monthly* 113 (1914): 178–86.

———. "Votes for Women and Other Votes." *Survey* 28 (June 1, 1912): 367–68.

———. "What Peace Means." 1899. In *Jane Addams on Peace, War, and International Understanding, 1899–1932*, ed. Allen F. Davis, 11–18. New York: Garland, 1976.

———. "War Times Challenging Woman's Traditions." 1916. In *Jane Addams on Peace, War, and International Understanding, 1899–1932*, ed. Allen F. Davis, 127–39. New York: Garland, 1976.

———. "What War Is Destroying." 1915. In *Addams's Essays and Speeches on Peace (1899–1935)*, ed. Marilyn Fischer and Judy D. Whipps, 61–64. Bristol, U.K.: Thoemmes Press, 2003.

———. "'Whoso Liveth to Himself': A Message to Believers in Peace and Freedom." 1924. In *Jane Addams' Essays and Speeches*, ed. Marilyn Fischer and Judy D. Whipps, 263–66. London: Continuum International, 2005.

———. "Why Women Are Concerned with the Larger Citizenship." In *The Woman Citizen's Library*, vol. 9, ed. Shailer Mathews, 2135–36. Chicago: Civics Society, 1913.

———. "Why Women Should Vote." *Ladies' Home Journal* 27 (January 1915): 21–22.

———. "Widening the Circle of Enlightenment." *Journal of Adult Education* 2, no. 3 (1930): 276–79.

———. "Woman's Special Training for Peacemaking." *Proceedings* 2 (1909), American National Arbitration and Peace Congress. In *Jane Addams' Essays and Speeches*, ed. Marilyn Fischer and Judy D. Whipps, 47–48. London: Continuum International, 2005.

———. "Women and War." 1915. In *Addams's Essays and Speeches on Peace (1899–1935)*, ed. Marilyn Fischer and Judy D. Whipps, 75–82. Bristol, U.K.: Thoemmes Press, 2003.

———. "Work and Play as Factors in Education." *Chautauqua* 42 (November 1905): 251–55.
Addams, Jane, and Emily Greene Balch. "Is a United Peace Front Desirable?" 1934. In *Jane Addams' Essays and Speeches*, ed. Marilyn Fischer and Judy D. Whipps, 353–56. New York: Continuum International, 2005.

Collections of Jane Addams's Writings

Addams, Jane. *On Education*. Ed. Ellen Condliffe Lagemann. New Brunswick, N.J.: Transaction Books, 1994.
Bryan, Mary Lynn McCree, Barbara Bair, and Maree De Angury, eds. *The Selected Papers of Jane Addams*. Vol. 1, *Preparing to Lead, 1860–1881*. Urbana: University of Illinois Press, 2003.
———. *The Selected Papers of Jane Addams*. Vol 2, *Venturing into Usefulness, 1881–88*. Urbana: University of Illinois Press, 2009.
Bryan, Mary Lynn McCree, Nancy Slote, and Maree de Angury, eds. *The Jane Addams Papers Project* (JAPP). 82 reels. Microfilming Corporation of America and University Microfilms International, 1984–85.
Cooper Johnson, Emily, ed. *Jane Addams: A Centennial Reader*. New York: Macmillan, 1960.
Davis, Allen F., ed. *Jane Addams on Peace, War, and International Understanding*. New York: Garland, 1976.
Elshtain, Jean Bethke, ed. *The Jane Addams Reader*. New York: Basic Books, 2002.
Fischer, Marilyn, and Judy D. Whipps, eds. *Jane Addams' Essays and Speeches*. Bristol, U.K.: Thoemmes Press, 2006.
———. *Jane Addams's Writings on Peace*. 4 vols. History of American Thought. Bristol, U.K.: Thoemmes Press, 2003. Facsimile edition.
Lasch, Christopher, ed. *The Social Thought of Jane Addams*. Indianapolis: Bobbs-Merrill, 1965.

Works on Addams's Philosophy and Ideas

Curti, Merle. "Jane Addams on Human Nature." *Journal of the History of Ideas* 22, no. 2 (1961): 240–53.
Deegan, Mary Jo. "Jane Addams." In *Fifty Key Sociologists: The Formative Theorists*, ed. John Scott, 3–8. London: Routledge, 2007.
———. *Jane Addams and the Men of the Chicago School, 1892–1918*. New Brunswick, N.J.: Transaction Books, 1988.
———. "A Very Different Vision of Jane Addams and Emily Greene Balch." *Journal of Women's History* 8 (Summer 1996): 121–25.
Elshtain, Jean Bethke. *Jane Addams and the Dream of American Democracy: A Life*. New York: Basic Books, 2002.

———. "Jane Addams: A Pilgrim's Progress." *Journal of Religion* 78, no. 3 (1998): 339–60.
Farrell, John C. *Beloved Lady: A History of Jane Addams' Ideas on Reform and Peace*. Baltimore: Johns Hopkins University Press, 1967.
Fischer, Marilyn, Carol Nackenoff, and Wendy Chmielewski, eds. *Jane Addams and the Practice of Democracy*. Urbana: University of Illinois Press, 2009.
———. *On Addams*. Belmont, Calif.: Wadsworth, 2004.
Hamington, Maurice. "Addams's Radical Democracy: Moving Beyond Rights." *Journal of Speculative Philosophy* 18, no. 3 (2004): 216–23.
———. *Embodied Care: Jane Addams, Maurice Merleau-Ponty, and Feminist Ethics*. Urbana: University of Illinois Press, 2004.
———. "Feminist Prophetic Pragmatism." *Journal of Speculative Philosophy* 23, no. 1 (2009).
———. "Jane Addams." In *The Stanford Encyclopedia of Philosophy*, ed. Edward N. Zalta (Summer 2007). http://plato.stanford.edu/archives/sum2007/entries/addams-jane/.
———. "Jane Addams and Ida B. Wells on Lynching." *Journal of Speculative Philosophy* 19, no. 2 (2005): 167–74.
———. "Jane Addams and the Politics of Embodied Care." *Journal of Speculative Philosophy* 15, no. 2 (2001): 105–21.
———. *The Social Philosophy of Jane Addams*. Urbana: University of Illinois Press, 2009.
———. "Two Leaders, Two Utopias: Jane Addams and Dorothy Day." *National Women's Studies Association Journal* 19, no. 2 (2007): 159–86.
Harkness, Georgia. "Jane Addams in Retrospect." *Christian Century* 77 (January 1960): 39–41.
Hunt, James B. "Jane Addams: The Presbyterian Connection." *American Presbyterians* 68, no. 4 (1990): 231.
Knight, Louise W. "Jane Addams's Views on the Responsibilities of Wealth." In *The Responsibilities of Wealth*, ed. Dwight F. Burlingame. Bloomington: Indiana University Press, 1992.
Leffers, M. Regina. "Pragmatists Jane Addams and John Dewey Inform the Ethics of Care." *Hypatia* 8, no. 2 (1993): 64–78.
Levine, Daniel. *Jane Addams and the Liberal Tradition*. Madison: State Historical Society of Wisconsin, 1971.
Pois, Anne Marie. "Foreshadowings: Jane Addams, Emily Greene Balch, and the Ecofeminism/Pacifist Feminism of the 1980s." *Peace and Change* 20, no. 4 (1995): 439–66.
Schaafsma, David, ed. *Jane Addams, Hull-House, and the Call to Education*. New York: Teachers College Press, 2008.
Schott, Linda. "Jane Addams and William James on Alternatives to War." *Journal of the History of Ideas* 54 (April 1993): 241–54.
Scott, Anne Firor. Introduction to *Democracy and Social Ethics*, by Jane Addams. Cambridge: Harvard University Press, 1964.
Seigfried, Charlene Haddock. "Introduction to Illinois Press Edition." In *Democracy and Social Ethics*, by Jane Addams, ix–xxxviii. Urbana: University of Illinois Press, 2002.
———. *Pragmatism and Feminism: Reweaving the Social Fabric*. Chicago: University of Chicago Press, 1996.
———. "Socializing Democracy: Jane Addams and John Dewey." *Philosophy of the Social Sciences* 29, no. 2 (1999): 207–30.
———. "Where Are All the Pragmatist Feminists?" *Hypatia* 6, no. 2 (1991): 1–19.

Whipps, Judy D. "Jane Addams's Social Thought as a Model for a Pragmatist-Feminist Communitarianism." *Hypatia* 19, no. 2 (2004): 118–33.

Biographies of Jane Addams

Brown, Victoria Bissell. *The Education of Jane Addams*. Philadelphia: University of Pennsylvania Press, 2004.
Davis, Allen F. *American Heroine: The Life and Legend of Jane Addams*. New York: Oxford University Press, 1973.
Diliberto, Gioia. *A Useful Woman: The Early Life of Jane Addams*. New York: Scribner, 1999.
Joslin, Katherine. *Jane Addams, a Writer's Life*. Urbana: University of Illinois Press, 2004.
Knight, Louise. *Citizen: Jane Addams and the Struggle for Democracy*. Chicago: University of Chicago Press, 2005.
Linn, James Weber. *Jane Addams: A Biography*. Urbana: University of Illinois Press, 2000.
Polikoff, Barbara Garland. *With One Bold Act: The Story of Jane Addams*. Chicago: Boswell Books, 1999.

Selected Works Addressing Addams in Context: Hull House, the Progressive Era, and American Philosophy

Alonso, Harriet Hyman. *Peace as a Woman's Issue: A History of the U.S. Movement for World Peace and Women's Rights*. New York: Syracuse University Press, 1993.
Barker-Benfield, G. J. "Mother Emancipator: The Meaning of Jane Addams' Sickness and Cure." *Journal of Family History* 4, no. 4 (1979): 395–420.
Bowen, Louise de Koven. *Growing Up with a City*. Urbana: University of Illinois Press, 2002.
Brown, Victoria. "Advocate for Democracy: Jane Addams and the Pullman Strike." In *The Pullman Strike and the Crisis in the 1890s: Essays on Labor and Politics*, ed. Richard Schneirov, Shelton Stromquist, and Nick Salvatore, 130–58. Urbana: University of Illinois Press, 1999.
Bryan, Mary Lynn McCree, and Allen F. Davis, eds. *100 Years at Hull-House*. Bloomington: Indiana University Press, 1969.
Chicago Unity. Hull-House Scrapbook (November), vol. 1 (1892). University of Illinois, Chicago, Special Collections Library.
Craig, John. "The Woman's Peace Party and Questions of Gender Separatism." *Peace and Change* 19, no. 4 (1994): 373–98.
Crunden, Robert M. *Ministers of Reform: The Progressives' Achievement in American Civilization, 1889–1920*. Urbana: University of Illinois Press, 1984.
Davis, Allen F. Introduction to *The Spirit of Youth and the City Streets*, by Jane Addams, vii–xxx. New York: Macmillan, 1930.

———. *Spearheads for Reform: The Social Settlements and the Progressive Movement, 1890–1914.* New York: Oxford University Press, 1967.
Davis, Allen, and Mary Lynn McCree, eds. *Eighty Years at Hull-House.* Chicago: Quadrangle Books, 1969.
Dawley, Alan. *Changing the World: American Progressives in War and Revolution.* Princeton: Princeton University Press, 2003.
Daynes, Gary, and Nicholas V. Longo. "Jane Addams and the Origins of Service-Learning Practice in the United States." *Michigan Journal of Community Service Learning* 11, no. 1 (2004): 5–13.
Deegan, Mary Jo. "An American Dream: The Historical Connections Between Women, Humanism, and Sociology, 1890–1920." *Humanity and Society* 11 (August 1987): 353–65.
———. "'Dear Love, Dear Love': Feminist Pragmatism and the Chicago Female World of Love and Ritual." *Gender and Society* 10 (October 1996): 590–607.
———. "Early Women Sociologists and the American Sociological Society." *American Sociologist* 16 (February 1981): 14–24.
———. "Hull-House Maps and Papers." In *Poverty and Social Welfare in America: An Encyclopedia,* ed. Gwendolyn Mink and Alice O'Connor, 386–87. Santa Barbara, Calif.: ABC-CLIO, 2004.
———. Introduction to *Women at the Hague: The International Congress of Women and Its Results,* by Jane Addams, Emily Greene Balch, and Alice Hamilton, 11–34. Classics in Women's Studies. Amherst, N.Y.: Humanity Books, an imprint of Prometheus Press, 2003.
———. *Self, War, and Society: The Macrosociology of George Herbert Mead.* New Brunswick, N.J.: Transaction Books, forthcoming.
———. *The Sociology of Race Relations at Hull-House and the University of Chicago.* Westport, Conn.: Greenwood Press, 2002.
———. "W. E. B. Du Bois and the Women of Hull-House, 1896–1899." *American Sociologist* 19 (Winter 1988): 301–11.
———. *Women in Sociology.* Introduction by Mary Jo Deegan. New York: Greenwood Press, 1991.
———. "Women in Sociology, 1890–1930." *Journal of the History of Sociology* 1 (Fall 1978): 11–34.
Deegan, Mary Jo, and Ana-Maria Wahl. "Introduction: Ellen Gates Starr and Her Journey Toward Social Justice and Beauty." In *On Art, Labor, and Religion,* by Ellen Gates Starr, ed. and intro. Mary Jo Deegan and Ana-Maria Wahl, 1–35. New Brunswick, N.J.: Transaction Books, 2003.
Degen, Mary Louise. *The History of the Woman's Peace Party.* New York: Burt Franklin Reprints, 1974.
Dell, Floyd. *Women as World Builders: Studies in Modern Feminism.* Chicago: Forbes, 1913.
D'Emilio, John, and Estelle B. Freedman. *Intimate Matters: A History of Sexuality in America.* 2nd ed. Chicago: University of Chicago Press, 1997.
Dewey, John. "Democratic Versus Coercive International Organization: The Realism of Jane Addams." In *Peace and Bread in Time of War,* by Jane Addams, ix–xx. Boston: G. K. Hall, 1960.
Edwards, R. A. R. "Jane Addams, Walter Rauschenbusch, and Dorothy Day: A Comparative Study of Settlement Theology." In *Gender and the Social Gospel,* ed. Wendy J.

Deichmann Edwards and Carolyn De Swarte Gifford, 150–66. Urbana: University of Illinois Press, 2003.
Faderman, Lillian. *Odd Girls and Twilight Lovers: A History of Lesbian Life in Twentieth-Century America*. New York: Penguin, 1991.
Feagin, Joe R., and Hernan Vera. *Liberation Sociology*. Boulder, Colo.: Westview Press, 2001.
Ganz, Cheryl R., and Margaret Strobel, eds. *Pots of Promise: Mexicans and Pottery at Hull-House, 1920–40*. Urbana: University of Illinois Press, 2004.
Gilman, Charlotte Perkins. *The Living of Charlotte Perkins Gilman: An Autobiography*. Madison: University of Wisconsin Press, 1935.
Green, Judith. "Building a Cosmopolitan World Community Through Mutual Hospitality." In *Pragmatism and the Problem of Race*, ed. Bill E. Lawson and Donald F. Koch, 203–24. Bloomington: Indiana University Press, 2004.
Greenwood, Janette Thomas. *The Gilded Age: A History in Documents*. New York: Oxford University Press, 2000.
Hamington, Maurice. "Jane Addams and Ida B. Wells on Lynching." *Journal of Speculative Philosophy* 19, no. 2 (2005): 167–74.
Harkavy, Ira, and John L. Puckett. "Lessons from Hull House for the Contemporary Urban University." *Social Science Review* (September 1994): 299–321.
Harkness, Georgia. "Jane Addams in Retrospect." *Christian Century* 77, no. 2 (1960): 39–41.
Haslet, Diane C. "Hull House and the Birth Control Movement: An Untold Story." *Journal of Women and Social Work* 12, no. 3 (1997): 261–78.
"Hull-House, Irreligious and Socialistic." *Chicago Chronicle*, September 16, 1903. In *100 Years at Hull-House*, ed. Mary Lynn McCree Bryan and Allen F. Davis, 120–21. Bloomington: Indiana University Press, 1969.
Jackson, Shannon. *Lines of Activity: Performance, Historiography, Hull-House Domesticity*. Ann Arbor: University of Michigan Press, 2000.
"Jane Addams Declares Ballot for Woman Made Necessary by Changed Conditions." *Chicago Record Herald*, April 1, 1906, 3.
Kelley, Florence. "I Go to Work." *Survey* 58, no. 5 (1927): 271–77.
Kleinberg, S. J. *Women in the United States, 1830–1945*. New Brunswick, N.J.: Rutgers University Press, 1999.
Lasch, Christopher, ed. *The New Radicalism in America, 1889–1963: The Intellectual as a Social Type*. New York: Norton, 1965.
Lissak, Rivka Shpak. *Pluralism and Progressives: Hull House and the New Immigrants, 1889–1919*. Chicago: University of Chicago Press, 1989.
Lynd, Staughton. "Jane Addams and the Radical Impulse." *Commentary* 32 (July 1961): 54–59.
Maohwald, Mary B. "What American Philosophers Missed: Jane Addams, Critical Pragmatism, and Cultural Feminism." *Journal of Value Inquiry* 31, no. 1 (1997): 39–54.
Marsoobian, Armen T., and John Ryder. *The Blackwell Guide to American Philosophy*. Malden, Mass.: Blackwell, 2004.
McDonald, Lynn. *The Early Origins of the Social Sciences*. Montreal: McGill–Queen's University, 1994.
———. *The Women Founders of the Social Sciences*. Ottawa: Carleton University Press, 1994.

———. *Women Theorists on Society and Politics*. Waterloo, Ontario: Wilifred Laurier University Press, 1998.
Menand, Louis. *The Metaphysical Club: A Story of Ideas in America*. New York: Farrar, Straus and Giroux, 2001.
Mink, Gwendolyn. *Settlement Folk: Social Thought and the American Settlement Movement, 1885–1930*. Chicago: University of Chicago Press, 1990.
Muncy, Robyn. *Creating a Female Dominion in American Reform, 1890–1935*. New York: Oxford University Press, 1991.
"Opens in Jolly Romp: Throngs of Children Besiege the Hull House Playground." *Chicago Daily Tribune*, May 5, 1895, 1.
Polacheck, Hilda Satt. *I Came A Stranger: The Story of a Hull-House Girl*. Urbana: University of Illinois Press, 1991.
Pratt, Scott. *Native Pragmatism*. Bloomington: Indiana University Press, 2002.
Quandt, Jean B. *From the Small Town to the Great Community: The Social Thought of Progressive Intellectuals*. New Brunswick, N.J.: Rutgers University Press, 1970.
Romano, Carlin. "Mulling (Not Hulling) Jane Addams." *Chronicle of Higher Education* 48, no. 29 (2002): B11.
Ross, Dorothy. "Gendered Social Knowledge: Domestic Discourse, Jane Addams, and the Possibilities of Social Science." In *Gender and American Social Science: The Formative Years*, ed. Helene Silverberg, 235–64. Princeton: Princeton University Press, 1998.
Rupp, Leila J. "Sexuality and Politics in the Early Twentieth Century: The Case of the International Women's Movement." *Feminist Studies* 23, no. 3 (1997): 577–606.
Sadovnik, Alan R., and Susan F. Semel. *Founding Mothers and Others: Women Educational Leaders During the Progressive Era*. New York: Palgrave, 2002.
Sawaya, Francesca. "The Authority of Experience: Jane Addams and Hull House." In *Women's Experience of Modernity, 1875–1945*, ed. Ann L. Ardis and Leslie W. Lewis, 47–62. Baltimore: Johns Hopkins University Press, 2003.
Schierman, Barbara. *Alice Hamilton: A Life in Letters*. Urbana: University of Illinois Press, 2003.
Schott, Linda. "Jane Addams and William James On Alternatives to War." *Journal of History of Ideas* 54, no. 2 (1993): 241–54.
Sherrick, Rebecca. "Their Father's Daughters: The Autobiographies of Jane Addams and Florence Kelley." *American Studies* 27, no. 1 (1986): 39–53.
Sklar, Kathryn Kish. *Florence Kelley and the Nation's Work: The Rise of Women's Political Culture, 1830–1900*. New Haven: Yale University Press, 1995.
———. "The Historical Foundations of Women's Power in the Creation of the American Welfare State, 1830–1930." In *Mothers of a New World: Maternalist Politics and the Origins of Welfare States*, ed. Seth Koven and Sonya Michel, 43–93. New York: Routledge, 1993.
———. "Jane Addams's Peace Activism, 1914–1922: A Model for Women Today?" *Women's Studies Quarterly* 23 (Fall–Winter 1995): 32–47.
———. "Religious and Moral Authority as Factors Sharing the Balance of Power for Women's Political Culture in the Twentieth Century." Paper presented at the hundredth anniversary of the founding of Hull House, Rockford, Ill., October 1989.
———. *Social Justice Feminists in the United States and Germany*. Ithaca: Cornell University Press, 1998.

Stebner, Eleanor J. *The Women of Hull House: A Study in Spirituality, Vocation, and Relationship*. New York: State University of New York Press, 1997.
Sullivan, Shannon. "Reciprocal Relations Between Races: Jane Addams's Ambiguous Legacy." *Transactions of the Charles S. Peirce Society* 39, no. 1 (2003): 43–60.
Tarbell, Ida M. *The Business of Being a Woman*. New York: Macmillan, 1912. http://manybooks.net/titles/tarbelli1657716577-8.html# (accessed March 23, 2006).
Taylor, Graham. "Jane Addams—Interpreter, an Appreciation." *Review of Reviews* 40 (December 1909): 680.
Terrell, Mary Church. *A Colored Woman in a White World*. New York: G. K. Hall, 1996.
Tomko, Linda J. *Dancing Class: Gender, Ethnicity, and Social Divides in American Dance, 1890–1920*. Bloomington: Indiana University Press, 1999.
Webb, Beatrice. "A Fabian Visits Hull House." In *100 Years at Hull-House*, ed. Mary Lynn McCree Bryan and Allen F. Davis, 61–62. Bloomington: Indiana University Press, 1969.
Wells, Ida B. *Crusade for Justice: The Autobiography of Ida B. Wells*. Ed. Alfreda M. Duster. Chicago: University of Chicago Press, 1970.

Contributors

VICTORIA BISSELL BROWN is the L. F. Parker Professor of History at Grinnell College. She is the author of *The Education of Jane Addams* (2004) and several articles and public presentations on Addams. Brown is the coauthor, with Timothy Shannon, of *Going to the Source: The Bedford Reader in American History* (2005, 2007).

MARILYN FISCHER is professor of philosophy at the University of Dayton in Dayton, Ohio. She is the author of *On Addams* (2004) and *Ethical Decision-Making in Fund Raising* (2000), which received two national awards for research in philanthropy. With Carol Nackenoff and Wendy Chmielewski she coedited *Jane Addams and the Practice of Democracy* (2009), and with Judy Whipps she coedited the four-volume *Jane Addams's Writings on Peace* (2003). She has published articles in journals including *Transactions of the Charles S. Peirce Society*, the *Journal of Speculative Philosophy*, the *Journal of Social Philosophy*, and the *National Women's Studies Association Journal*, as well as in a number of anthologies. She is currently writing a book on Addams's internationalism.

JUDITH M. GREEN is associate professor of philosophy and codirector of women's studies at Fordham University. She specializes in social and political philosophy, pragmatism, Africana philosophy, and feminist theory. She also serves as a consultant on citizen participation in urban planning. She is the author of *Pragmatism and Social Hope: Deepening Democracy in Global Contexts* (2008) and *Deep Democracy: Community, Diversity, and Transformation* (1999).

MAURICE HAMINGTON is associate professor of women's studies and philosophy as well as director of the Institute for Women's Studies and Services at Metropolitan State College of Denver. He is the author of *The Social Philosophy of Jane Addams* (2009); *Embodied Care: Jane Addams, Maurice Merleau-Ponty, and Feminist Ethics* (2004); and *Hail Mary? The Struggle for Ultimate Womanhood in Catholicism* (1995). He coedited *Revealing Male Bodies* (2002) and *Socializing Care: Feminist Ethics and Public Issues* (1995). His current projects include an edited volume on feminism and hospitality as well as one on care ethics and business ethics.

SHANNON JACKSON is professor of rhetoric and professor and chair of theater, dance, and performance studies at the University of California–Berkeley. Her publications include *Lines of Activity: Performance, Historiography, Hull-House Domesticity* (2000) and

Professing Performance: Theatre in the Academy from Philology to Performativity (2004) as well as dozens of essays in journals and collections in American studies, feminism, performance studies, art, and cultural studies. She is currently completing *Supporting Acts: The Infrastructural Politics of Performance* and *The Builders Association: Performance and the Politics of New Media*.

KATHERINE JOSLIN is the author of *Jane Addams, a Writer's Life* (2004, 2009). Her latest book, *Edith Wharton and the Making of Fashion* (2009), initiates a series called Reading Dress that looks at literature in the context of fashion, clothing, textiles, design, and production. She wrote *Edith Wharton* in the Women Writers Series (1991, 1994) and coedited *Wretched Exotic: Essays on Edith Wharton in Europe* (1993, 1996) and *American Feminism: Key Source Documents, 1848–1920*, 4 vols. (2003). A professor of English at Western Michigan University, she has received the Alumni Excellence in Teaching Award (1997), has directed American studies, and now co-chairs the President's Commission on Gender Equity. In 2008, Fulbright named her a Senior Specialist in the Study of the United States. Currently, she is writing a literary biography of Theodore Roosevelt.

LOUISE (LUCY) W. KNIGHT is an independent scholar and adjunct professor in communication studies at Northwestern University, where she teaches the history of rhetoric. The author of *Citizen: Jane Addams and the Struggle for Democracy* (2005), she has also published articles in the *Journal of Women's History*, *Gender and History*, the *Journal of Community Practice*, and *Affilia: Women and Social Work* and in various collections of essays, including Marilyn Fischer, Carol Nackenoff, and Wendy Chmielewski, eds., *Jane Addams and the Practice of Democracy* (2009), and reviewed books for the *New York Times Book Review* and the *Women's Review of Books*. In 2000 she received a fellowship from the National Endowment for the Humanities, and in 2007 *Citizen* received the Russell P. Strange Memorial Award for the best book on Illinois history from the Illinois State Historical Society. Knight's new full life of Addams, *Jane Addams: Spirit in Action*, will be published in 2010.

L. RYAN MUSGRAVE BONOMO is associate professor of philosophy at Rollins College. She is editor of the forthcoming *Feminist Aesthetics and Philosophy of Art: Critical Visions, Creative Engagements*, one of a six-volume set on feminist philosophy. Her work centers on the overlap of legal, ethical, political, and aesthetic value; her publications explore how these interweave within legal and sociopolitical philosophy, American philosophy, and feminist theory. Her recent work includes essays on feminist legal theory, epistemology and the arts, artist Nancy Spero's feminist modernism, pragmatist-feminist aesthetics, and Adorno's sociopolitical/aesthetic theory.

WENDY SARVASY teaches in the Department of Political Science at California State University, East Bay. Her publications include articles on John Stuart Mill's socialism and democratic theory, the feminization of poverty, postsuffrage feminism, Jane Addams's cosmopolitan thought, and social and global citizenship. She is finishing a book on democratic social politics and feminist theorizing from activism.

CHARLENE HADDOCK SEIGFRIED is a professor of philosophy and American studies at Purdue University. She is past president of the Society for the Advancement of American Philosophy and of the William James Society. She received the 2009 Herbert W. Schneider Award for Distinguished Contributions to American Philosophy and the 2005

John Dewey Society Outstanding Achievement Award. Among her publications are *Pragmatism and Feminism: Reweaving the Social Fabric* (1996) and *William James's Radical Reconstruction of Philosophy* (1990), and she edited *Feminist Interpretations of John Dewey* (2002). She has contributed to the recognition of Jane Addams's centrality to pragmatist philosophy by many articles and talks and by introductions to her *Democracy and Social Ethics* (2002) and *The Long Road of Woman's Memory* (2002). She is currently working on a book titled "Sympathetic Understanding and Cooperative Inquiry: Jane Addams's Social Philosophy."

ELEANOR J. STEBNER holds the J. S. Woodsworth Chair in the Humanities at Simon Fraser University. She is the author of numerous books and articles, including *The Women of Hull House: A Study in Spirituality, Vocation, and Friendship* (1997), and is coeditor of *The Westminster Handbook to Women in American Religious History* (2008).

JUDY D. WHIPPS is professor of philosophy and liberal studies at Grand Valley State University. She earned her Ph.D. in philosophy at Union Institute with her dissertation, "Philosophy and Social Activism: An Exploration of the Pragmatism and Activism of Jane Addams, John Dewey, and Engaged Buddhism." She also holds an M.A. from the University of Chicago Divinity School. Recent publications include "Learn to Earn: A Pragmatist Response to Contemporary Dialogues About Industrial Education" (*Journal of Speculative Philosophy*, 2008) and "Jane Addams: Pragmatist-Feminist Democracy in a Global Context," in *Democracy as Culture: Deweyan Pragmatism in an Age of Globalization* (2008). She is the coeditor with Marilyn Fischer of *Jane Addams's Writings on Peace* (2003), a four-volume edited set of Addams's writings. Recent publications include "The Feminist Pragmatism of Emily Greene Balch, Nobel Peace Laureate" (*National Women's Studies Journal*, 2006) and "Jane Addams's Social Thought as a Model for a Pragmatist-Feminist Communitarianism" (*Hypatia*, 2004). She also regularly presents papers about liberal education and interdisciplinarity.

Index

Adams, Henry C., 36
Addams, John (father), 3, 144, 205–6, 277
Addams, Laura Jane. *See also* aesthetics of Addams; Hull House; philosophy of art of Addams; religiosity of Addams; Rockford Female Seminary; sexual attitudes of Addams; *specific works*
   birth and early life of, 3
   career of, 4–5
   depression of, 39, 185
   illness of, 43, 187
   influences on, 41, 193, 205–6
   in late life, 45–46
   as literary woman, 32
   marginalization of, 1–2, 269
   Nobel Peace Prize of, 5, 42, 231
   as pacifist, 42, 210
   personal attacks on, 46–47
   as storyteller, 32–33
   theology of, 203–4, 210, 211–12, 216–17
   works of, 33–34
   as writer, 31, 42–43, 47–49, 67, 89, 126
"Addams's Radical Democracy" (Hamington), 281
"adjusted human relations," 165, 167–68
aesthetics of Addams. *See also* feminist aesthetics; pragmatist aesthetics
   contribution of, 118–20
   Emerson and, 116
   at Hull House, 109–18
   overview of, 108–9
Alinsky, Saul
   Back of the Yards organization, 255–56
   books of and biographies on, 268
   community organizing model of, 260–62, 269–70
   differences with Addams, 266–68
   importance of, 256, 270
   as radical, 268–69
   similarities with Addams, 262–65
All Sorts and Conditions of Men (Besant), 58
Anderson, Sarah, 206
androgyny, 192
Another Cosmopolitanism (Benhabib), 243–44, 251 n. 1, 252 n. 20
anti-antagonistic philosophy of community organizing, 258–59, 266
art. *See also* philosophy of art of Addams
   definition of, 108
   ethical dimension of, 114–15
   functions of, 61
   as libratory, 119
   social reform and, 57–60
"Art" (Emerson), 110
Art as Experience (Dewey), 109, 118
Art on My Mind (hooks), 113–14
Asia, trip to, 46, 76
authoritative discourse, 33

Bachofen, Johann, 187
Back of the Yards organization, 255–56, 260, 261–62
Bailey, Robert, Jr., 261
Bakhtin, Mikhail, 33
Balch, Emily Greene, 34
Baldwin, Margaret, 143
Barnett, Samuel and Henrietta, 189, 207
"A Belated Industry" (Addams), 8

Benhabib, Seyla, 224, 238, 243–45, 246–47, 251 n. 1, 252 n. 20, 281
Bérubé, Michael, x–xi
Besant, Walter, 37, 58
Bonomo, L. Ryan Musgrave, 63, 114
Booth, Heather, 256
Boston marriages, 193–94
Boulding, Kenneth, 269
"bounded communities," 243–47
Bowen, Louise de Koven, 190
Brieux, Eugene, *Damaged Goods*, 157 n. 62
Brown, Victoria Bissell, 20, 58, 70
Brown, Wendy, 163, 166, 178
Burgess, Ernest W., 265, 270
Busse, Fred, 128
Butler, Judith, 161, 163, 164, 169, 177, 178, 224

canon of philosophy, ix–xi
capitalism
    critique of, 113
    democracy and, 286–90
    A New Conscience and, 41, 129–30
care ethics, 13–17, 149–50
Carlyle, Thomas, 3, 206
Carpenter, Edward, 91, 95–96
"Cassandra" (Addams), 38–40, 65–66
Central Anti-Imperialist League of Chicago, 278
charity and lateral social progress, 11–12
charity practice
    Addams on, 213, 227–28
    criticism of, 167–68
    Hyman on, 262–63
    ideal type of worker for, 298–99, 300
"charm of words," 95–96
chastity, women and, 127, 137–39, 148–49
Chicago, 4, 255–56, 260
Chicago School, 265, 272 n. 1
Chicago Vice Commission, 128, 134, 137, 156 n. 55
childhood, government interest in, 165–66
children. *See also* devil baby tale
    delinquent, treatment of, 146–47
    movie theaters and, 63–64
    premature deaths of, 88–89
Children's Bureau, 165–66
choruses in Euripides' plays, 87–89
churches
    criticism of, 211, 212–13
    stained-glass windows in, 201–2, 217

citation practices, 85, 89
Citizen: Jane Addams and the Struggle for Democracy (Knight), 22
citizens
    arts-engagement and, 114–16, 120
    cosmopolitanism and, 297
    hospitality and, 227–28
    knowledge of others by, 16, 191–92
    as nonparticularized ideals, 280
    theory/activist dynamic and, 297–98
city housekeeping, 172–73, 174, 301–2
civic republicanism, 296–97, 299
clandestine prostitution, 139–41, 145
"clash of civilizations" analysis, 234, 239, 240–43
class hierarchy
    cross-class alliances, 294, 295, 298
    culture and, 62, 74–75
    democracy and, 278–79
    efforts to undermine, 72
classics, knowledge of, 84
collective bargaining, 10
collective memory, 43, 91–93
Collins, Patricia Hill, 7, 8
common good politics, 302–7
community organizing
    Addams model of, 257–60, 271–72
    Alinsky model of, 260–62
    common themes of, 262–65
    divergent approaches to, 266–68
    gender issues in, 268–70, 271
    companionship and devil baby tale, 96–98
Comte, Auguste, 67, 189, 207
connections, making, 93
Connelly, Mark, 127
cooperation as social reform theory, 189–90
cosmopolitanism
    "bounded communities" and, 243–45
    hospitality and, 248–49
    nationalisms and, 234–36
    peace-building and, 228–31
    political theory tradition of, 297
Cotkin, George, 5
creeds, 238–39
criminalization of prostitution, 144
cultivated persons, 75, 191
cultural colonization, 283–85
cultural malaise, 56, 74
culture
    art and social reform, 57–60

arts at Hull House, 112–13, 115–16, 117–18
"clash of civilizations" analysis and, 240–43
class and, 62
from elitist to human, 74–76
ethics and, 40–41
fine arts, valuing of, 60–65
global, hierarchical model of, 284–85
mutuality of interests across, 63
need for reform of, 56
social moral progress and, 17
women and, 65–69, 72–74

Dahl, Robert, 246
Damaged Goods (Brieux), 157 n. 62
Davis, Allen, 125, 209, 211
Dawes, Helen Palmer, 46
Deaconess Training School, 220 n. 38
death
　of children, 88–89
　of prostitutes, 135
Deegan, Mary Jo, 108, 110, 209, 215, 265
D'Emilio, John, 181, 183
democracy. *See also* citizens; *Democracy and Social Ethics*; social democracy
　books illustrating argument for, 41
　"bounded communities" and, 246–47
　capitalism and, 286–90
　evolution of views on, 276–79
　as evolving ideal, 225, 247–49
　human rights and, 280–82
　military missions and, 275–76
　postcolonial feminist critique of, 279–80
　reciprocity and, 93–94
　as social ideal, 226–27
　socializing care and, 16–17
　transnational, 289
　views of, 264–65
Democracy and Social Ethics (Addams)
　as beginning of argument for democracy, 41
　on blaming victims, 11
　Cassandra and, 39–40
　"Charitable Effort," 223, 227–28
　on charity workers, 263
　concepts of democracy in, 276, 277
　contemporary reviews of, 32–33, 40, 226
　James on, 32–33
　Joslin on, 67
　sympathetic knowledge and, 93–94
　Tolstoy and, 98

on unhappiness and unease, 55–56
　women's experiences in, 282, 288
"Democracy or Militarism" (Addams), 278
De Quincey, Thomas, "The Vision of Sudden Death," 57
"descriptive chauvinism," 284
"The Devil Baby at Hull-House" (Addams), 43–44
devil baby tale
　domestic violence and, 61
　folktales and, 90–91
　Greek tragedy and, 84–90
　Italian version of, 44, 82–83
　Jewish version of, 44, 83
　later tellings of, 83–84
　making connections and, 93–94
　origins of, 82, 83
　patterns of meaning in, 96–98
　race memory and, 91–93
　renunciation and, 98–100
　women as artists and knowledge makers, 94–96
Dewey, John
　Addams and, 5
　aesthetics and, 110, 118–19
　on art, 60
　Art as Experience, 109, 118
　Benhabib compared to, 243
　Ethics, 68, 226
　on nations as social formations, 240
　peace and, 248
domestic labor, women in, 8, 288, 302
domestic violence
　devil baby tale and, 61
　elevation of significance of, 81–82
　Greek tragedy and, 84–90
　social democracy and, 99–100
Dürer, Albrecht, 57–58
duty to care, 15–16

ecumenical movement, 212
education, views of, 267–68
"Education by the Current Event" (Addams), 63
The Education of Jane Addams (Brown), 20
Edwards, R. A. R., 209
Egypt, trip to, 45, 100
Eight-Hour Club, 305
Eliot, George, 59, 72, 191
Elshtain, Jean Bethke
　on Addams as theorist, 294–95

Elshtain, Jean Bethke (*continued*)
  Jane Addams and the Dream of American Democracy, 171–73, 174–76
  maternalism and, 299
  Public Man, Private Woman, 162, 171, 173, 175
  on religiosity of Addams, 209
Ely, Richard, 40, 41
Emerson, Ralph Waldo, 109–12, 114–15, 116, 118–19, 206
enforcement of laws, 304–5
Engel, Lawrence J., 265
erotic, meaning of, 194
ethics
  approach to, 299
  cultures and, 40–41
  essays on, 35–38
  feminist, at Hull House, 114–16
  seeds of in diary entries, 34–35
  social democracy and, 278
Ethics (Dewey), 68, 226
ethnic bias, 72
Euripides and His Age (Murray), 84, 85, 86, 92, 95
Europe, trips to, 3, 57, 70–72, 207
European Community, 237, 246
Ewing Congregational Church, 207
The Excellent Becomes the Permanent (Addams), 34, 202–3
experience, transformative possibilities of, 75–76

factory work, 62–63, 107–8, 113, 115, 287–88
Faderman, Lillian, 181, 182
family
  male-provider vision of, 149–50
  non-normative formations of, 174, 175–76, 178, 194, 195
  state normalization of, 177
  stereotypes of, 193–94
family claim, 37, 293–94, 296–97
female standard of sexuality, 148–49
feminism
  of Addams, 2, 89
  community organizing and, 271–72
  human welfare and, 224
  postcolonial, 282–83, 285–86
  prostitution and, 143
  state, 305
Feminism Without Borders (Mohanty), 280

feminist aesthetics
  contribution to, 116–20
  field of, 109
  at Hull House, 110–16
Feminist Aesthetics and Philosophy of Art (Bonomo), 114
feminist care ethics, 13–17
feminist political theory, 307–8
feminist pragmatism
  of Addams, 225–28, 290
  aesthetics of Addams and, 108–9
  devil baby analysis of, 90
  experience and, 94–95
  language and, 92–93
  lateral progress and, 9–13
  postcolonial feminism and, 285–86
  in *Twenty Years at Hull-House*, 66–67
  women's experience and, 82
feminist social politics, 295
feminist standpoint theory, 7, 8, 9
feminist theology, 213–17
Ferguson, Ann, 282
fine arts, valuing of, 60–65
Fiol-Matta, Licia, 160
Fischer, Marilyn, 19, 108, 117
folklore, 90–91
Foucault, Michel, 163, 166
Frankl, Viktor, 249
Freedman, Estelle, 181, 183
Freeman, Jo, 256

Gage, Matilda Joslyn, 213, 214
gay marriage, 164
gendered path, 295–302
"Gendered Social Knowledge" (Ross), 135–36
gender issues. *See also* men; women
  Alinsky and, 256
  in community organizing, 268–70, 271
  democratization and, 286–87
  Illinois Labor Law and, 304
  inclusive or lateral progress as, 11
  in philosophy, ix–x
  in social work, 265
  in treatment of delinquent children, 146–47
gender roles, 192–93
General Federation of Women's Clubs, 83
Gilman, Charlotte Perkins, 2, 149, 204, 213, 214–15
globalization, 241–42, 246, 289

Globalization and Feminist Activism (Hawkesworth), 284–85
Goldman, Emma, 129, 137, 149
Gordon, Mary, 47
Greek tragedy in devil baby tales, 81–82, 84–90

Hall, G. Stanley, 130
Halley, Janet, 163, 166
Hamilton, Alice, 34, 175, 190, 210
Hamington, Maurice, 281
Harding, Sandra, 6, 7
Harkness, Georgia, 210
Hawkesworth, Mary, 284–85, 287
Heathcott, Joseph, 266
Heilbrun, Carolyn, 41, 192
Held, Virginia, 14
Henrotin, Ellen, 156 n. 55
heroism
  ideal of, 74
  social, 3
hierarchical model of global cultures, 284–85
Hippolytus (Murray translation of), 99
His Religion and Hers (Gilman), 214
Holmes, Oliver Wendell, 40
hooks, bell, 113–14, 194
Horowitz, Helen L., 62, 76
Horwitt, Sanford D., 268
hospitality
  "bounded communities" and, 243–47
  as cause, 223–24
  citizenship and, 227–28
  cosmopolitan norms of, 248–49
  nationalism and, 238
  war and, 232–33
Hügel, Friedrich von, 212
Hull House. See also *The Second Twenty Years at Hull-House*; *Twenty Years at Hull-House*
  aesthetics at, 109–18
  cooperative efforts of, 189–90
  domesticity of, 194, 195
  fine arts and, 61–62
  founding of, 3–4, 70–71, 93, 185, 207, 225–26
  identity and function of, 4
  interior decoration of, 62, 110–11
  labor unions and, 301
  maternalist politics and, 160, 165, 173
  model for, 58, 76, 189, 207, 226
  neighborhood surrounding, 5–6, 38
  physical buildings of, 111–12

  privacy and publicity of, 169–71, 173–76
  proximity and, 12, 15, 168–69, 259
  public programs of, 12–13, 38, 64, 270
  queer domesticity of, 160, 169–71, 173–76, 178–79
  religiosity of Addams and, 207–8, 276
  spatial redefinition of, 170–71
  state feminism and, 304–5
  state welfare and, 159–60
  women's clubs of, 73–74, 75
Hull-House Maps and Papers (Addams and Kelley), 34, 110, 263–64
Hull-House Year Book, 258
humanism, 70
human rights and democracy, 280–82
Hunt, James B., 210–11
Huntington, James, 211
Huntington, Samuel P., 224, 234, 239, 240–43
Hurley, Joseph, 46
Hutchinson, Charles, 62
Hyman, Sidney, 262–63
hypernationalism, 238

Illinois Labor Law, 303–6
immigrants. See also devil baby tale
  civic republicanism and, 299
  class hierarchy and, 278–79
  cosmopolitanism of, 234
  cultural colonization and, 283–84
  hospitality and, 233
  household managers and, 302
  prostitution and, 134
  reciprocity toward, 83
"Immigrant Woman as She Adjusts Herself to American Life" (Addams), 83
imperialistic nationalism, 238
inclusive progress, 9–13
Industrial Area Foundation, 260–61
industrialization, 62–63, 107–8, 113, 287–88
Infant Welfare Society, 261–62
interdependent model of society, 215–16, 277
"international mind," 114–16, 118
intersectional location, 300–301, 307
Intimate Love (D'Emilio and Freedman), 183
intuition of women, 66
Italian version of devil baby narrative, 44, 82–83

Jackson, Shannon, 160, 194
James, William, 5, 32–33, 44, 226, 232, 237
Jane Addams, a Writer's Life (Joslin), 17

Index

Jane Addams and the Dream of American Democracy (Elshtain), 171–73, 174–76
Jane Club, 189, 258, 305
Jewish version of devil baby narrative, 44, 83
Joslin, Katherine, 17, 67, 69, 84, 126
juvenile delinquency, 15, 146–47
Juvenile Protective Association, 135, 146

Kant, Immanuel, 114, 235–36, 243
Keller, Evelyn Fox, 120
Kelley, Florence, 34, 154 n. 30, 190, 210–11, 305
Kenney, Mary, 258
kinship
  Butler and, 164, 177
  extended model of, 177
  Keller and, 120
  redefinition of, 170–71
  state welfare and, 161–62
Knight, Louise W., 22, 70, 93
knowledge
  arts-engagement and, 120
  of classics, 84
  of others by citizens, 16, 191–92
  as situated, 6–7
  sympathetic, 13–14, 93–94, 136, 257
knowledge-seeking practices, 119–20

Labor Museum, 112, 302
labor unions, 10–11, 287, 301
La Follette, Robert, 46
Lasch, Christopher, 209, 294, 295
lateral progress, 9–13
"Later Reflections on Peace," 230
Lathrop, Julia, 56, 157 n. 57, 165–66, 270, 300
League of Nations, 239
Left Legalism/Left Critique (Brown and Halley), 163, 166
lesbian experience, 181–82, 193–94
lesbian theory, 192
liberal feminist view of prostitution, 131, 132–33, 144
liberalism, feminist critique of, 280–82
Lines of Activity (Jackson), 160
Lippmann, Walter, 125, 143–44
literature
  as agent of social change, 60–61
  citation practices, 85, 89
  folklore as, 97
  moral function of, 57–59
  women and, 32

Little Theater Company, 83
Locke, Alain, 109, 245, 248
The Long Road of Woman's Memory (Addams)
  description of, 33
  devil baby tales in, 81
  introduction to, 84–86
  race memory concept and, 91–93
  standpoints and, 9
  women as storytellers, 42–45
Lose, Rebecca, 147
love
  as absorbing passion, 183
  affectionate, cooperative, 189–90
  functions of, 182–83
  of humanity, 190–92
  platonic, 186–87, 188–89
  romantic, intimate, 183–89

MacCulloch, J. A., 90–91
marriage and careers, 184
Martin, Patricia Yancey, 271
Marx, Karl, 260
Masaryk, Tomás, 279
"Master and Man" (Tolstoy), 98
maternalism, 299–300, 307
maternalist politics and Hull House, 160, 165, 173
Mazzini, Giuseppe, 37–38
McClure's Magazine, 128
McNally, Terrence, 194
Mead, George Herbert, 5, 265
Medea (Murray translation of), 88–89
Meeghan, Joseph, 260, 261
memory. *See also The Long Road of Woman's Memory*
  collective, 43, 91–93
  legendary wisdom and, 86
  race, 82, 91–93, 95–96, 100
men. *See also* domestic violence
  as agents of prostitution, 138–39
  male-provider families and, 149–50
Michelangelo, 59
militarism
  democracy and, 275–76
  peace and, 230, 278
  social equality and, 289
  war and violence against women, 89–90
Miller, Mike, 268
"A Modern Lear" (Addams), 60–61
Moers, Ellen, 32, 49

Mohanty, Chandra Talpade, 279–80, 282–83, 285, 287, 289
Monroe, Harriet, 33
moral conduct, 205–6
moral function of literature, 57–59
moral imagination, theory of, 117
morality and care ethics, 14–15
Morgan, Lewis Henry, 90
Mouffe, Chantal, 280, 283, 290
movie theaters, as vulgar, 63–64
Muncy, Robyn, 270
Murray, Gilbert, 83–89, 92, 95–97, 99
My Friend, Julia Lathrop (Addams), 34, 56

National Federation of Women's Clubs, 46
nationalism, 237–40, 279
A New Conscience and an Ancient Evil (Addams)
  abolition of prostitution and, 128–29, 143–45
  analysis of, 126–27
  capitalism and, 41, 129–30
  communal reforms in, 145–46
  contemporary reviews of, 133
  description of, 33
  evidence presented in, 133–37
  as ideological statement, 143
  increase in commercialized vice and, 130
  Lippmann on, 125, 143–44
  remedies offered in, 147–50
  social control and, 130–31
  vignettes in, 139–40
  white slavery and, 127–28
Newer Ideals of Peace (Addams), 33, 41, 228, 231–38, 278
Nobel Peace Prize, 5, 42, 231
North, Frank Mason, 212
Northbrae Community Church, Berkeley, California, 201–2
novel, genre of, 33
Nussbaum, Martha, 117, 284

"Objective Value of a Social Settlement" (Addams), 36, 38
Okin, Susan Moller, 280
On Addams (Fischer), 19
outsider, characteristics of, 7
"outsider-within," 7–8
Owen, Robert, 189

pacifism of Addams, 42, 210
Pan Pacific Union Congress, 76

Park, Robert Ezra, 265, 270
Pateman, Carole, 132, 280
patriarchy
  Addams and, 74
  in *Democracy and Social Ethics*, 40
  folklore and, 95
  marriage and, 127, 132
  militarism and, 89–90, 289
  in "A Modern Lear," 60–61
  prostitution and, 132
  religion and, 204, 213–14, 215
patterns of meaning in devil baby tale, 96–98
peace. See also *Newer Ideals of Peace*; Nobel Peace Prize; *Peace and Bread in Time of War*
  as cause of Addams, 223–24
  "clash of civilizations" analysis and, 240–43
  evolutionary peace-building, 231–40, 248–50
  military force and, 230, 278
  understandings of and writings on, 228–31
Peace and Bread in Time of War (Addams)
  democracy and, 279
  description of, 33–34
  female nature and, 283–84
  nationalism and, 237, 238
  social evolution and, 229–30
Philanthropy and Social Progress (essays), 34, 35
philosophical theories and human society, 58–59
philosophy
  of Addams, marginalization of, 1–2, 269
  epistemology and context of, 6–9
  feminist, ix–x
  gender issues in, ix
  public, 5–6
  re-reading canon of, x–xi
philosophy of art of Addams
  absence in relevant fields of, 108–9
  aesthetics at Hull House, 109–18
  overview of, 107–8
platonic love, 186–87, 188–89
"The Play Instinct and the Arts" (Addams), 109
Porterfield, Amanda, 209
positivism, 70–71, 72, 207
postcolonial feminist critique
  of concept of democracy, 279–80
  pragmatist feminism and, 285–86
  privilege and, 282–83
  social democracy and, 289–90
postmodern theory, 192–94
power relations philosophy of community organizing, 261–62

Powers, Johnny, 40, 258–59
pragmatism. *See also* feminist pragmatism; pragmatist aesthetics
  contributions to, 74
  experience and, 82, 110
  ideal of, 65
  philosophy as criticism of culture and, 76
Pragmatism and Feminism (Seigfried), 18, 94–95
pragmatist aesthetics
  Addams and, 109
  contribution to, 63, 118–20
  at Hull House, 110–14
Presbyterian Church, 70, 207, 211
private sphere and government, 164–66. *See also* public and private spheres
privilege
  postcolonial feminism and, 282–83
  sympathetic understanding and, 301
Progressive movement, 228
prostitution. See also *A New Conscience and an Ancient Evil*
  Addams's view of, 128
  clandestine, 139–41, 145
  communal reforms for, 145–46
  conclusions on, 288
  criminalization of, 144
  economic motives for, 137, 141–43, 147
  feminism and, 131–32, 143, 144, 149
  image of female victimhood in, 133–37, 139, 140–41, 143
  police role, advocacy for, 143–45
  remedies offered for, 147–50
  social control and, 130–31
  white slavery and, 127–28, 137, 138–39, 143
proximity and settlements, 12, 15, 168–69, 259
public and private spheres. *See also* public sphere
  Addams and, 4
  community organizing and, 269–70
  Elshtain on, 172
  entanglement of, 167–68
  government and, 164–66
  of Hull House, 169–71, 173–76
  "A Modern Lear" and, 60–61
  social democracy and, 293–94
Public Man, Private Woman (Elshtain), 162, 171, 173, 175
public philosophy, 5–6
public sphere. *See also* public and private spheres
  care ethics in, 16–17
  women in, 67, 272
Pullman strike, 60–61, 259

queer domesticity of Hull House, 160, 169–71, 173–76, 178–79
queer theory, emergence of, 161
queer welfare studies, orientation toward, 168–79

race, definition of, 90
"race life," 36–37, 43
race memory, 82, 91–93, 95–96, 100
radical feminist view of prostitution, 131–33, 149
Rauschenbusch, Walter, 201, 202, 208, 210, 211
reciprocity
  democracy and, 93–94
  devil baby tale and, 98–100
  settlements and, 167
  toward immigrants, 83
referendums, 305–6
Reitzes, Dietrich C., 268
Reitzes, Donald C., 268
religiosity of Addams
  baptism and, 70
  changes to, 206–7
  churches, criticism of, 211, 212–13
  The Excellent Becomes the Permanent and, 202–3
  feminist theology and, 213–17
  formation of, 204–6
  Hull House and, 207–9, 276
  interpretations of, 209–11
  Knight on, 69–70
  "renascent Christianity," 225–26, 249
  stained-glass windows and, 201–2, 217
  theology and, 203–4, 210, 211–12, 216–17
  understanding and deployment of, 249–50
  woman in pit story and, 215–16
renunciation and devil baby tale, 98–100
Re-Reading the Canon series, x–xi, 1
Reveille for Radicals (Alinsky), 268
revolutionary nationalism, 238
Rich, Adrienne, 181, 195
Rockefeller, John D., Jr., 135
Rockford Female Seminary, 3, 38–40, 65–66, 135, 184, 206
Roosevelt, Theodore, 4, 148
Ross, Dorothy, "Gendered Social Knowledge," 135–36
Ruether, Rosemary Radford, 216
Rules for Radicals (Alinsky), 266, 268
Ruskin, John, 3, 62, 191, 206

Salisbury, Rollin, 184
Sanders, Marion K., 268
scholarships, 305–6
School of Applied Ethics, 35
Schweitzer, Albert, 201, 211–12
science
    Addams and, 135–36
    role of, 67–68
Scudder, Vida, 211
The Second Twenty Years at Hull-House (Addams)
    context of, 42
    description of, 34
    as "honest reminiscence," 47
    "Play Instinct and the Arts," 62–63
    on "sense of futility," 45–46
    on sexual mores, 150–51
    Woolf quoted in, 47–48
Sedgwick, Ellery, 43
Seigfried, Charlene Haddock, 18, 92, 94–95, 108, 294, 295
Seligman, Edwin, 40
settlements. *See also* Hull House; Toynbee Hall
    common good and, 303
    community organizing and, 257–60
    description of, 4
    essays on, 35–38
    as lasting neighbors, 267, 272
    as part of "spiritual force," 208
    proximity and, 12, 15, 168–69, 259
    reciprocity and, 167
    state feminism and, 305
    women's clubs and, 73–74
"sex hygiene" classes, 146
sexual attitudes of Addams. *See also A New Conscience and an Ancient Evil*
    relations with women of neighborhood and, 150–51
    remedies for prostitution and, 147–50
    romantic, intimate love and, 183–89
    social justice and sexual purity, 129
    village mores and, 141
    women as naturally chaste, 127, 137–39, 148–49
sexual conduct of working-class women, 126, 139–41, 147
sexuality. *See also* lesbian experience; sexual attitudes of Addams
    changing history of, 195
    intimate love and, 183–89

sexual normalization and state, 163–64
Sicherman, Barbara, 59, 65, 66, 71–72
Sklar, Kathryn Kish, 209, 263, 304
Skocpol, Theda, 73
Smith, E. G., 34, 35
Smith, Mary Rozet, 45, 182, 187–88, 190, 194
"snare of preparation," 2–5, 37, 219 n. 24
social as space for practicing common good politics, 302–7
social Christianity, 70, 185
Social Creed of 1908, 212
social Darwinism, 12
social democracy. *See also* hospitality; peace
    as conceptual framework, 276–77
    domestic violence and, 99–100
    as ethical system, 277–78
    postcolonial feminist writing and, 289–90
    public and private spheres and, 293–94
    sympathetic knowledge and, 257
social evolution, 90
social gospel movement, 211
social heroism, 3
social inequality of women, 288–89
social philosophy of Addams, marginalization of, 1–2, 269
social reform
    art and, 57–60
    cooperation and, 189–90
social settlement movement. *See* Hull House; settlements; Toynbee Hall
social welfare common good, 302–7
social welfare responsibilities, extension of, 294
social work
    criticism of, 167–68
    experiential approach to, 59–60
    gender divide in, 265
    position in formation of, 176–77
    professional, 46, 259–60, 267–68
society, interdependent model of, 215–16, 277
song, writing as, 43
The Spirit of Youth and the City Streets (Addams)
    description of, 15, 33, 41
    Lippmann on, 143
    The Second Twenty Years and, 47
    sexuality and, 130
    standpoints and, 9
Stall, Susan, 269–70
standpoint theory, 7, 8, 9
Stanton, Elizabeth Cady, 213–14, 224

336   Index

Starr, Ellen Gates
  arts and, 112
  chapters on art by, 110
  friendship with, 184–85
  Hull House founding and, 226, 304
  interior decoration of Hull House and, 62
  as involved outsider, 7
  letters to, 35
  partnership with, 182, 185–86, 187
  pragmatist aesthetics and, 63
  religious adherence and, 206
  Society of Arts and Crafts and, 62
state feminism, 305
state welfare
  critique of, 162–63
  extended kinship and, 161–62
  Foucaultian understanding of power and, 163–64
  invention of, 159–60, 176–77
  private sphere and, 164–66
  situated understanding of, 162
Stebner, Eleanor, 23, 209
Stevens, Alzina Parsons, 305
Stoecker, Randy, 269–70
Student Nonviolent Coordinating Committee, 268
"The Subjective Necessity for Social Settlements" (Addams), 36–38, 208
suffrage
  city housekeeping and, 172
  commitment to, 148
  feminist pragmatism and, 13
  inclusive or lateral progress and, 11
  national mood and, 46
Sullivan, Shannon, 119
sympathetic knowledge, 13–14, 93–94, 136, 257
sympathetic understanding, 300–301

Taylor, Graham, 156 n. 55, 211
theology of Addams, 203–4, 210, 211–12, 216–17
theory/activist dynamic
  description of, 294–96
  gendered path and, 296–302
  social as space for practicing common good politics, 302–7
Third Presbyterian Church, Rochester, New York, 201
third world women
  critique of Western feminist thought and, 279–80
  as "other," 282–85

Thomas, William I., 265
Tolstoy, Leo
  on affection, 189
  critique by, 282
  ideals of, 232
  "last impetuous journey" of, 97–98
  "snare of preparation" and, 219 n. 24
  "Subjective Necessity for Social Settlements" and, 37
  visit to, 286
  writings of, 59, 191, 207
Toynbee Hall, 3, 58, 189, 207, 226, 276
Trachtenberg, Alan, 62
transnational democracy, 289
travel
  to Asia, 46, 76
  to Egypt, 45, 100
  to Europe, 3, 57, 70–72, 207
  life experience and, 56, 75–76
  to Russia, 286
The Trojan Women, Little Theater Company tour of, 83–84
Trolander, Judith Ann, 259, 270
twentieth century, prognosis for, 236–37
Twenty Years at Hull-House (Addams)
  "Arts at Hull-House" chapter, 109
  as classic, 1, 41
  context of, 69
  on cultivated persons, 191
  description of, 33
  last pages of, 59–60
  pragmatist feminism in, 66–67
  on School of Applied Ethics, 35
  on scientific methods, 68
  "snare of preparation" and, 2–5, 57, 59, 70
Tylor, Edward Burnett, 90, 92

Ulm Cathedral, 70–71
"Under Western Eyes" (Mohanty), 279–80
Unitarianism, 210
University of Chicago Settlement, 261–62
University of Illinois Press, 126
uplift model of women's clubs, 73
U.S. Immigration Commission, 128, 134

Verestchagin, Vasily, 59
Vice Commission of Minneapolis, 137, 155 n. 37
violence. *See also* domestic violence
  "devil baby" case and, 61
  dogmas and, 58

of Pullman strike, 60
war and, 89–90
"The Vision of Sudden Death" (De Quincey), 57
voices
  in chorus, metaphor of, 37–38
  as composites, 45
  of disenfranchised, 264–65
  gender of, 47
  of isolated, amplification of, 37
  of women, 43, 216–17

Wahl, Ana-Maria, 110
Wald, Lillian, 190
war and violence against women, 89–90
Watkins, Ferre, 46–47
Webb, Beatrice, 168–69
Weil, Marie, 271
Wells, H. G., 149
Westernization and cultural colonization, 283–85
"Westphalian" international world order, 252 n. 20
white slavery, 127–28, 134, 137, 138–39, 143
Wollstonecraft, Mary, 224, 297
The Woman's Bible (Stanton), 213–14
Woman's Peace Party, 83, 84
women. *See also* prostitution; third world women; white slavery
  of Asia, 76
  college experience and, 3, 38–40, 224, 293–94
  cross-class alliances of women, 294, 295, 298
  culture and, 65–69, 72–74
  in domestic labor, 8, 288, 302
  elderly, as artists and knowledge makers, 94–96
  intuition of, 66
  literary, 32
  as naturally chaste, 127, 137–39, 148–49
  as needing balanced lives, 71
  in neighborhood, 86–87, 92
  oppression of, 280–81, 286–87
  in public sphere, 67, 272
  sexual conduct of working-class, 126, 139–41, 147
  social inequality of, 288–89
  as storytellers, 42–45
  war and violence against, 89–90
Women and Economics (Gilman), 214
Women at the Hague (Addams, Balch, and Hamilton), 34
The Women of Hull-House (Stebner), 23
Women's Bureau, 270
women's clubs, 72–74, 75
Women's International League for Peace and Freedom, 4, 46, 229, 250, 289
Woolf, Virginia, 47–49
Woolley, Mary, 193–94
World War I, 4–5, 44–45, 83, 228–29, 279

youth of prostitutes, 134–35

www.ingramcontent.com/pod-product-compliance
Lightning Source LLC
Chambersburg PA
CBHW031543300426
44111CB00006BA/160